Mending the World

Mending the World

Social Healing Interventions
by Gestalt Practitioners Worldwide

Joseph Melnick and Edwin C. Nevis
Editors

A GestaltPress Book

published and distributed by
Routledge, Taylor & Francis Group New York.

GestaltPress
127 Abby Court
Santa Cruz, CA 95062

and

165 Route 6A
Orleans, MA 02653

www.gestaltpress.com

Distributed by: Routledge, Taylor & Francis Group

ISBN: 978-0-9882971-0-4

This book was printed in the United States of America.

Cover designed by Judy Robertson.

CONTENTS

Dedicated in Memory of

Paul Goodman

who taught us that the true aim of Gestalt therapy
is to create healthy citizens and nourishing communities

ACKNOWLEDGMENTS

For both of us this book is an attempt to return to our early roots in growing up with parents who were active union members and committed to social justice. This was reinforced through later mentoring by socially activist teachers in our early careers and, finally, through our life long immersion in the Gestalt approach. One of the authors (Nevis) was profoundly influenced by his study with Paul Goodman, to whom this book is dedicated. Some of the connection between the Gestalt approach and social change is described in Chapter One. However, the flowering of these dormant seeds took place at a conference on social change sponsored by the Gestalt International Study Center, in Cape Town, South Africa in 2006. There, we witnessed the work of Gestalt practitioners working across a wide spectrum of social change areas, such as the aftermath of the Tsunami in Southeast Asia, AIDS prevention interventions in South Africa, and many more. Our trip to the Robben Island Prison immediately following the conference heightened our energy and a commitment to create this book.

The prison on Robben Island sits just a few nautical miles from the thriving waterfront of Cape Town, South Africa. In an attempt to silence apartheid's domestic critics, Nelson Mandela and many of the leaders of the anti-apartheid movement were held in deplorable conditions for many years. For example, prisoners were only allowed to send and receive one letter every six months. Harsh beatings were common, inmates were forced to wear flimsy clothing that provided little protection from the harsh winds, and to perform mindless labor such as digging meaningless holes.

In 1999, it was turned into a UN World Heritage Site. This former prison has become a living museum, and visitors are ferried out regularly to tour the island and learn about this shameful chapter in South African history. One of the unique aspects of this experience is that the tour guides are all former prisoners. Our guide, a small, animated man, had been the youngest of all the males imprisoned on the island, having been sent there at the age of thirteen after having attempted to firebomb a post office. When one of our tour members expressed empathy for his experience, the guide replied with passion: "Don't be sad for me. I grew up in the hands of some of the finest, most compassionate people you would ever encounter. It was like going to a university behind bars. I learned history, geography, and social philosophy." As he told his story we, like most of the people on the tour, were moved to tears. Walking back to the boat, we turned to each other and agreed quickly to create a book that told the stories of individuals who, like the guide in Robben Island, have devoted themselves to creating social change.

Many people have supported us throughout this endeavor. Jochen Lohmeier and Chantelle Wyley, who helped create the South African Social Change Conference referred to above, provided useful insights about some of our concepts and the world of international social and economic development, many of which are reflected in their chapter below. Susan L. Fischer and Gloria N. Melnick worked indefatigably in preparing the book for publication in its current, second edition. Their editorial expertise and persistence were invaluable. Judy Robertson, responsible for this edition's production and design, is to be commended especially for her hand in the cover artwork.

Last, we would like to thank our wives, Gloria N. Melnick and Sonia March Nevis, who graciously supported their workaholic husbands through this laborious and gratifying endeavor. One of the themes we emphasize throughout the book is that the creation of change involves significant others. They are a powerful testimony to this principle.

Joseph Melnick, Falmouth, Maine
Edwin C. Nevis, Wellfleet, Massachusetts
May 1, 2011

*

As we were preparing the second edition of *Mending the World* for publication, Edwin Nevis died—on his 85th birthday (May 20, 2011). His death is not only a great personal loss, but also a loss to his family, many friends and colleagues, and the Gestalt and Organizational Development communities. Many of us throughout the world knew and loved him. His whole life was dedicated to supporting people to make a better world. I, along with many others, will miss him.

Joseph Melnick, Falmouth, Maine
July 10, 2011

FOREWORD

Philip Lichtenberg, PhD

Many years ago, social activists who were aiming for a better world would routinely say, "Comes the revolution . . ." Now, after we have seen many revolutions rise and fall, we have become wiser. And while still determined to pursue that goal of a better world, we are more sober and more humble but determined nonetheless. With the world entering a troubled time economically as this book makes its way to publication, the urges toward authoritarian and democratic social institutions and social systems vie with one another much as they did in the 1930s and 1940s. The welfare of humankind, indeed the very existence of humankind, is at stake today and we would do well to put our minds to making sure that things turn out well. This book, which comes from persons who identify themselves a Gestaltists—persons mainly relying upon the theory of Gestalt therapy who are active in other ways than psychotherapy—is a notable contribution that will inform persons concerned with intentional social change.

One of the strengths of this work is that the authors have a common theoretical orientation and yet have applied their efforts to many divers institutions and social arrangements. Herein are stories from many areas and countries: Africa, Brazil, Cambodia, Denmark, England, the North of Ireland, the Netherlands, Sweden, and the United States—even the United Nations (UN). So, too, there are many stories from working with people who have been hurt by the social arrangements surrounding them: poverty, drug abuse, the clash of socio-religious groups, and environmental disaster. Finding, empowering, giving voice to those most damaged by profound social institutions is a theme in this book, and it will be of good support to those who wish to be agents of social change.

Because I believe that all persons in any given social system are change agents, not only members of some subset such as the "proletariat," the fact that the authors of this book have so many and such various points of entry into social change efforts makes this a unique contribution to society. Of course, all persons resist change as well, which makes these efforts as difficult as they appear. But consider here only a sampling of such points of entry: a drug court with an activist judge; the agencies of the United Nations; a café in a London slum; families in the North of Ireland; refugees in centers in Sweden; leadership training in Cambodia; and a shanty town in Brazil. There are more. What is striking is the range of persons involved in social change: individuals in positions of power; those with specialized training such as social workers; on-through community actors in circles of the poor. This range includes the authors who are themselves powerful and supporters of those who act in a socially productive way; they are partners with those who are trying to create a better world.

Key to the work described in this book is the enhancement of awareness wherever activists are engaged. In line with consciousness-raising by the American feminist movement in the 1970s and the *conscientizacao* tactics of Paolo Freire in Brazil in the 1960s, enhanced awareness fostered by dialogue is a key to effective social change. With a more keen awareness of what is happening in their present situations, people are able to do things differently and make those situations more suited to human welfare. The Gestalt approach began from the focus upon unfolding awareness, including what limitations appear in becoming aware, and its various forms of practice continue to rely upon broadening persons' understandings in their lives.

Another central theme underlying the studies in this book is commitment to democracy and egalitarianism. The title of one chapter by Carolyn Lukensmeyer speaks directly to this matter: "Creating Democratic Spaces: Citizen Engagement and Large Systems Change in Post-Katrina New Orleans." When Judge Wheeler steps down from her formal seat in front of persons in drug court and sits in a circle with those persons being brought before her, she is implementing the egalitarian perspective in Gestalt. She does not forfeit her authority, and she can resume her original place when necessary, but she makes herself available for meeting persons affected by her on their level. In working in Third World countries, Lohmeier and Wyley emphasize participatory processes, a basic constituent of democratic living. Overcoming hierarchy in Cambodia, with special seats for authorities and monks, is critical to work with individuals damaged by a ruthless regime.

Depending upon her or his port of entry into social change, the reader will be stimulated to push further her or his own work. By following diverse efforts, readers may find themselves impelled to expand their own actions. This is a book that not only informs us; it is an inspiration to continue our efforts in these difficult times. Read it and grow with it.

Philip Lichtenberg, PhD is a licensed psychologist who taught at the Bryn Mawr School of Social Work and Social Research for more than thirty-five years. From 1983-2010 he served as a director and senior faculty member of the Gestalt Therapy Institute of Philadelphia. He continues on at GTIP as a faculty member and as Secretary of the Board of Directors. Lichtenberg received his formal Gestalt training with Erving and Miriam Polster and studied with Isadore From in New York. He has authored six books, including *Community and Confluence: Undoing the Clinch of Oppression,* and *Encountering Bigotry: Befriending Projecting Persons in Everyday Life.*

Contact: p-elichtenberg@ comcast.net

ABOUT THE EDITORS

Joseph Melnick, PhD, lives in Portland, Maine where he works as a Clinical and Organizational Psychologist. He is co-chair of the Cape Cod Training Program and Board Member of the Gestalt International Study Center. The founding editor of the *Gestalt Review*, he is the author of numerous articles and book chapters on intimate systems, group dynamics and organizational and social change. He trains and teaches worldwide. Contact: JosephMelnick10@gmail.com.

Edwin C. Nevis, PhD (1926-2011), was an organization development consultant for over 50 years. Together with his wife, Sonia, he co-founded the Gestalt International Study Center in 1979. He is the author of *Organizational Consulting: A Gestalt Approach* and several other books and numerous articles. He also spent 17 years at the Massachusetts Institute of Technology (MIT) Sloan School of Management as a faculty member and as Director of the Program for Senior Executives. In 2010, he was recipient of the Organizational Development Network (ODN) Lifetime Achievement Award.

CHAPTER 1

Introduction and Historical Perspective

Joseph Melnick, PhD, and Edwin C. Nevis, PhD

Introduction

This is a book for people who care about making a difference in the world. It is a book for people who want to have impact on others at a level beyond the individual. It is for people who believe that many crucial issues can be dealt with only on a broad societal level.

It is a book that will be useful to a broad range of readers: people who have never been exposed to the Gestalt approach as well as those who practice and teach from this perspective and method.

The framework of the book is very simple: it is built around stories about efforts to solve a social problem or alleviate a condition causing significant difficulty in the lives of many people. It is a collection of cases written by seasoned Gestalt practitioners. We have chosen to get our message across by presenting actual examples of their work. After discussing the origins of the Gestalt approach as it relates to social change, we will briefly present some theory that will help you understand the conceptual context that forms the underpinnings of each case. At the same time, we believe that the cases will serve as examples of the utility of our model for social change.

The cases vary and cover a range of situations across a wide section of the world. They deal with situations in Africa, Denmark, Holland, the UK (including the North of Ireland), Cambodia, Sweden, Brazil, as well as the United States. They deal with such diverse issues as AIDS reduction, trauma resulting from years of political conflict, poverty, the dilemmas of aging, the demise of labor unions, religious conflict, and intervening inside the UN.

The approach we have taken is to have the authors tell their stories of what they did and then reflect on how they utilized the theoretical principles. We have also asked the authors to discuss how their experiences have changed them. For some of these cases, the theory is obvious; for some, it is so deeply embedded in the work that it only emerges under close observation; and for others, it is blended with other theoretical models, resulting in a creative and unique approach.

Thus, this is a book for people who want to improve their understanding and skills for dealing with complex social issues. It is a book for people who have the energy and patience to get involved in what are often fuzzy boundary situations with unclear accountabilities, where being compassionate and caring about the people and the issues are not enough. It is a book for people who recognize that, perhaps, the major dilemma in the world is learning how to manage differences and influence the environment for social well-being.

Finally, it is a book for people who appreciate the tension generated by the two competing cultural drives that get played out in situations around the world over and over again: one for more interdependence and interconnectedness, and the other for increasing autonomy and independence.

Anyone who reads a newspaper, watches television, or listens to the radio is confronted daily with stories about local or global problems that, no matter what the content, have at their core difficulties in power relationships among people. This is true whether it is solving problems of famine, poverty, the conditions of women's lives, struggles for national self-determination, and devastating pandemics. Frequently the magnitude of problem is maintained by long-standing inter-group differences that produce highly embedded projections by one group about the other.

A core intervention issue is how to improve relationships that involve differences in influence among people. This might take the form of working with individuals so that they can understand better the deeply hidden feelings that drive their behavior, or in supporting the development of skills for achieving effective collaboration. It might include "shuttle diplomacy," or bringing in a third party such as the UN to help mediate. Or it might involve bringing together different stakeholders that are involved. But fundamentally, the problem cries out for better dialogue and more tolerance for diversity, and for confronting power differentials among people trying to deal with problems that affect all of the participants.

If you are reading this Introduction, it is safe to assume that you are among the many of us who care about making a difference in this world, about supporting human resilience and creativity, social justice, and human rights, and who want to diminish destructive conflicts, and eliminate social pain. Yet, often our tools feel weak, and our actions feel inadequate to deal with the many intransigent issues that call for action on a societal level.

One approach to social change stresses strategic and political conceptualizations and interventions. These tend to be utilized by those who have a background in law, political and social sciences, and politics. They take into account real differences in power and hierarchy, and look for *actions* that can be taken. They use *negotiation models* of decision-making that focus on a give-and-take approach to resolving conflicts.

Another approach, traditionally favored by psychologists and other helping professions, has to do with improving connectedness and mutual understanding. This approach emphasizes the broadening and deepening of *awareness* of self and other. Building connection stresses the development of *consensus* through expanded consciousness, bringing people of good will together to increase common understanding that can then lead to committed action. The Gestalt model traditionally has put more emphasis on this approach; though originally founded as "Gestalt Therapy," its creators at one time thought to call it "Awareness Therapy" or "Concentration Therapy" (Perls, Hefferline, and Goodman, 1951).

We believe that both of these modes need to be integrated for social change to be most effective. The most useful interventions pay attention to two types of social interaction, what we have elsewhere called the *strategic* and the *intimate* (S. Nevis, Backman, and E. Nevis, 2003). We think that the cases in this book show some understanding of this requirement.

Historical Perspective

We have chosen to highlight the Gestalt approach for a number of reasons. The obvious one is that it is what we know best. But more importantly, its focus on awareness-enhancing interactions through use of a robust intervener presence adds a powerful dimension. Moreover, we want to showcase Gestalt practitioners who work largely at system levels greater than the individual. In some ways it is a culmination of the work begun in the 1960s by Sonia March Nevis, William S. Warner, Joseph Zinker, Joseph Melnick, and Stephanie Backman in extending the Gestalt Model to work with couples and families (Wheeler and Backman, 1994; Zinker, 1994; Melnick and Nevis, 2005), and the work of Richard Wallen and Edwin Nevis (Nevis, 1987, 2005; Nevis, Lancourt, and Vassallo, 1996), in extending the approach to intervention at the organization level. These developments inspired Carolyn Lukensmeyer, John Carter, and Leonard Hirsch to extend the earlier work into larger levels of social system, such as the community, political, and educational arenas. The cases described in this book are the work of the students of all of the above pioneers, who, in turn, learned from the founders of Gestalt therapy.

From the first days of its inception, most Gestalt practitioners have had an interest in social issues and social change, even though they may practice psychotherapy or organizational consulting rather than do direct social change interventions. The creators and first teachers of what was developed as "Gestalt therapy" were largely Jewish professionals coming from families with socialist leanings or a strong social conscience. Though the original developers, Fritz and Laura Perls, came from educated and well-assimilated German families, they fled from Germany and settled in South Africa because of the rise of Hitler and the Nazis. After World War II, they saw the rise of apartheid in South Africa and immigrated to the United States. In the 1960s, Fritz Perls played a major role in creating the communal atmosphere at the Esalen Institute in California and after that helped set up a commune in Canada, partly in fear of what Nixon's authoritarianism would do to life in the United States. It is interesting to speculate on the possibility that they might have developed a "social therapy" if it were not for the fact that Fritz Perls had originally trained as a psychiatrist and psychoanalyst, and was driven by a strong desire to provide an alternative to the Freudian approach to psychotherapy.

Paul Goodman, generally conceded to be a powerful, conceptual contributor to the Gestalt model, was essentially a social critic, not a psychotherapist. Before he met the Perlses and became a collaborator on the book *Gestalt Therapy*, he had written numerous papers with a social utopian thrust, and on art, theatre, and architecture (Goodman, 1946, 1947). He had participated in experimental, educational communities such as the famous Black Mountain College (Katz, 2003). Though a large part of Goodman's explorations into psychotherapy were related to his intense desire to understand himself better, he believed deeply that psychotherapy was essential to producing better individuals *in the service of creating a better society*, rather than as an exercise in "self-development" (Perls, Hefferline, and Goodman, 1951). Goodman was something of a Renaissance person and more of a peaceful anarchist than a psychotherapist.

After completing *Gestalt Therapy* (Perls, Hefferline, and Goodman,

1951), he returned to writing and lecturing on education, management of people, and development of good citizens. His book *Growing Up Absurd* (Goodman, 1960) led to his becoming a hero on college campuses and thrust him into the forefront of the anti-Vietnam War movement in the 1960s. Along with Dwight McDonald and Norman Mailer he became a major advisor to organizers of war protests and the large protest gathering at the Lincoln Memorial in Washington DC (Mailer, 1968). In no little way, this book reflects the best hope of Goodman to encourage people to be involved in social change.

Among the first persons to join Fritz Perls, Laura Perls, and Paul Goodman in teaching Gestalt therapy to others was Isadore From. As a college student, From was influenced by socialism and the Social Labor Party. He also became part of a group of young intellectuals associated with Christopher Isherwood in Los Angeles. After completing his therapy with Fritz Perls, he was invited to become Perls's workshop assistant and accompanied him on teaching assignments in various parts of the United States. In his teaching of the next generation of Gestalt practitioners (including one of the editors, E. Nevis), he was ferocious in demanding that we push ourselves to use precise language and not use language to hide behind or to diminish powerful contact with others. He was particularly vigorous about this when it came to any statement we made about minorities (blacks, gays, women, etc.) or any stereotypical remark.

One of the first people trained in the Gestalt approach was Elliot Shapiro, a clinical psychologist who spent the most significant part of his working life as an administrator in the New York public school system. As a white administrator in Harlem, an African-American neighborhood in New York City, he saw his mission as creating a better society through improved education. He was the first person to apply Gestalt therapy to organization-level intervention and administration, pioneering ways to involve parents and the larger community in the education of children. His work is described in a marvelous book by Nat Hentoff (1967). He was an inspiration to Gestalt-trained people who came after him in applying the Gestalt model to the improvement of education, such as George Dennison (1969), George Brown (1971), and Janet Lederman (1969).

Like Paul Goodman, many of the young people who entered into the study of Gestalt therapy in the 1950s and 1960s also believed that through its practice and that of Lewinian Group Dynamics and Sensitivity Training, they would help to create a better world. As the post-World War II environment provided support for clinical psychologists and organization consultants, they directed their energy into becoming successful professionals. From being on-the-margin, soft revolutionaries, they became mainline practitioners. But their interest in social justice did not disappear entirely. It became expressed in their teaching of the next generation of practitioners, and in their direct participation in anti-war demonstrations and creation of food co-ops, free medical clinics and drug treatment centers, women and gay rights movements, and in AIDS action groups. A major motivation for producing this book is to share with a broad audience the emergence of a renewed commitment on the part of today's generation.

Although there is not much written by Gestalt practitioners concerning social change and social justice, one notable example is the work of Philip Lichtenberg. In two important books, *Community and Confluence* (1990) and *Encountering Bigotry* (1997), Lichtenberg has written about the psychological dynamics of the oppressor and the victim, and of the importance of looking into these roles in oneself, as well as about society in general. His insights into the dynamics of projection are a major contribution towards understanding social justice.

The Current Picture

The cases in this book represent an important forward movement. They are stories of direct involvement in social change by the generations that followed the early Gestalt practitioners and teachers; they are largely the work of our students. We believe that these cases are important examples of a burgeoning new direction. Our motivation for producing this book is to share this work with a broader audience. We were inspired to do so by hearing presentations of three of the cases at the Conference on Social Change sponsored in 2006 by the Gestalt International Study Center in Cape Town, South Africa.

It is interesting to note that only a few of the contributors to this volume were trained as psychotherapists in the traditional sense. Though experienced in applying the Gestalt approach, their basic fields of specialization include religion, economic development, law, organization development, and education. The range of case studies included in this book gives testimony to the growth of interest in applying the approach in the larger social arena, and to the growth of Gestalt education programs that train consultants interested in social change.

With the above as an orientation to the book, we move now to a brief discussion of some basic Gestalt concepts as they apply to intervening at a community or societal level. The remaining chapters will consist of the cases, and we will close with a discussion of implications and conclusions to be gleaned from studying the cases.

References

Baumgardner, P. (1975). *Legacy from Fritz: Gifts from Lake Cowichan.* Palo Alto, CA: Science and Behavior Books.

Brown, G. (1971). *Human teaching for human learning: Confluent education.* New York: Viking Press.

Dennison, G. (1969). *The lives of children.* Portsmouth, NH: Boynton/Cook Pub.

Goodman, P. (1941). *Stop-light: Five dance poems.* Harrington Park, NJ: 5X8 Press.

Goodman, P. (1946). *Art and social nature.* New York: Vinco.

Goodman, P. (1947). *Kafka's prayer.* New York: Vanguard Press.

Goodman, P., & Goodman, P. (1947). *Communitas.* Chicago, IL: University of Chicago Press.

Goodman, P. (1960). *Growing up absurd.* New York: Random House.

Hentoff, N. (with John Holt). (1967). *Our children are dying.* New York: Penguin Books. Reprint: (2004), Highland, NY: The Gestalt Journal Press.

Katz, V. (2003). *Black mountain college.* Cambridge, MA: MIT Press.

Lederman, J. (1969). *Anger and the rocking chair.* Toronto: McGraw-Hill.

Lichtenberg, P. (1994). *Community and confluence: Undoing the clinch of oppression.* Cambridge, MA: GestaltPress.

Lichtenberg, P., van Beuskom, J., & Gibbens, D. (1997) *Encountering bigotry: Befriending projecting persons in everyday life.* Cambridge, MA: GestaltPress.

Lichtenberg, P. (2007). Enriched awareness and fuller citizenship. *Gestalt Review, 11*(3), 170-181.

Mailer, N. (1968). *Armies of the night.* New York: New American Library.

Melnick, J., & Nevis, S. M. (1999). Gestalt family therapy. In R. Fuhr, M. Gremmler-Fuhr, & M. Sreckovic (Eds.), *Das Handbuch der Gestalttherapie* (pp. 937-952). Gottingen, Germany: Hogrefe.

Melnick, J., and Nevis, S. M. (1999), Gestalt family therapy. *British Gestalt Journal, 8*(1), 321-324.

Nevis, E. (1987, 2005). *Organizational consulting: A Gestalt approach.* Cambridge, MA: GestaltPress.

Nevis, E. C., Lancourt, J., & Vassallo, H. G. (1996). *Intentional revolutions: A seven-point strategy for transforming organizations.* San Francisco,

CA: Jossey-Bass.

Nevis, S. M., Bachman, S. and Nevis, E. (2003). Connecting strategic and intimate interactions: The need for balance. *Gestalt Review, 7*(2), 134-146.

Nevis, E. (1997). Gestalt therapy and organization development: A historical perspective, 1930-1996. *Gestalt Review, 1*(2), 110-130.

Orwell, G. (1946). *Politics and the English language.* London: Heritage Magazine.

Perls, F., Hefferline, R., & Goodman, P. (1951). *Gestalt therapy: Excitement and growth in the human personality.* New York: Dell.

Wheeler, G., & Backman, S. (Eds.). (1994). *On intimate ground: A Gestalt approach to working with couples.* San Francisco, CA: Jossey-Bass.

Wysong, J. (1985). An oral history of Gestalt therapy. Part four: A conversation with Elliott Shapiro. *Gestalt Journal, 8*(2), 3-24.

Zinker, J. (1994). *In search of good form: Gestalt therapy with couples and families.* San Francisco, CA: Jossey-Bass.

CHAPTER 2

Gestalt Concepts As Applied to Social Change Intervention

Edwin C. Nevis, PhD and Joseph Melnick, PhD

As we indicated in our introductory chapter, this is a book about practice, not about theory. However, like Kurt Lewin, we firmly believe that the most effective interventions are the actualization of good theory. In each of the cases that follow, the author's work was supported by assumptions embedded in Gestalt theory, or by related theoretical approaches consistent with this approach. In this chapter we present a brief overview of the Gestalt concepts most relevant to social change interventions. This can be used as a template or guideline for analyzing and making meaning of out of the cases. You may not see direct evidence that the authors were consciously aware of these concepts as they organized and conducted their work, but we believe that you will find many of them underlying the decisions and actions that the authors made.[1]

The concepts are organized into three categories:

1. Underlying Philosophical Perspective
   - Holism
   - Optimism
2. Principles of Learning and Change
   - Awareness
   - Gestalt Cycle of Experience
   - Multiple Realities and the Management of Energy
   - Completion of Unfinished Situations
   - Level of System
3. Centrality of Relationship Building in Creating Change

---

[1] For more detailed discussion of the Gestalt approach, the interested reader is referred to Nevis, 1987, 2005; E. Polster and M. Polster, 1973; Woldt and Toman, 2005; Wheeler, 1991; Zinker, 1977.

- Dialogue and Contact
- Presence and Use of Self
- Integration of Strategic and Intimate Interactions
- Joining in a Quest for a Superordinate Goal

Underlying Philosophical Perspective

Holism

The concept of holism embraces a fundamental principle: all living things actively strive for unity and completeness. This notion was of interest to Aristotle—"forms shape matter"—and other philosophers throughout the ages. It became a central aspect of the Gestalt approach through three streams: the work of Jan Christian Smuts (the South African soldier-statesman-philosopher who wrote the book, *Holism and Evolution* [Smuts, 1924]), the perception research of the early Gestalt psychologists, and the research of Kurt Goldstein (1934, 1995) with brain damaged soldiers in World War I. Fritz and Laura Perls became familiar with Smuts's work while Fritz served as an officer in the South African Army during World War II. Laura Perls became familiar with holism while doing graduate work with Max Wertheimer, one of the first Gestalt psychologists. Fritz Perls served as an assistant to Goldstein for a while.

Smuts postulated that "the coordinating principle of the universe is an impulse toward wholeness that manifests itself in each individual by a power of development, growth, or evolution from within." He defined evolution as "a rising series of wholes, from the simplest material patterns to the most advanced . . . with the aspect of unity, inner direction, and actual control always increasing." "Everything wants to be whole. Electrons, and protons, atoms, and molecules, inorganic and organic compounds, colloids, protoplasm, plants and animals, minds and personalities are but some steps in this movement of holism" (as quoted in Millin, 1936, pp. 397, 402). Smuts also talked about "the organism and its field," a notion very central to the Gestalt model.

During the same period of time that Smuts was developing his ideas, a number of European psychologists conducted groundbreaking research to show that people are not simply passive receptors of stimuli from the outside world (Koffka, 1935; Kohler, 1926, 1929, 1947; and Wertheimer, 1912, 1944, 1959). They found that human perception is influenced by an inherent biological drive towards "symmetry," "good form," and completeness. We see wholes before we take in the parts that make up the whole, and we "fill in" or add missing pieces in order to achieve a sense of wholeness. To capture this way of looking at the world, these researchers invoked the word "Gestalt," which means "whole" or "configuration." One of their key concepts was that of *pragnanz*, a German word best translated as *becoming*. This principle states that human beings are in a constant flowing stream of consciousness and of action directed toward making meaning of and enhancing their experience. Humans strive to organize their experience in the most positive way possible given their perception of their environment or "field."

Kurt Lewin and his students (Lewin, 1935; Zeigarnik, 1938, 1967) carried this further in their seminal work on the tension that living systems develop when problem-solving behavior is interrupted and "incomplete or unfinished situations" are created. Perls incorporated this into his techniques for helping clients to deal with "unfinished business" from the past, so that they could more clearly differentiate their present situation from the past. Until past hurts and disappointments are diminished, and the deeply held projections that they engender are dealt with, current progress is not possible.

Kurt Goldstein (1934, 1995) provided perhaps the most dramatic evidence for the importance of the concept of *pragnanz* and the striving for unity and completeness. He found that brain damaged soldiers were not passively resigned to their limitations but had amazing power to adjust through redistribution of function to other parts of the brain, albeit it with a more limited range of activity. Goldstein labeled this as the principle of *self-actualization*[2] and said that this was all one needed to understand the striving of human beings to fulfill their biological destiny.

The reader may be wondering what all of the above has to do with social change. The work discussed above was done mainly with individuals or small groups. However, we believe the holistic perspective has great relevance for the practice of social change. To begin with, the holistic perspective focuses on how the aspects of a social problem are related in a system; it helps in understanding the dynamics of how the system functions, and how the parts (stakeholders) relate to each other to create the overall "field." We are not as interested in diagnosing root causes, and cause-effect relationships as in bringing to light for all concerned the current patterns of thought and behavior that may prevent movement in dealing with a social issue.

Second, we believe that to try to ameliorate a complex social issue by

---

[2] Abraham Maslow (1954) is famous for popularizing the concept self-actualization, but Maslow, who was at one time an assistant to Goldstein, actually borrowed the concept from Goldstein.

dealing only with parts of the system will not be sufficient. This point is now acknowledged by most change specialists, and is a reason for the growing popularity of large-group interventions in which many groups are brought together to work on an issue. (See chapters by Lukensmeyer and Johnston and Mwelwa for examples of this point.)

A third belief that derives from the holistic principle is the assumption that everyone involved in social conflict is doing the best that they are capable of doing, given the conditions in their perceived field. This is a direct application of the principle of *pragnanz* to behavior in larger social systems. We assume that even those who fight against resolving a social problem in a particular way would prefer a better world than the one created by the problem. Stated simply: There are no "good guys" or "bad guys," no bystanders, no non-players. We are all part of the problem and all part of the solution. This perspective may seem naïve in the face of the existence of groups such as al Qaida and suicide bombers, but to remain stuck in projections of the "other" as evil has a limiting effect on our ability to understand and find ways to change things. (See Lichtenberg, 2002, for a thorough discussion of this phenomenon.) Many social conflicts are basically made of strong, emotionally loaded positions on the part of essentially well-meaning people. In these instances, it is a dysfunctional stretch to see the other as "evil."

Optimism

Given the principles of *holism* and *pragnanz*, one can see that the Gestalt orientation is a positive one and embraces a hopeful approach concerning what is possible for human beings to become and to achieve. Melnick and S. Nevis (2005) have written elsewhere about the power of these principles, which are incorporated into programs for professional practitioners and organization leaders conducted by the Gestalt International Study Center and others.

The Gestalt approach looks for what individuals do well and tries to create change by building on the competence and positive values of people. We know that all human beings and social systems have areas of competence and incompetence. But we also know that many change agents focus mainly on what is wrong and believe that eliminating what is wrong will solve the problem. We believe that a strong emphasis on the negative can be corrosive, especially at the beginning of a change process when trust is often low. Stated simply, a negative orientation diminishes and often totally stops people's energy. We know that dysfunctional behaviors need to be confronted, but we start by looking at what works within the system, and we try to get people to acknowledge this and use this "celebration" as a support for dealing with what might be wrong.

We believe that most social systems do not have an in-depth understanding of what they do well and are insufficiently appreciative of their strengths. Our approach, therefore, is to have people focus on strengths before looking at what might be improved or developed. This releases energy and helps to build the atmosphere of trust that is necessary for change to occur. Furthermore, we think that it is essential for leaders or facilitators of social problem resolution to model the faith that, if people engage in the process, something good will come out of it, no matter how dark things look at the moment.

Life by definition is improvisational in that no one can predict the future. The principle of optimism encourages us to take a stance of hope, and to inspire people to strive harder to become the best they are capable of being.

Principles of Learning and Change

Awareness

We believe that awareness *in and of itself* is a precursor for all change. A basic assumption of the Gestalt model is that the more an individual or group can achieve a robust and rich awareness about a situation, the more likely they are to see several possibilities for movement, and the more likely they are to become energized towards generating some action. Awareness includes a range of internal feelings, perceptions, thoughts, insights, fantasies, aspirations, and dreams. It embraces observations of external actions, and a full range of behaviors that catch one's attention during social exchange. It also includes becoming aware of environmental or contextual conditions that define what is possible to achieve at any given moment in time.

For social change to occur, it is necessary to create a sufficient amount of shared awareness that there is a problem, and how the problem manifests itself. Shared awareness results in the joint energy that serves as a catalyst for social action. Building shared awareness is not a simple process that moves in a linear manner toward resolution of what, to begin with, is usually a difficult issue of some duration. Sometimes, it is a one-time occurrence that paves the way for later interventions. Some issues are so impervious to change that they require years of various awareness-raising interventions before a "tipping point" is achieved. In any event, before unified, effective action can be attempted, it is essential to engage in what is often referred to as "consciousness-raising." If this process is not done well, or is curtailed in the interest of rushing to action, we severely limit the long-term effectiveness of our efforts. As you look at the cases that follow, we encourage you to give particular attention to ways in which awareness-raising was accomplished, and how this led to a successful outcome.

A pertinent example of an effective awareness-action sequence can be found in the history of the modern feminist movement in the United States. At the beginning of the twentieth century, there was an active feminist movement that included the opening of Margaret Sanger's birth control clinic in 1916, and the suffragette movement that led to the nineteenth amendment to the U.S. Constitution, which granted women the right to vote in 1920. There followed a period of relative inactivity—although birth control information was removed from classification as pornography in 1936, and the need for workers during World War II propelled women into new roles and new status. Several key events triggered a new round of consciousness-raising: President Kennedy's Commission on the Status of Women report on substantial discrimination against women in the workplace (1961) received wide attention because of its chairperson (Eleanor Roosevelt), and Betty Freidan published her book, *The Feminine Mystique*, in 1963. These events led to the development of women's consciousness-raising groups that were widespread among all levels of social class by 1970. Women talked to each other about what it was like to be a woman in American society. They voiced their experiences and created a lively shared awareness and a sense of "sisterhood." What seemed like isolated individual problems reflected common conditions calling for change.

The essence of the consciousness-raising group was summarized as follows by one of the movement's founders: "We assume that our feelings are telling us something from which we can learn—that our feelings mean something worth analyzing—that our feelings are saying something *political*, something reflecting fear that something bad will happen to us or hope, desire, knowledge that something good will happen to us . . . . In our groups, let's share our feelings and pool them. Let's let ourselves go and see where our feelings lead us. *Our feelings will lead us to ideas and then to actions*" (Sarachild, 1969).

The impact of this "awareness movement" cannot be overestimated; it paved the way for an amazing array of legislation, advocacy groups, and publications from 1968-1978, including the Supreme Court case *Roe vs. Wade* in 1973. It is apparent that it took a tremendous amount of awareness-building to support many personal, group, and political actions.

We are convinced that the actions that took place during those years would not have been possible without the intense awareness enhancement that took place earlier and continued through the 1970s.

The Gestalt Cycle of Experience

The process of generating awareness that stimulates human beings to move into action, and which may be seen as a *learning* process, is central to Gestalt therapy and its applications. At first, this was referred to as the "contacting sequence" (Perls, Hefferline, and Goodman, 1951, pp. 401-405). In the 1960s, the teaching faculty of the Gestalt Institute of Cleveland (William Warner, Erving Polster, Sonia Nevis, Richard Wallen, Marjorie Creelman, et al.) conceptualized it, mainly for didactic purposes, as the *Cycle of Experience*. The concept is now used broadly as a short but crisp way of capturing complex human phenomena: namely, attending to what is going on, finding out what is needed for adaptation and change, and organizing to take effective action toward goal attainment. The concept was first depicted in a circular diagram, but the editors and our colleagues have been picturing it as a sign wave.

Many of the chapters in this book make reference to how this concept informed their work. Practitioners often create a modified version as a guide to their particular work. Recent articles in *Gestalt Review* (Gaffney, 2009; Nevis, 2009) discuss various depictions of the Cycle, including the most recent one adopted by faculty of the Gestalt International Study Center. The important point is that all of these conceptualizations, no matter how they are depicted, are based on deep acceptance of the fact that *change begins with heightened awareness, and that energy and action that might be created is only as good as the awareness process of the "players" in a change intervention*. This is the reason why every one of the cases in this book starts with events designed to raise awareness.

Multiple Realities and the Management of Energy

One way of understanding the Gestalt approach is to see it as a model for understanding the process by which people, individually or collectively, manage energy in dealing with the problems and challenges of all aspects of life. It is not possible for action to occur without an optimum amount of intelligently focused energy, and it should be obvious that the things that stop us from mobilizing joint energy are what keep us from dealing with complex situations and dilemmas.

A social change intervention requires "joined energy." Not every member of an action group is energized by awareness to take the same action. One subgroup may want to "zig" in one direction, while another prefers to "zag" in a different direction. Once you begin to focus on mobilizing energy for change, you quickly come face to face with the reality of individual differences. In any interest group there will be different opinions and different thoughts, not to mention different levels of concern or varying interest in different aspects of the issue. Said simply, each of us creates our own picture of reality. If any movement is to be successful, these *multiple realities* have to be considered and embraced. Thus, there needs to be a respectful process for dealing with the differences, one that leads to some kind of acceptable integration. This is particularly important in settings where multiple stakeholders are involved in achieving any change.

A special challenge arises when the multiple stakeholders represent distinct cultures. Families, couples, and organizations have had a history together and have developed norms (good and bad) around how they deal with each other. We say they know the *rules of engagement* that define their culture. There is often a clarity of purpose and relationship. However, when dealing with social macro-systems there are numerous purposes and varying norms about relationships. Often, part of the dispute may be about the rules of engagement. Bringing different macro level systems together is to invite the possibility of a clash of cultures. Just look at the dismal record of success in many business mergers and acquisitions to see this phenomenon. For this reason, as well as the size and number of individuals and/or groups involved, continuing attention needs to be paid to making these differences explicit and understood by all involved, and as early as possible.

When working with a few people, it is relatively easy to create a joint figure or theme and move people toward the same direction. For the macro-level intervener, differences are often the starting point, while commonalities are in the background. Even with a particular constituency, there are often subgroups that might see a commonly acceptable position as diminishing their power, or violating the agenda of their followers. Because of the complex dynamics involved, it can take years to achieve enough joining so that this group is ready to meet with other constituencies. This dynamic is exemplified by the long and yet unresolved differences between Hamas and Fatah, the two major Palestinian subgroups. As long as these parties are at odds with each other, solid negotiations with Israel remain unattainable.

The Gestalt perspective has an advantage in these settings in that it not only tolerates differences but values them. We assume that differences are normal and are necessary for growth to emerge. Furthermore, any time that forces for change emerge, forces for stability and for maintaining the old ways are also generated. The job of an effective change agent is to respect these differences, to stay open and curious about them, and not to move into a judgmental, disdainful, or contemptuous place. Enhancement of awareness and appreciation of every viewpoint is an essential step on the way to change of any kind. Those trained in the Gestalt model will recognize this as a corollary of the *paradoxical theory of change* (Beisser, 2004): before change can occur, all parties need full awareness of what current reality is, including all variations of reality. The Gestalt model also sees resistance as a label put on people whose energy is not aligned with the direction in which an agent of change wants to move.

Though we are not familiar with all the details of the failed health care initiative of the first Clinton administration, on the surface it would appear that the leaders of the effort were so internally focused that they did not have a clear picture of the realities of important stakeholders. They may well have overestimated the readiness of these stakeholders to go along with a plan that they developed.

By contrast, an effective model for dealing with differences was developed by the Public Conversations Project (Chasin and Herzig, 2008). Some of their highly successful interventions involved an extended period in which people with opposing positions talked to each other but were not allowed to try to change the other's position. In one high profile intervention, they were able to get Boston-area leaders of both the pro-life and pro-choice movements to meet for several years while following these ground rules. This helped to defuse a tense situation following the killing of two members of pro-choice organizations. This approach has great merit in settings where opposing advocacy groups are highly locked into their positions.

Completion of Unfinished Situations

A great deal of social conflict reflects the perniciousness of past real and/or perceived hurts and insults. The recent and continuing conflict between the Serbs and Bosnians is related to something that happened six hundred years ago that left wounds that were never healed. The still unresolved conflict between the Turks and the Greeks around Cyprus goes back many generations. The conflict in the North of Ireland, as well as that between Israel and the Palestinians, are similarly supported by important past events that inhibit the ability of the antagonists to see each other clearly in the present moment. These conflicts remain alive through stories and memories of what happened in the past. Incomplete expression of wounded feelings and acknowledgment of differences that are left over from the past often get carried forward and impact how people see each other and their ability to interact differently in the here and now. A sad example of this kind of conflict occurred recently in Nigeria: a disputed presidential election between two members of different tribes ignited old tribal conflicts, resulting in much bloodshed.

By completion, we mean a diminished interest in hanging on to the past. While not necessarily forgotten, the past recedes into the background rather than being figural. (Melnick and Roos, 2007). But completing unfinished situations is very difficult and often requires giving up one's sense of being a victim. It also requires courage, as exemplified by Anwar Sadat's decision to address the Israeli parliament in 1977. This was an explicit acknowledgement that the past had to be healed in order for Egypt and Israel to move toward a peaceful relationship. Sadat paid for this courageous act with his life, but Israel and Egypt have been at peace with each other for over thirty years. By contrast, Yassir Arafat was not willing or able to accept the last peace accord worked out by President Clinton before leaving office in 2000. Though he apparently got a great deal of what the Palestinians were asking for, Arafat was not able to give up clinging to the past. Some experts say that, like Sadat, he would have been assassinated. Nonetheless, the Palestinian-Israeli conflict continues, as both sides stubbornly cling to the past.

Unfinished business, and the deeply embedded resentment that it generates, clearly interferes with any striving for holism, and for becoming the best that social groups are capable of being. Until the unfinished business is dealt with, progress will be limited. South Africa's Truth and Reconciliation Initiative (TRC) (Vora and Vora, 2004) is an example of an attempt to deal with the deep rupture of its apartheid past. Anyone who felt that he or she had been a victim of violence could come forward and be heard. Perpetrators of violence could also give testimony and request amnesty from prosecution. Though this program is controversial, and though there are doubters of its appropriateness or effectiveness, the TRC is seen by many to be an important component of the transition to democracy in South Africa.

Level of System

The goal of social change is to impact the attitudes and behaviors of large numbers of people. A critical issue is always that of where and how to start. Should we begin by working to change the leader or a few key individuals? There is a strong belief that starting "at the top" is the best way to get things rolling. Other evidence exists to show that significant change can begin at the bottom and work its way up. Yet other research shows that finding or positioning a significant group of "champions" throughout the stakeholders has an impact. And yet other evidence shows that building coalition groups or "cells" can help advance change. In his book *The Tipping Point*, Malcolm Gladwell (2000) has written about this matter. Beer, Eisenstat, and Spector (1990) have presented some case evidence of significant change that began in the middle or at the fringes of an organization. The fact is that entry can be made at various levels of the system. Moreover, both systems theory and much consulting experience tell us that change at any level of system can have a significant effect on other parts. An important tactical move is for social change interveners to select their point or points of entry, and when a significant intervention is made at a particular point, to anticipate the impact on other levels of system.

One entry point is to direct persuasive messages to a broad spectrum of *individuals* as is often done in political campaigns, or in initiatives to have people behave more safely at work, stop smoking, or practice safe sex. The message is disseminated through various forms of media, posters at the workplace, etc. Sometimes this approach is effective but often falls short in trying to change deeply ingrained patterns and habits, such as smoking. In these instances, a more direct intervention is needed, such as in individual psychotherapy or counseling. In the case of smoking, individuals could look at the reasons why they smoke, what stops them from quitting, the long-term physical implications of smoking, etc. A more powerful form of intervention might be to have the smoker meet with a significant other in a joint session, in which the partner discusses the personal impact of the smoking. In this case, one is intervening at a very important level: *the dyadic*.

A third, equally powerful level, is that of *the group*, insofar as it takes advantage of group dynamics. In a pioneering study in the 1940s, Margaret Mead and Kurt Lewin (Lewin, 1943; Wansink, 2002) were asked to work with the U.S. government on the task of encouraging housewives to buy less popular cuts of meats such as brains, tripe, and kidneys (prime beef was primarily being made available to the armed forces). Housewives who participated in-group discussions used the less popular meat at a much higher rate than a controlled group of housewives exposed to only lectures and written persuasion, such as brochures. Sharing concerns and objections and hearing some instances where those foods were used turned out to be a powerful motivator for those housewives. This study, and others conducted by Lewin and his students, led to what is now a widespread use of group participation in making important decisions.

Given the complexity of large-scale change efforts, one can say that, ideally, interventions should be made at all levels of system, from individual to dyadic, group, and community levels. Gestalt-trained OD consultants have been exposed to this perspective under the general heading of choice points and dilemmas. While, ideally, it may be best to work at all levels, in practice this is seldom possible; interveners must make choices as to what level will be their primary focus. In looking at the cases that follow, you will notice not only the variety of levels of choice, but also the specific conditions that helped determine where to intervene.

Centrality of Relationship Building in Creating Change

Dialogue and Contact

In order for social change to occur, effective dialogue among the stakeholders is essential. When there are strong differences or conflict among people, they stop engaging with each other in meaningful ways. They often focus on what is wrong with the other's position and engage in many projections. An essential ingredient in Gestalt therapy is to use methods to support authentic, congruent, and self-disclosing dialogue amongst all participants. In fact, one of the main reasons the Gestalt approach became popular initially was because it supported highly contactful conversations between client and therapist at the individual level, resulting in a process that produced much change and growth. One of the major contributions of Fritz and Laura Perls was their development of methods for actualizing what Martin Buber referred to as "I/Thou Communication" (Buber, 1947, 2002). Gestalt practitioners are highly attuned to the importance of dialogue and contact, whatever system level they are working at to produce change. In dialogue each can express and hear the other´s feelings, values, and aspirations. Dialogue involves much more than the speaking of words; it is the essential way people "reach" or "touch" each other. It includes how one talks, how one uses one´s body and, in fact, it encompasses one's whole stance. It is essential in order for trust to develop. One way to attack the mistrust among antagonists is to create settings in which meaningful dialogue can occur. This will not be easy to do at first try but examples, such as Sadat´s going to the

Israeli Parliament and the approach of the Public Conversations Project (Chasin and Herzig, 2008), show what is possible.

In building meaningful dialogue, it is essential to pay attention to the language used by participants. Gestalt consultants intervene to help people express themselves as directly and succinctly as possible. But words are cheap; not all talk is contactful. We want to achieve a give and take exchange, not to have people make speeches at each other. Practitioners help people reach across the barriers and impact each other as concerned, well-meaning human beings. To be successful, interventions must model and teach contactful use of language. In this regard we are reminded of Confucius, who was once asked what he would do if he were to be the ruler of the country. He replied that the first thing he would do is "to clean up the language of the country." Much of George Orwell's writings expressed his anger at how politicians used language to obfuscate and control things, keeping them from making good contact with each other (Orwell, 1946). The Gestalt way of working does not supplant good principles of diplomatic exchange, but it serves to loosen the restricting binds of overly formal institutional modes, and seeks a more direct human exchange.

Presence and Use of Self

To be effective, social change interveners must be able to use themselves as instruments of support and influence. They must act to support new awareness among stakeholders about their process, evoking an interest in what is working and what is missing, as well as modeling a way of solving problems and dealing with life in general. To accomplish this, Gestalt interveners must have some awareness of what they evoke in other people as a consequence of their being in the same space with them. Nevis (1985, 2002) defines this phenomenon as *presence*.

Presence is necessary for creating the conditions where others will notice, listen, and be interested in you. It is embedded in a commitment to being influential by living out one's values. It incorporates both a willingness to take a stand for integrity, commitment, and authenticity, and an ability to be equally curious about and respectful toward all the stakeholders. When interveners begin working with a group dealing with social change, they are often entering into situations where differences may be strong, or where the participants have low energy or little faith that something good can come out of the exercise. The first issue that an intervener has to address is: "Why should they listen to me?" "Why should they accept influence from me?" If thoughts such as these are not publicly expressed, they certainly go on inside the minds of participants. This is the case even if they have invited you to be a facilitator of their meeting. To deal with this given, it is very important to establish your *presence* at the outset. This is critical whether you are dealing with a couple of people, or working with a group numbering in the thousands.

Successful leaders seem to have an almost intuitive understanding of the above. They get the attention of their followers not only from their formal power but also from their compelling way of being. The challenge for interveners is how to present themselves so that participants in change efforts want to pay attention to what they say, and to how they behave. Using yourself to establish *presence* does not mean that, as a facilitator, you act to command the stage. After all, you are a stage manager, not one of the actors. You are a "third-party intervener," not a participant. This means that you act in an interesting way, and that you are enough like the participants to be acceptable, yet different in some compelling way. It involves how you introduce yourself, the language you use, and the way that you model being contactful with participants.

In order to have impact, you have to be seen as someone who is equally interested in all the parties involved and not just in certain viewpoints, while at the same time having something unique to add to the situation. You want to be seen as holding values that are acceptable to the participants so that they feel some trust and connection—yet different enough so that they are motivated to hear what you have to say. The stance you take will be an integration of your belief of how to be influential and your personal style in presenting yourself. Nevis has written extensively about these points in his book, *Organizational Consulting: A Gestalt Approach* (1987/2005).

Perhaps the biggest challenge for an intervener in this regard is how to remain neutral with regard to the *issues* being deliberated, while at the same time being a force that influences the *process*. One way is to get participants to see you for who you are and what you stand for, and not as an institutional symbol. One can reasonably assume that the participants' experiences with societal institutions have not often been very positive or have created ambivalent feelings. People will project onto you their history at different levels of system. If you are hired by a government agency to help with economic development in a province where people previously have had bad experiences with segments of government, they will project their experiences onto to you. If you are to help in this situation, you must find a way to undo this projection so that there is a clean picture of you and how you are there to be of help.

Using one's self in social change settings is an art of a high order. In reading the cases that follow, we suggest that you look closely at how each intervener established his or her *presence*.

Integration of Strategic and Intimate Interaction

A central concept in our teaching at the Gestalt International Study Center (GISC) has to do with the importance of connecting intimate and strategic interventions when intervening at any level of system. As we have written elsewhere (S. Nevis, Backman, and E. Nevis, 2003), intimate behavior helps build connection through mutuality and nonhierarchical exchange. The focus is on getting people to understand each other in the present moment while temporarily placing less attention on the outcome of the issue that initially brings them together. The behavior is directed toward understanding one another and focused less on task accomplishment. It is more focused on here and now interaction.

Strategic behavior focuses more on achieving a goal or completing a piece of work. It acknowledges that, in any social system, not everyone is equal in accountability for the output of interdependent behavior. There are differences of hierarchical responsibility. Parents are accountable for the behavior of their children, and heads of work units are accountable to their constituencies. Leaders of social, governmental, and educational organizations are accountable for the effectiveness of their organizations. All of these accountabilities are larger in scope and system importance than are the responsibilities of their followers. Strategic behavior is designed to get things accomplished.

In a general way, one can think of consensus models of decision-making as a form of intimate interaction, while negotiation models represent the outcome of strategic interactions. In the development of the Lewinian model during the early work in-group dynamics, the focus was primarily pointed toward ways of achieving consensus. The aim was to create a setting where people could share thoughts, feelings, and aspirations in a trusting atmosphere, one that would lead to a consensus around an issue (Lewin, 1948). This perspective also developed out of the practice of psychotherapy. Originally, the goal of psychotherapy was for individuals to learn to know themselves, and to become more connected to themselves. Paul Goodman's intense study of, and personal immersion in, psychotherapy was fired by his belief that highly self-aware individuals are needed to help create an enlightened society. Goodman believed deeply that, if we could gather enough of these people, we could build wonderful communities in which to work and live.

In past years, social change occurred mainly through strategic or structural interventions, often in the form of revolutions. Power was the primary tool, and as a result there were winners and losers. One unfortunate outcome was the unending resentment of the losers seen in the fact that many current conflicts are long standing. In more modern times, we have progressed toward trying to get the stakeholders into the room for face-to-face negotiations, and to have them understand that each has to give up something in order for a more lasting resolution to occur. In its original formulation, the Gestalt approach is somewhat underdeveloped in terms of its theory and use of power. Other than the early concept of "Top Dog/Underdog," and the examination of the power of the underdog, there is little mention of power issues. The closest we have come in recent years is to develop the notion of strategic behavior as a legitimate support for power differentials.

For long-term change to occur, stakeholders need to be able to talk to each other on both strategic and intimate levels. Both consensus building and negotiation may be required (Melnick, 2007; S. Nevis, Backman and E. Nevis, 2003).

Joining in a Quest for a Superordinate Goal

Strictly speaking, the concept of working with strong differences between conflicting groups is not a Gestalt notion. It is, however, closely related to the Gestalt concept of "joining": working with differing or diverse groups to find a goal important to all sides, and around which they each can muster significant energy. This is what is meant by superordinate goal: there is something each of us wants, but we cannot achieve it alone; we need to cooperate with one another. This concept received great attention during the days of the "Cold War" between the United States and the USSR. It was the focus of both research and inter-group relations teachings in the 1950s and 1960s (Sherif, 1971). Most interventions bringing diverse or "warring" groups together assume that a superordinate goal exists, but that people may not be aware of it or of what it takes to achieve it. The different groups may also need to come to terms with what they perhaps have to give up or alter in order to reach the common goal. The practice of mediation consists largely of working with people to identify a superordinate goal and to help them achieve it. There are undoubtedly other useful Gestalt concepts. We have selected these because we see them as being critical to success in social change efforts. We encourage you to look for their manifestation in the cases that follow.

References

Beer, M., Eisenstat, R.A., & Spector, B. (1990). *The critical path to corporate renewal.* Boston, MA: Harvard Business School Press.

Beisser, A. (2004). The paradoxical theory of change. *International Gestalt Journal, 27,* 103-107.

Bradford, L. P., Gibb, J. R., & Benne, K. D. (1964). *T-group theory and laboratory method.* New York, NY: John Wiley.

Buber, M. (1947, 2002). *Between man and man.* London: Routledge. (Original essay on I and Thou published in Germany in 1923)

Freidan, B. (1963). *The feminine mystique.* New York, NY: Norton & Company.

Chasin, L., & Herzig, M. (2008). *Fostering dialogue across divides.* Watertown, MA: Public Conversations Project.

Gaffney, S. (2009). The cycle of experience recycled: Then, now, next? *Gestalt Review, 13*(1), 7-23.

Gladwell, M. (2000). *The tipping point.* Boston, MA: Little Brown.

Goldstein, K. (1995). *The organism.* Cambridge, MA: MIT Press. (Originally published in the USA in 1939)

Kaplan, F. B., & Mead, M. (Eds.). (1965). *American women: The report of the president's commission on the status of women.* Government Printing Office.

Koffka, K. (1935) *Principles of Gestalt psychology.* New York: McGraw Hill.

Kohler, W. (1926). *Mentality of apes.* New York: Harcourt Brace.

Kohler, W. (1929, 1947), *Gestalt psychology.* New York: Liveright.

Lewin, K. (1948). *Resolving social conflicts: Selected papers in group dynamics.* New York, NY: Harper & Row.

Lewin, K. (1943). Forces behind food habits and methods of change. In *The problem of changing food habits, 1941-43. Bulletin of the National Research Council, 108* (pp. 35-65). Washington, DC: National Research Council and National Academy of Sciences.

Lewin, K. (1942). The relative effectiveness of a lecture method and a method of group decision for changing food habits. Unpublished document.

Lewin, C. (1935). *A dynamic theory of personality.* New York, NY: McGraw Hill.

Maslow, A. (1954). *Motivation and personality.* New York, NY: Harper & Rowe.

Mead, M., & Lewin, K. (1943). *The problem of changing food habits, 1941-*

1943. Bulletin of the National Research Council, 108. Washington DC: National Research Council and National Academy of Sciences.

Melnick, J. (2007). Managing differences: A Gestalt approach to dealing with conflict. *Gestalt Review, 11*(3), 165-169.

Melnick, J., & Nevis, S. M. (2005). The willing suspension of disbelief: Optimism. *Gestalt Review, 9*(1), 10-26.

Melnick, J., & Roos, S. (2007). The myth of closure. *Gestalt Review, 11*(2), 90-107.

Millin, S. G. (1936). *General Smuts.* London: Faber & Faber.

Nevis, E. (2009). Commentary: Gaffney's cycle of experience recycled. *Gestalt Review, 13*(1), 37-42.

Nevis, E. (1987, 2005). *Organizational consulting: A Gestalt approach.* Cambridge, MA: GestaltPress.

Nevis, S. M., Bachman, S., & Nevis, E. (2003). Connecting strategic and intimate interactions: The need for balance. *Gestalt Review, 7*(2), 134-146.

Perls, F., Hefferline, R., & Goodman, P. (1951). *Gestalt therapy: Excitement and growth in the human personality.* New York: Dell.

Polster, E., & Polster, M. (1973). *Gestalt therapy integrated.* New York, NY: Brunner/Mazel.

Sarachild, K. (1969). *Feminist revolution.* New York, NY: Redstockings.

Smuts, J. (1924). *Holism and evolution.* New York, NY: Macmillan.

Vora, J., & Vora, E. (2004) "The effectiveness of South Africa's truth and reconciliation commission: Perceptions of Xhosa, Afrikaner, and English South Africans". *Journal of Black Studies, 34*(3), 301-322.

Wansink, B. (2002). Changing eating habits on the home front: Lost lessons from World War II Research. *Journal of Public Policy & Marketing, 21*(1), 90-99.

Wertheimer, M. (1944). *Gestalt theory.* New York:

Wertheimer, M. (1959). *Productive thinking.* New York: Harcourt Brace.

Wheeler, G. (1991). *Gestalt reconsidered: A new approach to contact and resistance.* New York: Gardner Press (The Gestalt Institute of Cleveland).

Woldt, A., & Toman, S. (Eds.). (2005). *Gestalt therapy: History, theory and practice.* London: Sage.

Zeigarnik, B. (1927). Über das Behalten von erledigten und unerledigten Handlungen (The retention of completed and uncompleted activities). *Psychologische Forschung, 9,* 1-85.

Zeigarnik, B. (1967). On unfinished and finished tasks. In W.D. Ellis (Ed.), *A Sourcebook of Gestalt Psychology* (pp. 300-314). New York,

NY: Humanities Press. (Original work published 1938)

Zinker, J. (1977). *Creative process in Gestalt therapy.* New York, NY: Brunner/Mazel.

CHAPTER 3

When Poor is Rich: Transformative Power of I-Thou Relationships in a Brazilian *Favela*

Mary Grace Neville, PhD

Editors' Introduction

Humans are social creatures. We are deep wired to not be alone, to connect, to belong, to be in relationship, and to be in community. Yet at the same time, as a species, we are also deeply competitive and hierarchical, which often results in both economic wealth and power resting in the hands of a few.

In this chapter, Neville conveys her personal journey of venturing into Quatro Varas, an economically poor community in Brazil. She documents how the community members' relational lives challenge our narrow, conventional notions of wealth, as she discovers a community built on the joining of people who refuse to relate in traditional hierarchical ways based on education, social class, and finances. Instead, she finds a community that challenges our conventional notions by creating relational wealth.

Neville, using the stories of its members, explores how this community is able to transcend poverty by living fully in relationship. Through transformative cooperation, a web of connections is created. A social network that includes individuals, institutions, and programs is formed, and it supports this community and its members. This fostering of humanness through authentic relationship, or what Buber calls I-Thou (1970), builds wealth not only in the traditional ways but also in terms of something less concrete and tangible. This economically poor group of people builds wealth in terms of connection, cooperation, self-esteem and identity—ways that are, at their core, truly transformational.

The communal spirit, the building of authentic interaction through community, has been an essential value of the Gestalt approach from the beginning (Goodman, 1947; Baumgardner, 1975). As Neville says in her conclusion, the Quatro Varas community represents Gestalt practice at its best.

Introduction[3]

This ethnographic case study considers the role of relationship and humanness in creating wealth through well-being in a socio-economically marginalized community. Though I am classically trained in business to conceptualize "wealth" in financial terms, I understand wealth linguistically as "that which brings value." What is explored here, then, is the "value" created in individual lives through the transformative power of individuals who not only honor themselves and their life experience, but also honor others as equals. Doing this work requires that individuals come to know themselves beyond the boundaries created by social projections and economic labels (e.g., "dangerous drug addict" or "filthy poor people"). These relationships, grounded in profound and authentic humanness, can best be characterized by Martin Buber's "I-Thou" interactions (Buber, 1923/1970). Traditional interactions for *favelados*, the people of Brazilian *favelas* (shanty towns), are hierarchical relationships (Buber's "I-It" relationships), both with other classes of society and among themselves. The shift to I-Thou interactions brings value to the experience taking place *between* individuals, rather than locating wealth either in the individuals or in their possessions.

The emphasis on value found through relationship by honoring self, co-creating experience among people, and dialogic creation of meaning, also undergirds Gestalt therapy theory (Yontef, 2002). Gestalt theorist Wulf (1998) explains: "[T]he fundamental fact of human existence is the human being with the human being, i.e., a person is always in relation to something, or somebody. In Buber's anthropology, communication is what makes human beings human beings. Genuine dialogue begins when the 'I' enters into the presence of the 'Thou'" (p. 89).

This study explores how one group of socio-economically marginalized people (e.g., "the poor") creates holistic riches by cultivating that fundamental fact of fully being human, that I-Thou interaction. Its hypothesis is that transformation from a schema designed on projections, to a schema based on an experiential capacity and courage for human encounter, emerges from the experience of people being authentically in relationship with one another. This transformation includes valuing the humanness of others and learning from one another as everyone builds self respect, self-esteem, and, in the case of poverty, economic sustenance. The hypothesis will be explored through the stories the people in and of

---

[3] This study is reprinted, with permission, from *Gestalt Review, 12* (3), 248-266.

a community in northern Brazil related to me during fieldwork carried out in 2001. By way of conclusion, an emergent theory of transformative cooperation will be posited.

Background

When I first visited the village Quatro Varas in 1994, the spirit and grace of the people starkly contrasted with the physical squalor of the neighboring *favelas*. I arrived in an air-conditioned tour bus as part of an American delegation of business students wanting to learn about international trade, though from the sanitized perspective of banks and four-star hotels. Perhaps in an attempt to thwart a particularly parochial chaperone, I immediately volunteered for "treatement" [*sic*] offered through the broken translation of a local healer. Three healers set to work on my various pressure points and chakras, as my chaperone worried on the other side of the drape about her personal liability if I contracted disease from the locals' touch. With no shared language but that of a transcended tongue of the heart, the healers and I encountered each other in what Buber calls an "I-Thou" relationship, a reverent state of presence co-created with the other. I experienced an unconditional acceptance never imagined in my otherwise privileged life. These women, with every reason to resent me—from the vehicle in which I arrived, to the indignant chaperone, to the icon of privilege possibly projected onto a foreign business student—transformed our socioeconomic inequities through their human touch. The healers conducted a particular current of love transcending not only socioeconomic boundaries but also personal life injustices, backgrounds of drug abuse, violence, and other burdens. This was my first—my pivotal and my transformational— experience with the village Quatro Varas. From there, I became curious. My deep regard for their web of relationships and humanness only grew as I repeated contact with the community in 2001.

I studied Quatro Varas—a community, a project, and finally a metaphor—in order to understand the phenomenon of wealth as well-being. This phenomenon compels people to discard their individualistic and hierarchical power perspectives and change into interconnected human beings who honor themselves and others. Their rich existence is particularly intriguing when contrasted with the socioeconomic poverty context of the relationships. Here, two middle-class brothers transcend social boundaries in ways that catalyze indigenous healing and strength among a local population excluded from even the hope of having economic or social parity with any proximal social group. I now understand the community of Quatro Varas[4] to manifest itself in three ways: the project grounds as a physical location, the programs held on and sponsored through the project grounds to reach people, and the rhythm of how work gets done by the community.

The Project Quatro Varas

The project Quatro Varas is a therapeutic center in an urban *favela,* slum or shanty town, in one of the poorest regions of Brazil with the highest rate of illiteracy, the lowest level of income, and the greatest incidence of malnutrition and infant mortality nationwide (Roett, 1999, p. 228).[5] The project is located on private land in Pirambu, the 250,000 person urban "periphery" on the north side of the city of Fortaleza in the northeastern Brazilian state of Ceará. Within Pirambu, different neighborhoods and *favelas* have evolved. One of the *favelas* was coincidently near an abandoned manufacturing site.

Years after the site was "baptized" a community by squatters, foreign grant support was secured to buy the property.[6] This geographic area has come to be known as Quatro Varas. The site of Quatro Varas remains the abandoned manufacturing site, but the community now privately owns both the land and the buildings that have been converted into appropriate program spaces.

Quatro Varas emerged during the 1980s as a place of hope, with a community-based program of primary care therapies and skill learning. Blends of spiritual traditions actively guide the therapies and healings. The project is run as a collective where the proceeds any one individual generates are shared, half with the particular community project, and

---

[4] The Portuguese word *comunidade* can be translated as either "the community" or "the commonwealth." The distinction between these two words in English illustrates a distinction made in this paper. In interviews, we find that "the community" is used to refer to the project Quatro Varas, the people associated with Quatro Varas living in surrounding neighborhoods, as well as the commonwealth or entire class of poor people nationwide. This blended intention of both structured community and communal spirit of living mirrors Paul Goodman's intention in his book of 1947, *Communitas.* By this time, Goodman's thinking was already shaping that of Fritz and Laura Perls and of early Gestalt therapy theory. Victor Turner (1969), cultural anthropologist, later explores the experience of "comunitas" from individual existential, group cooperative, and social model perspectives in *The Ritual: Process Structure and Anti-Structure.*

[5] For an in-depth academic discussion of Brazilian *favelas* and the *favelados'* migration patterns in São Paulo, see Perlman (1976), *The Myth of Marginality.* For a journalistic story about the *favelas* of Rio de Janeiro, see Rambali (1993).

[6] The purchase of property in Brazil increases the social standing of poor people among their peers according to Sarti (1995, p. 117). Many symbolic statements made by individuals and neighborhoods with regard to their relative self-worth appear in the stories told throughout this paper.

half to reward the person's efforts. The project is open to a wide range of involvement, and its participants explain it structurally as a spider's web of relationships touching approximately 12,000 people annually. As a primary figure in the community reveals in a story, "the spider is nothing without his web and we are nothing without community." People hear about Quatro Varas through word of mouth and come because someone they know has been there. "People come here because of pain; they get here because of faith," stated one visitor. The joining of people and stories creates a web of relationships central to the community's identity and transformative potential.

The community's web metaphor forms what I refer to as *relationality*. Relationality extends beyond simply relating to another; it also includes a state of humanness that coexists with the experience of being in relationship. The interactions described here, and the stories related that others have shared, highlight two common conditions people tell me relationality heals: loneliness and social ostracism. A common experience for the people interviewed was discovering, "I am not alone." To be "in relationship" in this context implies a reciprocal way of being, whereby one seeks to learn from the other as well as to share respectfully parts of oneself with the other. By giving voice to their experiences, the people of this community come to find that they are not alone, that they do in fact belong to the community. The second term that emerges frequently is *humanism*, the condition of being fully human. In this context, humanism represents the potential for good and for the realization of uncertainty, fallibility, or evil in every person. Relational life and humanism are at the center of the stories that people tell.

Method

During the fieldwork for this study, I lived in the guesthouse called "the house of refuge," which was located on a hill at the ocean side of the project's common grounds. Anastasia White, another student of organizational behavior, and I were engaged in participant observation and conducted interviews for eight days in the spring of 2001. We shared our observations and opinions during our weeklong visit, and we reflected upon our impressions, experiences, interpretations, and the meaning that could be made from the interpretations. In addition to conducting interviews, I gathered photographs and children's artwork and experienced healing practices. We maintained separate field notes, and we made audio-tapes of our dialogues each evening. We acknowledged on arrival that our ability to hear people's stories about their experiences would be, in part, dependent upon our ability to gain acceptance into the community. No doubt, our fields of experience differed enormously each from the other and from those of the community members. Therefore, our primary liaison "presented" us to the community through stories of introduction and arranged for us to stay in the community itself.

Living in the community created opportunities to watch daily comings and goings of people, socialize informally by "hanging out" with community members, participate in massage therapy and healings, and consume local tonics for circumstantial ailments. We experienced an increasing level of trust from others as we participated in community activities and simply respected the rhythm of interactions.

Given that our life experiences shape our perceptions and interpretations in qualitative research (Schwartzman, 1993; Reinharz, 1992), it is necessary to outline our backgrounds here. I am a white, upper middle class, American woman, raised in a liberal and socially active academic family in the Southern United States. This was my third trip to Brazil and my second visit to Quatro Varas. I am classically trained in business; I am also religiously and socially conditioned in the power of human experience. This convergence of fields not only exposes me to traditional economic and scientific thinking, but it also gives me a sense of identification with the twentieth-century German philosophers who challenged the scientific establishment and influenced the Gestalt movement.

Anastasia White is a white South African raised in a black, South African community during the end of apartheid and the birth of the new South Africa. She grew up as a freedom fighter for the anti-apartheid movement and subsequently trained as a peacekeeper and negotiator in identity-based conflicts. Coming from a religious family who continually gave everything they had to people who needed it more, she is comfortable with ambiguity, familiar with poverty, accustomed to multiracial situations, and flexible where she does not understand the spoken language.[7] This was her first trip to Brazil, which she found culturally similar to her home country.

Our open-ended interviews, anchored in appreciation for positive aspects of the individual and the collective whole (Cooperrider and

---

[7] South Africa has eleven official languages and twenty-two commonly spoken languages; however, it is rare for any one South African to speak all the languages. It is common, on the other hand, for two or more people to have a conversational interaction or a non-verbal interaction in which the parties do not speak the same language. Therefore, a cultural familiarity exists in situations where communication beyond language is required.

Srivastva, 2000), were conducted in English and Portuguese in the presence of an interpreter.[8] The interviews themselves were designed to make stories surface about the ties that bind individuals to the project of Quatro Varas. Because storytelling is common in the therapeutic methods of many programs within the project, it is a familiar way of interacting for the people. After returning to the United States, I followed Strauss and Corbin's (1998) grounded theory analytical approach to the identification of themes and concepts. A prevalence of relationality and humanness through personal transformation emerged inductively as the dominant contributor to the creation of wealth through well-being.

Quatro Varas and Its People

Quatro Varas translates into English as "four canes" or "four sticks." *From the Sertão to the Favela*, a book researched, written, and illustrated by the children of the village as a therapeutic project to strengthen their identity by honoring their field of heritage, tells the story of these migrant people's arrival in Fortaleza. The book begins with a description of the proud people's agricultural heritage prior to seasons of drought that had forced outward migration:

> After an exhausting journey, the migrants finally reach the city in pursuit of their dreams. Straight away they find out that far from solving the problem, they are about to face a whole range of much more dramatic difficulties. These include finding shelter, putting up with the stench of the sewers and the uncovered rubbish heaps, having to endure constant noise and live in confined spaces, and coping with disease as well as all the violence and aggression that are a feature of life in the *favelas*. The city's indifference to so much suffering induces feelings of violence against life since their right to belong to society goes unrecognized [*From the Sertão*, p. 65].

As they migrate to the city and become its urban poor, these people undergo an identity shift: their initial identity forged by land and agriculture becomes conditioned by isolation and domination. Secondly, some of these migrants organize themselves into what evolves into Quatro Varas. The children's book tells of repeated police attacks and the

---

[8] All interviews were audio-taped. Interviews conducted in Portuguese were translated into English, including interviews conducted with an interpreter present. Two translators were tested, and their work was validated for accuracy by an independent Brazilian familiar with the approach and methodology used for the study. One translator was selected to render all interviews.

migrants' collective resistance. It then recounts an ancient legend that goes as follows. Having a presentiment of his death, a very poor man summoned his four children and said, "I am going to die and I don't have any material goods to bequeath as a legacy. However, I am going to leave you a very important message." He then told each of them to bring a stick. When they did so, he broke each stick individually and sent his sons for more sticks. When they each returned, the old man put the sticks together and ordered each of his children to break them. Nobody could do so when all the four sticks were together. "All right, this is my message: while they are joined together, no one can destroy them" (*From the Sertão*, p. 149). At a people's meeting, the occupied *favela* began to be called "Community of Quatro Varas" (*From the Sertão*, p. 149), a metaphor that expresses the power of choosing to exist in interdependent relationship with others.

Today, the name "Projecto 4 Varas" is proudly painted on a double width car gate around the corner of a washed out yet active, dirt street. The boundary to this community land is symbolic; a doorway next to the car-gate is always open, and fencing marks only three of four sides of the property. The project grounds are located along the ocean in the heart of the Pirambu *favela*. The project comprises buildings for various activities and gardens, as well as a large covered space for community meetings. The grounds feel energetically peaceful and restorative in the midst of urban density; yet, the Brazilian heat and humidity are oppressive and exhausting. Self-esteem, identity, and economic possibilities are co-created around the individuals; the eight programs run from the project grounds, and the collective of relationships now spanning middle class and people of the *favela*. The stories of some of these people and their programs provide examples of these relationships.

Airton Barrato—A Lawyer in the *Favelas*

Airton Barrato is a central individual who creates relationships in Quatro Varas. He grew up in the Sertão in a family of ten children, with a deep regard for human beings. Airton's transformation occurred early in the life of the community. Once he found a wallet in a trash pile. He was elated, until his mother scolded him for his delight by saying, "For you to have found it, someone else must have lost it." He describes his own childhood resentment toward workers who begged for food, because when his parents consistently invited waywards into their home, Airton's portion of dinner became smaller. Interestingly though, Airton's own adolescent entitlement shifted into a horizontal, relational way of being-in-the-world as he saw injustices being done, and as he came to know the people of the *favela* as individuals. Today, he lives in the *favela* as a lawyer and runs a near-free human rights legal aid project in Quatro Varas. He shares a small office with two others in a secondhand furniture and electronics warehouse, which supplies thrift shops throughout Pirambu.

His family migrated to Pirambu when his father's job changed during the drought. Airton tells stories of being embarrassed by his family's economic limits when they moved to the city; he thought, "The favela was the place of poor and dead people." His projection shifted from that of "those poor people" into a "thou" paradigm, which he now articulates by asking, "What makes me different from those children? These adults? Why should I be different?" Two stories exemplify how he integrates his experiences by honoring self and others as equals, i.e., relationality through humanness.

At first, Airton was exploring career possibilities through school. One day, while waiting for a bus, he watched as a boy sniffed glue from a paper bag. A policeman rubbed the boy's face in the bag. The boy screamed. A street bum, as Airton describes him, asked the policeman why he did that, and the police, in turn, arrested the bum for interfering with police work. Airton went to the police station as an eyewitness for both the boy and the bum but was told, "You go away or you're going to jail." Airton said he learned that "it's good to see, hear, and shut up;" the world was the way it was because people did not want to interfere. He said that he felt like a coward for having left. He asked, "How am I going to change the world if I'm uncomfortable to come forward? Had I been a lawyer and had I known the law, I would have had more power to help the two of them, the kid and the man." From a relational perspective, Airton was identifying with part of an alienated population oppressed by societal contempt for I-It relationships. His career goal was not so much to become a lawyer as to find a career that allowed him to engage in human relationships, and so move toward a Gestalt wholeness leading to social change.

In the second story, Airton had befriended Louisa, a young woman living in a shanty in the *favela* with two younger brothers and no parents. Whenever he could, Airton gave Louisa or the boys spare change and bits of food. Louisa sadly describes the day when Airton passed by saying, "I have nothing to give you." She called out to assure him that it was his friendship they wanted, not his money. Not long thereafter, Louisa developed tuberculosis. Airton took her to the hospital. While they waited, two wealthy women arrived and jumped the line. They expressed a devaluing pity for Louisa, alleging that she had gotten tuberculosis in the streets and through working with straw. They voiced how hard it was for them to find servants and, at the same time, emphasized what good lives servants have—a roof over their head and food to eat. Airton exploded in anger: "I think she ought to die thin instead of fat and a slave to you people! You just want slaves. They work very hard for you, but they're not treated like people. So I prefer that she dies in the street." The wealthy woman promptly hit Airton with her handbag in response to his perceived insolence.

Airton was discovering through exchanges like these that how he related to poor people mattered more than what he or anyone else could give them. The rigid identity boundary that Airton had originally felt was now becoming invisible to him. He was not "helping" people across a hierarchical boundary out of piousness or pity, but rather he was being transformed as much as he was transforming others relationally.

Airton's presence in Quatro Varas symbolically, and through services provided, creates I-Thou wealth. The mainstream opinion that wealthy people are entitled to privileges because of the control that money brings kept anyone other than Airton from confronting the wealthy woman who ignored the people in the hospital line because they were of lower socio-economic status. Similarly, the social normalness of police abusing poor people who have no access to legal protection keeps others from standing up for those being abused. The collective reinforcement of social norms in culture is precisely what makes cultural change so difficult; it explains why social change through transformative cooperation requires authenticity, courage, and time. Airton has the option to leave the project by virtue of his education, but he chooses to stay for the wealth of relational life and humanness.

Adalberto Barrato—A Psychiatrist

Adalberto Barreto, Airton's brother, is a psychiatrist trained also in religion and medical anthropology. He treated some *favelados* free for his lawyer-brother early on. Soon found he needed to go to Quatro Varas, where as many as thirty to seventy people would show up for help at the same time. "I'm not here to resolve your problems," he explained. "I come here to resolve *my* problems." Adalberto was positioning himself with the community, not as a medical expert with I-It encounters over patients, but rather in a horizontal relationship, where he too genuinely was seeking help. He tells the following story:

I need you . . . I am here ill also. People say, "Why? What kind of illness? You are here to cure [my] Universitarian alienation." Are you are content with the physicians, the doctors you have? "No, because they don't talk with us, they don't touch the hand, they are just prescribing drugs, they don't talk with us." Okay, and so [I] come here to learn to be a good physician.

This horizontal relationality aligns with Marianne Gronemeyer's (1992) notion of "helping." Gronemeyer explores the oppressive power relationship between haves and have-nots through the haves' attempt to "help" others "less fortunate," thus objectifying the have-nots. The subtle shift Gronemeyer advocates for is attitudinal; it calls for treating others with dignity and regard for their humanity. It requires revisiting our beliefs about what support entails. Adalberto did not come to the "poor" people and try to "help" or fix them. Instead, he cultivated his own ability to be in co-created relationships.

Community Therapy—A Foundational Program of Quatro Varas

"People who have had their lives transformed by belonging to the community in their turn invite others to join their group," explained Adalberto. The premise of community therapy, he went on to say, is that 80% of the psychosocial problems of the community can be resolved within the community by evoking the competence of the people. Therapy ground rules exist, fostering the dialogic and relational process. The group collectively chooses the issue to be worked during a given session, everyone must speak only in "I" statements, and each person's experience is respected as valid. In fact, experience is seen as equal to medical opinion here, a perspective embedded with social status. By focusing their awareness on themselves both as experts and as people in need, community members foster authentic relationships (see Brown, 1980, regarding integration of conflicting personality aspects). Moreover, instead of functioning as a lawyer or a doctor and seeing their work as "helping" the other through the arrogance of a specialist's knowledge, Airton and Adalberto join the interdependent posture of relationality and humanness.

In parallel fashion to the Gestalt therapy movement's rebellion against traditional psychoanalysis, this practice is "firmly rooted in a basic belief in the power of human capabilities" (Yontef, 1993, p. 6). As in Gestalt therapy, Adalberto "emphasized what people knew and what people could learn by focusing their awareness" (Yontef, 1993, p.

7) in his systematically relational approach. This stance does not negate the power of education and expertise, something from which isolated populations like *favelados* are historically excluded (Blau, 2000). In fact, Adalberto seeks to build horizontal relationships systematically by identifying community members who have the potential to be trained as "community therapists" in an extension course at the local University, where Adalberto holds a faculty position. This effort transcends educational as well as socioeconomic boundaries, resulting in the creation of community therapists capable of providing services in the larger Brazilian economy. In fact, the model has been so successful that it has been replicated in more than seventeen communities in Brazil. The leader of the Brazilian health department has recently invited community representatives to help the government learn how to provide better health care for Brazilians nationwide.

Casa de Cura—The Healing House

The Casa de Cura is a traditionally thatched hut on the ocean edge of the common grounds where people from many neighborhoods come. The women healers explain that the people of the community wove the bamboo canes with jute string to build the circular walls and then thatched the reed roof. The only non-permeable wall in the house is embedded with clay figurines of heads and body parts. The clay pieces are called "ex-votos" and represent an ancient healing practice of giving thanks to St. Francis, the patron saint of the people from the hinterlands. The ocean and the rain can be heard inside the house, and when there is a breeze, it too comes through. These structural elements keep the human experience grounded in nature and community, thereby honoring integration and wholeness.

Dona Francisca, now a healer, is a testament to the possibility created by I-Thou relationships. She arrived at the community desperate for help. Through the community therapy, and eventually through the massage certification program, Dona Francisca has now lived and worked in Quatro Varas for eight years. She recalls:

When I arrived, we had meetings under this tree and Adalberto practiced here. When I first arrived, I did not talk to him . . . just slept. When I awoke, I looked at him and asked, "Are you a psychiatrist?" He answered, "Yes." I said, "What is your name?" He said, "Adalberto." I said, "I want to talk to you." He said, "Yes, you can talk to me." I was embarrassed to tell him all my story at first, so only told him what was absolutely necessary . . . that there was no reason to live. I wanted to commit suicide. There were a lot of unpleasant experiences in life, but [I] wanted him to treat me so I would get better. I was a housewife with kids. But, didn't want to live this life of anguish, sadness, and craziness. And he took me off all medication and gave me an adequate treatment.

All that is gone. I live the present. I'm cured and serve the people with lots of love and affection. I have lots of dedication to people and owe my health to Adalberto. He treats many people, including my family. He is a very special person. He does not treat only with medicine. He treats your self-esteem. He did an amazing job with me. To me the most beautiful word that no one in my family ever said to me, was when Dr. Adalberto said, "Francisca, you are not alone."

Pharmacia—A Local Innovation for Health and Economy

An extension service of the local university, Federal University of Ceará, teaches about herbal plants and experiments with remedies. Adalberto brought the university pharmacist together with "root specialists" fromthe village, as well as with traditional indigenous healers now living in the *favela*. The knowledge shared and exchanged generated a cadre of women trained formally in making herbal remedies (tonics from plants grown on premises). The remedies have been carefully selected and analyzed to ensure safety and effectiveness. Locally grown in the common gardens, the ingredients in these remedies also have the advantage of creating jobs in the garden and in the lab, as well as of producing a product affordable to local residents.

Although Dona Ierina had a preexisting interest in medicinal plants, she lacked self-esteem and opportunity. She now works in the pharmacy and shares her story of transformation. She tells it this way:

I really wanted to know what it was, Quatro Varas. So, I came with that . . . I had been without earning any money and I was suffering a lot because of [my] divorce and surgery, so they invited me to come and teach crochet to the children through a program. And through this work, Dr. Adalberto, he got to know me even more. It had been some time since a person had left that had been doing that living pharmacy. And so he invited me. I said, "No, I don't have good health." So on the third time when he invited me to come and work here in this project, I accepted, I came. And I said to him, "I'm going to give this experience one month." And now I've been here almost nine years.

Art—A Program for Youth

The art therapy program started with the existing talent of young people already in the *favela*. Adalberto tells of holding a special therapy session for young people who were victims of abuse, children of alcoholics, or on the street. Seventy children showed up at the first meeting. As Adalberto arrived, he noticed some young boys scribbling cartoons on trash; they crumpled up the drawings when they saw Adalberto—it was simply child's play. Adalberto asked to see the cartoons; reluctantly, the boys showed him what they had been doing. He thought the drawings were beautiful. Adalberto convinced the boys that there was value in their drawings, particularly if they were to draw on clean paper, folded over such that someone might use the drawing as a note card. The boys began to produce hand drawn cartoon cards, which Adalberto would take to medical conferences off-site and sell. Now, cards are also sold to visitors, researchers, and tourists who come to the community, as well as to the middle-class clients of Thursday morning community therapy programs. Both the children's internalized projections about their lack of ability, and the social circumstances isolating them further, had to be transcended in order for them to shift their own self-conception. By honoring their human potential and using his own socioeconomic status, Adalberto created wealth, and then well-being, within the boys themselves.

Neves was one of the early adolescents drawing on the cards. Now he lives with his wife and children below the art house, still on the project grounds. His story illustrates the power of being genuinely seen rather than merely objectified through projection; as well as transformation made possible through human encounter. He tells his story in this way:

I stayed in the beginning because I didn't have anything else to do. But what made me stay was that it was the first place that somebody said to me, "You are capable." First time that somebody had said that I had the possibility to accomplish something, to actually do something. Here, nobody saw me as the son of an alcoholic, but as an artist, a drawer, a painter, and that's what made me stay. And my function is to relay, demonstrate my experience to the others who arrive, the children . . . There are people who stay six months and they go away. What's important is that while he is here, he becomes educated, understanding things, so that when he leaves, he does not have to stay in the street doing drugs.

Neves played an active role in the children's multi-year art and cultural history project resulting in the above-mentioned book, *From the Favela to the Sertão*. He explained that some French people had contracted for the book to be made, and that the result was profound for both the children and the community. He stated:

> Here in Brazil, as in any other part of the world, the only thing that's valued is what comes from outside. People give privilege to what comes from the outside. The stuff from here people don't really like a lot. And the French really enjoy Brazil, so they came up with this idea of making a book from here but they were going to sell it there . . . for us, it was a jump, a great achievement.

Faviana, a healer and pharmacist, also celebrated the transformative role of the book project when we interviewed her. She explained:

> The day that they began the book, all of the kids, they studied hard and they worked hard and it was a big thing for them. They launched it by taking it to the Cultural Center of Banco de Brasil. It was a victory for the people that live here in the *favela*, to have your name in a book, this book, and it's published in two or three languages, and it's a chance for people to learn about another country or another culture. Without that, we were nothing. It gave us a chance to be something. I was so happy. I was very happy.

The children's artistic exploration of their heritage and identity began with deep regard for the child's identity and fosters a *thou* status within society.

Interpretation—Transformative Cooperation

A web of transformative cooperation is created through the journeys, the relationships, and the programs that are connected through what is denominated the Projecto Quatro Varas. The web extends through the links of interpersonal relationships emerging from unconditional and deep regard for other human beings. The web includes all the programs— anyone who researches there, touches lives, or is touched by the lives of people or programs. In academic literature, the web is akin to a social network (Wellman and Frank, 2001), and to relational wealth (Johnson, Smith, and Gambil, 2000).

Paradoxically, through awareness of their own humanity, these people transcend their poverty. The baseness of poverty is precisely what generates their holistic wealth. The web allows the members of this marginalized social class, who do not have access to a local economy, to live in and support themselves through relationship. Living "in relationship" implies a reciprocal way of being, living into the energy *between* individuals, seeking to learn from the other as well as to respectfully share parts of oneself with the other. By giving voice to their experiences, the people of this community come to find that they are not alone, and that they do in fact belong to humanity.

The power of Quatro Varas is its ability to "provoke a break in a model which concentrates power" in the hands of very few. In the existing dominant model, money and access to its equal power, which is culturally synonymous with success. In his community therapy model, Adalberto argues, "We change the passive individual object into an active, pattern of subjects." In Gestalt thinking, this active pattern of subjects matters: "I make the difference that makes the difference" (Wulf, 1998, p. 85). Interdependences and respect for self and other equal success. With success, otherwise marginalized individuals become active community members who both honor others and honor themselves. From this shifted stance, enormous holistic wealth emerges because of the "psychical whole formed by [this] structuring of the perceptual field" (Wulf, 1998, p. 86).

Transformative cooperation, as experienced here, arises for these people as sequences of I-Thou experiences over time, particularly across identity boundaries. The experience has the potential to create a bond or a social link of a different significance than when it is formed within one's proximal reference group. Each extension of self—both giving and receiving connection—seems to establish a link in a growing web, or social fabric, of relationship. Both individuals stress feeling the transformative experience of the trans-boundary connection as a shift from I-It relationships to I-Thou relationships. The shift generates an awareness that "you are not alone," which in Quatro Varas makes the difference between identifying one's worth or potential and one's hopelessness. From a Gestalt perspective, Buber advocates shifting human consciousness in order to initiate social change (Doubrawa, 2000, p. 25). When this pattern of relationality that transcends boundaries in order to find mutual benefit for all parties is considered as an emergent theory, it suggests that the cumulative experience of increased links in a web or social fabric may enable transformative cooperation to occur at an entire societal level.

Implications and Conclusions

The anarchist roots of German existential philosophers who influenced Gestalt early on show up here. By authentic interaction, these subservient classes of society can indeed rise in their own humble and honorable esteem, co-creating the ability for response. The people and programs of Quatro Varas are transforming lives by seeding and cultivating respect and innovation. This is Gestalt practice functioning at a community and societal level. The work of Quatro Varas expands the interdependencies of the web. As the interdependencies and respect grow, the community's success also grows. This transformative rippling effect demonstrates Laura Perls's notion of Gestalt as a "therapy in society," of the shift in human consciousness as a means for creating social change (Doubrawa, p. 20).

The generative core of Quatro Varas is the reciprocity of and human engagement in the relationships that knit together the web of community. Through authentic human interaction the community builds, and self-esteem, self-worth, and pride in special gifts are generated. Through community, everyone knows, "I am not alone." The web's knit transcends socio-economic boundaries such that social ostracism, abuse and injustice made from fear, and individual loneliness are redesigned. Souls are caught as they fall, making healing encounters into a local economy, and a newly constructed local economy into a healing process.

Paulo Freire, a Brazilian author and scholar of education who grew up poor during difficult times, portrays the historical context of landowners and workers in terms of oppressive power relationships of "haves" towards "have-nots." Freire also argues that to transform the world is to humanize it (1973). The children authors, who could now be considered urban victims of their history, are indeed choosing to paint the landowner in compassionate terms to draw out positive capabilities and self-respecting lessons from their own heritage.

This philosophical perspective emulates what Buber (1923/1970) explores as a movement from objectifying others in "I-It" relationships (landowner as oppressor; vertical dominance) to honoring the sacredness in all people and things, or what he calls "I-Thou" relationships (landowner as co-creator and one who empowers; horizontal collaboration). An "I-Thou" stance forms the foundation of the Gestalt paradigm. The Gestalt experience of meeting and being met at the boundary of contact, drawing on inherent wisdom of each individual's lived experience, and honoring "what is" as a basis for change are emblematic of the structured and organic self-esteem therapies of Quatro Varas. The resulting web symbolizes the organismic response of a community healing itself and others. From a social change perspective, this shift shapes current and future generations. Here, today's children learn about dignity, justice, and responsibility for reaching across potentially divisive boundaries in order to create honorable circumstances, rather than waiting for the larger national system to change and honor them.

The rhythm of the project is helping a community to step outside of the relentlessness of the culture of poverty, what Freire refers to as the "culture of silence" (Collins, 2001). Adalberto asks people, through community meetings, to step outside of the poor mentality to join him in transcending the boundary created by projections and introjections. He asks people to take pride in their life-knowledge as a valued commodity. He asks people to identify with their heritage, a time when they were valued as individuals and had a culture of pride. By so doing, he gets people to step outside of their objectification, boundaries that they have placed on themselves and that society has placed on them. The collaborative work moves them outside of being marginal in Brazilian society and into being pivotal in their own lives and in the lives of those around them. The "web" becomes the new referential society. As part of the web, people then come from a social place of importance and belonging and can identify with being *Brazilian*—with part of their identity—without being Brazilian *favelados*. In these ways, the rhythm of how work gets done has a fiery core.

Authentic relationship—reciprocally listening, learning and attending to—shows up at the contact boundary, and acceptance of humanness—vulnerabilities, gifts, and emotion—builds value immeasurable in traditional ways. Our traditional notion of wealth as that which can be measured and economically leveraged must change. The depth and richness of the economically poor people of Quatro Varas illustrates the potential power of transformation available to all humanity, if only we would choose it. In this case, poor is very rich indeed.[9]

---

[9] I am grateful to the people of Quatro Varas for sharing their stories with me; to the Social Innovations in Global Management project at Case Western Reserve University's Department of Organizational Behavior for financially supporting this research; and to my teachers, colleagues, and friends for reflecting with me as I analyzed, wrote about, and edited this work.

Mary Grace Neville, MBA, PhD, is currently a teacher-scholar at Southwestern University in Texas. Her ongoing research includes positive change in business and society, well-being and interdependence as catalysts of holistic wealth, and paradigm shifts in business education to foster global citizenship. Prior to her work at Southwestern, Neville was a manager in the strategic services practice of a global management consulting firm and served as a non-profit executive in education. She has extensive training in Human Development through the Gestalt Institute of Cleveland.
Contact: *nevillem@southwestern.edu*

References

Blau, J. R. (2000). Relational wealth in the commons: Local spaces of work and residence in a global economy. In C. R. Leana, and D. M. Russeau (Eds.), *Relational wealth: The advantages of stability in a changing economy* (pp. 217-232). New York: Oxford University Press.

Brown, J. (1980). Buber and Gestalt. *The Gestalt Journal, 3*(2), 47-56.

Buber, M. (1970/1923). *I and thou.* (W. Kaufman, Trans.). New York: Charles Scribner's Sons.

Collins, D. (2001). Adapted from *Paulo Freire: His life, works and thought.* Retrieved from http://nlu.nl.edu/ace/Resources/Freire.html.

Cooperrider, D. L., & Srivastva, S. (2000). Appreciative inquiry in organizational life. In D. L. Cooperrider, P. F. Sorensen, Jr., D. Whitney, & T. F. Yaeger (Eds.), *Appreciative inquiry: Rethinking human organization toward a positive theory of change* (pp. 55-98). Champaign, IL: Stipes Publishing.

Doubrawa, E. (2000). The politics of the I-thou. *The Gestalt Journal, 23*(1), 19-37.

Friere, P. (1973). *Pedagogy of the oppressed.* New York: The Seabury Press.

From the Sertão to the Favela. (1999). Projecto Quatro Varas, Universidade Federal do Ceará.

Goodman, P. (1947). *Communitas: Means of livelihood and ways of life.* Chicago, IL: University of Chicago Press.

Gronemeyer, M. (1992). Helping. In W. Sachs (Ed.), *The development dictionary: A guide to knowledge as power* (pp. 56-69). London: Zed Books.

Johnson, O. E., Smith, M. L., & Gambill, D. Y. (2000). Reconstructing "we": Organizational identification in a dynamic environment. In C.

R. Leana & D. M. Russeau (Eds.), *Relational wealth: The advantages of stability in a changing economy* (pp.153-168). New York: Oxford University Press.

Perlman, J. E. (1976). *The myth of marginality: Urban poverty and politics in Rio de Janeiro.* Berkeley, CA: University of California Press.

Rambali, P. (1994). *In the cities and jungles of Brazil.* New York: Henry Holt & Company.

Reinharz, S. (1992). *Feminist methods in social research.* New York: Oxford University Press.

Roett, R. (1999). *Brazil: Politics in a patrimonial society.* Westport, CT: Praeger Publishers.

Sarti, C. (1995). Morality and transgression among Brazilian poor families: Exploring ambiguities. In D. J. Hess & R. A. Damatta (Eds.), *The Brazilian puzzle: Culture on the borderlands of the western world* (pp. 114-133). New York: Columbia University Press.

Schwartzman, H. (1993). *Ethnography in organizations: Qualitative research methods series 27.* Newbury Park, CA: Sage Publications.

Strauss, A., & Corbin, J. (1988). *Basics of qualitative research: Techniques and procedures for developing grounded theory.* Thousand Oaks, CA: Sage Publications.

Turner, V. (1969). *The ritual process: Structure and antistructure.* Piscataway, NJ: Aldine Transaction.

Wellman, B., & Frank, K. (2001). Network capital in a multilevel world: Getting support from personal communities. In N. Lin, R. Burt, & K. Cook (Eds.), *Social capital: Theory and research* (pp. 233-273). New York: Aldine De Gruyter.

Wulf, R. (1998). The historical roots of Gestalt therapy theory. *The Gestalt Journal, 21*(1), 81-96.

Yontef, G. (1993). *Awareness, dialog, and process.* Highland, N.Y. The Gestalt Journal Press.

Yontef, G. (2002). The relational attitude in Gestalt therapy theory and practice. *International Gestalt Journal, 25*(1), 15-35.

CHAPTER 4

Extraordinary Skills for Extraordinary Circumstances: Supporting Parents, Children, and Caregivers in the Transition from Armed Conflict in the North of Ireland

Bríd Keenan, MA, MBCAP, and Rosie Burrows, PhD

Editors' Introduction

The cost of war goes far beyond the physical destruction and the lives lost. As Burrows and Keenan point out in this chapter, war generates trauma that isolates, separates, objectifies. It locks people in the past, ties up their energy, and limits their possibilities. In the aftermath of war, trauma creates a confusing and chaotic situation for individuals. They behave in many ways "as if" the war is still going on, although they know that it is not. Burrows and Keenan go beyond the usual conception of trauma as an individual experience. They recognize that it impacts the family, not just in the present, but also for generations to come, as it also affects the community and society itself.

Although they work in the heart of a traumatized society they retain their optimism; they know that even in the worst of circumstances there is potential, not just for recovery, but for growth and development. They understand that, with the right support, resources can be unleashed, of which individuals and the community were not aware.

They challenge the dominant understanding of trauma support, which is primarily individualistic. Instead, they work with community groups and intervene on multiple levels—the intrapsychic, interpersonal, and societal. They demonstrate that by working with many segments of society in artistic, cultural, community, and political activities, the complexity of traumatic responses can be understood and integrated.

64

Introduction

To hold traumatic reality in consciousness requires a social contex that affirms and protects the victim and joins victim and witness in a common alliance. For the individual victim, this social context is created by relationships with friends, lovers, and family. For the larger society, the social context is created by political movements that give voice to the disempowered. (Herman, 1992, p. 7)

Herman's article describes our work as Gestalt practitioners/ researchers[10] in the North of Ireland from 2002-2008 (see Keenan and Burrows, 2004, 2006).[11] During that time, we focused on working with groups that were involved in the lives of children. To do this we had to extend our knowledge and practice of trauma, co-facilitation, and group process. The research aspect of the work required that we devise a method to capture the practice data in order to contribute to the thinking and practice in the field of trauma support. We believed that our work would extend our knowledge and practice, as well as that of the wider field of Gestalt therapy. In this chapter, we intend to outline that learning. After describing our first meetings and the context out of which we worked— including the individual, familial, and community aspects, the war, and the aftermath of the conflict—we will focus primarily on trauma, not just as an individual event, but also as a societal response to overwhelming experiences. We will also describe the difficulties we faced as co-facilitators and members of the community.

How We Came Together

When traumatic events are of human design, those who bear witness are caught in the conflict between victim and perpetrator. It is morally impossible to remain neutral in this conflict. The bystander is forced to take sides. (Herman, 1992, p. 7)

We met in an organizational development supervision group in 1996. We had trained as Gestalt practitioners in the early 1990s and were

---

[10] Our research was supported throughout these years by our supervision group (Joëlle Gartner, Mary Kay Mullan, and Mary Slattery) and by our supervisor, Seán Gaffney. They have been an integral part of this work.

[11] Keenan and Burrows (2004) documents the mental health needs of a community and informs a ten-year community, voluntary and state strategy. The title of the report comes from a story told by a grandmother in a quilting group, one of the ten groups we met within the area. In describing the absence of state services and the hostility from the local town, the grandmother remarked on the daily trudge to and from the town: "You needed arms like an orangutan to carry your shopping home."

private practice both as psychotherapists and as consultants
.'s for community and voluntary organizations. For some years,
had been manager of a parent support project in Barnardos (a
·luntary children's organization), and Keenan had been working
ommunity projects providing training for the early years. We came
.her in the Barnardos project ("Parenting in a Divided Society")
2002 (the post-ceasefire era), with Burrows as project manager and
.eenan as consultant. As parents we were, and still are, committed to
nelping to create a better environment for our children, for we believe
that the quality of life of one child is dependent on the quality of life of
others. Therefore, we believed that as a community, we needed to learn as
quickly as possible about conflict-related and transgenerational trauma
in order to develop effective ways of supporting people to integrate
terrifying events and engage with the present.

As we began talking about the work, we were concerned with what we
were teaching our own children, arising out of our having grown up in
the midst of armed conflict. We grew up in different traditions. Burrows
was raised in a Protestant family in the Unionist/Loyalist tradition; at that
time, she was married to a Catholic raised in the Nationalist/Republican
tradition and raising their children in the Catholic school system and
in a diverse secular community tradition. Keenan had been raised as
a Catholic in the Nationalist/Republican tradition, and was raising her
child in an Irish language school. Clearly, this ground informed who we
were. As mothers, we wondered if, or how, we were helping to reproduce
a frightening environment by not paying attention to what the changing,
present circumstances were demanding: to act *as if* the ceasefires had
not been declared. There was still clear evidence of danger, but certainly
not to the same degree as before. As Gestalt practitioners, aware of the
organism/environment relationship, we wanted to understand more
about this phenomenon, and how to deal with it.

Based on the importance of the parent/child relationship in the
development of resilience (Newman, 2002), we believed that parents
were generally best placed to provide the continuing care needed in this
time of transition. It seemed, however, that parents were often caught
by two opposing views: they were expected either to know exactly
what to do for their children because, after all, they were parents; or to
know nothing, because they were only parents! What, in fact, did we
need to know in order to be able to deal with this terrible time? Our
own development told us that by supporting parents to work with their
own experiences of the conflict, and to obtain the care and support

they needed as parents, they could develop what we came to ref
"extraordinary skills for extraordinary circumstances." In the sar
as other parents, our understanding of those skills and circums
has grown and developed over the years.

Historical Context of Our Work

To understand the setting in which our work was done, it will
useful to know something about the recent history of political confl
in the North of Ireland. While the conflict began in the nineteen
century, we focus here on the period beginning in 1968 with an intens
Civil Rights Movement. Figure 1 presents a time line of political event
through the 1998 "Good Friday" agreement, which culminates in the
2005 IRA declaration to end a military strategy (middle section of the
figure). To see the picture fully, and to grasp the personal meaning of our
involvement in this work, we have added our own political involvement
time line to Figure 1. We want the reader to get a picture of who we are
and of how this work is that of highly passionate practitioners, each of
whom has her own history of experiences that have guided our path and
undoubtedly influenced our intervention practice.

Timeline: Brid				
Involved with Civil Rights Movement whilst at school 1967-70.	Studied and lived in Menorca. Daughter born. Began studying Marxism and ideology. Uncle interned. Wrote regularly to him. Collected money for internees.	Discovered Gestalt theory in teacher training. Active in Republican politics, women's movement, anti-racism. Joined Women and Ireland. Returned home regularly. Continued political involvement at home as well. Wrote on Ireland, racism, ideology and culture.	Heard of the death of Bobby Sands on BBC world services. Came home for most of 1980-81. Father died 1983, brother shot, injured 1984. Came home for good. Joined Sinn Fein. Met partner in Long Kesh, 1987. He was released on licence 1990. Son born 1993. Brother died 1994 just before the cease fire.	Many friends and colleagues killed, injured. Continued political involvement. Worked in community education with Open University. Initial training in Gestalt therapy 1991-94. Mother died 1995. Began working as a psychotherapist, first as a volunteer in the nationalist community and then in private practice. Met and began working with Rosie, 2002-2007.

Political Timeline								
Outbreak of conflict		Prison struggle and conflict		Ballot box and Armalite	Beginning of peace process	Political process and peace building		
1968-69	1971-75	1976	1977	1980-81	1992-93	1994-97	1998	2005-
Civil rights	Political detainees interred without trial; 14 unarmed civilians killed by British army on Bloody Sunday	Withdrawal of political status for prisoner and criminalization strategy	The IRA Long War declaration	Hunger Strike for political status in the prisons	Hume-Adams talks made public	Cease fires	Good Friday Agreement establishing local assembly	IRA declaration of the end of military strategy

loose. Exploding ally know. Dead , of bodies, body ouses, bullets, riots, ices. Nowhere safe - at ol or wider environment. .rtan gangs fighting each J the 'other side.' Following bands with a Union Jack for ıse of group. Leaving religion, e drinking, punk rock and ple hair. In a lot of 'trouble.' .cking off school, risk taking, leav- ng home in a hurry. My father, only breadwinner, made redundant, un- employed for a year then becomes a prison warden. Home more scary as security staff are a target. Courting a republican, courting a Loyalist, venturing out. Working as a cham- bermaid, waitress, disillusionment, not working, going back to college. Reading a lot including existentialist writers. Feeling on the margins, outside the main political blocks. Dancing a lot. Leaving family and wider community I grew up with.	Start university, fringes of femi- nist and socialist politics, close in on bohemenian/punk scene and Belfast Anarchist Centre for disillusioned young people to meet, dance, imagine. Catholic/ nationalist friend shot dead in '81. Disillusion with university and the north, escape to Bristol to live in anarchist collective, drink cider and travel round free music festivals. Anti-racist marches. Challenging 'straight.' Homelessness, injury. Early death of some friends. Return- ing to Belfast to work with en- vironmental organization then return to university. African drumming and ethnomusicol- ogy friends. Meeting anarchist/ musician partner from Catholic background. Daughter born in 1989. Living and working in working class republican community. Anti-poverty, com- munity playspace campaigning, traditional music scene.	Campaigning for childcare for mature students. PhD. Gestalt training 90-94. Work- ing in adult education, community develop- ment including in pris- ons with IRA women and men, loyalists and others. Daughter born 1993. Continuing to feel unsafe. Deaths, injury, addiction nearby. Developing parent support, work for 'positive parent- ing' alternatives to physical punishment and Gestalt supervi- sion. Working as psychotherapist part time. Working with Brid. Separated 2005. Father died after long illness in 2006. Eldest daughter left home in 2007.

Figure 1: Political Timeline

It is also important to understand that the community is small in Belfast. The extended family is a resource of support as well as the mechanism that has brought the conflict into the heart of everyone's life. The existence of an extended family network and of close social and cultural connections means that everyone is connected in some way to someone who has been directly affected by death, injury, and imprisonment of combatants and noncombatants, intimidation and harassment, unemployment, burned-out homes, and community displacement. All of this took place in the context of generations of well-documented, institutionalized discrimination against the Catholic community.

The Context of the Peace Process

The challenge to any civilized society is to find ways to both contain the excesses of violence, suffering and deprivation, and to provide an umbrella under which children can be raised without being brutalized, victims can get redress for their grievances and people can grow old without becoming helpless. (Van der Kolk, 1996)

The 1994 IRA ceasefire produced a significantly different environment in the North of Ireland, albeit one in which the major unfinished business of national unity continues in a political context. We had entered the period of the Peace Process,[12] which initially appeared publicly in 1993 with the Hume-Adams talks. There followed a gradual reduction in armed conflict culminating with the IRA statement in 2005,[13] requiring all IRA units to "dump arms" and instructing all "Volunteers to assist the development of purely political and democratic programs through exclusively peaceful means."

As the peace process progressed, a number of painful political concerns emerged about how to understand and work with the continuing impacts of the past. It soon became clear that political negotiations move—sometimes at a rapid pace or at a snail's pace—but differently from the psychological and emotional condition of individuals, families, and communities. In the post-ceasefire era, the climate began to open up. Both personally and professionally, we wanted to understand the changes that were occurring at the level of community, and how we, as adults, were part of them. In some areas violence was still going on, but generally speaking the community seemed physically much safer. As a result, people were beginning to feel the impact of the armed conflict more acutely, i.e., realizing the impact of violent death and injury and that they had held their grief, pain, and fear in check for years in order to manage daily life.

Now people were beginning to talk where previously there had been silence. Victims and former prisoners' rights and support groups were appearing rapidly throughout the region. However, at the same time, the adults—us included—seemed to act as if armed conflict was still happening. We were becoming aware of other forms of violence that hitherto had been less figural or hidden for years, i.e., domestic violence, attacks on the LGBT (Lesbian, Gay, Bisexual, and Transgendered) community, child abuse, and, more recently, racism. There was a greatly reduced need for most people to behave as if at any moment a life-threatening situation could develop, and yet often we continued to do so. Most worrisome, we were seeing increased risk-taking by young people, car theft, antisocial activity, and misuse of alcohol and other drugs. It

---

[12] This term was used initially by Republicans to describe the period of political initiative which became figural after the Hume-Adams talks and includes all political engagement since then. The term denotes commitment to continuous engagement with difference in support of the development of politics.

[13] "All IRA units have been ordered to dump arms. All Volunteers have been instructed. Volunteers must not engage in any other activities whatsoever." For the full statement see: http://www.anphoblacht.com/news/detail/10583

was as if our adult coping strategies, developed over years, were spilling out into this new generation and being made more shocking by the intensity of the effect on young lives. What could we do?[14] Many people began asking the questions: "What was it all for? Was it worth it?" And others queried: "The price was very high. How do we continue towards our goal?" Often these questions reflected, respectively, the experience of the Protestant/Unionist/Loyalist community (P/U/L) and that of the Nationalist/Republican/Catholic (N/R/C) community. But not always. Often, they also reflected the response to the unfinished business of the conflict, and what it had cost everyone to survive. At the same time, they also realized that many had not survived, or had done so with physical and psychological injuries. In addition, what constituted trauma, who experienced it, and who deserved support, was a central aspect of political negotiation, enmeshed as it was in the contested ground of who is the "victim" (Perls, Hefferline and Goodman, 1953).

Now, some fifteen years after the first ceasefire, and specifically between 2002 and 2008, we have co-facilitated groups of young people, parents and grandparents, and adults working with or in the environment of children, including policy makers and strategic planners. In doing so, we have tried to identify how trauma, and conflict-related trauma in particular, shapes not only individuals but also the community itself. In the light of our growing understanding of trauma theory and Gestalt practice, we speculated that the individual experience of trauma was materializing at the level of the community. The emerging social phenomena we were witnessing was not, as it is so often judged to be, the fault of bad parenting, personal weakness, or moral failure. Many of the social features found in the aftermath of conflict in other parts of the world were becoming more obvious here: for example, an increase in "non-conflict" related violence; suicide; self-harm; domestic violence; sexual, racial, and homophobic attacks; and fragmentation within communities.

Vitally important, however, was the recognition that people survived and were resilient. Evidence, as revealed in art and culture, community development, and political action, indicates that the experience of trauma also transforms and, as part of the human condition, can also be a powerful resource for life. This was also part of the field of the work. We wanted to address what seemed a disconnection between a common understanding of (a) trauma as a medical condition, i.e., mental and/

---

[14] We were later to realize that this experience was not unique to our country. Many places in transition from armed conflict experience similar problems embedded in their cultural uniqueness.

or physical ill-health of an individual; and (b) trauma as a community experience generating a wide variety of survival strategies.

A Gestalt Framework for Understanding Trauma

Before looking at the work we did, it may help to present our conception of trauma, and how it influenced the design of our interventions. Levine (1997) defines trauma as

> an internal straitjacket created when a devastating moment is frozen in time. It stifles the unfolding of being, strangling our attempts to move forward with our lives. It disconnects us from ourselves, others, nature, and spirit. When people are overwhelmed by threat we are frozen in fear. It is as if our instinct of survival energies "are all dressed up with no place to go." (p. 1)

In order to look at the impact of trauma on the community, we believed it was necessary to understand how it affects the individual, maintaining as we did that the structure of the impact of trauma and the experience of fight/flight and freeze was being felt and seen at the level of the community.

Perls, Hefferline, and Goodman (1953) contrast traumatic "fright" and "ordinary fear" in the context of a sudden danger:

> The most clear-cut case of healthy anxiety is fright, the choking off of the feeling and movement in which one is fully engaged in order to meet a sudden danger.
> In fear, the dangerous object is foreseen; one is deliberate and defensive with regard to it; therefore, when it is necessary to withdraw because the danger is too great, the approach to the environment is still open; and later, with increase of knowledge and power, it will be possible to confront the danger again and avoid or annihilate it. In fright, the threatened pain and punishment loom suddenly and overwhelmingly large, and the response is to cut off the environment, that is, to play dead and withdraw within one's skin. The anxiety, the excitement which was suddenly muscularly dammed up, continues to shake for a long time, till one can breathe freely again." (p. 410)[15]

As Gestalt practitioners know, cutting off new experience and damming up excitement and feeling results in *fixed Gestalts* (Yontef,

---

[15] Although fear is discussed in the context of parent/child relationships, it seems highly relevant for our understanding of what happens when any overwhelming power is encountered, producing the fear of annihilation.

1988). Toward the final days of the project, as our learning was beginning to be more integrated with Gestalt theory and practice, we began describing trauma as a fixed Gestalt experienced at all levels of the organism and in relationship. It is the fixed Gestalt together with and as part of the unfinished business (the incomplete Gestalt) from the past that gives rise to the "symptoms" of complex post-traumatic syndrome and leads people to seek support. We asked ourselves, "How could a person integrate the experience?" and "Is closure ever possible? What does it mean?" (Melnick and Roos, 2007) These were not just therapeutic concerns for the individual and therapist but relevant at all levels of the social and political systems of support.

Creative adjustment is another Gestalt concept that had great utility for us. We tried to apply a particular use of the term to describe the moment between the traumatic event and living in the aftermath (Perls, et al., 1953). We have supported the view that there is no value applied to the term "creative," but that it merely refers to whatever had to be done at that moment to ensure continued survival. Often we heard group members talk about adjustments that were considered to be "good" (for example, people who denied their own needs to rear children when a husband was in jail for many years; and those who became involved in political and community support groups).

We also wanted to support people to be in the here and now, recognizing the terrible events in their lives; and also to know better their capacity for resilience and appreciate their ability to do the ordinary and extraordinary things that make life possible. We wanted to support their choices about what they needed to do next. One woman described how she survived the murder of her child. When leaving the graveyard at the time of the burial, she told her child she would be back when the other children had grown up. Thirty years later, we met her in a group when she had begun revisiting the grave. Whilst having suffered migraines for years, she was a great support to more recently bereaved women in the group.

Sometimes the adjustments drew compassion or pity from the group, for example, "She really couldn't cope afterwards and was never really right again." Often, we heard criticism that involved people "taking up drinking"; or losing interest in themselves and their children, splitting the family; or becoming personally reckless and losing the run of themselves after some terrible event. We frequently talked to the groups about our own lists of good and bad adjustment. This approach has allowed us to support group curiosity about *how* we judged, rather than simply to go to judgments and self-recrimination in relation to what was done and being done. In so doing so, we all began to see the full impact on children. As Van der Kolk (1996) puts it: "Although both adults and children may respond to a traumatic event with generalized hyperarousal, attentional difficulties, problems with stimulus discrimination, inability to self-regulate, and dissociative processes, these problems have very different effects on young children than they do on matured adults" (p. 184).

Research on Trauma and Resilience

Following the surge in trauma research in recent years, there are some general statements we can make about trauma, and which we have used as the basis of our approach. These come from a synthesis of the works of James (1989), Herman (1992), Levine (1997), Cosolino (2002), Siegel (1999), Rothschild, (2002), and Melnick and Roos (2007).

- Trauma is a natural occurrence in the lives of human beings. Our systems are designed to integrate traumatic events. Sometimes, however, for various reasons this does not happen.
- Trauma is integrated, not cured. Nor can the person/family/ community be restored to the condition prior to the experiences.
- Trauma has many origins and after-effects. It is anything that represents a threat to survival: where we are overwhelmed beyond the normal capacity to cope, and we separate our safe sense of self from the world around us.
- Trauma is in the body, not in the event or circumstances. This is one of the most significant discoveries in recent years. When trauma occurs, the natural involuntary response of fight and flight arises. Where these are not completed the physiology remains frozen at the moment of the experience. This frozen experience continues to structure the lived experiences of the survivor. The present moment, therefore, is the only context available for working with the experience.
- Each person experiences trauma uniquely even though the physiological experience is similar across human beings. The meaning given to experiences makes the experience unique.
- Unintegrated, traumatic events are manifested uniquely by the person involved and often appear as symptoms and syndromes, which are treated often as maladaptive behavior or illness.
- Everyone who has survived trauma has had to do something creative and unique in order to survive.

- Our understanding of trauma now goes far beyond the definition of Post-traumatic Stress Syndrome in the standard psychological nomenclature (DSM IV). We can now talk about complex post-traumatic stress syndrome, which includes not only the unique experience of the person involved but also the context of the experience, the response of the community, and the trans-generational working out of events.

Not all frightening experiences result in post-traumatic stress, and not all people are traumatized by an experience even when they have a shared experience with someone else who has suffered a traumatic response.

- People seek support when the survival strategy has become problematic, i.e., has become symptomatic and/or is interfering with the person's ability to relate to others.
- The will to speak out about terrible events and the will to stay silent is the central dialectic of trauma. "Truth recovery" therefore is essential to trauma integration.
- The transformative nature of trauma is present in the experience as well. Resilience and creativity in ordinary life manifest in community action, the arts and culture, and the continual experience of hope. (Keenan and Burrows, 2006)

Recent developments in neuroscience and in traumatology clearly point to the whole organism's response to overwhelming circumstances, and we now have a fuller understanding of the psychological, emotional, cognitive and behavioral impacts of trauma.[16] Our interest in the specific physiological aspects of trauma arose from people in our practices and in groups reporting not feeling any better despite telling the story again and again: "Just talking does not help. I've told this story so many times and it just feels stuck"; and they would clutch or hold a part of the body. Indeed, our own personal experience provided us with an experience of trauma that was locked in the body. We knew that this persistent physical experience was also part of the ground of relationship that gave rise to a variety of strategies for "just getting on with it." When the human system is frozen in this involuntary way, a person will try to manage the physiological experiences of trauma, for example, adrenaline,

---

[16] "Since the creation of the diagnosis of PTSD, it has become clear that the long-term effects of trauma are numerous and complicated. Intrapsychic, relational and social factors are not the only issues that contribute to the long term adjustment to trauma; the biological consequences of traumatization have a different impact at different stages of development as well" (Van der Kolk, 1996, p. 184).

hypervigilance, and related symptoms and behaviors, as they continue in the present.

Supporting awareness by slowing down and staying with the phenomenology of the experience, as well as having the experience with others, offer the possibility of integrating unfinished responses more satisfactorily even when there are persistent physiological and medical conditions. Because it isolates and objectifies, trauma causes people to lose their "ordinariness" and to gain a "specialness" that is directly founded on the event itself. We believed that trauma support programs, including our own, are needed to support people to become ordinary again without minimizing the terrible events they have experienced.

Sustained, respectful, and careful work that addresses the specific needs of the injured is required. The work must also address the context in which these people live their lives. To support reconnection with the environment, the work must support the social context. The intergenerational impact of the conflict will be affected by how we deal with the current situation. The work also needs the support of sound political structures that recognize the complexity of recovery (Keenan and Burrows, 2006).

With regard to reconnection, we have experienced on many occasions how the telling of a story of terrible events resonates in the room. The same is true when someone tells of a heartwarming experience. Given the fundamental connection between us as human beings physiologically and culturally, we knew that individual experiences of trauma had to have a reciprocal and dialectical relationship with the wider community. We believed that the experience would be manifested in larger systems and particularly across generations. As a result, we began to reconsider social phenomena as expressions of persistent attempts to manage the unfinished physiological and defensive orientations of fight and flight, for example, addictions, social violence, and community fragmentation.

The naming of creative adjustment and making it explicit as a survival response provided the ground for discussion, and for working with "symptoms" without embarrassment or shame. Most importantly, it allowed the groups to reconsider their responses as actions that reflected their capacity to bear what seemed unbearable at the time. This helped people to realize that telling their story was very supportive, even if the memory of the trauma did not disappear.

In addition to work on trauma, studies on the concept of "resilience" demonstrate that recovery from the effects of trauma is most likely to *need for safety in grief/trauma to work through *

occur when children and young people are supported by their families, and when they are able to perceive that their immediate caregivers are able to exert agency over their circumstances. Moreover, evidence indicates that those who are best placed to maintain positive mental health in the face of distressing events are those able to:

- identify with a community and the aims of that community; and
- have the opportunity to take part in meaningful social rituals that affirm their cultural values. (Hodes, 2000)

The Role of Storytelling and What is Remembered

From our research on trauma, we gained a new appreciation of the importance and limitation of telling one's story of traumatic happenings. When terrible things happen, people frequently want to tell the story as if telling it could resolve the grief and pain. We Irish have a strong oral tradition, but during the time of armed conflict silence often had to be maintained for reasons of safety. After the ceasefires, people wanted to talk and be heard. Indeed, trauma recovery requires:

- speaking out the unspeakable (saying that this happened to me and that it cannot be denied);
- bearing witness (hearing from others that what happened was a terrible thing);
- remembering (knowing in detail what my experiences were);
- mourning the losses incurred as a result of what happened (I can't go back to how I was before); and
- reconnecting with life and the future (I survived, I will stay connected to others with this in my history, and I can grow from this experience). (Herman, 1992)

When working with traumatic events, however, the simple act of retelling terrible events does not support integration but may in fact "flood" the teller, as contact with the present is lost. A culture in which oral tradition of storytelling is prominent will rely heavily on the recounting of the ordeal or the silencing of it as the solution to the distress, or as proof that there can be no solution. The fixed Gestalt of the repeated story, almost hypnotically retold, can serve as a means of fixing the event even more rigidly in the present. We slowed this process up by asking the teller and the listeners the following question at regular and significant moments: "How is it for you to tell/hear this story now with us?" Consistent with the Gestalt approach, we dealt with the story phenomenologically in the present in small, contained units of experience, and worked with individuals, small groups, or the whole group.

In this context, we worked with memories as representing the only possible meaning at that time. To this, we added the idea of explicit memory (subject to recall) and implicit memory (what is present physiologically) (Seigel, 1999). Physiological symptoms or conditions were often figural in the groups and served as a means of sharing experience and/or as a metaphor for describing "what it feels like to be me." Physiological responses on many occasions became a way of talking about the unfinished business and of exploring more deeply the impact on relationships.

We frequently encountered people who could not remember details, had a fragmented memory of what had happened, or had no memory at all. The role of the narrative was poignantly illustrated in the first group of parents with whom we worked, as they described the terrible events they had witnessed in the company of their children. They talked about the stories they told each other about the shared experience, the story they told the world, and the story they told their families, recognizing the difference in the stories told by the children. One woman was very distressed about how one day she had had to protect her child in the face of the terrible actions of others. So scared was she of what her daughter would see, she was surprised when her daughter told her that the only thing she remembered was her mother's covering her head with a coat.

Working with Parents and Caregivers

In light of the above, we concluded that with specific awareness and training, parents and caregivers could provide continuous support to their children as part of the home environment. Furthermore, with increased information, parents would be better placed to obtain support and resources from the relevant agencies involved with children and their families. Our interventions followed from this reasoning.

We were concerned when we heard it said that it would take generations for the impact of the conflict to work itself out of the community. Our children were part of this "working out." We wanted to know how this working out was going to occur, and what we could do to protect our children and communities during the process. There was little or no locally gathered, relevant research available to offer any guidance to parents and caregivers, or to those whose decisions affected the lives of children and their families and communities.

We wanted to address the complex parent-child relationship. We were concerned that, where child trauma was recognized and support available, the response tended to mirror what was available for adults: individualized support with counseling and/or medication through access to the often overstretched health service. Here, in other words, the child was the focus of treatment. In our view reconnection—a vital element in the process of trauma integration—was in danger of being weakened by the system itself. Therefore, we wanted to work with the cultural centrality of the family, extended family, and community as the most significant support systems for the child.

Four major features of the environment indicated that we should do this work in groups.

1. The unique cultural structure and role of groups in Irish society
2. The need for safety and reconnection in the aftermath of trauma
3. Scarce financial resources, and an absence of state intervention strategies for trauma recovery
4. The pathologizing/medicalizing of the aftermath of traumatic experiences

Although individuals experienced dramatic events uniquely, whole families and communities had been affected collectively by the conflict for at least thirty years. The need and urgency seemed so great that we also wanted to do something effective that would reach large numbers of people as quickly as possible. The traditional route of individual counseling or psychotherapy, whilst clearly necessary in many cases, did not seem to offer a good solution. Having said that, however, we continue to work in private practice with individuals where support for the unique experiences can be addressed.

In Ireland, generally, we still live within extended families and small communities. Many people had experienced the direct impact of events through family and community connections. Individual experiences often had an extensive impact on the community. We knew this through personal experience, and there was substantial anecdotal evidence to support it. So, we believed that the reverse could also be true: if we could work effectively with a group in a community, that experience could have an effect far beyond the group participants.

Whole communities in some cases were the focus of life-threatening experiences, e.g., a street of houses was burnt down; communities fleeing in fear were forced to become "internal refugees"; the effects of British army and police search operations across whole sections of the community; bomb or gun attacks in the heart of communities, or the fear of them. It seemed illogical, therefore, to focus on isolated individuals rather than on groups who had shared experiences. At the heart of trauma is the experience of never being the same again, of isolation, of being marked in some way that separates a person from others. Focusing on the individual, though necessary at times, seemed to support isolation of the experiences, thereby cutting people off from the opportunity to re-establish connection (Herman, 1992). People need to reconnect with life after terrible events. A group offers the opportunity to be with others in a mutual experience

Indeed, the need to feel safe inside families and communities had become very necessary throughout the years of conflict, and we were aware of the need to establish safety as a key element of any work in the aftermath of trauma. Since group members needed to feel safe, the groups we worked with were generally self-selected and self-organized. This was obvious with some groups toward the end of the project, which had not been self-selected but chosen by various agencies to attend our talks and workshops. In these instances, establishing safety was extremely difficult. And, of course, children lived in extended families and attended schools inside their own communities. Young people gather naturally in groups, particularly in adolescence, as they are disembedding themselves from the family and peer relationships become important (McConville, 1995). Thus, it seemed to us logical and practical to interact in the various groups where parents and children lived and worked.

We also wanted to challenge the dominant understanding of trauma support that was heavily individualized, seeming to fall within a medical model focused on treating symptoms. This approach can be summarized generally as pathologizing, individualizing, and medicalizing (Keenan and Burrows, 2006), i.e., designed to treat the symptoms (outward signs of traumatic experiences) as illness, sometimes physical, sometimes mental, often both. According to this model, the illness is located within the individual, and therefore the individual carries the problem. It seems to follow that if we "cure" the individual, we somehow get rid of the problem—the normal response to being overwhelmed in the environment. Drug treatment (i.e., sedatives, antidepressants, mood regulators) is often offered when symptoms have been isolated (Keenan and Burrows, 2006).[17] This was particularly alarming when mothers reported that their children had been prescribed strong medication to help with night terrors and bed-wetting following frightening experiences. Alternatively, there was limited availability of individualized therapy and counseling aimed at restoring clients to health and supporting them to move on.

Working With Different Levels of System, 2002-2008

Sustained long-term work with over 140 groups, organizations, networks, and state bodies was made possible primarily through the organizational structure of Barnardos. The work involved:

- continual fundraising and negotiating with state and other funders, as funding cycles are short-term (2002-2008);
- consulting with a wide range of organizations and communities on need (ongoing);
- reviewing the literature on trauma and political conflict, locally and internationally (2002);
- setting up and maintaining an advisory group made up of senior state representatives, head of the Victims Unit, health authority/ State Trauma Center clinical psychologist/researcher, head of the University Social Work Department, director of an interface project, youth organizations, and community representatives (2002-2008);
- initially working with two self-selected community groups in interface areas (2002-2003);
- writing up the work into a resource for workers and publishing it (2003-2004);
- disseminating the resource, "We'll Never Be the Same" (Burrows and Keenan, 2004) to organizations internationally and locally (2004-2008);
- developing training and skills workshops with community groups, educational providers, nursery and early years workers, and all those concerned with the quality of life of children, young people and parents/grandparents (2004-2008); and
- receiving further trauma training in somatic experiencing in the Netherlands (2003-2005).

[17] People in the North of Ireland/N. Ireland are at greater risk of mental health problems than those in England or Scotland; they visit their Doctor/GP twice as often and GPs give out two to three times as many tranquilizers and antidepressants (Health and Well-Being Survey, DHSS, 2001). The health and well-being of certain groups is more at risk: the young, women, the divorced/separated, Catholics, ethnic minorities, Travelers (gypsies), those with a (learning) disability, gays/lesbians, and deaf people (Health and Well-Being Survey, 2001).

We worked flexibly in order to respond to varying group needs, for example, presentations to management, day workshops, residentials, and specific interest groups. Often there was an overlap where workers were also those who had been affected by the conflict. Just as often we met those who believed that either they had been unaffected, had not had such severe or direct experiences, or wanted to distance themselves from those overwhelming events. The work consisted of three main components:

1. Self-help groups or support groups—making sense of personal experience with parents, grandparents, adults, self-help groups (such as suicide prevention and family support), groups for those bereaved and injured in the conflict, former combatants, young people aged fifteen to nineteen, and former prisoners.
2. Skills and knowledge development in relation to how people, groups and communities were affected by trauma, supporting the development of skills of self-regulation to help their contact with clients. Since many frontline workers had also been directly affected by the conflict, much of this took the form of staff development. We worked with staff groups who provided direct support and engaged in the group as part of developing service provision. We also collaborated with workers in the community and voluntary sector, who provide direct support for conflict-related need/ issues, such as community-based counselors, therapists and complementary therapists, health and youth workers, various self-help organizations, student-teachers, teachers, social workers, and youth workers.
3. Information-giving/awareness-raising with managers at all levels, including policy makers and strategic planners.

Generally, our groups were organized around one of two beliefs. The first is that bringing "warring" communities together (usually in the context of a training framework) by neutral facilitators who encourage the exploration of similarity and difference will produce new perceptions and openness to dialogue. This work was sponsored by the State through government and European Union funding. To obtain funding, groups had to demonstrate their commitment to include the "other"; often special projects targeted the setting up of "cross-community" and anti-sectarian work. Group participants were supported to work together in various life contexts, to uncover and explore personal sectarianism, to learn to respect the "other"—and, in so doing, to create the possibility of a more peaceful co-existence. Alternatively, some groups held that religion and politics have little or no bearing on their work, or that their work had transcended personal political and religious issues. Those who saw the issue more as one of psychological healing supported this approach.

At the heart of both is the belief that sectarianism is a result of personal ignorance or individual failure, which can be overcome through goodwill and education. This implies that, somewhere or somehow, the absence of sectarianism can be achieved through education, goodwill, and a meeting with the "other." In this approach, facilitators from different backgrounds working together often model one community's tolerance of the other. The assumption is that the facilitators have managed to overcome their differences, or they have found a way not to let them get in the way.

In applying Herman's (1992) approach to working with trauma, we maintained that we could not be neutral in relation to the experiences of the participants in the various groups. In addition, we had to develop a way for us to work with the political context of trauma—by speaking out or staying silent, and seeing the implications for the community in general, as well as for the group and for ourselves as members of the community.

Containment and Safety in Co-facilitating the Groups

We knew that establishing safety was a prerequisite for doing work with trauma. Contributing to the creation of safety in the group meant that we had to be prepared continually to deepen our own awareness and that of our co-facilitating system, in order to support the group where it needed to go (Lichtenberg, et al., 1994). Throughout the work we were in personal therapy; and we wrote separately after each meeting about our individual experiences of the group, exchanged our reflections, met and reflected again as a pair, and then took supervision. In addition, we were aware that the context of the group meeting—the world outside—would also influence the group environment.

Much of the supervision we received focused on our relationship and the struggle we had in becoming a co-facilitator system. Our task was to facilitate groups that were embedded in a society which, for at least forty years, had emphasized similarity rather than difference as a vital mechanism for survival. Recognizing "your own" was crucial to personal safety, and many social signals existed to ensure that you knew where you were and whom you were with outside your own place of safety. Our personal agendas were considered and set aside early in supervision, allowing us to attend fully to the group, attention that was central to developing our own awareness of the impact of trauma, as well as that of the group.

The "outside world" as a system also influenced the work of the group. We noticed that if the members in the groups felt supported and contained by their community, it was easier to establish safety in the group and the work seemed to reach greater depth and integration. This was more often the experience of members of the Nationalist/Republican (primarily Catholic) community, where the historical experience of discrimination and exclusion laid the ground for a greater sense of community cohesion. Conversely, if the group was not supported by the community, the participants experienced greater levels of fear and fragmentation. This was generally our experience of the Unionist/Loyalist community. Following our own histories, this was reflected in our co-working. We experienced feelings of being out on a limb, sometimes enmeshed with the groups, other times checked out by members through contacts outside the group. Sometimes we were an unknown quantity and untraceable; other times, we had an advance introduction to the group through other community connections; and still others we had to prove the usefulness of the work before being accepted.

In addition, because we were also of the wider field of Belfast and the conflict, we could use our responses in and out of the group to track group themes, particularly the unspoken ones; this gave us greater insight into the life experiences of the group members and how best to offer support. We constantly asked the following questions during or after sessions: "If I/you/we/ was/were feeling this or that, what does it mean for the group? How is it reflected in the group? How is the group reflected in us?" In this experiential process, the group brought its expertise in respect of living with the impact of traumatic events; and we brought specialist knowledge and skills from our training, as well as from our life experiences, in support of the group's awareness. Together, then, we produced something new for all of us: a collective experience that informed all our understanding of how they (and others) continued to live with traumatic experiences. Co-facilitation was an environment that supported the group's safety, awareness, and integration, rather than a means of changing or restoring participants to better health and well-being. This dialogic process respects and values equally everyone's experience and expertise and places it at the disposal of the group in the interest of producing new, fully participative understanding (Freire, 1973).

Though our different backgrounds and life experiences were generally

cf white/black re oppressed/oppressor

dialogue under projection?

enriching, they sometimes made the work difficult. Therefore, we had to devise alternative ways of working together to support the essential sense of safety needed for the work. Take, for example, when we worked with the first two groups from the interface in Belfast, one Protestant/Loyalist, the other Catholic/Nationalist/Republican. It became clear very quickly that it would be impossible for both of us to be present together with each group in the same way. The following case illustrates this dilemma, and how we handled it.

Belfast 2002: A Loyalist Group

We have chosen this group primarily to illustrate what we learned about the role of the facilitator during ongoing conflict, and to challenge commonly held myths about the "neutral" or "objective" facilitator who can and "should" be able to work anywhere. We facilitated two groups each for ten weeks. Both were parent groups whose participants, together with their children, had experienced sustained violent events. In Burrows and Keenan (2004), Burrows states:

> I worked with a well-known Belfast Loyalist interface community, with Bríd as support in the background, for review and planning, due to safety issues in working with the group of mothers and grandmothers whose families were linked to rival feuding intra-communal Loyalist armed groups. These families experienced terror, horror, and betrayal, being put out of their homes by "their own," and feeling scapegoated by state and church groups, and the media. In the aftermath of an eighteen-year-old who had been shot dead by one of "his own," and in the absence of a state or political response, one grandmother asked: "Are we nothing to politicians and the rest of them? Are our lives worth nothing? That could have been my son, and it would have been completely ignored, invisible, as if it hadn't happened at all." (p. 39)

The work with this group was frightening due to the extreme states of fear, terror, horror, and violence within the community as the "enemy" became "their own"; and due to my current primary identification with Irish Catholic/Nationalist/Republican culture (the "enemy" of this group). However, my grandfather had been born and raised in this community, and these class and family roots provided ground for me to work alongside the group, not as some "objective" other. Struggling with complex identifications and alienations was particularly pertinent with this Loyalist/Unionist group. It clarified changes happening in the field, as this group felt increasingly betrayed by the state they had previously supported, having sacrificed their "loyal" sons through two World Wars on the British side. Wall murals on the end of gable walls displayed these military battles with the poignant ironic words, "Lest we forget."

Slowly, in the absence of a strong human rights culture and with minimal community development (Burrows, 1991), people were beginning to speak out about the extent of unresolved trauma and the ongoing fear in their fractured community. The work was primarily focused on trauma and psychosocial education, in order to help support safety in the moment, given the prevalence of high levels of silence, mistrust, despair, contempt, desire to forget, shame, lack of cohesion, and isolation; what Herman (1992) locates as the earliest phase of trauma recovery, with minimal sense of physical or emotional safety for remembering and mourning or reconnecting. The group has gone on to reposition itself as a learning and support organization for ex-prisoners' families, instead of being primarily a "victims' group." Keenan states:

> It was impossible for me to work with Rosie in the Loyalist area group at that time. The community was fragmenting and the group members were frightened and angry, and feeling betrayed and helpless. My presence would have introduced inappropriately into the life of the group a wider conflict at a time when the group was greatly distressed by the violent fragmentation of its own community. This would have been, at the very least, insensitive and increased the already high levels of fear, anger, and distress in the group. We wanted to support some basic level of safety within the group that would allow its members to find a way to work with the distress. We devised a method of working where we talked together in detail about the group, and then Rosie facilitated it. Afterward, we met and talked again about her experiences with the group and my experience outside it. (Burrows and Keenan, p. 39)

The Nationalist Community

In the groups based in the Nationalist community, Rosie and I were both present though I took the lead a lot in work. Once again, group safety was the focus. And again, the danger was outside as well as in the collective and individual memories and physiology of the group members. On two occasions, we had to abandon the group because of bomb scares and we had to pass through a very hostile environment to get to the group. I felt very safe in the group, as people had traced my connection to members of their community. So, we had a strong affinity. This was not true for Burrows, who could not be traced, except to Barnardos. However, we noticed that, as the group progressed, safety in being different became an important theme. It became part of the discussion particularly when the group explored the desire for revenge against the Loyalist community who had brought so much terror to their children. By paying attention to the desire for revenge, and giving the figure time to emerge, the members began to differentiate between Loyalism and Protestants by remembering school experiences, family weddings, or the faces of people who had supported them and their children from inside the Loyalist community. At this point, Burrows spoke briefly of her own history in the Protestant community:

> I felt a loss of self in not sensing enough ground and emotional safety to speak freely in this group—at this heightened time in the aftermath of an international human rights crisis—about my earlier experiences of the Protestant community and complex identifications with both the Nationalist/Republican and Protestant communities. I felt that the group was overwhelmed enough and that, at times, I was dealing with a painful sense of disconnect and shame in the partial identifications I brought to supervision.

Later, in supervision, we explored the inclusion/ exclusion theme of the group through the dynamic between us and as a co-working pair in relation to the groups. As a result, we began to understand the continuum existing between polarities of experience; the group could experience itself at any point along the continuum depending on circumstances at the moment. We often reflected the polarities that were in the group, which supported our understanding of what was happening, not just in the group, but at the level of the community and across communities.

Flying Horse, Model Farm and New Model Farm Community: 2004

We have selected this whole community intervention to illustrate how Gestalt practice influenced state, voluntary and community responses to mental health in the short and longer term.

Between February and June 2004, we worked with a rural Nationalist/ Republican community located near the Mourne Mountains "that sweep down to the sea," as the famous song goes. We had a four-month action research contract (and an additional six weeks to write the final report) to work with the state health organization and local community forum engaging with people on the mental health needs of the community, and to form a ten-year strategy. We facilitated and recorded ten groups in the community, including young people, parents and children, younger women, ex-prisoners, drugs/alcohol group, disability group, older women/prayer group, community forum, a rural network, and an Advisory Group. We also interviewed representatives of the main state and voluntary organizations serving the area. Our interest was to find ways to challenge a generally patronizing and pathologizing stance towards the community, and to support awareness of transgenerational and conflict-related trauma. This would be a lens through which to view ongoing manifestations of both distress and resilience.

The significance of transgenerational issues emerged in hearing how the first generation of internal refugees/displaced families had been intimidated or physically put out of their homes in Belfast, and relocated in a rural housing estate thirty miles from Belfast with no social infrastructure. Rows of uniform, public housing stood two miles from a local town, whose people looked down their nose at these incomers or "Frankies."[18] Moreover, situating the community beside a large state mental institution, whose involuntary "patients" were often released into the community, built a strong interest in health and well-being.

We began by proposing an Advisory Group made up of a range of relevant organizational representatives from whom we could get support and feedback. Our approach was focused on resilience: on identifying the strategies and structures that had supported people to keep going during decades of struggle for basic needs and rights. Working with different levels of system involved:

- The groups the community itself had formed (and not formed; for example, there was no group for young people who were lesbian/gay, nor for those experiencing domestic violence)—The community had organized to meet many of its needs in what we recognized as "structures of well being," for example, mother and toddlers groups, youth groups, older people's groups, Gaelic sports and cultural activities.
- Extended families—What struck us were the experiences of many of the older generation who took pride in making a heartless shell

---

[18] This term emerged during the Second World War to refer to people from Belfast who were evacuated to Downpatrick. The local people resented the presence of the city people and substantial animosity existed between the two groups. When people queued at the post office to have the ration books "franked" (i.e., stamped), the Belfast people had to form a separate queue away from the local people. Thus, people displaced from Belfast became known as "Frankies."

into a living community, and who found common identity in the face of external threat. Differences between the generations brought comments from the grandmothers such as: "The young mothers don't know how to cook or budget," and "The young men are drifting." Parents and grandparents expressed uncertainty as to how to support children and young people in more peaceful times: "I was throwing bricks at the army and peelers at their age. What do I know to teach them now?" Meanwhile, the young people often experienced the community as unable to provide or sustain the activities they wanted to do, nor to accept their ordinary playing of football in front of the houses.

- The structures formed by state and voluntary agencies to provide services to the community, and how the community perceived these services—In order to be supportive, we were careful to honor the contract we had made with the groups not to alter how they spoke about these structures, nor how they described what created poor mental health. They wanted to be sure that their experience would be present in the final report. To optimize our influence with these state and voluntary sector agents, we utilized selective international reports, which added legitimacy to our work in a competitive commissioning culture of "evidence-based" research.

Our differences as practitioners provided solid ground for the work. The report, "Out of Town, Out of Sight," is being used by the community for strategic and operational planning, and for drawing down further state and other resources. Gestalt practitioners are being contracted on an ongoing basis to work with different groups within the community; and to support strategic approaches between the state, other agencies, and the community.

Summary: What We Have Learned

- It is possible to work with small units of experience and have significant impact at every level of the system. Through our interventions as the peace process took hold, parents and children began to act as though their world was safer.
- Parents/caregivers want to know what else they can do to support their children, and many are willing to learn what we called "extraordinary skills for extraordinary circumstances."
- When individuals with unresolved trauma in their history are in a group, we are more aware of what they bring to the group

experience. We are also more aware of the process of resonance, and how people in the group may be triggered by the experiences they are reporting and hearing.

- The importance of survival and resilience as a vital focus of group experience. We work with the meaning of survival strategies as creative adjustment, as the group is expressing them in the moment. We now recognize that finding "closure" and "moving on" are less useful concepts than focusing on current lived experience and offering relevant support for the integration of experience.

- Specific and precise knowledge and skills for working with the part of the brain responsible for survival, including physiological involuntary responses as well as voluntary responses of fight, flight, and freeze. This supports the de-pathologizing of instinctive responses that are involuntary, and of meaning-making in the present. Within our environment, people are generally unsupported in making other than pathologizing meanings of their own instinctive responses to traumatic events (e.g., there is something wrong with me/the other). * projection as flight response to trauma?

- The importance in Gestalt training for providing an understanding of the embodied response to life events.

- We can teach about the physiological experience of trauma and support the development of skills for self-regulation in the present.

- We are more aware of our own process as we resonate with the group experience, and through our skills of self-regulation are able to contain and hold the boundary of our own co-facilitation system with more ease.

- Raising the possibility that what one generation learns in relation to another can also be understood as the unfinished effort of previous generations to handle overwhelming events. This allows us to support parents to become more aware of how they hold their own life experiences when they are rearing their children.

- Working with parents and caregivers in groups changes the focus to a systems level and reduces concentration on individuals as victims who require therapy.

→ projection as unfinished business / overwhelm / trauma — projected. ont — requiring dialogue + integration

for me → connected to (un) certainty / unsure. being

Bríd Keenan, MA, MBACP, (British Association for Counselling and Psychotherapy), has been working since 1996 as a Gestalt psychotherapist, primarily in the greater Belfast area. She has a particular interest in developmental and transgenerational trauma. In 2005, she received the Somatic Experience Practitioners Certificate from the Foundation for Human Enrichment. With Rosie Burrows, she has co-authored a number of resources in relation to trauma, aimed at parents and adults, one of which received a commendation in the BACP research awards in 2004. Keenan has a daughter and a son, lives with her partner in Belfast, and continues to be politically active.

Contact: *b.keenan70@ntlworld.com*

Rosie Burrows, PhD, is an independent Gestalt practitioner working with young people and adults, families, groups, and organizations. She has a background in community and women's education, community development, and parent support. She is the mother of two adolescent daughters and is committed to living and working in ways that support engagement with life and with transformation in the North of Ireland.

Contact: *rosieburrows@ntlworld.com*

References

An Phoblacht 18 July, (2005) *http://www.anphoblacht.com/news/detail/10583n*

Bloom, S. (1997). *Creating sanctuary: Toward the evolution of sane societies.* London: Routledge.

Burrows, R. (1991). Unpublished report: Community development in Protestant areas.

Burrows, R., & Keenan, B. (2004). "We'll never be the same": Learning with children, parents and communities through ongoing political conflict and trauma. A resource *http://www.barnardos .org.uk*

Burrows, R., & Keenan, B. (2004). Bearing witness: Supporting parents and children in the transition to peace, *Child Care in Practice, 10*(2), 107-125.

Cosolino, L. (2002). *The neuroscience of psychotherapy: Building and rebuilding the human brain.* New York: Norton.

Danieli, Y. (1998). *International handbook of multi-generational legacies of trauma.* New York: Plenum Press.

East Timor: *http://www.bbc.co.uk/radio4/womanshour/05/2007_51_tue. shtml*

Farlane, A. C., Weisaeth, L. (1996). *In traumatic stress: The effects of overwhelming experience on mind, body and society.* New York: The Guildford Press.

Freire, P. (1973). *Education for critical consciousness.* Cambridge, MA: Center for the Study of Development and Social Change.

Gaffney, S. (2006). Gestalt with groups—A developmental perspective. *Gestalt Journal of Australia and New Zealand, 2*(2), 7-19.

Gaffney, S. (2008). Supervision in a divided society: Theory, practice, perspectives and reflections. *British Gestalt Journal, 17*(1), 27-39.

Gostin, L. (2001). Beyond moral claims. A human rights approach to mental health. Special section: Keeping human rights on the bioethics agenda. *Cambridge Quarterly of Healthcare Ethics, 10*, 264-274.

Herman, J. L. (1992). *Trauma and recovery: From domestic abuse to political terror.* London: Pandora.

Hodes, M. (2000). Psychologically distressed refugee children in the United Kingdom. *Child Psychology and Psychiatry Review 5*(2), 57-67.

James, B. (1989). *Treating traumatized children: New insights and creative interventions.* New York: Free Press.

Keenan, B., & Burrows, R. (2004). "Out of town, out of sight?" Action research report on the mental health needs of the community in the Flying Horse, Model Farm and New Model Farm areas of Downpatrick, commissioned by Down Lisburn Trust and the Flying Horse Community Forum.

Keenan, B., & Burrows, R. (2006). Do you think we're mental? A therapeutic approach to group work with young people. *http://www. contactyouth.org*

Kepner, J. (2001). *Body process: A Gestalt approach to working with the body in psychotherapy.* Cambridge, MA: Gestalt Press.

Levine, P., & Poole-Heller, D. (2003). Unpublished training manual. Foundation for Human Enrichment.

Levine, P. (1997). *Waking the tiger: Healing trauma—the innate capacity to transform overwhelming experiences.* Berkeley, CA: North Atlantic Books.

Lichtenberg, P., Gibbons, D., & van Beusekom, L. (1994). Working with victims: Being empathic. *Clinical Social Work, 22*(2), 72-85.

McConville, M. (1995). *Adolescence: psychotherapy and the emergent self.* San Francisco, CA: Jossey Bass.

McConville, M. (2003). Lewinian field theory, adolescent development, and psychotherapy. *Gestalt Review, 7*(3), 213-238.

Melnick, J., & Roos, S. (2007). The myth of closure. *Gestalt Review, 11*(2), 90-107.

Newman, T. (2002). *Promoting resilience: A review of effective strategies for child care services.* Unpublished Report: Barkingside, N. Ireland: Barnados.

Parlett, M. (2000). Creative adjustment and the global field. *British Gestalt Journal, 9*(1), 4-16.

Perls, F., Hefferline, R., & Goodman, P. (1953). *Gestalt therapy: excitement and growth in the human personality.* London: Souvenir Press.

Rothschild, B. (2002). *The body remembers. The psychophysiology of trauma and trauma treatment.* New York: W.W. Norton.

Save the children fund. (1999). *Inside the gates: Schools and the troubles— how schools support children in relation to the political conflict.* Belfast: Save the Children Fund.

Seigel, D. (1999). *The developing mind: Towards a neurobiology of interpersonal experience.* New York, NY: Guildford Press.

Van der Kolk, B. (1996). The complexity of adaptation to trauma: Self-regulation, stimulus discrimination, and characterological development. In B. Van der Kolk, A. Mcfarlane, A. & D. Weisaeth (Eds.), *Trauma and stress* (pp. 182-213). New York: Guilford Press.

CHAPTER 5

Creating Democratic Spaces: Citizen Engagement and Large Systems Change in Post-Katrina New Orleans

Carolyn J. Lukensmeyer, PhD

Editors' Introduction

Carolyn Lukensmeyer is a deeply skilled and experienced Gestalt practitioner who has devoted a major part of her career to improving political process and citizen engagement. She has been a consultant to United States congressmen, senators, governors, and Presidents, as well as serving as chief of staff to a governor of Ohio (USA). The work described in this chapter reflects her work in melding Gestalt awareness development in individuals with large group decision-making around critical social problems. It indicates how a shared reality can be created out of the multiple realities that exist when diverse stakeholders are involved. The approach reflects the growing popularity of large group interventions in organization development and social change.

Key to the AmericaSpeaks approach is the ability to respect all positions and values, whether the intervener agrees with them or not. This requires authentic and powerful use of self; the facilitator must make good contact with a wide variety of people. And it requires the ability to tolerate and make good use of the strong emotional reactions that emerge in this process. The reader will see how this process builds on being able to interact with people on both an intimate and a strategic level.

---

[19] America*Speaks* is known as Global Voices when the Twenty-first Century Town Meeting model is used outside of the United States.

Introduction

This chapter presents an in-depth case study of how America*Speaks'* Twenty-first Century Town Meeting®[19] helped create a unified voice for the citizens of New Orleans after the Hurricane Katrina disaster. The case explores how a demographically representative gathering of New Orleanians—both those living in the city and those displaced to more than sixteen cities across the country—was realized; and how the recommendations that emerged had an impact on city, state and federal officials. The case also follows the story of New Orleanians who, two-plus years later, are still being left behind in the recovery process and in the strategies used, to ensure that their collective voices reach the systems charged with supporting them. The chapter highlights the theory of change and the conceptual frameworks that underlie the work. It includes a discussion of how the Twenty-first Century Town Meeting model builds on a basic Gestalt principle: creating a robust, shared awareness by accepting the validity of multiple realities can lead to effective joint action on the part of a large group of diverse citizens.

Aspirations and Actuality of the American Democracy

The Founding Fathers of the United States had a deep and abiding belief in the ability of people to self-govern. These aspirations for democracy have since occupied a near mythic power in the American imagination. We rely on them to describe our sense of what is right and what is fair; we rely on them to organize our work, our play, and our family lives. Yet since the earliest days of our nation, there has always been a tension between the aspirations of our democracy and its reality: a disconnect between the vision, the words and the structures, and the extent to which citizens have been truly empowered to self-govern. To cite just a few examples: our Founding Fathers chose a Republic instead of a Democracy, and a Senate selected by members of the House and not the electorate; African Americans and women were disenfranchised for more than a century. As a nation we have made great strides in closing some of the gaps between the aspirations expressed in our founding documents and our everyday realities: we ended slavery, converted the Senate to a publicly elected body, and enfranchised the full population.

Yet, as we move into the second decade of a new century, there has been discernible erosion in our democracy. Money and special interest groups more easily capture the attention of decision-makers than do the voices of citizens. Previously public functions like our technology infrastructure and aspects of our national defense have been privatized; we too often fail to take ownership of pressing common good concerns such as the environment, health care, and education. Rather, elections focus on sideshow, incendiary issues that affect small numbers like abortion, gay marriage, and "English only." Large percentages of our citizens do not vote. In the late summer of 2005, the disconnect between our aspirational democracy and our actual governing system was laid bare for the world to see when Hurricane Katrina hit the city of New Orleans. Our government "of, by, and for the people" failed, and we watched in horror as fellow citizens, abandoned on their rooftops, called out: "How can this be happening to me? I'm an American."

New Orleans After Hurricane Katrina: An Epic Failure of Democracy and a Reason for Hope

Our aspirational democracy calls for an authentic and productive relationship between individuals, systems, and institutions; it requires that citizen voices be firmly embedded in the public's business. Yet for decades, the city of New Orleans in Louisiana has embodied much the opposite. New Orleans has been a place in which the individual right to participate in a functioning democracy has been routinely ignored. For twenty years, repeated requests for federal funds to maintain the city's levees were rejected by Congress; the city's public education system, among the worst in the nation, has been left to fail. Corruption in the public sphere and years of citizen disenfranchisement has been accepted as simply "characteristic" of the city instead of a call to action. Hurricane Katrina brought into sharp relief the simmering crisis of democracy in New Orleans and, by extension, in our nation. The storm exposed deep and long-ignored racial and economic disparities as we literally watched our government abandon fellow citizens before our eyes. More than a year after Katrina, virtually no federal dollars beyond what was required by law had been released for the recovery and rebuilding of the city. The response in post-Katrina New Orleans was a profound example of what happens to individuals in a dysfunctional governing system.

Sixteen months after the hurricane, and following several unsuccessful attempts to plan for recovery, the national nonprofit organization America*Speaks* brought a unique, large-scale citizen engagement effort to the city that was able to unite people and decision-makers behind common priorities, and develop a blueprint for rebuilding that would finally release the federal dollars vital to recovery. Efforts are ongoing with those citizens of New Orleans still being left behind in the recovery process to help them build a collective voice and thereby substantially increase their impact on the institutions and governing systems charged with their care and safety. This success in revitalizing the citizen-governing system relationship provides good reason for hope, not just for the people and city of New Orleans, but also for American democracy and possibly other nations. The crisis of Katrina was a call to look deeply at the failures of our systems and decision-making processes and to commit to institutionalizing new governance mechanisms that will move us closer to our aspirations. Supported by an understanding of systems and human behavior and how they interact, the lessons from New Orleans make it possible to take another step on the long journey to meaningful self-governance.

Large-Scale Citizen Engagement and the Rebuilding of New Orleans[20]

The Aftermath of Hurricane Katrina

Hurricane Katrina shattered New Orleans: more than 70% of the city's housing was damaged and entire neighborhoods were virtually destroyed; schools, hospitals, and police stations were shut down. Much of the city's infrastructure was decimated, and the city faced financial losses of enormous scale. Almost 100,000 jobs were lost following the Hurricane and, eighteen months later, more than half of the city's population still had not returned. Those who remained struggled to survive. In the chaos, decision-makers at all levels scrambled in crisis mode and quickly found themselves to be in conflict about rebuilding priorities and how to proceed. The failure of public officials at all levels to respond quickly and effectively to the hurricane and flooding, as well as the disparities along racial lines in how New Orleanians fared in the immediate aftermath, profoundly affirmed and deepened the already long-standing citizen distrust of government. The citizens of New Orleans, whether at home or dispersed around the country, faced, and continue to face, untold challenges in reconstructing their lives.

Early Struggles in Citizen Involvement

Citizens met early recovery planning efforts were met with suspicion anger, and protest. One month after the hurricane, New Orleans Mayor Ray Nagin's *Bring New Orleans Back* (BNOB) initiative convened an elite,

[20] This section draws from a case study previously published by the author (Lukensmeyer, 2007).

appointed commission to oversee a team of external planning experts. Without public consultation, the planners proposed not rebuilding many neighborhoods based on flood levels. The BNOB plan faced great public opposition, lost momentum, and was not able to go forward. Following this, the New Orleans City Council's Lambert Plan, while praised for its neighborhood-level participation process, did not include any of the people in diaspora and did not have the funding necessary to consider the larger, citywide issues. As a result, it was not able to respond fully to the recovery needs of the city.

Understanding the Challenges

In this challenging environment, the parameters of what it would take to launch and sustain viable recovery planning in New Orleans seemed daunting. Representative participation of those still living in the city, as well as of the many people dispersed around the country, was needed. Participation would have to overcome extreme skepticism and fatigue among citizens about planning efforts; and a strong legacy, recently intensified, of racial mistrust and socioeconomic division. Given the urgency of the situation on the ground, any new process would have to move quickly and simultaneously at both the citywide and planning district levels.

In the spring of 2006, officials began to conceptualize a strategy for addressing these many challenges. That summer, following months of intense negotiation, the Mayor, the City Council, and the City Planning Commission endorsed a new planning process: The Unified New Orleans Plan (UNOP).

Selecting a Citizen Engagement Model

Recognizing the need to engage the full diversity of the citizenry at levels sufficient to ensure credibility of results, the foundation overseeing the UNOP planning process invited a national organization with considerable experience in this area to join the team. Founded in 1995, the nonprofit America*Speaks* has worked to reinvigorate democracy by engaging citizens in public decision-making via an innovative model that links them with decision-makers and governance systems. In New Orleans, the methodology was selected to ensure that a large, demographically representative group of citizens, dispersed across twenty-one cities, could reconnect with each other and plan for their future. With key decision-makers listening, these citizens would determine shared views in a number of critical areas: ensuring safety from future flooding, empowering residents to rebuild safe and stable neighborhoods, providing incentives and housing, so people could return, and establishing sustainable, equitable public services.

The Twenty-first Century Town Meeting Process

America*Speaks'* Twenty-first Century Town Meeting® is a public forum that joins technology with small-group, face-to-face dialogue. The method not only engages large numbers of people (many thousands at a time) in deliberations about complex public policy issues but, by design, makes citizens and government co-owners of specific action plans. By bringing together a diverse cross-section of those affected by a given issue, and equalizing their opportunities for participation, the model restores balance to the political playing field. The methodology has been used by the Mayor of Washington, D.C., the Governor of California, the city of Port Phillip, Australia, and by many other municipalities, states, and regions across the country and around the world. The use of this methodology has not been limited to the public sector; it has also been successfully applied by large nonprofit associations. The World Economic Forum (Davos) and the Clinton Global Initiative have used modifications of the process to engage global leaders in developing action steps for addressing today's most complex issues.

The power of the Twenty-first Century Town Meeting lies in the way it integrates several critical elements, many of which have their theoretical basis in Gestalt principles. Prior to the meetings, key decision-makers from across all of the affected systems are brought into the process. Demographic outreach targets are set so that diverse citizen participation is ensured, and all receive essential background information so they can fully understand the issues and options and participate in the discussion. Experts are also made available to answer questions or clarify points. The heart of the process involves a combination of small, facilitated table discussions (with about ten people in each group) and electronic, real-time aggregation of these "intimate" conversations so that they are available to a larger group for consideration. Some of the group facilitators, who remain neutral through the discussion, are Gestalt-trained practitioners. The strategic use of advanced technolog (video teleconferencing, webcasting, networked laptop computers, voting keypads, etc.) enables ongoing interplay between the small groups and the whole community of participants. In the end, the small-group facilitation, and its connection to the larger group process, allows the work to bridge the multiple realities of the many participants and create a shared narrative that leads to decision-making and commitment to action.

Application of the Model in New Orleans: A Massive Effort

In preparation for two Twenty-first Century Town Meetings— Community Congress II, held on December 2, 2006, and Community Congress III, held on January 20, 2007, America*Speaks* worked in close partnership with more than fifty local organizations on a massive outreach campaign that ultimately registered and engaged thousands of citizens in New Orleans, Baton Rouge, Houston, Dallas, Atlanta and sixteen other cities. In addition to generating large numbers of participants, outreach efforts captured a demographic that matched the pre-Katrina population of New Orleans (67% African American, 28% White, 3% Hispanic, 2% Asian; 37% with annual incomes below $20,000). Elected officials and other key decision-makers were engaged in the outreach process, enhancing the legitimacy and credibility of the project and giving them co-ownership with citizens of the outcomes. More than 500 volunteer facilitators led citizens' face-to-face discussions.

Immediate Results:
Citizens and Leaders Work Together Toward Common Goals

With its unprecedented levels of citizen engagement, the Community Congresses yielded a number of immediate, powerful results:

- *Large numbers of citizens made substantive contributions to complicated policy issues.* Citizens publicly declared their priorities for rebuilding their city, raised concerns that accurately reflected weaknesses in the planning process, and were willing to accept trade-offs and additional responsibilities as well as make individual sacrifices.
- *Decision-makers found the process and emerging roadmap credible.* Twenty New Orleans leaders said that the representative mix of citizens and the conversations across demographic differences meant the results were a reliable basis for action.
- *Equal voice was given to the most disenfranchised.* Diverse participants said they were "very comfortable" speaking their minds at their tables (96%), and that people listened to each other "very well" (91%).
- *The deliberation had an impact on citizens:* 80% said hearing from people in the other cities made a "big impression" on them; 33% felt their views had changed as a result of the table deliberations.

- *Citizens committed to staying involved:* 93% of citizens at the second Community Congress said they would stay engaged, creating a constituency for further participation and for holding decision-makers accountable for taking action on the results.
- *Hope was ignited.* New Orleans and its citizens had been through a devastating trauma and left to languish without a concrete action plan for almost a year and a half. The Unified Plan process helped to bring back hope.

Impact on Large Governing Systems

The work of the Community Congresses reestablished the value of incorporating citizen voice in New Orleans' governance. All of the governing authorities involved (the City Planning Commission, the City Council, the Mayor, and the Louisiana Recovery Authority) approved the public's plan and then successfully used it to secure release of $216 million in relief funds in October 2007.

Continuing its work, America*Speaks* helped facilitate a meeting of 700 city employees with Recovery "Czar" Ed Blakely. The meeting enabled employees to hear about the Unified Plan, to review their individual and collective responsibilities for implementing it, and to provide feedback about how to make it a success. The session was also used to rollout the city's new evacuation plan. Nearly half of the attendees volunteered to help in future evacuation efforts, a remarkable commitment that again demonstrates the power of relinking citizen voice, in this instance "employee voice" with governance.

Further Building the Citizen System Connection: Ongoing Work in the Gulf Region

Taking on the Housing Crisis

As described, the work of the Unified New Orleans Plan was culturally transformational for New Orleans in many ways. At its conclusion, America*Speaks* felt a moral obligation to respond to requests to continue providing a supportive and unbiased presence in the work that would come next.

During the Community Congresses, strong relationships had been established with survivors and evacuees in four Diaspora cities. Further raising these voices would help sustain the momentum needed to ensure that New Orleanians could begin to rebuild their lives. Following Community Congress II, America*Speaks* brought together 30 diaspora leaders to determine an agenda for ongoing action. Their top priority was to help citizens who were still living in Federal Emergency Management Agency (FEMA) trailer parks: nearly 500 trailers remained in one park, "Renaissance Village," and dozens of other parks throughout the state kept tens of thousands in temporary housing. For over two years, these New Orleanians had been unable to reestablish their lives due to isolation from jobs, public transportation and support networks. Families as well as the disabled and senior citizens were living in spaces too small to accumulate household items, and they continued to fight the stigma associated with living in emergency housing. The absence of consistent and constructive case management made it nearly impossible for these residents to access resources and navigate the "helping" system. Further intensifying their struggle was a severe shortage of affordable housing.

In 2006, America*Speaks* engaged with a survivor/organizer to begin community-building and leadership team development on the grounds at Renaissance Village Trailer Park. The following work was accomplished:

- An array of local, state, and federal officials, agencies, and organizations met with more than 350 trailer park residents to hear a citizen-developed plan of action. Follow-up strategy sessions strengthened communication and coordination between trailer residents and agency staff.
- The American Red Cross established a presence at Renaissance Village, helping to address the needs of many residents by, for example, providing funds to purchase a vehicle. Other agencies stepped up as well.
- The Louisiana Recovery Authority (LRA) initiated weekly meetings among various state agencies and increased efforts to establish negotiations with FEMA and the Department of Housing and Urban Development (HUD).
- Renaissance Village resident leaders led trailer site visits for LRA staff and a delegation from the federal Government Accounting Office.
- Tulane law students and their counterparts from universities across the country in the "Student Hurricane Network" helped oppose a proposed City Council ordinance that would criminalize living under the I-10 Bridge in a tent—a necessary arrangement for many of the city's displaced residents. Legal aid agencies and law student organizations from other universities came to the table to work with a growing coalition of advocates.

- As a FEMA deadline approached to close the largest trailer park group sites in Louisiana, Mississippi and Alabama, efforts were made to create broader awareness of the unresolved problems residents faced, and FEMA extended the deadline.
- In response to the voices and issues raised at Renaissance Village, the LRA requested over $20 million from FEMA to implement coordinated case management for trailer residents. Unfortunately, the case management system was never implemented, for reasons never fully acknowledged.

Resident leaders who have moved out of Renaissance Village continue to advocate for their community and for others across the Gulf Coast. Given all of the progress in such a challenging environment, the Louisiana Recovery Authority has asked America*Speaks* to replicate and continue its work. Our ongoing priority is to continue helping position survivors and evacuees to sustain, over time, the work of self-organizing and engaging with governance officials.

A Unique Strategic Approach

America*Speaks*' work with displaced residents has capitalized on, and sustained, their enthusiasm for the participatory role in governance they experienced during the Twenty-first Century Town Meeting process. Taking advantage of the "neutral broker" role America*Speaks* played in the development of the Unified New Orleans Plan, the work diverges from traditional advocacy methods that are based largely on exerting pressure from the outside. Instead, it has deliberately sought to build relationships between citizens and the local, state, and federal agencies involved, so that America*Speaks* and the trailer park residents can be experienced by these agencies as partners and resources.

The community organizing work has also focused on the common good of the whole instead of tackling a specific problem in a specific location. This was a key message from citizens engaged in the UNOP process: the importance, to the community, of regaining its sense of wholeness.

The work with trailer park residents is taking on some extremely daunting systemic challenges. Yet, these efforts seek not only to leverage critical change in service delivery and the responsiveness of government. In addition, the work hopes to instill in citizens an expectation that they will continue to participate in the decision-making that affects them, and to nurture their capacity for the kind of participation that brings results.

Building citizens' and communities' capacity to speak with a collective voice and take action on public policy *over time* is the key to realizing a democracy that is truly of the people, by the people, and for the people.

Advancing the Citizen Engagement Field: Moving Toward our Aspirational Democracy

In the field of civic engagement, the work in New Orleans was, and continues to be, groundbreaking. It is securing substantial and representative participation in a "hardest case" environment: citizens have been openly skeptical of planning efforts and angry with public institutions, and the majority have been living in a post-disaster crisis mode. The Unified Plan effort, in particular, drew participation on a geographic scale that few have attempted, bringing citizens together across twenty-one cities simultaneously. The Twenty-first Century Town Meeting's strategic use of advanced technology clearly demonstrated that dispersed geography need no longer hinder face-to-face participatory processes.

The work is also succeeding in giving equal voice to the most disenfranchised: low-income citizens—African Americans in particular, who were disproportionately represented among the victims of Katrina, but who had been largely unheard in early recovery planning processes— and New Orleanians who had been given no opportunity whatsoever to participate dispersed to other cities.

The work concretely demonstrates two key tenets of civic engagement: that average citizens *can* make substantive and worthwhile contributions to complicated policy issues; and that reluctant decision-makers *can* be effectively brought into these processes. Finally, efforts in the trailer parks, in particular, demonstrate the capacity for sustainability: cumulative, ongoing impact following from a single-point-in-time engagement.

Theory of Change and Application of Gestalt Principles

The social change interventions undertaken in New Orleans (and in other America*Speaks* projects) are built on a conceptual framework solidly grounded in systems theory and Gestalt philosophy. Gestalt is so deeply embedded in the organization's methodology, that even staff members who are not formally trained in it apply the principles effectively.

Embracing Systems Theory

Meaningful and lasting social change is only possible if change occurs in *all* of the involved systems. In the case of post-Katrina New Orleans, this included systems from the individual and family level to the state and federal government. For months following Hurricane Katrina, the federal government claimed it would not release funds appropriated for recovery and rebuilding because of competing signals from the various levels of jurisdiction operating in New Orleans—the City Council, the Mayor, and the state-level Louisiana Recovery Authority, among others. When America*Speaks* made the decision to work toward significant change in New Orleans, it was clear that it would be critical to develop meaningful relationships with all these local decision-making systems, with other influential stakeholders, and with those systems involved at the federal level, such as FEMA, HUD, and the relevant congressional committees. To attempt to make progress without a full-system engagement would only reinforce the neglect, finger pointing, and lack of accountability that had been so persistent.

An analysis was conducted to identify all the points of leverage that had the ability to influence the flow of resources needed to rebuild the city, and the initiative strategically engaged with each in a deliberate and substantive way. America*Speaks* worked with each decision-maker and stakeholder group until they were willing to make a public commitment to acting on the citizen priorities that would emerge from the engagement. With project teams in five cities, the relevant social service agencies and elected officials in those cities were also actively involved. In the end, the large number and representativeness of the citizens who were deliberately brought together both enticed the necessary range of decision-makers and systems to become involved and, critically, gave them confidence to act on the results.

Bridging Multiple Realities

One of the primary mechanisms through which the Twenty-first Century Town Meeting helps citizens and decision-makers tackle a pressing concern is by ensuring that those directly involved have the opportunity to create a shared reality and narrative that includes all relevant and diverse perspectives. There are several core components of the model that work to this end:

- The small group, facilitated, face-to-face discussions at the heart of the process enable the intimacy necessary to explore differences and find commonalities. When these small discussions are fed into large-group decision-making, the developing narrative can then be experienced and collectively worked on by everyone in the whole community.

- Regardless of the specific issue or policy matter on the table, the Twenty-first Century Town Meeting always begins with a values discussion, first within small groups and then across the larger body of people assembled. The unified reality that is created is generally strong enough to hold participants together when the social and political issues they next discuss might tend to push them back to their fragmented realities.
- Small and large-group voting, cross-city theme development, and transparent display of the entire process result in a declaration of shared priorities on a key public concern.

In all these ways, the Twenty-first Century Town Meeting process actualizes the Gestalt principle of effectively working with multiple realities through the stages of recognition, respect, and, ultimately, reconciliation and/or creating a new shared reality. In New Orleans, multiple realities were bridged on two different, yet intertwined, levels of system. At the team level, the diverse group of people involved in planning the Community Congresses had to find bridges across individual members' unique experiences. As the team worked, they experienced many of the tensions and realities acutely felt in greater New Orleans and the diaspora cities. Issues of race and racism surfaced as they established leadership roles and work assignments, figured out how to share housing, and managed relationships in the context of an exceptionally grueling schedule. In the end, the commonly held experience of having survived Katrina served as a foundation; through open communication and respectful confrontation, the team succeeded in bridging its realities and accomplishing its goals.

At the level of the larger group of participants in the Community Congresses, a key bridging of multiple realities was also achieved. While the results related to rebuilding plans and resources for the city were specific and concrete, perhaps the more profound result for the 4,000 citizens and many decision-makers who participated was creation of a shared experience and narrative based on their commitment to rebuild their deeply beloved city. Indeed, several months later, when the City Planning Commission held hearings on the recovery plan, hundreds of people attended in order to make sure their recommendations and shared story were not lost in the cacophony of competing interests.

Completing the Unfinished Situation

In the United States, we place high value on our ability to move forward, take action, and not bog down in the past. A consequential weakness of this aspect of our culture is a reluctance, too often, to embrace sufficiently community rituals that enable mourning and closure. Yet, recovery from a significant trauma requires an opportunity to grieve and heal. Stated in Gestalt language, by first acknowledging and honoring the change that has taken place, we can then allow ourselves to find and/or create a new ending to the situation that was interrupted.

In post-Katrina New Orleans, a primary undertaking of the Community Congresses was to acknowledge the city's extraordinary need for healing by actually embedding this goal into the design of the work. A series of large-scale meetings that asked citizens to simply look at planning documents and make decisions would not suffice. Instead, it was critical to set an emotional tone in the room that would make it safe for participants to express authentically what they needed to express in order to grieve and move forward. Core elements of the model were designed to accomplish this goal.

- Strategically arranged table seating, and small and large-group introduction practices, diminished the power differentials that inherently exist in such a diverse group, and that often result in skipping the necessary work to achieve satisfactory closure.
- Highly skilled facilitators created a climate of emotional safety at each table, helping people appropriately express their internal state of being, and express their needs.
- In response to the uniquely tragic circumstances underlying this engagement process, local counselors were on site to talk privately with those who needed a quiet space to do so.
- To address the urgent needs and angers, every participating city had constituency services tables. Appointments were made and immediate needs addressed so that participants could focus on the planning decisions during the meeting.
- Finally, the physical environment was meticulously attended to, so that people would do this difficult work in a space that had key symbols and energy expressive of their common experiences and values. Participants in the Community Congresses were surrounded by the poetry, images, music, food, and culture of New Orleans. Second-line musicians (a long-standing tradition of the city) played people into and out of the room to profound effect.

The Community Congresses did not, of course, finish anyone's grieving process. However, they did allow a publicly shared, authentic honoring of those who had died, and enabled everyone in the room to carry some of the grief so that all could then join in the planning work that followed. This stands in marked contrast to common public meeting scenarios in which participants fight over whether to attend to healing or to planning. In those situations, the "haves" in the room are often on the side of moving forward and the "have-nots" on the side of grieving and healing. In the end, an understanding of the importance of respecting healing as a basis for moving forward enabled people to work productively and collectively.

Leadership through Presence and Use of Self

Effective Gestalt-based interventions rely on the leader establishing a "presence" that, while completely authentic to the individual, also deliberately serves two critical purposes: establishing a connection to, or familiarity with, participants, and creating a level of knowledge and authority that is interesting and compelling to them. In short, strategic use of self is key to a successful intervention.

As lead facilitator of the large-scale Twenty-first Century Town Meetings in New Orleans, it was critical that I establish that the space in which the day's dialogue would occur would honor people's authentic emotions, call on them to remain as present as possible, and then build on this presence to create a different kind of result—one that could be shared by the large number of people participating.

New Orleanians were deeply appreciative of all the help coming to them from around the country. But they were also painfully aware that the helpers too often believed they could grasp what had been experienced during and after Katrina. Understanding this dynamic, I deliberately began these participatory processes by acknowledging not only what had befallen this group of people, but also that no human being who had not been there at the time could ever really fathom the experience. Further, I emphasized that in order to survive and flourish, people needed to know that their voices—the true expression of their experiences—would finally be heard.

Not frightened by my own authentic emotion, I took the risk to come from all of myself. In doing so, I created safety and inspired other people to take similar risks. This shifted the room's energy, allowing people to be there with their whole selves, not just with their heads thinking about planning issues, nor with just their hearts angry about what had happened to them. To show the importance of simple things, an example early in the project was that my northern pronunciation of "New Orleans" was creating a breach in my position as a well-meaning outsider. I quickly learned to say "Nawlins," and residents were then able to hear me in a more positive way. In my experience over the last ten plus years leading large-scale citizen deliberations, it is clear to me that my authentic presence has an immediate and important impact on the proceedings. Participants routinely say that they knew, after the first five minutes of a Twenty-first Century Town Meeting, that what would happen would not only be different, but that it would make a difference.

Awareness at Strategic Moments

As noted in Chapter Two, a social intervention's success can hinge on application of the Gestalt principle of awareness: seeing "environmental or contextual conditions that define what is possible to achieve at any given moment." America*Speaks* applies this concept at three different levels simultaneously:

- *Awareness among stakeholders.* Awareness is critical if stakeholder groups are to maintain ownership of the process, and remain open to taking responsibility for the common good, not just protecting their own interests. In New Orleans, the stakeholder groups included business and government leaders, elected officials, representatives of the media, the planning team itself, and citizens from every neighborhood (both those who had returned and those who were still living in diaspora around the country). It was critical that we both generate awareness across these groups and balance respect for each stakeholder position with awareness of the overall needs of the city.
- *Awareness as a design principle.* All of the activities leading up to a large-scale participatory event, and the minute-by-minute events during the meeting itself, must be based on an understanding of the awareness necessary to reach the preliminary outcomes that will lead to the ultimate outcomes. In New Orleans, a common belief among decision-makers was that citizens would want to rebuild in their old neighborhoods, even if they were in a flood plain. It came as a surprise (a new awareness) that citizens were willing to discuss land swaps or other fair alternatives. By deliberately designing opportunities for citizens to discuss openly all options we were able to shift decision-makers' awareness so that planning discussions could proceed from this new perspective. In another example, it

became clear as this work progressed that a key shift in awareness that would inspire energy and mobilization among participants would be recognizing that, as a community, they were "on their own;" that no one was going to save them. By incorporating trusted community members into the design of the day to present the reality of where help was coming from and *not* coming from, we were able to help people move from a victim to a survivor stance and sensibility from which they could better take action.

- *Awareness at the individual level.* A key goal of this work is to create the circumstances that will empower people to build the future they want, to support citizens and decision-makers in coming to a new awareness of what is possible. During Community Congress II in New Orleans, a dramatic example of this took place with New Orleans Mayor Ray Nagin. The Mayor's opening speech that day was mostly a repeat of a speech he had given many times—he spoke but had very little investment in the words. It was clear that the cumulative trauma of the experiences surrounding the Hurricane and its aftermath had made it difficult for him to be in the present, open to his authentic emotions and fully aware of the possibilities. During the course of the day, however, Nagin experienced the people in the room (and across the sites) coming together with new life and new energy. He broke through his fog and by the end of the day was "back," aware of, and able to connect once again to his own passions, and able to join his community's energy and focus on planning for the future.

In all of these ways, America*Speaks*' work in the citizen engagement field reflects a robust application of Gestalt philosophy and theories of change.

Conclusion

Use of the Twenty-first Century Town Meeting with more than 145,000 people over a ten-year period has shown the power of the approach. It has also taught us some critical lessons.

Without full participation, results lose their power. If a citizen engagement effort does not bring all voices to the table, the work will not give leaders a reliable basis for action; the results will always be vulnerable to charges that they do not represent the views of various key constituencies. Unfortunately, getting a real commitment to full participation is often more difficult than might be imagined. Although democracy requires it, very few leaders who hold positional power are truly willing to do what it takes to ensure fully representative participation in decision-making.

Attending to issues of trust is vital. Around the world, the trust between people and their governing institutions is severely strained, if not, in many places, fully broken. For change interventions to rebuild this trust successfully, several components are key:

- Full transparency *at every step* is essential.
- Leaders and facilitators must use themselves authentically and compellingly, so that participants trust they can speak their truth and be heard.
- Building safe, democratic, and neutral spaces for this work is vital. True neutrality means believing that at any given moment, all parties—from political leaders and interest groups to the "average citizen"—are doing the best they can.

The work is highly adaptable across cultures. While the Twenty-first Century Town Meeting model was developed in the United States and has been primarily used to address serious deficits in American democracy, its principles and approaches are highly adaptable. People all over the world are seeking greater voice in government decision-making. America*Speaks*/Global Voices has been honored to apply adaptations of the model on four continents, and has learned that with a keen awareness of cultural, political, and structural differences, as well as with a full understanding of the history and context of the issues at stake, no matter where you are, it is possible to bring everyone to the table and influence policy.

By slowing down, we can speed up. Ironically, the Twenty-first Century Town Meeting process has shown that by deliberately slowing down—attending to multiple realities and creating awareness at every juncture—effective citizen engagement has actually been dramatically "sped up." The model can now be implemented without tremendous lead-time, and dramatic results can be achieved in a relatively short period. Speed is a necessity in a policy world so driven by fast-paced legislative calendars and the twenty-four-hour news cycle.

By adhering to these lessons learned, we can increase our capacity to produce effective joint action by large groups of diverse citizens. It is vital that we do so. Our choices in the coming years will determine whether our world is environmentally sustainable, spiritually fulfilling and socially just, or whether the consequences of actions we have collectively taken over the centuries will lead to our demise. It is therefore essential that we transform the way we conduct our global community's business; that w commit to working in urgent timeframes, at large scale, and with a level of inclusivity and participation that will empower us all and ensure we thrive into the future.

Carolyn J. Lukensmeyer, PhD, is an innovator in deliberative democracy, public administration, and organizational development. She is Founder and President of AmericaSpeaks, a nonprofit that develops and implements innovative deliberative tools, engaging more than 145,000 people in governance, in all fifty states and globally. Lukensmeyer was Consultant (1993-1994) to the White House Chief of Staff, and Chief of Staff (1986-1991) to Governor Celeste of Ohio. Lukensmeyer earned a PhD in Organizational Behavior from Case Western Reserve University and completed postgraduate training at the Gestalt Institute of Cleveland.

Contact: *cjl@americaspeaks.org*

Reference

Lukensmeyer, C. (2007). Large-scale citizen engagement and the rebuilding of New Orleans: A case study. *National Civic Review, 96*(3), 124-132.

CHAPTER 6

Community Psychotherapy in a Social Context: Gestalt on the Streets of London

Nigel Copsey, PsyD

Editors' Introduction

A basic Gestalt axiom is that growth and development come from the meeting of differences. When not addressed properly, however, differences can lead to scapegoating, polarization, disenfranchisement, and even war. In this chapter, Copsey describes what happens when a once stable community becomes thrown into a rapid change process over which the citizens have little control. The result is polarization along many fronts, including faith and religion, the wealthy and the poor, and the new residents and the indigenous population, as well as between the mentally challenged and the community as a whole.

Throughout this chapter, Copsey describes a number of interventions that his team made. In all of them, there is a focus on support and dialogue. Above all, he demonstrates the importance of staying in contact with those with whom one has profound differences. Copsey describes the task of the Gestalt community activist as that of being able to live in the middle and create relationships built on mutual respect. Copsey's work is a wonderful example not only of community action at its best but also of how to make a difference. It demonstrates how a small group of caring individuals can impact a community where polarities threaten its sustainability.

The Setting

London will be hosting the 2012 Olympics; the area in which I work covers that part of inner London where the event will be staged. My specific area of responsibility is within the mental health services of East London where I seek to ensure that all users have access to the necessary spiritual support whilst they are receiving care. East London has a long history of welcoming new communities from all over the world. As a result, the area is the most diverse in the UK: the uniqueness of the community is that it embraces a wide spectrum of ethnic groups as well as the many Faith traditions that form part of those groups. The area also has high levels of social deprivation.

Alongside the changes that have taken place over the last thirty years, with waves of new populations moving into and settling in the area, a new trend has begun to emerge. London has become the world's financial centre, with the result that the City of London has expanded into areas of East London. You can walk through what were at one time old disused docks that have now been transformed into a mini "Manhattan." Along the riverfront there has been an explosion of property building, with new developments aimed at the new financial community. There is also an airport created in the center of the old docks that were once the largest in the world; British Airways has recently announced that they will be shortly launching a new business-class-only route from this airport to New York. If you consider the size of the investment needed to establish the new infrastructure for the 2012 Olympics, then you can imagine the next seismic change that will be affecting the area. Whilst there are obvious major benefits to the community from all these developments, a dimension has not been predicted. The developments over the last decade have led to a number of polarizations: between those with wealth and the poor, between the new communities and the indigenous populations.

Polarization and Gestalt Therapy

As I have already indicated, inner London is increasingly becoming polarized at many levels with no sign of a desire to create meaningful dialogues between communities. As I write, a number of British Muslims are before the British courts on terrorism charges. These young men are highly intelligent, deeply religious believers from East London. In the current climate, the polarizing of the communities will become even more deeply entrenched. My hope is that the contents of this chapter will awaken hope that it is possible for change to take place at "street level." The developments predicted in the coming years will only increase the process of polarization. In this chapter, I am going to look at two of these trends and explore the ways in which a Gestalt perspective can provide a framework to support change that avoids polarization.

There has been a welcome focus in the recent Gestalt literature on developing an expanded understanding of the theory of polarities. Maurer (2002) has applied this particular Gestalt insight to illuminate the process of working within organisations. He shows how it is possible to identify polarities from a "figure-ground" perspective and enable change to take place. Evans (2007) has developed this perspective even further by outlining a "new paradigm," where he applies the theory to conflict situations within the Middle East. He develops the idea of "You are, therefore I am" within a context of stressing the "interconnection and interdependence" of all races. By linking these ideas with those of Buber, he makes a strong statement concerning the need to challenge traditional polarized ways of relating.

Despite its utility, the Gestalt approach has not been able to get recognition within the National Health Service, where the therapeutic focus is driven by brief therapy with short-term, evidence-based outcomes. As a result it, along with other humanistic theories, has remained on the edge. One way to bring humanistic theories into the mainstream is to reclaim the early tradition of the Gestalt approach and combine it with a robust and accepted research model. The tradition I am referring to is that of *community engagement.* Gestalt theory emerged out of community. I myself was first attracted to the Gestalt approach because I became a member of a training community as well as a therapeutic community. In stark contrast to my earlier experiences of training, I felt the power of healthy community, where the centrality of relationship was the focus to learning. That key insight is needed today more than ever. Once a person has received psychological help founded on the healing experience of the therapeutic relationship, that person needs to be able to be supported through the experience of being part of a community. Most that leave clinical help have no community to return to.

Two Stories

In the following two "true stories" I will be recounting, I describe working with communities by using the core principles outlined above. They are examples of developing "communities of support" for those who are cut adrift from community. Gestalt theory is ideal when applied to these community situations. It provides a map to describe a process of change. I have attempted to find language which will reach those in these settings, as I believe that the Gestalt model can be applied in any setting. The two communities with which I have been working represent the challenge presenting itself in our inner cities. How is it going to be possible to live with difference? How can we release the natural caring of the ordinary person? How are we able to sustain community support in an environment where it is absent? I have been using Action Research methodology to develop this work, as I think it is the only possible research methodology to use when "on the streets" and when stimulating change.

A Café

Just opposite the newest development in "Docklands" (the largest exhibition center in London) is perhaps the most deprived neighborhood in the district. As you leave the train, you can either cross the railway line and the road north to this poor neighborhood, or you can walk across a newly built bridge south to the wine bars, hotels, and dockside developments adjoining the exhibition center. If you were to head north, you would walk along a road where all the shops are protected with heavy metal shutters after closing time. There have been two murders on the streets in the last year: one, where a young man challenged a gang that was abusing him. They then followed him to his home where they shot him in front of his wife and young child. In this last week alone, there have been three stabbings on the streets which will go unreported by the press, as such tragedies are commonplace; in one of the incidents the youths slashed the tires of a police car. The local secondary school is under special measures with deeply committed teachers unable to find an answer. I could continue in the same vein, providing you, the reader, with a picture of a community which local residents themselves call a "war zone" and "wasteland." Only thirty years ago, this neighborhood was a proud and safe area with a settled community that consisted of extended families who had lived in the area for generations. Those who now remain who were once part of that community live in fear. Those who leave the train and walk south to visit the expensive hotels and restaurants will be unaware that a completely different world exists on the other side of the railway line!

Situated in the "war zone" is a community café. The Garden Café was at one time a local shop that sold fruit and vegetables. With the advent of a new supermarket, the owners were unable to continue. They decided to turn the shop into a community café. The vision for the Café was to create a safe environment where those most isolated and on the edge could find a place of hope and peace. Those who use the Garden Café include: local people suffering from mental illness and distress, young people with learning disabilities gaining work experience, street kids with nowhere to belong, those alone and isolated and needing somewhere to be accepted and loved, and those who need support whilst challenging faceless authorities. As I paint the picture, I am sure that you, the reader, can begin to appreciate that this special couple who had transformed their store into a community café would quickly become casualties unless they themselves were supported. The nature of support has evolved in a number of ways.

The most important area of support for this couple was to train and equip them as well as to establish a team to work with them. They both undertook a range of different trainings. Bill joined the program that we offer to the community through the mental health services. This training, which is jointly provided with the psychology department of the local university, is founded on a core syllabus shaped by Gestalt theory. Using the Cycle of Experience as foundational, students learn through experiential learning and discovery.

Each training group consists of a range of local people drawn from a wide range of different ethnic backgrounds. A core value of the group is to learn by respecting, valuing, and celebrating the differences within the group. The importance of experiencing real relationships, and understanding the blocks to real contact, form a core aspect to the experience. In addition, we include contributions from colleagues within the mental health services to cover the range of understandings necessary to have a framework with which to help others. We provide students with an understanding of the wide range of support networks that are available to them. In the case of the café, we undertook to establish links between Bill and Eve and the local community mental health team. We have ensured that they both have twenty-four hour access by phone to a mental health practitioner, if required. Throughout the training program a high value is placed upon providing support and developing a system which could sustain the work undertaken by Bill and Eve. I have already mentioned that the secondary aim was to train a group of volunteers who would work as a team with them. At this moment, five people have completed our training program and work as part of the team with Bill and Eve. We have also undertaken to provide monthly supervision for the team.

The key point here is that, for any social undertaking to succeed, there needs to be a high level of support. Those who use the Café enter a safe community. They know that they can "be themselves" and not be judged. They know that they will experience a quality within the relationships, whereby they can receive genuine support from the "Café Team" who accept and love them for who they are. At a very deep level, they know that the team has a genuine interest in their lives. This level of commitment flows from their deeply held spiritual beliefs about the importance and uniqueness of every person.

I have witnessed the impact this "safe community" has had upon the neighbourhood. When all the statutory agencies and professionals leave their workplace to return home, the Café remains as a beacon of hope and support. Many would not be alive today if it were not for this community. Others have been prevented from being admitted to psychiatric hospital. Many find only in the Café the support that they need when leaving hospital. The irony is that such community ventures fight to survive and rarely obtain funding from statutory bodies. Kurt Lewin (1946) believed that training was part of the cycle of research and action. The Café has been an experiment in effecting change. I will look at the implications of this radical approach in my concluding remarks.

The uniqueness of the Café is the creation of a "safe community" built upon a high level of relational support that is not "clinical." The reason why the support offered at the Café is so important is that the relationships established are not restricted to "professional boundaries." The quality of relational contact founded on community begins to meet the deep relational needs within the person. The following example illustrates this uniqueness:

> One of the greatest needs for those who leave the psychiatric wards is to feel that they "belong." The community into which people are discharged is a hostile environment. The majority of those who leave a hospital without family or friends find themselves living in hostels, flats, or a bedsit. Whilst the basic needs of food and shelter are met, the deeper relational ones seldom are. The result is that there remains a high level of isolation. The only contact is with "professionals" who limit the level of their relationship. As many are coping with major complex mental health needs (such as schizophrenia), such persons often return to a hospital as the symptoms reappear.
>
> In the last six months, our team has been aiming to continue the relationships established within the hospital setting into the community. Many remain in hospital for up to six months, during which time a volunteer from the Café visits them at least on a weekly basis. As they move into a hostel or a flat, one of our volunteers continues to visit them. We then invite them to join us for an activity at the Café.
>
> One recent example has been the supporting of a man who has an interest in music. Each week one of our volunteers picks him up and takes him to the Café where another volunteer has been helping him to explore his musical gifts. This person now looks forward every week

to the afternoon at the Café where he is always welcomed. When he arrives, there is always a mixture of local residents and volunteers who are aware of the particular support that he needs. Those volunteers are local residents who have completed the one-year training provided by the university's mental health services. They are also members of a monthly support group. In addition, members of the mental health team (psychologist, social worker, community psychiatric nurse) include the Café as an integral part of the support for a person leaving hospitals. Our vision is that many individuals will be supported by this partnership between mental health services and faith groups.

Ramadan

In a different part of East London is a neighbourhood where the largest Bangladeshi community in the UK lives. Just along from the road where our mental health centre is situated is the largest mosque in Europe. The community is almost completely Muslim and is the largest in the UK. We have a team of six people working in that area, two of whom are Muslims.

The recent tragedies caused by the London bombings have caused many to question our understanding of a multicultural society. Indeed, many of the Muslim community have suffered greatly from Islam phobia. We are at a crossroads: there is a very real danger of increased polarization between the different communities of inner London. There is, at the moment, little hope that the different communities will enter into dialogue with one another and learn from each other. Since many of the London bombers were young British Muslims, there is an even greater suspicion of young "fundamentalists." I would like to share a story that should bring hope amidst the polarizing that is taking place.

Close to one of our mental health facilities is one of the largest colleges that form part of the University of London. The largest student group within the university is the Islamic Society. The group meets not only to have weekly prayers, but also to reflect upon the interface between their faith and living within western culture. We had been finding it difficult to establish any meaningful dialogue with the leaders of the Mosques. Instead, one of our team made contact with the President of the Islamic Society at the university. To our surprise, he responded with great enthusiasm to our request for contact. The result was the beginning of a series of training programs which introduced the students to an understanding of mental health alongside discovering a respect for the differences of other faith traditions. A number of the students continued their study and completed the same university program as Bill from the

Café. In truth, some of the students found it very difficult to engage in this type of learning through dialogue; however, a number have persisted and, consequently, have made a major impact on the mental health services.

For example, over the last two years a number of students working together with our team organized the culturally appropriate diet for Muslim patients on the wards in the period of Ramadan. When they first began to work with us, they wanted to ensure that all Muslim patients received the correct level of support throughout Ramadan. They were soon to discover that hospital budgets and ward routines would not permit patients to have the right food at the right time. Our team helped them to understand the resistance in the system. They then convinced the owner of a local restaurant to donate food that was then delivered every evening throughout Ramadan at the breaking of the fast. This made a significant difference to the patients.

In addition, this same group of students began running a weekly discussion group for Muslims as well as weekly Jumma prayers. These students have not only taken the risk to train in spiritual care with those from other faith traditions, but they have also discovered that it is possible to continue to remain true to their own beliefs as well as learn about others who are different from themselves.

The most moving moment in the training was the occasion when the Muslim female members wearing the veil sought to explain their reasons for covering their faces. The context was a media and political debate that was very critical of such a practice. Although the group looked as if it might disintegrate, the members were able to work through the struggle, with the result that their relationships were transformed. The link between the mental health services and the Islamic society is now stronger than at any time.

There has been a long tradition within East London of a polarization between the mental health services and the Faith Communities of the area, particularly between the Asian Faith-based communities and the psychiatric services. The main reason is the polarization of belief systems. The Asian Faith Groups believe in the supernatural, whereas the mental health services are predominantly Western, secularised, and Eurocentric in their belief system. The training program established between our team and these communities is designed to create a dialogue between these two often-polarized belief systems.

Each year, members of our team make a presentation to the Islamic society, the largest in the university. From that initial meeting, a group of students attend an introductory course with members of our team; the course consists of participants drawn from all the faith traditions. It is always a challenge for those who never meet with those from other faiths to join an experiential group where the aim is to learn from each other whilst remaining in a relationship of respect. From this initial group, two or three decide to commit themselves to further training, through which we seek to help them connect their faith system with an understanding of mental health. Although this is a new experience for all of them, there is always a willingness to engage with this process. From the training, the students become registered volunteers and begin to support our team members on the wards.

I believe that the relationships being established will have a lasting impact upon multiculturalism in our small area of East London. My hope is that, as we develop stronger links of trust, we will be able to explore the many subjects that for the moment are a taboo area: how is it that sincere young Muslims born in the UK can identify with radical views that underpin the justification of bombings? The core Gestalt principle that has influenced us is the belief that it is possible to stay in relationship whilst at, the same time, understanding our differences. In a context where the pull is to move to polarized positions, it is hard work to remain in contact around such profoundly different belief systems. It also involves great risk for those willing to explore beliefs not accepted by the community from which they originate.

Reflection and Implications

When first introduced to the Gestalt tradition, I was deeply impressed by the emphasis found in the work and life of Paul Goodman, namely that Gestalt theory could be applied to a social context. I was also inspired by Kurt Lewin's (1946) emphasis on change following from research. It was therefore a great sadness to me that, during the period of my training as a psychotherapist, the profession was steadily becoming an elitist profession. Both the cost and length of training excludes all but a few from joining this elite club. The march towards accreditation and regulation, whilst perfectly understandable, is in grave danger of stifling the spirit of helping and of limiting help to a profession of counselors, psychologists, and psychotherapists. The implication of this trend is that it will not be long before only those with postgraduate qualifications will be admitted to the profession. Over the last twenty years university qualifications have become the benchmark for recognition. The majority of training programs now seek university status: those not holding such a qualification are often seen as "amateurs."

Herein is a very serious problem. In the areas I have been describing in this chapter, the majority of support provided to the most vulnerable sections of our community is given by ordinary people, many of whom have themselves experienced mental health problems. Once someone has left the consulting room in a hospital, mental health centre, or other facility, that person has to then survive in the "war zone" until he or she sees the professional helper again a week later. If the person has been in hospital, he/she has to return to a "wasteland" infected with violence, crime, and drug abuse.

Those helpers who provide the support throughout the week do so either in a voluntary capacity or on a low income. They often do so without any support from being a member of a multidisciplinary team, and will often be unsure if the agency for which they give their time will be funded the following year. In contrast to the professional helpers who are only available by appointment, this group of helpers is available when needed most. Another major difference is that professional helpers seldom live in the area where they work. Indeed, it is often seen as important to keep a professional distance from the client, and it would be considered as inappropriate to have contact with any client outside of clinical time. The volunteers in the Café, in contrast, live in the area and are themselves from that neighborhood: many have themselves experienced similar problems as those they are helping.

Herein lies the problem: those who often provide the most creative, committed and sacrificial type of helping, and who are supporting the most vulnerable in their community, are perceived by the professional helpers as "amateurs."

The Gestalt movement was not the only one to have its roots in community. Person-Centered counseling also began with an ideal of sharing its insights with as many helpers as possible. Many working on the front line were often trained with person-centered skills. There was no desire in the early days to create a psychotherapy profession. Many psychological theories have originated to give a meaning to human experience. The development of a profession of helpers accredited with the necessary qualifications has resulted in a body of experts who hold the necessary knowledge and power. Instead of this body of knowledge being shared with the most vulnerable, there has been a narrowing of helping to certain groups of suitable clients.

I hope the two examples I have given in this chapter illustrate the need to return to the original principles of helping. I am arguing against a polarization between the professional and the volunteer. There needs to be a mutual respect between the two groups, whereby each sees the importance of the work done by the other. To achieve this, there has to be an elevating of the importance of work undertaken, for example, by those who give their time at the Café and at the Islamic society. We need to be able to "give away" our knowledge generously, so that the maximum help can be given to the most vulnerable. There needs to be a partnership between those engaged in "street therapy" and those in the more established professions. Such a partnership will enable those in the professional bodies to learn from those on the street. There would be a dismantling of hierarchy. A truly I-Thou relationship could then be established.

Is this vision too idealistic? As I have been writing this reflection, I have come to realise that we have created a polarization amongst the helpers that reflects the polarization that is developing in the other areas of society. Our value as Gestalt practitioners is to live in the middle and create relationships built on mutual respect. My hope is that the partnerships we are creating between very different groups in East London will inspire you, the reader, to think and practice "out of the box." The bringing together of Gestalt theory, training, and Action Research has resulted in the mobilization of psychotherapeutic theory into social action.

Let me conclude with one final example of the way in which these three areas come together. I have already highlighted the need for training founded on Gestalt principles and values to underpin the community action we have embarked upon. On one training program the students concluded that it was not the world outside the mental institution that was normal but those within it! This came about because of a number of sessions where the group members (drawn from a mixture of faith traditions) shared their inner worlds with one another. They had never done so before at that level, and certainly not with others drawn from such diverse backgrounds. From these discussions, a series of action research cycles began whereby groups were established within the hospital; those who attended could be themselves as they shared their inner spiritual journeys in a setting which provided safety even amidst a wide spectrum of difference. At the end of each group, participants are encouraged to share ways in which their experience could be improved. The challenge for us is to develop this idea into a community context where "normal society" expects persons to conform to rigid sets of beliefs.

I am on a journey of discovery. The examples I have given in this

chapter reflect my stage of learning at this moment. The most impo[...]
truth I am discovering is to stay in relationship even within the mo[...]
difficult of settings, where polarization has become the norm. I have
also discovered that in order for me to achieve this goal, I need to create
a community around me of those who are also willing to work and be
committed to the same set of values as I am. I need to be able to model
in my life as a practitioner the willingness to remain in relationship
with those with whom I have profound differences. I am also more
committed now, than at any other stage in my life, to community action
by mobilizing the gifts of the ordinary person without demanding that
those special people conform to a form of professional elitism. I want to
be able to release the brilliance of the ordinary person.

Nigel Copsey, PsyD is the Team Leader for Spiritual
Care within the Mental Health Services of East
London, England. He leads a team of ten drawn from
a wide spectrum of Faith traditions. Their task is to
ensure that all those who use mental health services
have their spiritual needs met within the context
of holistic care. Over the last twenty years, Copsey
has established three departments in spiritual care
within the National Health Service. He is an ordained
minister in the Church of England as well as being an
accredited psychotherapist. He is a program leader
at the University of East London where he teaches
spiritual care and mental health. He is also a visiting
lecturer at the University of London.

Contact: *N.copsey@ btopenworld.com*

References

Evans, K. (2007). Living in the 21st Century: A Gestalt therapist's search
for a new paradigm. *Gestalt Review, 11*(3), 190-203.

Lewin, K. (1946). Action research and minority problems. *Journal of
Social Issues, 1*(2), 34-46.

Maurer, R. (2002). Managing polarities. *Gestalt Review, 6*(3), 209-219.

he Human Face in the Eye of the Rhetoric: A Dialogue on Same-Sex Marriage

Patricia Perry, PsyD

Editors' Introduction

This chapter illustrates the application of a cornerstone of the Gestalt Approach, namely: the use of fairly intense dialogue to improve understanding and contact among people or groups holding diverse or conflicting positions. As Perry indicates, other conceptual frameworks have been developed, and she shares with us her experience using the "Creative Conversations" approach of the Public Conversations Project (PCP), along with use of her Gestalt training. As with the Gestalt approach, "Creative Conversations" derived from the principles and methods of psychotherapy: a practice designed to facilitate difficult conversations. This case, and many others, illustrates the power of applying these methods to social issues.

One thing that stands out in this case is the sobering reality that many people with strong positions on an issue are not willing or ready to engage in dialogue with people who hold different or opposing positions. This reality raises the importance of preparing individuals for engaging in difficult conversations. While some people can ease into tense situations without difficulty, in most cases some unhurried "warm-up" may be required. Perry ponders whether her intervention would have been better if she had devoted more time to such a "warm-up," thus alerting practitioners to the tricky business of laying the groundwork for this kind of intervention. The chapter portrays a sensitive practitioner as she weaves back and forth between awareness of her participants and herself.

Introduction

A quiet, young woman from a two-parent, heterosexual family, with her first child in kindergarten, looked at the group of nine other parents around her and said: *"He's only five! I had no idea what to say to him when he came home from school and asked me why two men would be married to each other. He'd never seen that, heard of that. I didn't have any warning from the school. We don't talk about that sort of thing. He was just looking at me waiting for an answer. I didn't know what to say."*

This mother, part of the "very conservative" group in the school system, reluctantly had agreed to attend one in a series of "Constructive Conversations" aimed at calming a major confrontation over a discussion in her son's elementary school about same-sex marriage. Her words, and the confusion and anxiety on her face, suddenly shifted the wary mood in the room. Several of the mothers "from the other side" nodded slowly, seeming to acknowledge painful familiarity with finding themselves in difficult conversations with their children. Contact[21] had been made. A small window had opened.

This chapter will describe an intervention in this school system, the ideas and theories behind the design, some of the outcomes, and a reflection on the nature of dialogue, resistance, contact, awareness, and the potential power of both understanding, and not understanding (Gurevitch, 1989), in the face of deeply value-laden social conflicts.

History and Description of the Conflict

On May 17, 2004, the fiftieth anniversary of Brown vs. the Board of Education, same-sex marriage became legal in Massachusetts. On that day, at Jefferson School, an elementary school in a primarily middle/upper-middle class suburb of Boston, Massachusetts, the Principal's morning announcement included a statement about both of these historic events. During the day, many of the teachers had discussions of the meaning of these events in their classrooms.

When the children went home and reported that they had talked about same-sex marriage, there was an outpouring of highly charged, diverse community reactions, expressed by parents and teachers in a

---

[21] "Contact" is a concept used by Gestalt practitioners to describe a point at which boundaries shift and change occurs. For more information on training and learning opportunities in the Gestalt model, see www.gisc.org (Gestalt International Study Center, South Wellfleet, MA) or www.gestaltosd.org (Gestalt Organization & Systems Development Center, Cleveland, OH).

volatile community meeting and in civil and uncivil exchanges on an electronic "bulletin board." Reactions ranged from acclaim for the school's commitment to teaching and valuing different kinds of families, to outrage at the content of the discussion and anger at not being given advance warning. Many members of the school community spoke of feeling deeply hurt and devalued because of the communication that took place in the days and weeks following the announcement.

While this situation in and of itself was the cause of much pain and controversy, other factors added to the complexity. Four years earlier, at the same school, a first grade teacher had responded to his first grade class's persistent questions about his family by talking about himself and his male partner. This "coming out" to his class led to angry letters to the editor in the local paper and a confrontation of the superintendent, who responded by saying: "I support my teachers." Since it happened near the end of the school year, nothing further happened about the issue, but it remained underground and resurfaced in the current situation as an accusation that the entire school system had "a gay agenda."

Some additional factors that are part of the whole include:

- Jefferson School is located in the most working class neighborhood in the district and saw the closing of the Catholic Church that served it, due to the financial crisis following the priest pedophile scandals.
- The school has the largest number of "activist" teachers in the school system, but there is also a wide diversity of views among teachers.
- The GLBT teachers in this system are among the most highly regarded by *all* of the parents.
- The school system as a whole has a "Respect for Human Differences" mission statement that identifies a "commitment to respecting and valuing human differences."

After unsuccessfully trying to manage the conflict internally, the Superintendent of Schools and Principal of Jefferson decided that they needed some outside help. At that point, they contacted Public Conversations Project (PCP), a Boston-based group that works nationally and internationally, designing and conducting dialogues about divisive social issues (for further information, see www.publicconversations. org). Having worked with PCP on a number of different projects over many years, I was asked if I would be interested in being part of a two-person facilitation team. My co-facilitator would be another associate of the organization whom I had first met in 1994, at a training of facilitators for a series of public dialogues on abortion. We agreed we were both interested in this project.

Public Conversations Project, Gestalt, and Me

Before going further into a description of what we did, I want to take a moment to add to the context. When I was invited to write this chapter for a book on Gestalt and social issues, using my Public Conversations Project (PCP) work as the case material, I chose a project that had happened subsequent to my participation in an eighteen-month Organization Systems Development program at the Gestalt Institute of Cleveland (1996-1998).

Project chosen, I faced the dilemma of how to talk about Gestalt concepts when I also was steeped in PCP's models, which initially grew out of family systems thinking and narrative theory. The more I thought about this issue, the more I kept coming back to the fact that what seems to "work" in the dialogues I have done with PCP is what seems to work when I have facilitated a process with my Gestalt lens in place. What began to interest me was looking at what happens in the conversation when an unlocking and opening to new viewpoints occur. Which core concepts, whether from Gestalt and/or PCP, might help me understand and build a framework to use at those other dreaded moments when the conversation stays cold and closed?

Old Stories and Stuck Conversations

From my long-ago training at PCP, one particular core idea has stayed with me over the years and become part of how I think about what is in the room when people come together in dialogue. Drawn from work by Michael White and David Epson (1990) on narrative therapy, and adapted to PCP's model by Sally Ann Roth,[22] the basic concept is that we

---

[22] Sally Ann Roth is a founding member of the Public Conversations Project. In her work as a family therapist, she applied narrative concepts to couples and family therapy: "When partners are at an impasse in their relationships, their individual and couple stories have become predominantly narratives of limitation." The question then becomes: "How can they each develop narratives of possibility or gain the freedom and agency to create narratives of choice?" (Roth and Chasin, 1994, p. 190). Carrying this idea into polarized debates, she and her colleagues at PCP suggest that the movement from debate to dialogue occurs when: "Participants witness those whom they had objectified as 'other' engaging in struggles similar to their own—struggles to construct meaning and coherence from contradictory experience and struggles to manage the tension of having experiences, feelings, and beliefs that their constructions do not accommodate" (Roth, et al., 1992, p. 48).

all have many old stories that we have adopted as "the truth" about our values and ourselves. These stories may cause us personal pain ("I will always be a loser") or be a source of personal affirmation ("I am really good at anything I do"). They define us ("I am a person of strong moral beliefs") and they reassure us ("I know what is the right thing to do"). In order to keep our stories in place, whether positive or negative, we may selectively choose to hold onto experiences and interactions that leave these narratives unchallenged and allow the whole (the "Gestalt") to become fixed. When this occurs we close down our ability to take in any new "data" that might disconfirm our story. This may be especially true when the belief is one held by our families and/or the communities within which we live. Much of the PCP method and the Gestalt approach are designed to allow for the possibility that the fixed Gestalt might be loosened, or at least opened to reexamination.

The problem arises when my story not only conflicts with your story but, more frightening, when your story calls into question my whole fundamental belief system and sense of identity. My willingness to stay present during this kind of conflict depends on many things, including the nature of my relationship to you (stranger or friend), the degree of threat to me (both physical and psychological), the rigidity or flexibility of my internal belief structure, the safety of the "container" in which the conflict occurs (home, work, community), and the "level of system"[23] at which the interaction is happening (person-to-person, person-to-institution, group-to-group).

In any given situation, based on all of the factors mentioned above, there is the possibility that I will listen, reflect, inquire, test my assumptions, and rewrite my story in a way that creates "contact" (with myself and with you); and there is also the possibility that you and I will continue to reiterate our viewpoints with more and more fervor, becoming increasingly locked into an unchanging conversation. Some of the characteristics of "stuck conversations on polarized issues" (included in a handout used by PCP [Public Conversations Project, 1997]) are:

• The conversation is unvarying and predictable.

---

[23] "Level of System": The four primary levels of system (as described in a handout for Organization and Systems Development, Class XII, Session 7, by the Organization & Systems Development Center, John D. Carter & Associates [1997]) are: 1. self or individual; 2. self and other (interpersonal); 3. subgroup (dyad or triad); and 4. group. One way of breaking this down further shows the nested levels of system: individual, dyad, group, organization, community, institution, and culture. A critical part of any intervention at one level of system is considering the consequences on all other levels.

- Conscious proactive choice becomes limited as reactive emotional responses increase.
- Blaming and attack reign, fueled by righteous passion, feelings of victimization, disempowerment, and disqualification.
- Members of an opposing alliance seem to all be alike; the most extreme leaders are seen as representative of the whole group.
- Partisans believe that the "problem" would disappear if the adversaries would.
- When members of opposing sides do listen to each other, they scan for flaws, rarely attempting to deepen their understanding of the other.
- Fixed and simple convictions are openly displayed. Complexity, ambivalence, confusion, and inner conflict are concealed.

It Looks Like Resistance to Me

As I thought about which concepts from Gestalt apply to similar phenomena described in different theoretical models, I was reminded of *Beyond the Wall of Resistance* (1996) written by Rick Maurer, a Gestalt-trained organizational consultant. While he speaks primarily about the use of Gestalt in dealing with resistance to change initiatives in organizations, his comments on the nature of resistance help to describe what happens in the kinds of polarized conversations that are core to PCP's work. Resistance is a natural phenomenon, a normal reaction to something new or different that might prove to be harmful. In the case of a long held belief (story) that is core to our sense of self and/or our sense of belonging to a like-minded community, Maurer (1996) suggests that resistance may be a valid form of protection. It is just trying to help us "stay ourselves." If we give up that belief we might not know who we are, and the communities or families that we need to survive might ostracize us.

Resistance is also energy. Having watched people involved in debates on the hottest social issues, there is no doubt that they are tuning forks of energy. Tap them with a different viewpoint, and the angry buzz they emit can puncture your eardrums. The question is, what else can you do with that energy? Sometimes, if you are feeling safe enough, you can join it by asking a question, sharing a personal story, making an observation, or allowing yourself to sit with it. Sometimes, however, that feels impossible. There are different levels of resistance in Maurer's framework. Important about this idea is that we often try to respond to all resistance with the same hammer and nail and then wonder what went wrong. The three levels he describes are:

- *Level 1:* This is a "low-grade resistance" to a new idea where people oppose a change because they just do not like the idea or understand it; they do not think their ideas were taken into account; they like things as they are. Generally, this kind of resistance can be dealt with on an "intellectual" level by giving people more information and/or giving them a voice in the change. While this is rarely the level at which most deeply felt social conflicts occur, it is sometimes the way in which social conflicts are dealt with, and it rarely works. Telling people how and why you are going to introduce a book on gay and lesbian families into the elementary school curriculum will not put an end to parents' resistance to the whole concept.
- *Level 2:* Level 2 resistance is bigger than any particular change being suggested. It has to do with loss of power, status, and/or respect. It often triggers fears of isolation or abandonment and stirs up mistrust of those proposing the change. Sometimes it is just plain weariness with too much change. Often, resistance at this level can be managed by helping people feel heard and valued.
- *Level 3:* Level 3 resistance is the most deeply embedded and entrenched. The stories are often old and filled with ancient pain. It represents significant disagreement over values and reflects different cultural, religious, ethnic, racial, and gender realities. This is the level of the social issues most difficult to surmount. Yet, Maurer (1996) believes that even Level 3 resistance is open to hope. Tentative bridges can be built through humanizing the conflict and searching for common ground.

The Power of Not Understanding

Before continuing with the discussion of the process at Jefferson School, I want to bring in one final paradoxical idea (from a paper used in the training at PCP) that has to do with the "power of not understanding" (Gurevitch, 1989, p. 164). While I agree with Maurer that putting a human face on the rhetoric and working to find out what we have in common can often lead to contact, there are times when that is not enough—when the effort to understand leads us into a place where "the other is not unexplained, but is instead inexplicable" (Gurevitch, 1989, p. 164). At those moments, despair is inevitable *and*, at the same time, may be the only door left open.

I remember attending a "Diversity Training" workshop many years ago, full of good intentions and the sense of myself as a deep and committed listener. At one point on the second day, I was engaged in a dialogue (my word) with a young African-American male who had grown up on the streets, become a street worker, and was starting his studies in social work. It was not a dialogue. I was asking him question after question, convinced that I could understand his life, sure that we could find places of connection as human beings. He was struggling to answer. In my determination to connect, I did not notice the pain on his face. The workshop leader put out her hand towards me and said, "I'm going to stop you. Your questions are not going to help. You will never be able to understand his experience."

Even as I write this now, I can feel my outrage, indignation, anger, and shame at her words. *"What did she mean I could never understand?? I could always understand. I was really good at putting myself in someone else's shoes. I was known for my ability to step across boundaries. I really cared. I was trying so hard!"* I could not bear to sit with what Philip Gurevitch calls "the inability to not understand" (1989, p. 163). I wanted to be able to hold this young man in a framework of familiarity, of what was understandable from my own life experiences of hurt and hope. My questions were aimed at finding those underlying similarities. I assumed that "by striking up a conversation and by declaring a will to overcome differences and to lay down a basis of understanding, dialogue will succeed" (Gurevitch, 1989, p. 162).

Contact, however, is a funny thing. Sometimes it refuses to be herded so easily. Sometimes it requires the willingness to face the "not-me" and accept that I do not understand. It may mean letting go of my story not only about me, but also about the other. In that encounter, there can be no easy assumptions of sameness, or projections onto the other of what I think I already know about him or her. More than that, it inevitably means that I take the risk of seeing myself through the eyes of someone else, something I was not ready to do with the young man in the diversity workshop.

I have often thought about that intervention. I sort of "got it." I knew that the facilitator was holding out a possibility to me and I had a glimmer of what she intended. I understood it better in the light of Gurevitch's article. I can think of it now as an example of "the paradoxical theory of change" (discussed in chapter 2 of this book), with its suggestion that it is only in accepting the *disconnection* that connection becomes possible. But part of me still wants to fight it. How can good intention not be enough? What if I, we, the world, become stuck in the not understanding and there is no bridge, no contact?[24]

The First Steps in the Process

These kinds of questions and concerns were always standing in the shadow for me as we began the process of working with Jefferson School, especially given the "stuckness" of their current conversation and the degree of frustration and helplessness that many people were experiencing. In addition, the intensity of the debate on same-sex marriage at local and state levels provided a constant backdrop to any conversation that was happening in this school. This was not an issue that was going to go away or be easily resolved, and it was happening at every level of system: national, state, whole school system, whole community, particular school, parent community of that school system, teacher groups, school administration. In intervening, we needed to be aware that anything we might do with this individual school community could send ripples up and down through the larger system, potentially amplifying both positive and negative outcomes.

Our first step was to understand the conflict. PCP talks about "mapping the conflict." Gestalt practitioners talk about entering the Cycle of Experience, beginning with "scanning the environment" and gathering data to create a "shared picture of the conflict."[25] In this case, some people had thought a great deal about their version of the issues and were ready to leap to action, while others in the community were still relatively unaware of the conflict. We wanted to clarify what had happened, identify the stories and where they had become stuck, and begin to plant the idea hope was possible. Dialogue or "constructive conversation" would be the vehicle, and we emphasized that part of building a container that could safely hold their differences would involve the use of "community agreements" (see Appendix 2) and a structure and process that would encourage genuine inquiry, self-reflection, and personal speaking (Public Conversations Project, 1997).

We began with the Steering Committee, a diverse group of parents

---

[24] Fritz Perls contributed to an understanding of this dilemma by encouraging Gestalt trainees to give up trying to show empathy but, rather, to show interest in the differences and just listen to the "different" person as a means of taking in his or her story (personal communication, E. Nevis, 2008).

[25] These terms are taken from a version of the Gestalt Cycle of Experience (Kepner, 1996) used by the Gestalt Institute of Cleveland in the Organization and Systems Development Program I attended. Another version has been adopted by the Gestalt International Study Center. A visual picture of the version of the Cycle used in this chapter can be seen in Appendix 1.

and teachers who initially had been chosen by the Principal to pick a consultant, but who ended up staying with the project through the community dialogues. Following individual interviews of all the committee members, we held a meeting in which we looked at their goals and expectations for the dialogues, discussed the themes from their questionnaires, and clarified the focus of the dialogues.

Recurring themes were:

- *Issues of trust and respect*—Finding ways to bring a diversity of opinions to the table in open, genuine, and direct communication;
- *Finding ways to deal with differences*—Of values, political beliefs, the right to expression of teachers/parents, and the roles of parents/ teachers; and
- *Need to clarify expectations and boundaries*—Personal and professional.

The goals they identified for the community conversations were:

- *Discover how to work together while still remaining connected to deeply held beliefs;*
- *Find new ways of communicating that diminish stereotyping and promote caring;* and
- *Dispel simplistic polarization and respectfully share deeply held concerns.*

Reflection: This first meeting with the Steering Committee felt like walking on eggshells. We reported out, anonymously, some of the things different individuals had said in their interviews. Some of these individuals immediately identified themselves, defensively saying that everyone would recognize their "voice" anyway. While they ended up being relatively comfortable with this group knowing what they had said, they were very wary about their words going out of the room. They spoke of how anxious they were about being labeled and of potential repercussions. They worried about the success of the community dialogues. I wondered if we had not been careful enough about setting the boundaries. I appreciated this instant mirror into the lack of trust that we would probably encounter throughout the system.

Following this meeting, we had a Community Meeting, where everyone who was part of the school community was invited to hear about what was being proposed for the "Constructive Conversations," to learn about PCP, to meet us, and to ask questions. We explained that there would be eight three-hour Conversations, starting in a week, each one facilitated by one of us. We described the process and intention of dialogue, what would come from the meetings, and the logistics for signing up. People were tense and had a lot of questions about how we would make it safe. It turned out that the most anxious group was that of the teachers, in particular the gay and lesbian teachers. The next day many of them contacted the Principal with questions about how they would be protected from angry parents during and after the conversations; whether they were speaking as teachers or as individuals; how many teachers would be in each small group; and whether there would be recriminations if they did not attend.

Further Reflection: The flood of concern from the teachers made me wonder about the speed with which everything was happening. As often is the case in schools, the rhythm of the school year sets a schedule that can seem to have a life of its own. We started discussions at the end of the summer, submitted our work proposal in September, and were not able to meet with the Superintendent until October because of all the start up work of the year. The Steering Committee meeting was on November 4, and everyone wanted to do the dialogues before Thanksgiving.

Yet, at one of the meetings, someone had said: *"Trust for the process is not there. It seems that some people are not ready to participate fully."* At this point, I found myself agreeing with the speaker. It felt like we were racing through the Cycle of Experience, failing to build ground in a way that would create enough safety to ensure the kind of participatory process we had envisioned. It seemed we would be better off if we could do more work with the teachers alone before putting them in mixed groups with parents. In addition, although everyone was committed to making the dialogue groups as representative as possible of the different viewpoints in the community, there was not enough time to reach out to the more conservative parents, who, as the minority group, were reluctant to put themselves in the face of additional conflict. My comment in a memo to my co-facilitator was: "I feel like the bride who knows she shouldn't go through with it, but can't stop the momentum." The schedule stayed in place.

"Constructive Conversations"

Participants were required to pre-register. In an effort to create groups that were as diverse as possible, they were asked to indicate whether they were a parent, teacher, or administrator. In addition, they were asked to indicate on a five-point scale from "strongly agree" to "strongly disagree" whether they thought the all-school announcement about the passage of the same-sex marriage bill was appropriate.

From these registrations, the Principal put together eight groups of ten, making sure that there were at least two teachers in each group. She also tried to maximize the diversity of viewpoints, although that turned out to be difficult as there were fewer who had signed up who were "strongly opposed" than who "strongly agreed," a point that would be discussed in the debriefing. As a result, the mix was often a subtler blend of agreement and disagreement. There were four conversations a week for two weeks, and then we were done.

As with all my work since I first began approaching it from a Gestalt frame, the most critical step for me at the beginning is to become absolutely clear about my intention. By this step I mean not just the goals for the encounter, but also, even more, the deeper possibilities for this group of people at this point in time. Once I have that, I can create a design or agenda that I hope will take us there. Then, even if things go awry (an exercise not working, people refusing to do something I want them to, loss of energy, all the myriad "untidy" behaviors that occur in any group), I trust that coming back to my intention will help me find my way back to the group. For me, at Jefferson School, I had two core intentions:

- Give people an opportunity to have a "new" conversation about the issues (with themselves and others).
- Engage people as individuals, not as a point of view.

As facilitators, we also agreed that we wanted to:

- create a safe space for dialogue;
- explore the differences;
- generate community building ideas; and
- encourage them to make personal commitments.

The agenda for the dialogues reflected all of these ideas and included:

- *Welcome* and clarification of intention of the conversations;
- *Introductions,* including their hopes for the evening;
- *Discussion of community agreements;*
- *First Go-Round* when participants had a few minutes to reflect and write, and then had three minutes each to speak without interruption to a question about "the heart of the matter" for them as individuals;
- *Second Go-Round,* with time to reflect, write, and then speak to a

question about an experience with being misunderstood or judged for having a different point of view;

- *Open Conversation* with exploration of the differences they had just heard or expressed;
- *Community Building Ideas* with time to reflect, write, and post ideas about how to be the kind of community they wanted to be in, and personal commitments they wanted to make to help that to happen; and
- *Final Reflection.*

Reflections on What Happened

Each of the conversations had a different feel to them. Some of the voices I remember were:

- A working-class mother in a two-parent, heterosexual family, with three children in the elementary school, who talked of feeling disrespected and unheard and deeply offended by someone talking about her as a member of a "privileged" group of "oppressors" (heterosexuals) just for being who she was;
- An upper-middle class, gay, partnered father of third and fifth graders, who spoke with strong emotion about how grateful he was to the teachers who made his kids feel proud of their family;
- A middle-class father in a two-parent, heterosexual family with a second grader, who had been shocked by the announcement and the ensuing discussions, and who said in closing: *"This process changed my mind a little. Hearing other people's stories opened my eyes. I didn't want my second grader to hear about men loving men and women loving women, but then what about his classmate who has two moms?"* and
- A teacher of five years who told the group what it was like to try to figure out what to do when one child called another "gay" or snickered when a classmate described his vacation with his two dads. She spoke of how hard it was to separate her personal beliefs from what she believed was her role as a teacher, and her own ideas about age-appropriate classroom discussions. Her fear was of being labeled "homophobic" by other teachers if she did her anti-bias work in a different way from them.

I began to notice that often as each person told his or her personal story, uninterrupted, bodies began to shift, settle, and relax a little. In the open discussion, there would be a lot of surprised comments: *"I never thought of it that way." "I didn't realize how hard that might be." "I knew how I felt, but it didn't occur to me that you might feel the same way."* For these groups, in those moments, the human face was seen, not the rhetoric that had separated them. There was some understanding, and sometimes there was a movement past the "incident" to agreement that what mattered were the kids—all the kids, every kid—and finding ways to help them to feel respected, and safe and valued. They had moved, for however long, from not understanding to understanding, and then to their belief in common that they needed to make the kids the center of attention. Those moments felt good and valuable. There were other moments that did not feel so good, when the multiple realities seemed incomprehensible, when old arguments remained fixed, when people talked too much or not at all, when the questions asked were not questions of concern or curiosity, but disguised judgments. *"Do you really think that it's OK for kids in families with two moms or two dads not to be able to talk about them in school?"*

One group stands out for me. After the initial introductory go-around, it became clear that the participants were rather closely aligned with each other on the "liberal" side. One of the mothers said she was disappointed that there was not more diversity in the group and suggested that everyone might as well go home rather than just talk to each other. She had come with clear intentions of listening and understanding different viewpoints and was upset not to have that opportunity. Unwilling to disband them right away (I remember thinking: *You can't decide to just leave me!*), I asked the mother who had spoken up if she would be willing to spend some time exploring what she *would* have asked those other people, had they been there? What did she want to know or understand better? She started with the rhetorical question I mentioned above: *"Do you really think that it's OK for kids in families with two moms or two dads not to be able to talk about them in school?"* When we looked at the question and talked about it as a group, she realized that it was more of a statement than a question. She tried again: *"If you knew how much it might hurt some children to not be able to talk about their families, would that change your mind?"* The group thought that was a little better, but still had an implied judgment in it. Also, it did not ask anything about how the other person felt or thought. One more time: *"Can you explain to me why you would think it's OK to not create a safe atmosphere for kids from gay families?"* Almost as soon as the words were out of her mouth, she stopped. A stunned look crossed over her face. She said, with great emphasis: *"You know what? I actually don't want to know anything about*

[handwritten annotation: ! me ! my family ... you're wrong !]

them. I think they are just wrong, and I don't believe there is anything they can tell me that will make it OK. What I really wanted is a chance to tell them how wrong they are." She stopped for a second, and then went on: "I can't believe this is me. I'm horrified! I thought I was such an accepting person."

What she had come up against was herself. In that moment of contact, she had not only encountered the "inability not to understand" (which requires a willingness to let the other be fully "other"), but her own lack of interest in understanding. Her "aha" not only gave her a new piece of insight into herself, but also allowed the rest of the group to bring forward their own blocks to listening. The ensuing conversation was rich and led to an exploration of subtleties in the viewpoints that were in the room, as well as a determination to keep exploring the closed doors in themselves.

Feedback

[handwritten annotation: open/closed souls]

The evaluations from this series of dialogues showed that:

- *Overall, it was a positive experience.* People felt relieved, appreciative, and hopeful. They valued hearing others speak from their personal connection to the issues and learning how deeply different individuals were affected by them. Most participants felt respected, listened to, and, sometimes, that something in a story led to a shift in understanding on both sides.
- *Many parents would work to continue the dialogue.* When asked about individual commitments they would make to carry forward the work of the Constructive Conversations, some talked about reaching out to people they did not normally speak with, especially people who had been reluctant to attend, hoping that one-on-one connections might allow for new stories to emerge. Others wanted to continue small group conversations, using the "ground rules" and the time to reflect as ways to encourage dialogue and not debate.
- *It was a good start, but . . .* Many felt there was still a lot of work to be done, especially around involving a more representative group of parents in the next steps. The surface had been scratched, but they wanted more time to talk. Some expressed concerns about the challenges these issues posed in terms of complexity and polarization.
- *The structure helped.* Participants found the slowed down pace of having time to reflect and write, speak without interruption, and

focus on understanding rather than persuasion, gave them an experience that was different from many of their conversations on controversial topics.

Completing the Cycles of Experience

It was helpful to think in terms of all the overlapping cycles as we moved through this process. One unit of work[26] had been completed with the parents and teachers who had attended the Constructive Conversations. There were, however, many other levels to this system that were still involved in the process. Subsequent work was aimed at them.

- *Steering Committee Meeting:* This happened about two weeks after the final Conversation. They looked at the evaluations and the copious recommendations for "Building Community." They disbanded and turned the process over to the School Council (an elected group). Three subcommittees were formed out of the data.
  1. Clarifying the Respect for Human Differences Mission Statement
  2. Communications
  3. Community Building
- *Community Feedback Meeting:* Held a month later, participants had a chance for small group discussions about the results from the Conversations and were encouraged to sign up for one of the subcommittees.
- *Teachers' Meeting:* At the same time, the teachers at Jefferson wanted to do more work as a group. They had a half-day retreat to discuss their concerns and ideas for how to teach in a way that respected not only the differences in the school, but also the differences among themselves.
- *Meeting of Principal and Teachers:* Held two months later, the focus was on what language (within staff) teachers experienced as polarizing and causing misunderstanding and how to change it.
- *Ongoing Work:* Throughout the following fall and winter, School

---

[26] A "Unit of Work" is described (in a handout titled *Notes on the Cycle of Experience and A Unit of Work*, for Organization and Systems Development, Class XII, by Elaine Kepner, 1996) as "a coherent, assimilable experience; it may be the completion of a task, the resolution of an issue, or a learning experience. A successful unit of work creates energy that is sustained and purposeful." Kepner further talks about the stages of a unit of work as: "Assessing What Is, Choosing What to Attend to, Acting on the Choice, Closing Out the Activity." In any given project, there will be multiple units of work being started and completed at all levels of the system.

Council subcommittees continued to work on their topics. The group that was focused on the Respect for Human Differences Mission Statement developed a "Frequently Asked Questions (FAQ)" document that outlined how the school would approach a broad range of diversity issues, including same sex families.

- *Elementary Principals' Meeting:* In December, all of the elementary school principals from the system met to hear about what had happened at Jefferson and engage them in a conversation of the FAQ document, and how they might use it in their schools.
- *Community Meeting:* That spring, the FAQ document was presented to the Jefferson School community and became a living document for subsequent development of the Respect for Human Differences curriculum.

Over the course of those two years, the Jefferson community, administrators, teachers, and parents remained actively engaged in identifying the steps they could take to address gender differences within the context of its overall commitment to respect human differences. It was a juggling act that called for ongoing openness to multiple viewpoints in order to turn the dialogue into practices that everyone in the community could live with. I doubt that the difficulty of that juggling act has changed. Although we completed our consultation in 2006, the work has continued. As noted on the school website, the FAQ document was finalized and distributed as part of the Parent Handbook by the beginning of the following year. It then became a cornerstone for ongoing learning projects and meetings scheduled continue through 2010.

Final Reflections and Questions

The biggest disappointment for participants from both sides of the issue was the under-representation of the more conservative voices. Clearly, a group of parents existed in the school that strongly disapproved of the actions the school was taking around gay and lesbian families. Some of these parents were comfortable approaching the administration to express their anger. Some of them chose the relative anonymity of an electronic conversation to vent their feelings. A number of them attended the Constructive Conversations. However many, we were told, felt unsafe to sign up for the dialogues, feeling that they held a minority view in a highly liberal town, and that nobody would listen to them. I am not sure how to address this problem of representation, although I would note I saw something similar in the public dialogues *is the people who matter most.*

that PCP held on abortion. In those dialogues, we required an equal number of participants from pro-choice and pro-life viewpoints. We often had difficulty finding enough people from the pro-life viewpoint to participate. Some of the things we heard that might explain this situation included: not wanting to be seen "talking with the enemy,"[27] fear of being "talked out of" their viewpoints, feeling that they did not need to defend or be questioned about their deeply held beliefs, and believing that those with opposing views would not listen or understand. The problem with those explanations, however, is that they could apply to anyone (with any viewpoint) who chooses not to take part in a dialogue on a heated, social issue. Perhaps the reader has other ways to think about the dilemma of under-representation of the conservative voice.

At the same time, a different group that was under-represented in the Jefferson conversations included the GLBT teachers. While several took part in the dialogues, we learned that a good percentage chose not to because their fears of repercussions had not been addressed sufficiently. Hearing this led me again to wonder about the timing and the rush, particularly because subsequent conversations revealed that there was additional history that might have helped explain their reluctance. Perhaps, if I had stuck with my gut instinct to slow things down and spend more time mapping the system and building the ground, we could have done a better job of responding to their concerns and encouraging their involvement. In talking about dialogues he had conducted, Gurevitch notes:

> Dialogue with the other as a legitimate other threatens to disintegrate a former self, which has been securely encrusted around some conviction, justification, identity, cause, or the like, which led to a packed, enclosed understanding of the issues at hand and of the self within them that denied the legitimacy of the other. Therefore, a long pre-negotiation debate may occur over whether or not one should enter into the dialogue. (1989, p. 165)

Reading this statement and reflecting on the dialogue processes, both at Jefferson School and in the abortion dialogues, I wonder if there is any set of rules to ensure contact in the face of so many fears. Does one slow down and spend meeting after meeting building ground and setting up

---

[27] "Talking with the Enemy" (January 28, 2001, *The Boston Globe*, Section F, p. 13) describes a private dialogue facilitated by PCP between leaders of the pro-life and pro-choice movements, following the shootings at the Planned Parenthood Clinic and Preterm Health Services in Brookline, MA in 1994. At the same time as the high level dialogue was being held, ongoing single meeting dialogues were being facilitated for the public. For more information, see: www. publicconversations.org.

the process? Can it only happen over time? Is a single meeting a laughably short time in which to expect any meaningful change to occur? Is it worth undertaking these kinds of conversations if only a small portion of the community is represented? The answer to these questions is, of course, "yes" and "no."

Similar to the Constructive Conversations, the public abortion dialogues were single meetings. They began with a meal together (during which time nobody identified their position), followed by a three-hour structured conversation. All participants had a pre-meeting phone call with a facilitator in which they were introduced to the ground rules and concepts of dialogue. Their willingness to engage using those understandings was an essential component. Like some of the groups at Jefferson, there were times when participants left feeling frustrated and like little had happened. At other times, a new awareness developed, sometimes about oneself, sometimes about the other. The following are some comments from participants.

- *During dinner, all of us were trying to figure out who was pro-choice and who was pro-life. One person who was very sophisticated and fit my mold of pro-choice turned out to be pro-life! That really made me question my assumptions.*
- *The best sharing was when people were talking about their own experiences with crisis pregnancies. Telling stories is a form of dialogue tool to build bridges. To see two people who disagree share their stories is more compelling than a debate.*
- *I'm really grateful for people's honesty and willingness to talk about this in a way I've never experienced before. It has served as a reminder of the complexity of this issue in that I can hear people speaking about things that I value and yet they come to a different conclusion on it.*

Perhaps, in the end, it is about taking all the care possible to inform and ground people and then stand back and appreciate the power of baby steps. Each step is both miniscule in terms of actual ground covered, and monumental in terms of a developmental moment that will have ongoing implications and reverberations. The very fact of showing up at a dialogue is a step. Sitting in the face of an unacceptable viewpoint is a step. Catching even a glimmer of the human being behind that viewpoint is a step. Recognizing a personal blind spot is a step. Going back into your community after these experiences and answering questions is a step. None of these steps are guarantees of major shifts, but each represents a moment of possibility.

Implications

Much is happening in the world of dialogue. Models continue to evolve, drawing on multiple theoretical frameworks.[28] As noted at the beginning of this chapter, several of these frameworks were useful to me and have been blended in my thinking about the interventions we designed. However, in summary, I would like to look at those Gestalt ideas that remain the most powerful for me. For all those facilitators, leaders, and citizens involved in conducting dialogues on highly charged social issues, questions of boundaries, resistance, and contact are always going to be foremost. The work takes place in the realm of those values and beliefs that are core to a person's identity and, as such, are not to be taken lightly. As became increasingly clear to me during this process, the willingness even to be in dialogue is a leap; as a facilitator, I need to honor that point by going slowly and paying careful attention to the ground that is built and the figures that emerge from the participants themselves. Yet, the stakes are often very high, and it is easy to become caught in the urgency of finding resolution or encouraging reconciliation. Gestalt, in its emphasis on staying in constant contact with myself as an intervener, helps me resist premature solutions by showing me the parts of my own identity that are being threatened by what is unfolding.

As the need for talking and listening at the edge of our boundaries grows, the capacity to be changed by what we hear (contact) becomes increasingly important, whether the shift is in beliefs, judgments, or actions. To be open to both influencing and being influenced are two sides of the same coin, and both can be difficult to do. As a society, we value the power of being able to influence others. Some are comfortable with that, and others are not. On the other hand, many people like to think of themselves as open to listening and being influenced by what others have to say and, like the "liberal woman" in the "liberal group," would be surprised to discover that they were as closed to a new perception of the other as they assume the other to be towards them. Yet, her moment of recognition of her lack of openness is as powerful a moment of contact, albeit intrapersonal, as anything that might have occurred between her and another participant.

The Gestalt framework creates the space for this kind of unexpected moment to happen, the essence of dialogue. This comes from embracing

---

[28] For readers interested in learning more about what is happening in the world of dialogue and deliberation, a comprehensive website is run by the National Coalition for Dialogue and Deliberation at: www.thataway.org.

the intention to stay in contact in spite of difference, and from valuing resistance in oneself and the other. It comes from slowing down to see the face of the stranger and rejoicing in discovering the eyes of a friend. In our current world of ever-shifting social boundaries and high stakes dialogue, where the fate of an individual, community, or nation rests on the capacity to tolerate differences, the Gestalt approach invites practitioners and participants to be as fully themselves as possible, knowing that this may be the only way they can come to see the human face in each other.

Patricia D. Perry, PsyD, is a consultant with over twenty years of experience working with individuals, groups, organizations, and communities. She has worked on a broad range of initiatives involving high stakes dialogues across divisive social issues, sustainable planning for schools, and community wide civic engagement processes. A graduate of Stanford University, Harvard University, and the Massachusetts School of Professional Psychology, she received additional training at the Gestalt Institute of Cleveland in the Organization and Systems Development Program.

Contact: *pldperry@comcast.net*

Appendix 1

Gestalt Cycle of Experience*

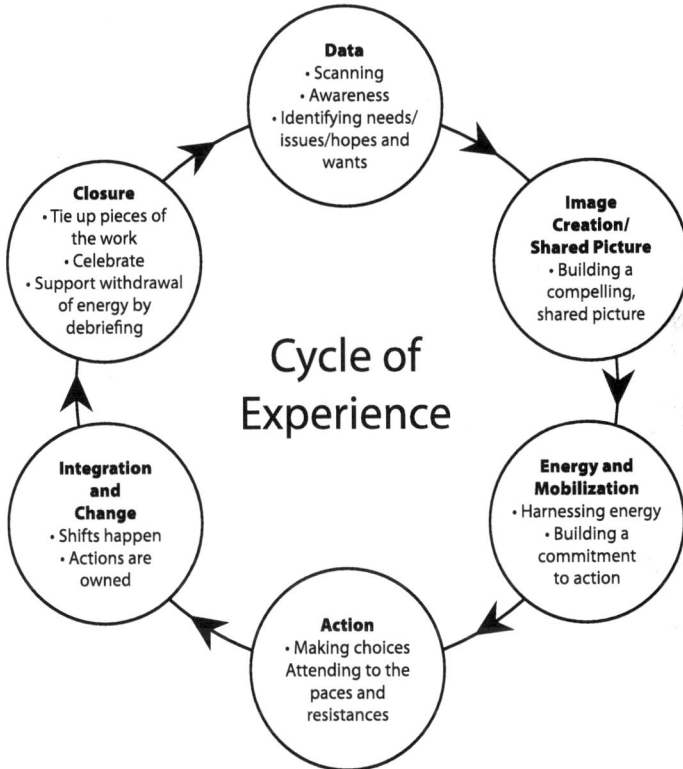

Data
· Scanning
· Awareness
· Identifying needs/
issues/hopes and
wants

Image Creation/ Shared Picture
· Building a compelling, shared picture

Closure
· Tie up pieces of the work
· Celebrate
· Support withdrawal of energy by debriefing

Energy and Mobilization
· Harnessing energy
· Building a commitment to action

Integration and Change
· Shifts happen
· Actions are owned

Action
· Making choices
Attending to the paces and resistances

Cycle of Experience

*Adapted by the author from E. Kepner, (1996)
Unpublished Teaching Material

Appendix 2

Jefferson School Community Agreements

- Confidentiality: we will speak only of facts that have been agreed upon at the end of this meeting. We will not attach names or content comments outside this meeting when discussing this with others.
- Pass (if are not ready to speak)
- Don't interrupt
- Speak for one's self, not a group
- Give everyone time to speak; share airtime
- Listen actively
- Don't blame
- Allow for misinformation to be corrected
- Don't make assumptions; rather ask clarifying questions
- Be honest and reflective
- Be positive; think of ways you can contribute
- Use language that does not invite defensiveness

References

Carter, J. (1994). Teaching notes. Gestalt Institute of Cleveland Organizational Development (OSD) Program, Cleveland, OH.

Gurevitch, Z. D. (1989). The power of not understanding: The meeting of conflicting identities. *The Journal of Applied Behavioral Science, 25*(2), 161-173.

Kepner, E. (1996). Unpublished teaching material. Cleveland, OH: Gestalt Institute of Cleveland.

Maurer, R. (1996). *Beyond the wall of resistance: Unconventional strategies that build support for change.* Austin, TX: Bard Books.

Public conversations project. (1997). *The basics of our approach.* Available online at www.publicconversations.org

Public conversations project. (2001). Talking with the enemy. *Boston Sunday Globe.* Globe staff. [Available online at www.publicconversations.org]

Roth, S., Chasin, L., Chasin, R., Becker, C., & Herzig, M. (1992). From debate to dialogue: A facilitating role for family therapists in the public forum. *Dulwich Centre Newsletter, 2,* 4148. Available online at www.publicconversations.org

Roth, S., & Chasin, R. (1994). Entering one another's worlds of meaning and imagination: Dramatic enactment and narrative couple therapy. In M. Hoyt (Ed.), *Constructive Therapies*, Volume I (pp. 41-48). New York: Guildford.

White, M., & Epston, D. (1990). *Narrative means to therapeutic ends.* New York: Norton.

CHAPTER 8

A Sisyphean Task:
Managing Porous Boundaries During
OD Interventions in UN Agencies

Raymond Saner, PhD, and Lichia Yiu, EdD

Editors' Introduction

This chapter is unusually interesting in several ways. First, it discusses interventions in one of the most diverse and complex organizational systems that currently exist: The United Nations (UN). The UN currently consists of 192 member states and over 50,000 employees. Though the work described was done in subsystems, the report clearly indicates how the interventions were impacted by forces outside the level at which they were performed.

Second, the authors share two cases in which the outcomes were less than highly successful. Most of the time, we want to publish instances of our success and share with colleagues what we did that worked well. While there is great liveliness in talking to others about "the fish that got away," it is another story to put in writing instances of our work that do not meet our expectations. Saner and Yiu are to be complimented for sharing these cases with us, for there is great learning to be had in studying them.

Finally, this chapter raises the hard, possibly distasteful, possibility that the optimistic intervention stance of most OD approaches, and certainly a Gestalt-oriented one, has real limitations in settings where power dynamics are a large part of the setting. The cases presented herein force us to think long and hard about getting better at doing work in these situations, and at learning to be more strategic in producing readiness for others to open themselves to our values and methods. And maybe we will have to admit that there are settings where we are not going to be able to intrigue people with our "magic."

Introduction

Organization Development (OD) is an established socio-technical method with a long history of field application in the private and public sectors of Western economies, dating back to the early fifties and the work of Kurt Lewin. Though a substantive literature exists on OD interventions in private and public enterprises, as well as in the field of public administration, little work has been documented regarding OD projects in international, multicultural organizations in general and in the United Nations (UN) system in particular. Practically no publication exists reporting OD work in UN organizations based on a Gestalt-oriented frame of reference.[29]

Drawing on two case studies of OD consulting projects in UN specialized agencies, this chapter illustrates the particular difficulties of using the OD method in a highly politicized environment where porous organizational boundaries pose a formidable challenge to both OD specialists and Gestalt-oriented OD experts. The chapter first describes the challenge of applying OD methods to large systems, and then summarizes key features of the UN and its environment, characterized by porous institutional boundaries and a multitude of power factors which need to be addressed by OD consultants. Two case examples of past OD interventions in two UN agencies are narrated in a subsequent section. Based on the description of the two cases, the authors identify the potential congruence and incongruence of established OD approaches in the light of cultural differences, be that at the national or organizational level. The final section closes with reflections on specific challenges of using OD approaches in UN agencies in general, and of applying Gestalt-based OD principles in complex multicultural settings.

Gestalt-oriented OD: Strong at Micro Level, Weak at Macro (Large System) Level of Intervention

Gestalt therapy principles have been applied to Organization Development for almost fifty years, but it is only in recent times that we see practitioners applying them to interventions in large, complex systems. Most of Gestalt therapy was developed for work at the therapeutic micro-level, i.e., for individual, couple and group therapy. Pioneering steps towards an application of Gestalt Therapy principles to

---

[29] This article draws on analyses developed in two articles previously published in *Gestalt Review*: R. Saner (1999); and R. Saner and L. Yiu (2002).

organizational development and change go back to the work of Richard Wallen[30] and Edwin Nevis in the 1960s, and by extension by their students, particularly Carolyn Lukensmeyer, John Carter, and Leonard Hirsch in the early 1970s. S. Herman also applied Gestalt to OD early on. Nevis and Herman, however, did not publish their work until much later (Nevis, 1987, Herman, 1988).

Describing the growing trend towards technical and system-oriented OD at the cost of person-related awareness and consultant-client interaction, Edwin Nevis (1997) states that:

> It is safe to say that the work of increasing awareness in individuals and small groups will continue, but there may now be an opportunity to build heightened awareness through interventions with a larger focus. There is no reason why a focus on awareness and a focus on action (usable results) cannot be integrated at the larger system level. But this achievement will depend on our ability to give up old assumptions and to be creative in developing a new synthesis. (p. 129)

Nevis (1997) further observes that: "one of the major aims of OD consulting has been to show action-oriented managers how they can act better by stretching their consciousness before moving into action (p. 124).

What follows is a narration of two OD interventions at the large system level of major UN agencies. The consultants-authors worked as OD experts in organizational bureaucracies characterized by politicization and porous boundaries. There was no attempt to structure the intervention as uniquely "Gestalt-oriented"; instead, the approach used was based on traditional OD theory and practice. However both consultants, being trained in Gestalt therapy, tried to use their own experiences as tools to guide themselves when faced with a multitude of resistances; some easily identifiable, others very opaque and defuse, as is typical in large system functioning. Hence, this chapter tells the story of how the two OD interventions were designed and implemented, and what led to their failure. Lessons are drawn using Gestalt-oriented insights and concepts.

Importance of Well-functioning UN Agencies for the World Community

---

[30] Wallen was both a founding member of National Training Laboratory (NTL) and the Gestalt Institute of Cleveland. He interested Nevis, already familiar with the work of Kurt Lewin, to work together in integrating the two approaches.

In this world of growing conflicts, few people question the need for a strong role of the UN. Many, however, express their wish to see the UN and its specialized agencies improve their management effectiveness and efficiency. While acknowledging the role the UN plays, and will continue to play, in many parts of the world, criticism and concerns against perceived shortcomings of recent UN leadership have been expressed in various influential publications. For instance, the United States government raised criticism about the role played by the UN Secretary General Kofi Annan, who ended his eight-year term on December 31, 2006; and in regard to UN agencies said to be ineffective due to a lack of reform of their swollen bureaucracies, or considered slow in responding to the needs in the field.

Size and Scope of the United Nations and Its Agencies

The UN is the best-known international organization. Its system is also the largest, most diversified, and most complex, counting 192 member states in 2008. In 1991, for example, the fifteen UN organizations employed some 50,000 people who were assigned to over 140 countries, working at some 600 different places throughout the world and using six major official languages (Slater, 1992). Fifty-two percent of the UN staff work for the UN secretariat and its programs. The remaining 48% are employed by the fifteen specialized or related agencies such as the International Labor Organization, the World Health Organization, and the World Bank. These agencies report annually to the Economic and Social Council in New York. The IAEA, established in 1957, reports annually to the General Assembly and, when appropriate, to the Security Council (e.g., after the Gulf War) and the Economic and Social Council. The GATT, a multilateral treaty laying down trade rules accepted by its member states, has a secretariat in Geneva, which helps organize occasional new trade negotiations (e.g., the recent Doha Round).

These inter-governmental agencies are separate, autonomous organizations related to the UN by special agreements. They collaborate with the UN and with each other through the coordinating machinery of the UN Economic and Social Council. Their secretariats, composed of international staff representing over 160 different nationalities, work under the direction of the executive head of the respective agencies. Their functions are to provide either a forum for negotiations and decisions (e.g., international conventions in respect of trade, labor, human rights, etc.) or specific services (e.g., health, institution building, agricultural development, etc.).

Organizational Context Characterized by Multiple Layers of Political Influence Creating the Effect of "Porous Boundaries"

Public management and public organizations are characterized by distinct features. Rainey (1991) has summarized the most commonly known aspects, namely: reliance on governmental appropriations for financial resources; presence of intensive formal legal constraints; presence of intensive external political influences; and greater goal ambiguity, multiplicity and conflict. The UN system has to function within similar characteristics. Each specialized UN agency has its own decision-making body involving a multitude of governments and related constituencies, which together approve annual budgets and influence the major directions of the agencies' programs and activities. Hence, the decision-making process can be very complex; it presents major obstacles with respect to the clarity of purpose, effectiveness, and efficiency of management; and the unity of staff (Sochor, 1989).

Continuous external pressures, combined with complex decision-making processes, weaken organizational boundaries and open the UN agencies to the power plays of multiple external and internal constituencies. Power plays an important role in the total management process of the UN system; it cannot be overlooked and needs to be understood in its complexity. The factor of political power in private sector organizations has been studied and analyzed by management scholars: e.g., Jeffrey Pfeffer (1981); and Henry Mintzberg (1984), who developed a typology of configurations of organizational power and proposed one possible relationship between external and internal coalitions, which he believes fits the context of the UN system best.[31] Mintzberg hypothesizes that different relationships might be expected between different stakeholders within and without organizations who form internal and external coalitions. He states concisely: "A divided external coalition encourages the rise of politicized internal coalition, and vice versa (p. 209). Drawing on Mintzberg, this means that conflicts in one of the coalitions can spill over into the other. For example, political activity in the internal coalition might encourage internal actors to enlist

---

[31] The other three configurations are: a dominated external coalition that encourages the rise of a bureaucratic internal coalition; a personalized, ideological, professional, or bureaucratic internal coalition that encourages the rise of a passive external coalition; and other combinations of the coalitions, as well as non-dominant mixtures of the internal forms of influence, that encourage moderate or intense levels of conflict in an organization.

the support of different outside stakeholders and, conversely, conflicting external coalitions might result in pulling parts of the internal coalition in different directions, potentially leading to a breakdown of more legitimate forms of influence like formal authority or certified experts.

The board members of UN agencies, namely the various member governments, have been (and continue to be) divided over general and particular issues. The most apparent divisions occurred during the cold war period. The current divisions center on the North-South divide, trade block conflicts, and issue-by-issue conflicts, whatever is at stake at the moment for the governments concerned. Member governments exert pressures on leading heads of UN agencies and vice versa. The respective director generals use their political weapons to counterattack real or perceived threats to their power. De Cooker (1990), citing various secondary sources reports, gives an example of such maneuvers:

> Mr. Saoma, the head of FAO, is accused of having politicized and mismanaged his organization, of practicing coercive and terrorist tactics and of running a reign of terror in the secretariat. In addition to the United States, the UK, Australia, and Canada have suspended further payments to the organization pending budget reforms. These countries are applying financial blackmail to the organization, in order to obtain the right to approve or veto its budget level.

This continuous building and shifting of coalitions weakens the decision-making process of UN agencies and causes negative consequences in regard to staff cohesion and internal functioning. UN agencies' external and internal boundaries remain weak, porous, and continuously open to manipulations by multiple interest groups and stakeholders.

Building on Rainey (1991), Sochor (1989), and Mintzberg (1984), the present authors propose a definition of "Porous Boundaries" in Figure 1, below.

Potential Conflict Regarding Loyalty of UN Agency Staff

The tendency towards external and internal coalition building is further heightened by the multinational and multicultural composition of the UN staff, who represent a rich linguistic, national, religious, and cultural mixture. This built-in diversity can create insecurities with respect to staff loyalty, which in turn can further increase the likelihood of conflict and coalition building. Under ideal circumstances, those working for the bureaucracy should be politically neutral, recruited on the basis of merit, and subject to uniform standards regarding conditions

Stakeholders	Multitude of actors, for example, governments, NGO's, intergovernmental institutions, who compete over use of financial and human resources of the organization.
Leadership	Elected or reinstated by members of governing body through process of bargaining and coalition building. Elected leadership enjoying relative autonomy during times of power parity in between budget cycles.
Goals	Negotiated compromises often remaining ambiguous in order to satisfy the needs and objectives of the stakeholders.
Financial Resources	Results of bargaining process, often approved, rejected, altered or amended on a yearly basis.
Human Resources	Recruitment based on official or unofficial quota system Standards adjusted to accommodate divergent competence levels of international staff.
Organization	Hierarchical, dominance of legal and bureaucratic measures as a defense against shifting alliances and external pressures.
Culture	Traditional, non innovative, defensive, security-minded, clanism combined with idealism resulting in frequent power fights.

Figure 1: A Definition of "Porous Boundaries"

of employment. But, in reality, the international civil servants are subject, like their national counterparts, to the political conditions of their environment.

The conflict regarding loyalty is built into the system by two articles of the UN Charter which can lead to possible tension. Article 100 reminds international servants not to seek or receive instructions from any government or other authorities external to the UN organization. It also reminds member states not to influence the staff and to respect the international character of their work and responsibility. Article 101 on the other hand, while not putting into question Article 100, asks for due geographical distribution of the UN staff. Both articles have been actively resisted at times by main member states for different reasons.[32]

The result of these continuous changes in its external environment, combined with possible reactive or even proactive shiftiness of its internal environment, makes UN agencies an especially difficult if not challenging place for leadership and management control. Any OD intervention in such a volatile environment has to face many forms of open and subtle resistances. Failure is common, small successes give rise to a consultant's celebration but, overall, the task of conducting OD intervention in UN agencies can best be characterized as "Sysiphonian."

Limited Theoretical Understanding of the Impact of the "Porous Boundary" Factor on OD Work in Agencies Like the UN

A major contributing factor to the politicized environment are the multiple stakeholders, who constantly vie for power and directly influence the UN agencies' mandate and, at times, intervene in their day to day functioning. How to understand and work within a context of multiple stakeholders is of paramount importance. Useful comparative information and insights have been summarized and described by Derick Brinkerhof and James Gage (1992) in regard to the understanding of the role of multiple stakeholders in development projects.

UN agencies are also subject to extensive interference by external stakeholders but, in contrast to development projects in developing countries, the UN agencies' stakeholders are mostly governments of developing and developed countries alike. This particular "cocktail" of stakeholders presents a unique situation requiring special analytical attention to the resulting loose or "porous organizational boundaries" which make any change effort tentative, if not impossible.

Organization Development, or simply change projects, conducted in such a complex and shifting environment, are difficult to design and even more difficult to implement successfully. The relevant fields of knowledge offer little guidance with respect to change projects in such complex and highly politicized environments. Developments in the field of large system change (Pettigrew, Ferlie, McKee, 1992; and A. Mohrman, S. Mohrman, Ledford, Cummings, Lawler, et al., 1991) are helpful but not instructive enough, since most of their theoretical concepts apply to large-sized private sector companies that certainly face complexity too, but are not to the same extent subject to the instability of their external and internal environments.

---

[32] For instance, based on President Truman's Executive Order 10,422 of 1952, U.S. citizens used to have to obtain full field security investigations before being "cleared" for work in the UN organizations. This political control has since then been abolished.

In contrast to the private sector, OD projects in the public sector are faced with more bureaucracy, and with more entrenched behavioral patterns and values, which present special obstacles to change efforts. For instance McConkie (1985), quoting Golembiewski (1969), states that:

> the nature of the public institutional environment clearly places some constraints on achieving OD objectives. The public sector is webbed by multiple accesses to multiple authoritative decision makers, a phenomena designed to ensure that public business gets looked at from a variety of perspectives. (p. 138)

Aspects of the "porous boundary" factor have been described by David Brown (1983), whose work in the development field offers excellent insights and suggestions on how to resolve conflict at organizational interfaces, for example, between communities or between external stakeholders and organizational actors. Brown (1983) states that conflict is particularly important at the interfaces because interfaces are between social units, authority, and responsibility; and appropriate behaviors are often unclear (p. 16). Hence, values and norms that might exist within one organization cannot be extended to external organizations that are arranged and managed according to different norms and values. When organizations come into contact—a bit like tectonic plates rubbing against each other—visible and invisible forces can cause organizational boundaries to fracture, with resulting conflict that often requires skilled interventions to mediate. What is missing is a closer look at change processes within the specific context of UN agencies; and how the organizational boundaries at times become porous due to cross-organizational power politics played out by internal and external stakeholders, and by inter-organizational differences in values and norms leading to conflict.

Description of the "Porous Boundary" Phenomena through Two Case Studies of UN Agencies

The two interventions described below focus on inter-group relations and total system intervention. Both OD interventions could be characterized as failures seen from a short-term perspective. However, the solutions developed and proposed in the first case were later on implemented by the client organization after a "cooling-off " period of three years.

Handy (1978) developed a typology to define four types of organization cultures:

1. *Apollo* (role culture, highly formalized, centrally directed, bureaucratic)
2. *Zeus* (power culture, "old man" in center, informal lines, verbal, intuitive)
3. *Athena* (task culture, matrix organization, formalized but decentralized)
4. *Dionysos* (atomistic, bonds of affection and respect, free spirited, independent)

In order to safeguard anonymity, the present authors apply Handy's typology to describe the two UN agencies under discussion, which are comparable to *Zeus* and *Athena* types of organization.

Case I: Efficiency Improvement at Zeus

Zeus organizations, according to Handy, are comparable to a spider web: the spider is in the center of the web consisting of several layers formed by informal colleagues who are "on the same wavelength" as the old man. One can compare it to traditionally run enterprises, organized around a brilliant founder or leader. The organizational culture of *Zeus* is verbal and intuitive despite possible bureaucratic webs surrounding the informal and personalized reporting relationships.

The core mandate of this UN-*Zeus* focuses on the upholding and renegotiation of international conventions. *Zeus* is also involved in technical cooperation projects in favor of developing countries. Established before World War II, it now counts about 3,000 staff stationed in different countries around the world. More than 150 states are members of *Zeus*, and the annual budget varies around several hundred million dollars.

Summary of OD Intervention

The OD intervention lasted four months, during which over eighty people were interviewed individually as well as in groups, some once, others several times, as appropriate and necessary. The OD intervention followed traditional steps of OD consulting.

I. Entry Conditions

The organization's management studies unit called for consultancy inputs in regard to perceived inefficiencies of its recruitment of consultants and experts. Up to 600 external consultants per year were used by *Zeus* to develop, attend, manage, and evaluate its multiple projects in developing countries. There was a perception that the recruitment function had been handled inefficiently and needed to be reviewed, in order to find alternative solutions for the near future. A branch within *Zeus* consisting of about twenty permanent staff had the formal responsibility to prospect, interview, recruit, and manage external consultants and experts. This branch, previously part of the Personnel Department, had been moved out of the Administrative Department and put under the Department of Technical Cooperation fifteen months prior to the OD consultation. The stated reason for this structural change was to centralize management related to technical cooperation, under a newly created department that reported to the Assistant Director General responsible for technical cooperation.

II. Contracting

A competitive tender was organized by *Zeus* and won by the authors' consultancy firm. The terms of reference were further defined and agreed upon. The project was to be started without delay.

III. Diagnosis

The consultants organized initial orientation meetings with appropriate top management officials, scheduled individual and group interviews with concerned units, developed a questionnaire, administered it to all units involved in technical cooperation and recruitment of external experts, collected the data, and proceeded with the analysis.

The major findings confirmed most of the comments heard at the initial contracting meetings. The recruitment function was inefficiently organized, the work methods were outdated and slow, and most units involved with technical cooperation projects duplicated the branch's activities. Each unit involved in technical cooperation projects created its own, isolated recruitment function and consultants roster within the boundaries of its own organization. The results were duplication of effort, fights over external resources, hoarding of information and de-motivation of staff at the recruitment branch.

IV. Feedback

Meetings were organized with heads of branches and departments concerned, and initial findings communicated. The goal was to feed back key diagnostic results, to have the findings validated, and to collect additional information for further clarification. At the same time, the feedback sessions were used to get initial suggestions for possible solutions.

V. Planning Change

Taking the previous steps into consideration, the consultants prepared a draft of the final report and developed a list of possible solutions to the documented problems. The solutions consisted of the following options:

a. Decentralization (all units engaged in technical cooperation would be given not only authority and resources to recruit consultants and experts but also full accountability)
b. Recentralization (branch to be reintegrated into main personnel department)
c. Information sharing (consultancy rosters would become accessible to other units, and candidates' background like CVs, references, etc., available through computer linkages)

It was agreed that the internal consultant would conduct the next step without direct participation of the external consultants.

VI. Intervention

The internal consultant presented to the respective authorities the draft report prepared by the external consultants. The reaction to the diagnosed problems and the proposed solutions was positive on the part of all members of top management, except for the head of the department directly responsible for the recruitment branch. Proposals for improving performance efficiency, either through decentralization or recentralization, were rejected by him, and subsequent briefings of top management officials were cancelled at the last minute. The report was subsequently finalized, filed away, and made inaccessible to managers responsible for technical cooperation.

VII. Evaluation

Despite the blocking by the department head, the report was widely read and became a sort of "underground" reference document. The "secret" report was quoted widely, and many of its solutions were implemented over a period of four years. The consultants, however, both internal and external, were excluded from follow-up reviews.

Postscript

At the time of the OD intervention, the consultants did not know that, at the time of his nomination as department head, the recruitment branch was actually moved out of the central Personnel Department. This shifting of a whole branch from one department to another increased the head's power, since it added budget and human resources to his "kingdom." But at the same time, it created new problems in regard to internal coordination and supervision of *Zeus*-wide recruitment function. Using informal influencing mechanisms, the department head resisted the application of the consultants' change propositions. Yet, his resistance weakened over time. A new Director General has since been elected, and the expert recruitment branch is now again part of the general personnel department. The new Director General also shifted the UN Agency's main activities, including main budget means from technical cooperation to the organization's core business.

Discussion and Reflections

The OD intervention could have been designed and conducted differently. The external consultants could have undertaken the intervention itself, thereby leaving the internal consultant with the possibility of supporting and complementing the intervention process proper. A longer interval also could have been envisaged between diagnosis and presentation of solutions, thus leaving more room for internal coalition building between the heads of the indicated departments, responsible for the acceptance and implementation of the external consultants' proposals.

Both alternatives, however, remain hypothetical since the manager most concerned with the problem, and the possible impact of the proposed solutions, short-circuited any attempts at either gaining time or reopening discussion within the organization's top management. Instead, he used the approaching summer holidays to break off the consultation project and, subsequently, to file away the final report as "classified" and "restricted" material. He overstepped other departments' areas of responsibility and authority, and even neutralized the Deputy Director General in charge of administration and personnel.

The internal "porous boundary" phenomena, on hindsight, consisted of his using informal power (direct personal access to the Director General) to cut across established departmental lines and to suspend functional line responsibility, including even officials situated at higher levels of the *Zeus* hierarchy. Thus, line responsibility was bypassed and hierarchical authority disregarded. The final report was simply blocked and shelved without the "bypasser" entering into a substantial discussion of the report's findings. This, in itself, was a remarkable expression of informal power despite the fact that *Zeus* was characterized by a strong bureaucratic culture.

The internal "porous boundary" effect seemed possible because of the manager's informal link to the Director General. The bypassed high-ranking managers could muster only little formal and informal power, despite the fact that most of them had the necessary professional training and background. The organizational weaknesses of the bypassed managers can be attributed to the fact that most of them were from different national and cultural backgrounds, while the manager enjoyed personal as well as cultural links with the Director General. As international civil servants approaching the end of their careers, and having few alternatives with respect to employment opportunities, the managers' power was weak and subject to informal pressures. Most officials of UN agencies are expatriates living in a foreign country and experiencing a form of cultural isolation which, combined with the absence of real job alternatives, makes them especially vulnerable to informal pressures and the effects of "porous boundary" manipulations.

Organizational effectiveness should be viewed as a reflection of the values and cognitive bases of powerful actors in the organization. The fact that the bypassed manager was a relative and countryman of the Director General made it possible for him to create and benefit from the internal "porous boundary" phenomena. In addition, it is known that the internal "porous boundary" phenomena flourishes in organizational environments like "Zeus," which lack clear accountability and are without formalized feedback mechanisms in terms of management efficiency and effectiveness.

Knowing the above suggests that Gestalt-oriented practitioners who work in these kinds of environments might pay much more attention to the informal "political" aspects of the situation. If we had done that in this case, we might have recognized that the relationship with the Director General would "make or break" our interventions. But even if we had known it, we would have needed a connection to the Director General to have any influence. We did not have a connection to the Director General; moreover, we thought it inappropriate to go above the head of our direct client, since it would drag us into the same power games that were common practice of the upper management. This is not to suggest that we lacked the influence to make the intervention work, or that we should not have undertaken it. But it does suggest that we need to lower our expectations and our measurement of success. The fact that our report influenced people at lower levels of power, and that many of our recommendations were later implemented, indicates that we did achieve some modicum of success, even though our services were discontinued.

Case II: Interorganizational Team-building between *Dionysus* and *Apollo*

This case focuses on a team-building intervention at two offices of a UN agency whose mandate concentrates on humanitarian efforts in developing countries. Applying Handy's terminology, the headquarter culture of this UN agency could be described as an *Athena* culture characterized by a matrix type organization, several task forces, organizational decentralization, and more or less formalized roles defined according to professional competencies (e.g., health services covered by medical staff, irrigation and water supply by engineers, etc.).

Athena has two European-based organizations that report to different division heads in the United States. These two organizations share the same building and the same client system. At the time of the OD intervention, both averaged thirty to forty permanent staff. The two sister organizations were loosely grouped together as *Athena's* European Office, but were in fact completely independent of each other. The overall organization employs several thousand full-time staff operating in more than 220 locations around the globe, with many stationed in various countries of the developing world. The organization's total budget of almost a billion dollars is raised through governmental and private contributions, through the organization's own efforts in raising funds privately, and through commercialization of the humanitarian aspect of its development work.

The first office's responsibility was to serve the National Committees on a global basis and help them in their efforts of advocacy, education, and fund raising in favor of *Athena's* humanitarian efforts. Additionally, it was expected to liaise with non-governmental and inter-governmental agencies in Europe, and to organize fund raising campaigns as ways of reaching the greater public for financing purposes.

This UN agency's organizational functioning had been strongly influenced by American management practices, such as task forces, decentralization, staff initiative, and regular management reviews. At the time of the OD intervention, the office was headed by a South-European Director who had held the post for one year. This European office had seen a lot of transition and instability over the previous three years, which had ended with the arrival of the new director. Management practice and organizational arrangements were marked by a mixture of voluntarism, professionalism, passion, independent thinking, and interest in media and creativity. Handy has named such an organization after the Greek God *Dionysus*.

The second office was organized according to traditional business standards similar to a typical small enterprise of the service industry. Its goals were simple and straightforward, namely creating sellable products that could generate revenues for *Athena* and help to increase *Athena's* public relations impact and image recognition in the wider public.

For many years in the hands of a general manager of Southeastern European background, this office was characterized by clearly established roles and a systematic-bureaucratic organization of its workflow. Handy would label such an organization based on clear pillars and organizational architecture as an *Apollo* culture.

Summary of OD Intervention

The team-building intervention extended over four months. Both offices (*Dionysus* and *Apollo*) were involved, separately at first, then jointly. Overall, twenty staff of *Dionysus* and *Apollo* participated throughout the project. The main steps of the OD intervention are summarized below.

I. Entry

The head of *Dionysus* already knew the consultants. They had conducted a successful team-building intervention in another *Athena* office in the Middle East region, which at that time was under his regional responsibility. He felt confident about the consultants' competence and invited them to conduct an interoffice team-building intervention for *Athena's* two European headquarter offices.

The organization chart of *Athena's* European headquarters office depicted the head of *Dionysus* as being one level higher than the head of *Apollo*. The consultants took this at face value. In fact, it turned out later that the reporting lines between both managers were unclear, leaving room for ambiguity and setting the stage for conflicts over power and authority.

II. Contracting

The head of *Dionysus* issued the annual contract in more or less open-ended terms. The details of the contract were further spelled out at a later stage in the invitation letter to the participants of the team-building workshop, which was held after the completion of the initial fact-finding interviews. The head of *Apollo* was briefed by the head of *Dionysus* about the goals of the team-building project and asked to give his full support.

III. Diagnosis

Following standard practice, the consultants conducted preliminary interviews with representatives of both organizations. The semi-structured interviews were based on questions relating to perceived strengths and weaknesses of both organizations separately and then jointly concerning their inter-organizational cooperation.

IV. Feedback

The consultants analyzed the information collected during the interviews according to Weisbord's Six Box Model (1978).[33] They prepared a feedback process for a two-day off-site workshop which grouped together staff from both organizations.

The major findings of the individual interviews were aggregated to protect anonymity and presented to the workshop participants. After validation of the findings, the consultants formed mixed *Dionysus-Apollo* work groups whose task was to further analyze the current inter-organizational cooperation and come up with possible solutions to improve the identified problem areas.

The main areas of commonly agreed problems were lack of inter-office communication and coordination, lack of coordination regarding interdependent tasks (e.g., relations to National *Athena* Committees), and lack of clear mission statement regarding the joint *Dionysus-Apollo* European office of *Athena*.

The mixed team generated twenty proposals that were presented in public to representatives of top management of both organizations. Thirteen proposals were subsequently adopted for implementation; two were rejected by the leaders of both organizations, and it was said that the remaining five would be studied further.

The workshop output was extensive, an atmosphere of cooperation emerged, and both teams seemed to get along well with each other even though many of the individuals had never worked together previously. The only drawback was the absence of the head of *Apollo*, who opted out

---

[33] In Weisbord's model, the organization is represented by six boxes: purpose, structure, rewards, helpful mechanisms, relationship and leadership. Client organizations are diagnosed in terms of how its formal and informal systems affect the functioning of the six boxes.

at the last minute and had *Apollo* represented by his deputy.

V. Planning Change

One month later, the consultants organized a special feedback session for both organizations' top management. The goal this time was to have both top managers and their respective deputies jointly assess the proposals developed during the workshop. Both teams listened to the feedback the consultants provided. They reacted to the key proposals and discussed the next steps that needed to be undertaken.

The meeting wavered back and forth between confrontation and cooperation. No definite decisions were taken in regard to implementation of the proposals. The group disbanded with a vague agreement to meet again at a future date. Both sides, however, agreed that the consultants should be invited back within six months to conduct an evaluation of the whole team-building effort.

VI. Intervention

The inter-organizational cooperation never evolved further and none of the proposals was implemented. Both directors pushed in opposite directions and tried to outmaneuver the other, to the dismay of their respective staff.

VII. Evaluation

A follow-up session was conducted with the heads of the two organizations. The consultants were informed about improved inter-organizational cooperation at an operational level among lower-ranking managers. However, no agreement was reached in regard to key issues, namely elaboration of a common mission statement; clarification of each organization's roles and responsibilities with respect to interdependent tasks affecting both offices; and procedures for interoffice communication and coordination.

Postscript

The two heads of both organizations tried to win the stalemate by using lobbying and influencing tactics on *Athena's* global constituencies (or stakeholders). The influencing was aimed at heads of National Committees, Inter-governmental Organizations, Government Officials and, of course, *Athena's* top management at headquarters in New York.

The head of *Apollo* won the fight; the head of *Dionysus* was moved, i.e., promoted, to headquarters in the United States. The mandate of *Dionysus* was subsequently trimmed down by the U.S.-based headquarters, which centralized global coordination with National Committees at headquarters in the United States.

Discussion and Reflections

Much could be said about this OD intervention, which seems to have been flawed from the beginning. For instance, the consultants should have spent more time during the entry phase with the two heads of office to clarify the obviously ambiguous structural relationship between both parties. In addition, relations between *Dionysus* and *Apollo* vis-à-vis *Athena* should also have been further clarified as much as possible, taking into account the fact that the work was done with *Dionysus* and not *Athena* who, of course, had the final say concerning structural rearrangements between the two European organizations.

It might also have been better to cancel the workshop as long as the head of *Apollo* could not, or did not wish, to attend. Even though he delegated his deputy, the commitment level of *Apollo* was obviously weakened. The covert message of "no cooperation" given to participants of *Apollo* could have been neutralized by insisting on his presence, or by postponing the workshop to a later date convenient and acceptable to both decision makers.

In retrospect, this may be a case where the consultants might have asserted their "power" by refusing to go along with a tenuous agreement. In Nevis's model (1987/2005, pp. 124-39), this would be a *provocative act*, but one that would have tested the "give" in the relationship between *Dionysus* and *Apollo*. Frequently, under such circumstances, both clients and consultants have their awareness enhanced about the current situation, and about whether both are ready to take on the project as initially defined. In short, the consultants' *use of self* enhances awareness of all concerned. In line with this approach, the consultants might have attempted to engage both *Dionysus* and *Apollo* in an examination of their readiness for the project using a formula of resistance to change defined by Beckhard and Harris (1987), whereby:

$C = (A \times B \times D) > X = C$ (change)
A = level of dissatisfaction with the status quo
B = desirability of the proposed change or end state
D = practicality of the change (minimal risk and disruption)
X = "cost" of changing.

Applying this definition to the change process described above, the following reflections can be made:

A: *Level of dissatisfaction with the status quo*
During the diagnostic and feedback process, and again during the workshop phase, it became apparent that the middle management of both organizations was interested in improving the inter-organizational relationship, which the great majority considered ineffective and inefficient.

B: *Desirability of the proposed change at end stage*
Proposals for change were elaborated and solutions prepared, which were supported by the great majority of the managers of both organizations.

D: *Practicality of the change (minimal risk and disruption)*
Mixed working groups were developing mutually beneficial solutions, which would not have caused great disturbances to day-to-day business of either organization.

X: *"Cost" of Changing*
The change process became a power struggle between the heads of *Apollo* and *Dionysus* first, and second, between the head of *Athena* in the United States and the head of *Dionysus* in Europe. It turned the change process from minimal organizational costs to maximal gain or loss of personal power. The OD process failed largely because of the personalized power factor linked to the porous boundary factor. Both leaders, representing *Apollo* and *Dionysus*, could mobilize external stakeholders to further their positions, while attempting to weaken the position of their opponent. This maneuvering included attempts to involve *Athena* headquarters in their bilateral power struggle, thereby defeating the attempts of the OD consultants to find mutually acceptable solutions that might have benefited both organizations, although they might have been seen as a loss of "influence" by either of the two leaders.

Power and the Internal "Porous Boundary"

Tushman and Nadler (1982) defined political power in organizations as consisting of the following sub factors:

a. Reward power
b. Coercive power
c. Legitimate power
d. Referent power
e. Expert power

f. Control over critical resources power
g. Avoiding "routinization" power
h. Access to powerful others power
i. Assessed stature and gaining visibility power
j. Group support power
k. Exchange as a source of power (trading favors)

Applying these factors of power to both protagonists, we see that the head of *Apollo* appears to have had more power at his disposal than the head of *Dionysus*. The following power analysis could be drawn up:

I. Reward Power

Salary and bonus systems are tightly set by UN bureaucratic rule; hence, both heads had equally limited reward power.

II. Coercive Power

Again, dismissing staff in UN agencies is difficult, if not impossible. Staff is well protected by International Civil Service rules, and both heads could not easily draw on this power factor.

III. Legitimate, Referent and Expert Power

While both heads had long-standing professional track records in the *Athena* organization, a difference existed which give the head of *Apollo* a power advantage. His reputation was based on many years of successful management of a commercial organization, which had generated for *Athena* a continuous and predictable source of revenue and image recognition. The head of *Dionysus* had less visible evidence of success and lacked the many years of successful "survival" that his opponent could demonstrate. Despite some positive field records, the head of *Dionysus* was new to the situation. His leadership style being "Latin," he could not, or did not want, to turn his organization into a tightly controlled bureaucracy.

IV. Control Over Resources

Since the staff of *Apollo* was mostly of traditional, clerical, and commercial background, few opportunities were available to change jobs within *Athena*. The opposite was the case for staff of *Dionysus*, whom we regularly rotated to other assignments around the world. They could move, and furthermore, their job assignments were decided at headquarters in the United States, not in Europe. Hence, the head of *Dionysus* had less control over resource power than his opponent.

V. Avoiding "Routinization" Power

Routinization leaves a manager with less power. This power factor could have been the most important influencing tactic for the head of *Dionysus* had the head of *Apollo* agreed to a closer cooperation, which in the end would have put his organization under the influence of *Dionysus*. *Apollo* knew how to avoid this danger by refusing to cooperate.

VI. Access to Powerful Others Power

Both heads had access to decision makers in the United States with different degrees of effectiveness. *Apollo* was for *Athena* a steady and non-threatening subsidiary and ally. *Dionysus*, had it been successful in absorbing *Apollo*, could have been seen as a political threat to headquarters control. Hence, headquarters sided with *Apollo* and dropped support for *Dionysus*.

VII. Assessed Stature and Gaining Visibility and Group Support Power

Both heads suffered from a mixed reputation. The head of *Apollo* was seen as too traditional and bureaucratic; the head of *Dionysus* as too emotional and unpredictable. While the head of *Dionysus* clearly had more charisma, he was new on the job and overall was seen by the staff as stirring up too many new issues. Hence, he was seen as leading to a lot of uncertainties without guarantees of political support from headquarters in the United States.

VIII. Exchange as a Source of Power (Trading Favors)

No previous "indebtedness" existed between both heads. In addition, the head of *Dionysus* could not yet offer established "credits" either from internal or external sources that would have been seen by the head of *Apollo* as important for survival. It appears understandable that the power factor was weighted in favor of the head of *Apollo*, who played out his superior power advantages successfully.

The internal "porous boundary" phenomena in this case were made possible by the institutional ambiguities left open by headquarters in the United States. *Athena* did not clearly specify the relationship, either between *Apollo* and *Dionysus*, or between itself and *Dionysus*. Such structural ambiguities can lead to creative adjustments or, as was the case, to destructive power struggles.

External "Porous Boundary"

"Open systems must maintain favorable transactions of input and output with the environment in order to survive over time," writes David Nadler (1982). What is true for private sector companies also applies to UN agencies; the difference is that, instead of an environment of clients and suppliers, the environment of UN agencies consists mostly of government and non-governmental institutions.

Capitalizing on his established network built over many years of cooperation, the head of *Apollo* skillfully used his good relations with various National Committees against his competitor. Informing them of his power struggle with his opponent, many National Committees took sides with him and used their influence at *Athena* headquarters in the United States. The head of *Dionysus* was outmaneuvered and had to give up in his attempt to absorb *Apollo* into his own organization.

Reflections from a Gestalt Perspective

Looking back at the two OD interventions, the following comments can be made from a Gestalt-oriented OD perspective.

With regard to the *Zeus* OD intervention, the highly politicized environment made traditional Gestalt-based OD intervention techniques—such as sharing of observations, attending to awareness, and engaging clients in interactions—largely ineffective. Transparent data collection and proposals for change were shortcut by backstage political maneuvers, which the consultants could not address within their limited mandate. More time should have been spent creating a Gestalt interactive cycle, showing a strong joining around a group figure with a group selection of their preferred solution to the diagnosed problem (Nevis, 1987/2005, p. 36). However, as the mandate ended, and the summer holidays started, spending more time and withholding closure would have had to be renegotiated with the client system. Having seen the choices available, the key client preferred to let the mandate end in the expectation that the solutions put forward by the consultants, and discussed with lead department heads, would be shelved and forgotten. The proposals were indeed shelved and labeled "top secret." Nevertheless, it was reported that the proposals and the consultants' account were often cited and referred to. In fact, after a three-year suspension, the report was "resuscitated," and all proposals for change and improvement were implemented.

With regard to the case of *Athena*, the difficulties encountered by the consultants were manifold. First, conflicts between the two European subunits labeled *Apollo* and *Dionysus* needed to be addressed. Following the traditional OD work of collecting data from in-depth individual interviews, the data feedback meeting with both sub-unit heads and staff turned out to be inconclusive. Borrowing the concept of the Gestalt Awareness Cycle and Flow of Continuous Experience (Nevis, 1987/2005, pp. 2-3), the consultants were not able to help the client systems complete the Gestalt Cycle, insofar as both sub-units avoided direct contact, and instead used tactical moves with Headquarters in the United States to turn the bilateral contact into a triangular one. The consultants, not having a mandate to include the "invisible" hand, were not able to create sufficient trust and support for *Apollo* and *Dionysus* to agree on cooperation on a bilateral level. Instead, they made the third party (United States Headquarters) intervene and impose an organizational solution from outside.

Conclusions

UN agencies, and others like them, are necessary and will continue to play important roles in world affairs. Due to the multiple stakeholders involved, the organizational environment of UN agencies is, and will continue to be, politicized for the foreseeable future. Hence, the "porous boundary" phenomena described above will continue to survive.

Improving existing and future UN agencies' performance will require OD interventions for a long time to come. In order to secure success for all parties concerned, the main points of this article should be considered: change strategies and tactics should be designed which can successfully overcome the UN system's "porous boundary" phenomena. Practitioners with a Gestalt orientation will be more effective interveners in these settings if they can pay more attention to power and political issues, and integrate them with our values for authentic communication (e.g., rich, honest, trusting contacts among people). The Gestalt approach has much to offer, but consultants will have to use themselves more effectively in dealing with people who have not yet been brought into this perspective. We will need to pay more attention to negotiating and bargaining models than we tend to give to consensus models.

Faced with porous boundary phenomena, Gestalt-oriented practitioners with clinical practice might benefit from a comparison of porous boundaries with clients who have borderline personality characteristics. In both instances, boundaries are fluid, frustrating the practitioners in establishing contact with the client or client organization, respectively. Attempts at structuring the fluid situation can lead to aggressive responses by the individual or client organization, which can then result in defensive reactions by the practitioner. This weakens the intervener's presence, which may then be interpreted by the client as "having defeated the powerful expert." In a similar vein, we were attempting to structure the ill-defined environment, but by so doing, we became pulled inadvertently into the power games played by the clients. Being "defeated" results in immobilization of the practitioner's flexibility to respond and tends to diminish ability and motivation to keep seeking client contact. This is what the client is searching for, but has learned to deflect or disown when contacting brings feelings of discomfort. Finally, the above lessons teach us that we cannot easily change things in any social system if the leaders are not ready for it.

In conclusion, both case studies highlight the fact that large system interventions make traditional micro-based Gestalt OD interventions difficult, if not impossible. Change in large organizational and social systems need to be made possible through indirect means and mechanisms. To use Gestalt terminology, large system OD is somewhat comparable to being faced with a fuzzy canvas where neither figure nor background are identifiable, and where the interventions often need to be based on attempts to change or modify the larger context within which figure-ground distinction can be made possible.

Raymond Saner, PhD, is Professor of Organization and International Management at Basle University, Switzerland, and teaches at Sciences Po, Paris, and Geneva University. He is Director of Diplomacy Dialogue, a branch of the Center for Socioeconomic Development in Geneva, Switzerland, a not-for-profit foundation focusing on socioeconomic research and public sector reform. He was a member of the New York Gestalt Therapy Institute (1980-1984), was trained in Gestalt, Psychodrama, Existentialist and Phenomenological Psychology, and has published on Gestalt-oriented OD and social development since the mid-1980s.

Contact: *saner@diplomacydialogue.org*

Lichia Yiu, EdD, is President of the Center for Socioeconomic Development, a Geneva-based research and development institute (since 1993). She has designed OD projects for multinational companies on cross-cultural leadership and international negotiations. She has also designed and implemented institution development platforms to support public sector reforms in China, Slovenia, Vietnam, Russia, and English-speaking African countries for different UN agencies and donors. Her publications include books and articles in major journals. She was trained in psychodrama and Gestalt therapy in the United States and founded the Taiwan Psychodrama Troupe in 1980.

Contact: *yiu@csend.org*

References

Beckhard, R., & Harris, R. T. (1987). *Organization transitions: Managing complex change* (2nd ed.). Reading, MA: Addison-Wesley.

Brinkerhoff, D., & Gage, J. (1992, April). Natural resources management policy in Africa: Implementation challenges for public managers. Paper presented at the American Society of Public Information (ASPA) Conference.

Brown, D. (1983). *Managing conflict at organizational interfaces.* Reading, MA: Addison-Wesley.

De Cooker, C. (1990). *Law and management practices in international organizations.* Amsterdam: Martinus Nijhoff.

Golembiewski, R. (1969). Organization development in public agencies: Perspectives on theory and practice. *Public Administration Review, 29,* 367-77.

Handy, C. (1978). *The gods of management.* London: Souvenir Press.

Herman, S. M. (1988). Reflections on 25 years with OD. *OD Practitioner, 20,* 1-3.

Lewin, K. (1997). *Resolving social conflict & field theory in social sciences.* American Psychological Association.

McConkie, M. (1985). Organization development in the public sector. In E. Huse & T. Cummings (Eds.), *Organization Development and Change* (pp. 418-26). Egan, MN: West Publishing Co.

Mintzberg, H. (1984). Power and organization life cycles. *Academy of*

Management Review, 9(2), 207-24.

Mohrmann, A., Mohrman, S., Ledford, G., Cummings, T., Lawler, E., et al. (1991). *Large scale organizational change.* San Francisco: Jossey-Bass.

Nadler, D. (1982). Implementing organizational change. In D. Nadler, M. Tushman, & N. Hatvany (Eds.), *Managing organizations* (pp. 440-49). Boston: Little, Brown.

Nevis, E. (1987, 2005). *Organizational consulting: A Gestalt approach.* Cleveland: Gestalt Institute of Cleveland Press.

Nevis, E. (1997). Gestalt therapy and organization development: A historical development, 1930-1996. *Gestalt Review, 6*(2), 110-130.

Pettigrew, A., Ferlie, E., & McKee, L. (1992). *Shaping strategic change: Making change in large organizations.* Thousand Oaks, CA: Sage.

Pfeffer, J. (1981). *Power in organizations.* New York: Pitman.

Rainey, H. (1991). *Understanding and managing public organizations.* San Francisco: Jossey-Bass.

Saner, R. (1999). Organizational consulting: What a Gestalt approach can learn from Off-Off-Broadway theater. *Gestalt Review, 3*(1), 6-21.

Saner, R., & Yiu, L. (2001). External stakeholder impacts on third-party interventions in resolving malignant conflicts: The case of a failed third party intervention on Cyprus. *International Negotiation, 6,* 387-416.

Saner, R., & Yiu, L. (2002). Porous boundary and power politics: Contextual constraints of organization development change projects in the United Nations organizations. *Gestalt Review, 6*(2), 84-94.

Slater, T. (1992). UN personnel policies support world body's unique organizational values. *Public Personnel Management, 21*(3), 383-84.

Sochor, E. (1989). Decision-making in the international civil aviation organization: Politics, processes, and personalities. *International Review of Administrative Sciences, 55,* 241-59.

Tushman, M., & Nadler, D. (1982). V.C.V.A. The informal organization/political concepts. In D. Nadler, M. Tushman, & N. Hatvany (Eds.), *Managing organizations* (pp. 377-84). Boston: Little, Brown.

Weisbord, M. R. (1978). *Organizational diagnosis: A workbook of theory and practice.* Reading, MA: Addison-Wesley.

CHAPTER 9

Witness for the Client: A Judge's Role in Increasing Awareness in the Defendant

Joyce Wheeler, JD

Editors' Introduction

The astronomical social and financial cost of crime, in this case drug abuse, begs for judicial innovation and change. Traditionally the judge's relationship with the client has ended with sentencing. Judges have not been trained or expected to take responsibility for outcomes after the sentence has been imposed. In this chapter, Wheeler talks about her experience in Drug Court, an innovative program that also provides treatment after sentencing. Operating within this new paradigm, Wheeler must grapple with the professional, ethical, and personal issues associated with communicating with persons not only as defendants, but also as clients involved in a process of rehabilitation. To shift away from the traditional judicial stance involves major psychological and professional changes for judges whose training and role have been based on objectivity and detachment.

In this new model, judges have to do more and be more. They need to have a deeper knowledge of context, of the field in which the defendant operates. They have to witness as well as judge. This new process, though still heavily outcome-oriented, is also deeply relational. Judges must be able to switch back and forth from a detached I/it stance to an I/thou one. They must be aware of feelings and biases, and they must be able to manage and relate to an interdisciplinary team with different training, biases, and perspectives. Wheeler does a masterful job describing how her Gestalt training has supported her movement from the traditional role of judge to a more fluid one, in which she finds new ways to organize her experiences as a judge that add depth and creativity to a traditionally reified process. What is unique about this chapter is that Gestalt theory is utilized (i.e., viewing self as part of the field, heightening awareness, supporting dialogical exchange) within a legal structure that is a far cry from a typically supportive Gestalt environment.

Introduction[34]

Justice does not depend upon legal dialectics so much as upon the atmosphere of the courtroom, and that in the end depends primarily upon the judge.
—Judge Learned Hand (*Brown v. Walter*, 62 F.2d 798, 800 [2d Cir. 1933])

My participation in a new drug treatment court during the last few years signifies a transformation of this judge's use of herself in the courtroom. I have moved from the traditional role of judge to a more fluid role in which I begin from the stance of witness for the client and, when necessary, move to the more traditional decision-making responsibility of a judge. Awareness of the change occurred over time, and was clearest in the context of an adult drug treatment court, which integrates drug and alcohol treatment and the criminal justice system.[35]

A number of factors support the change in my judicial stance. First, this is a treatment court that requires new and different skills be brought to bear on criminal behavior related to substance abuse. Second, the colleague with whom I share the responsibility for this drug court has taught me that it is all right to make contact with criminal defendants, and in doing so, to relate to the defendants as clients. I use the term "contact" here in the Gestalt sense of being "open in a broad and deep way to the other's experience" (Melnick, 1997, p. 5). Third, my training in Gestalt therapy over the last eleven years has provided me with the necessary tools to organize my experience in drug court. Fourth, working collaboratively with the drug court team expands my awareness of what

---

[34] This study is reprinted, with permission, from *Gestalt Review*, 9 (2), 144-161.
[35] The change began when, at the conclusion of trials of separating and divorcing parents, I summarized for the parties what I heard them say during the trial, acknowledged their accomplishments as parents, and identified areas to develop for their more effective parenting after the trial and the custody decision. At that time, I did not perceive my role as witness; rather, I was experimenting with some Gestalt tools for developing awareness.

the client needs, provides more creative approaches for addressing crime and addiction within the judicial system, and supports a greater likelihood for rehabilitation. And finally, the fact that the defendants have already accepted responsibility for their crime by pleading guilty, and that they know the "best" and "worse" deals depend on the outcome of their participation in drug court, means that the punishment aspect of criminal justice has been met, and we can focus on rehabilitation.

A drug court session describing my experience—and maybe the clients' experience—illuminates this expanded structure for judging. But first, descriptions of the drug court, the role of the judge, and the concept of judge as witness will provide a context for the drug court session that follows.

Adult Drug Treatment Court

Drug courts first appeared in the late 1980s to stop abuse of alcohol and other drugs and related criminal activity. By May 2004, there were 1,160 drug courts nationwide, including adult, juvenile, family, and tribal drug courts (Office of Justice Programs Drug Court Clearinghouse and Technical Assistance Project, 2004). Drug courts use the coercive power of the court through judicial supervision and oversight to encourage offenders to stay in treatment and out of trouble.

Maine initiated an adult drug treatment court (ADTC) with six locations throughout Maine in 2001.[36] The ADTC is based on a post-conviction model that focuses on offenders who demonstrate a high risk of criminal recidivism and a moderate-to-substantial substance abuse problem. In entering drug court, the offender enters a plea of guilty to a crime or probation violation, receives a "best deal" and a "worst deal," depending on the outcome of drug court, agrees to delay sentencing until he or she either successfully completes or is terminated from drug court, and enters a contract agreeing to the conditions contained in the drug court contract. These conditions include abstinence, daily telephone check-ins and weekly meetings with the adherence case manager, meetings with probation, random drug testing, substance abuse treatment,[37] and attendance in weekly drug court sessions presided

---

[36] In 4 M.R.S.A. §§ 421-423, the Maine Legislature authorized the Judicial Branch to establish an Adult Drug Treatment Court.

[37] The Office of Substance Abuse and the Department of Corrections cooperatively researched and developed a Differential Substance Abuse Treatment System (DSAT) for Maine's adult substance abusing offender population. DSAT provides for standardized substance abuse screening and comprehensive follow-up assessments for adult offenders, and then primary treatment for the adult drug court client. The treatment

over by a judge. There may also be other conditions such as individual counseling, maintaining a stable residence, concurrent participation in a certified batterers program, maintaining employment, paying child support, compensating the victim, and performing community service.

Drug courts combine judicial supervision and community-based treatment to change offender behavior. Before each weekly court session, the judge meets with the drug court team, which includes treatment providers, the adherence case manager, probation officers, and prosecutor to assess the status of each client. Sometimes, in order to understand better where the client is, the team invites the client and his or her counsel to join the team in the pre-court session. The team develops a coordinated strategy for keeping the client in treatment. The weekly drug court sessions occur in the open courtroom at the conclusion of the pre-court team meeting. The judge wears a robe and sits on the bench. Each client comes before the court to speak with the judge and to report on the outcomes of drug and alcohol testing, how many AA/NA meetings were attended, and other activities of the prior week.[38] Members of the team may also speak, adding relevant information concerning each client.

Drug court uses a system of graduated rewards and sanctions over at least a one-year period. In the court sessions, the client's progress is acknowledged with verbal praise from the judge, the team, and other clients. Praise may be received for a range of behaviors including negative urine tests, resisting an overture from a "friend" to use drugs or alcohol, obtaining a job, finding housing, or positive participation in a treatment session. A client's failure to comply with the conditions of his or her drug court contract results in sanctions. Violations that result in the imposition of sanctions include a positive urine test, missing a treatment session, failing to make daily call-ins to the case manager, missing a weekly drug court session, or new criminal conduct. Sanctions

component consists of Motivational Enhancement Treatment and Intensive Treatment Phase, including Intensive Cognitive/Behavioral Groups, a Maintenance Phase, and a Re-evaluation prior to discharge. DSAT is research-based, utilizes best treatment practices for adult substance abusing offenders, and is designed to produce positive treatment outcomes. Initially, there was great resistance in the treatment community to the DSAT model. After working with this model for the past few years, many treatment providers find that it works, and they have integrated the tools from this model into their work with other clients.

[38] Clients report that they find it difficult to speak with the judge in drug court because they are not used to relating to a judge in this manner, since their prior experience involves communicating with the court through their attorney. It is not necessarily any easier for the clients to sit with the judge, prosecutor and probation officer in the circle format that is described later in this article, but the clients appear more open in this less formal courtroom environment.

for violations range from warnings and admonishment from the bench in open court, to writing assignments to increased monitoring, or to escalating periods of jail confinement, and ultimately, termination from the program and reinstatement of the regular criminal court process.

A cornerstone principle is that each court event and process, including the application of rewards and sanctions, has a therapeutic purpose and value. The purpose of drug court is to motivate the adult substance-abusing offender to change addictive and criminal behaviors (State of Maine Policy and Procedure Manual, 2002, p. 26).

Relapses are expected and, like other violations, are addressed through a series of graduated sanctions. "Becoming sober and drug free is a learning experience, and each relapse [of alcohol and other drug use] may teach something about the recovery process" (National Association of Drug Court Professionals, 1997, p. 23).

"There is a growing body of evidence indicating that drug treatment—especially intensive, long-term treatment—can successfully reduce drug use and criminality, even when treatment is involuntary" (Johnson, Hubbard, and Latessa, 2000, p. 71). Although there is limited research to support the widespread effectiveness of drug courts, outcome findings for some drug court models suggest lower incarceration rates, longer times to re-arrest, and less frequent re-arrest among participants (See, e.g., Goldkamp, 1994; Hepburn, Johnston, and Rogers, 1994; Peters and Murrin, 2000; Peters, Haas, and Murrin, 1999). Other studies disclose that some drug court programs have failed to show evidence of effectiveness. It is difficult to evaluate drug courts, in part, because there are different drug court models and variations in the style of the particular judge. Johnson (2000) points out that "[a]lthough it is difficult to determine why some programs are failing to show evidence of effectiveness, the correctional treatment literature provides a strong case that the quality and content of the treatment programs may have an effect" (p. 72).

The Role of the Judge

Key components of a successful drug court include judicial oversight, immediate treatment intervention, and frequent alcohol and other drug testing (see National Association of Drug Court Professionals, 1997, p. 4). Recognizing that "[o]ngoing judicial interaction with each drug court participant is essential," best practices have been recommended for that judicial interaction (National Association of Drug Court Professionals, 1997, p. 27). Best practices include encouraging appropriate behavior and discouraging inappropriate behavior, communicating through ongoing supervision that someone with authority cares about them and is closely watching them, conducting frequent status hearings so that the participant is aware of how he or she is doing in relation to others, and having a significant number of participants in the courtroom to provide the opportunity to educate both the client speaking with the judge and the other waiting clients about the benefits of compliance and the consequences for non-compliance. (See National Association of Drug Court Professionals, 1997, p. 27.)

The relationship between the judge and the participant in drug court is innovative. The relationship "challenges the time-honored role of judicial impartiality" (Satel, 1998, p. 47). Traditionally, a judge remains objective and detached enough to carry out the responsibility of making decisions that are objective and reasonable and based on the evidence presented and the applicable law. This occurs in a single event in the courtroom; it involves the judge listening to the evidence and arguments of prosecutor and defense counsel, sometimes hearing from the defendant and the victim, and then, imposing the sentence. In contrast, the drug court judge actively and continuously supervises the client's progress in treatment, and engages the client directly, not only about successes and failures in treatment, but all aspects of the client's life (see Satel, 1998, p. 47.)

Judicial self-assessment reflects that judges value the relationship between themselves and the participant (Satel, 1998, p. 52). Satel (1998) warns, however, that the unconventional nature of the relationship with the participants can engender complex reactions in the judge: There is the possibility of "judicial" counter-transference (p. 54). "Classically, these reactions are unconscious—that is, outside the awareness of the judge (or therapist), but are manifested in ideas, feelings or behaviors that are inappropriately intense (in the positive or negative direction) or somehow not fully rational" (Satel, 1998, p. 54).

In this article, I will add to the discussion of the relationship between the drug court judge and the participant by exploring the space between the judge and the client that contributes to the change in my judicial stance. It is in that space that the concept of witness for the client arises.

The Stance of Witness for the Client

A drug treatment court offers an opportunity to move the criminal justice system from a dualistic view (in which the judge stands here and the defendant over there) to a unified field view (Parlett, 1997): the defendant is not the crime or addiction, but rather the crime or addiction forms part of a whole person who exists within systems of relationships—

individual, family, community, and other groups, including drug court. The use of the term "defendant" allows the judge to stand separate from the defendant, and this position is often necessary to carry out some of the traditional and important judicial responsibilities, such as sentencing. In contrast, the use of the term "client" creates a different relationship between judge and defendant, one in which the two—and the larger community—work together to create change and support for the client. From the vantage point of the unified field view, the judge, the team, the clients, and the drug court are all part of the field. "Adopting the unified field perspective wholeheartedly entails individuals recognizing that they are not just *in* a group but *are* the group. They constitute the systems they are in; they are part of the system's existence as the system is of theirs" (Parlett, 1997, p. 30). As such, we co-create the community of which we are a part, and we share responsibility for how the community and the individuals within the community operate.

The concept of judge as witness for the client can support the judge in this new role in the community, and also support the client in changing habitual patterns and in risking living life differently, free of addictive substances. I intentionally use the term witness because it both challenges the traditionally defined neutral role of a judge and describes my experience in drug court.

The Gestalt therapy concept of awareness informs my use of the term witness. From a Gestalt therapy perspective, awareness is part of phenomenology, a method for "bracket[ing] off our biases and assumptions as much as possible" and depending instead on our ability to observe and describe "the phenomena of the self, the other(s) and the interpersonal dynamics that occur" (Melnick, 1997, p. 5). "Gestalt therapy emphasizes that you can only know that which you experience and considers all experience as legitimate phenomena" (Melnick, 1997, p. 5).

As a witness, I can contribute to increasing a client's awareness of "what is," a precursor for change. In Gestalt therapy, it is the paradoxical theory of change that postures that "change occurs when one becomes what he is, not when he tries to be what he is not" (Beisser, 1970, p. 77). Like the therapist who "enables the client to amplify *what* she does and *how* she does it in the *here* and *now*" (Matzko, 1997, p. 42), a judge can make it possible for drug court clients to see what he does and how he does it in his daily life. The judge can do this by carefully listening and watching, paying attention to the "interaction of [her] senses and the external or internal world as simply a way of learning" (Nevis, 2001, p. 7) about the client so that she can find out what is needed. Then, the judge, to paraphrase Beisser, can use the client's own words to make more prominent what the client has said so that he or she might see choices perhaps not seen before (Beisser, 1997, p. 11).

I am also increasing my awareness. Edwin Nevis (2001) describes the process of awareness as wandering around in our environment without a particular goal, enabling us "to maintain an unjudgmental posture," allowing "one or more of our senses to become aroused and for our interests to grow in response," and because of this, encountering "unforeseen or serendipitous learning" (p. 7). As witness, I wander around and remain fully open to what the client has to say about what happened when, for example, the client relapsed, where the client is now, and what the client thinks he or she needs to maintain sobriety or comply with the drug court requirements. By listening to the client, I increase my own awareness and learn something new that did not come up during the pre-court team meeting, which contributes to a greater understanding of what is needed for the client and from the team.

The stance of witness allows me to suspend judgment and wander for a while with the client, to meet the client where the client is and to try to understand the client's experience. Expanding my understanding of where the client is enables me to assist the client in gaining greater awareness of where the client is and what the client needs, and to support the client in making new and different choices. This stance then supports my moving more fully into the role of judge where I will make a decision informed by the client and the drug court team, which will support the client's recovery and will hold the client accountable for his or her behavior.[39]

A Drug Court Session

Out of nineteen clients in drug court today, four clients are in jail, having been arrested for violations of the drug treatment court contract. Two will have to be addressed today in a sanction hearing; the other

---

[39] An interesting tension has developed in the work of the drug court team. The team, in its pre-court session, tries to reach consensus on how to deal with a client based on the information available to them in the pre-court session. Other professional demands of some team members prevent them from staying for the drug court session. The outcome is sometimes dramatically affected by what occurs in the drug court session. Those team members who are not present for the session often find it difficult to understand the decision actually made and feel as if their views were not taken into consideration when the decision is made. As a team, we have struggled to gain greater awareness of this experience, and to develop greater understanding when this happens.

two will be put off until defense counsel and additional information are available. But today—in addition to the fifteen who have been towing the line—there are these two. One has transgressions that are minor, really, when compared to where he has come from, failing to check in weekly in person and failing to call in daily. Also there is the non-payment of fees that he agreed to reimburse the shelter where he lived during another sanction.[40] The other client's problems are more serious: He tested positive for cocaine for the third time in the last seven months. Each has compelling stories that will get developed and filled in during today's drug court session. But for technical reasons (no clerk available to record the sanction hearings until later in the day), we address first those clients who have had a successful week. Each week with no use of drugs or alcohol and compliance with the other drug court requirements is a success that merits acknowledgment by the court, and sometimes an expansion of privileges.

Each client is in drug court because he or she committed a crime and has a serious drug or alcohol problem. Drug court offers them, over the course of a year, an opportunity through a system of graduated sanctions and rewards to become clean and sober, and to meet their responsibilities to their family and community. If they succeed, their criminal cases come to completion generally without any jail, but if they fail, they will serve a period of incarceration that could be substantial, depending on the nature of their crime.

Each client's story is quite remarkable. Today I am able to learn a bit more about each of them. Two of the clients have been clean and sober and in compliance since they began drug court—one having completed nine months and one week, and the other ten months. Both are contemplating graduation in a couple of months; the average length of a stay in drug court is one year. Another, who should have graduated last month if time in drug court alone mattered, seems to have let go of his struggle about whether his positive tests for cocaine are reliable, turned his attitude around, and showed his vulnerability and desire to succeed. Another is honest about not feeling great, and we discuss the health issues that interfere with her ability to read or do ordinary things to get through the day. Others relate stories of their success in strengthening their connections with their family and children, and how those connections support them in remaining free of drugs. When asked

---

[40] We have been fortunate to have the ability to house some clients at the local shelter, which provides a safe, structured, residential environment for those in early stages of recovery, until they experience some success and learn to take care of themselves.

whether they used alcohol or drugs this past week, each responded "no" and added that they had attended two, three, or even five AA sessions this past week, attended their group DSAT session, and reported as required. Some recount stories of what keeps him or her sober. One who is a full-time college student and taxi cab driver sees the drunks who ride in his cab. Their condition reminds him of why he wants to stay sober. Another has buried a second friend who died a drug-related death. The consequences of using, the impact on their children's lives—these are powerful motivations for staying away from drugs and alcohol. These are the lucky ones this week. They may have slipped in the past, but this week they can claim to be a success. Each has found support—within and without—to make healthy choices, including, for one client, the choice not to take an apartment on her own because it is not time yet in her recovery. She is developing the ability to manage her impulsivity. As each tells his or her story of this past week, I listen, point out the new skills he or she is developing, and then congratulate each client on his or her successes this week. The District Attorney, the case manager, the treatment provider—all part of the drug court team, alternately offer words of encouragement and respect for the choices these clients have made. Two of the clients are offered the most improved journal award this week because of the honesty and frankness their journals reflect. They are using their journals in a way that supports their recovery.

It has been a long morning. It is now noon—two hours since we began the weekly in-court sessions at 10:00 a.m., during which each client came before the court and shared with the judge and the rest of the team members and clients his or her experiences during the prior week. And it has been three and one-half hours since 8:30 a.m. when we began the drug court team pre-court meetings when the team meets to discuss the progress of each client and whether a reward or sanction is merited.

These pre-court team sessions are a departure from the typical handling of criminal cases. In the team meetings, the judge, prosecutor, probation officer, treatment provider, and case manager talk about each client, usually without the client or his attorney present. Each of the team members stands on equal footing as we struggle over those clients who are not in compliance. When a client encounters serious problems, the defense attorney and the client meet with the team or members of the team. During the pre-court session, the team weighs all of the information, trying to reach consensus. These discussions are not always easy—sometimes there is great disagreement about what should be done. Each team member comes with his or her own professional and personal experiences and perspectives. There is a lot of ground to cover at each pre-court session, with nineteen clients to review, prospective clients to screen, and rewards and sanctions to be discussed. In the end, however, the ultimate decision about the sanction to be imposed is left to the judge who, after pre-court team discussions and after hearing in open court from the prosecutor, the client, and his attorney, makes the decision.

Contact with Sam

The two clients today who are not in compliance illustrate the difficulty of these discussions. Sam[41] is only twenty-four years old and spent much of his adolescence and the first three years of his adulthood in prison. Altogether, Sam has been in drug court for 379 days and is still in an early phase of treatment because of violations of his contract. He experienced serious problems in the early part of drug court. He sustained one of the longest sanctions, 120 days, for packing an adulterated urine sample. He just missed being terminated from drug court when one of his good friends was terminated from drug court and sent to prison. Sam was given another chance, a chance well worth the gamble because he has been sober and out of trouble with the law for the last five months. Yet, he is not meeting all of the requirements of drug court, which expects much more of its clients than just sobriety. He has been late for appointments and not shown for check-ins, failed to make payments and, in general, just not paid attention to the details. These details are important because compliance with them demonstrates, to some degree, the client's stage of recovery. Sam was warned in August that he was on thin ice because of his failure to pay attention to these details and told that he needed to come up with a backup plan for how he would ensure his reporting to the case manager when work interfered with his ability to get to the appointment. He failed to submit the backup plan and now he has missed the last two weeks of meetings with the case manager, failed to check in daily by telephone, and failed to start making the payments he agreed to make to the Shelter. In the pre-court session, the team was unanimous that Sam was getting away with too much and that some jail time was necessary to impose upon Sam the importance of compliance.

It is noon before we reach the two cases requiring a sanction hearing. I see Sam's attorney in the courtroom in connection with another client whose sanction hearing is put off until another day because of lack

---

[41] Although drug court sessions are open to the public, the names and details have been altered to protect the clients.

of information on the extent of that client's violation—the possible commission of a new crime. I advise Sam and his attorney that Sam is facing a jail sanction, and ask them to speak with each other and some of the team members before the sanction hearing. I release the clients who reported to the court earlier in the morning and adjourn the drug court session for a few minutes. Most clients leave, but one, Alan, remains for the next stage of today's proceedings.

Sam's sanction hearing begins. The prosecutor asks for seven days in jail and outlines all of Sam's failures. Sam's attorney pleads for an alternative to jail. He points out that this is the longest period in his life that Sam has stayed out of jail. He outlines Sam's successes. He argues that Sam is handicapped because he spent so much time in jail[42] that he does not have the skills to make choices which, for many of us, seem simple, such as remembering in the midst of a busy workday schedule to call to say that he will be late, or to tell his ride or his employer that he needs to check in by 6:00 p.m. Many of the drug court clients have lost their right to operate a motor vehicle, and Sam fits this category. For these clients, it is difficult to get rides for work and to meet the drug court requirements. It takes some skill and perseverance to manage it all. After the attorney speaks, some of the team members speak, clarifying what Sam did or did not do, and offering further insight into what might support Sam in drug court.

Gina, Sam's girlfriend and the mother of Sam's two young girls, comes into the courtroom. She has missed most of the proceedings, but quickly understands that there is a risk that Sam will go back to jail. She has been a strong support for Sam; yet, she has held him accountable, not letting him move in with her and the girls until he stopped using drugs. And now she is upset that he may go to jail because, as she explains to me, she has known Sam for ten years, and this is the best he has ever done; he is trying so hard, and jail is not the way to change his behavior. She points out how hard it is for them because they both work, they have two little girls, and Sam does not have his driver's license and has so many

---

[42] There is a basis for this argument. "Many addiction specialists believe that emotional development ceases at the beginning of chronic drug abuse" (Matzko, 1997, p. 59). This certainly seems to be true for many of our drug court clients such as Sam, who finds it difficult to perform tasks that are easy for many of us because we learned them early in our lives. Matzko postures that emotional development of those who abuse substances "is greatly diminished much earlier, namely when emotional abuse begins" (Matzko, 1997, p. 50). Regardless, in drug court, we focus on the client's experience in the present, and the history of the client is part of the ground from which the work that we do arises.

commitments for drug court. She is right. It is very hard. They are very young and doing all of this alone.

It is Sam's turn to speak. He is very emotional. His eyes fill with tears. He is frustrated and is not sure where to begin. He does not understand, because he thought he was doing well in drug court. He does not want to admit that he is overwhelmed, but then he does. He describes what happens to him when he is at work and his employer moves him from one job site to another in one day; and how difficult that makes it for him to remember about his drug court obligation, and then to follow through on that obligation. I begin to see what happens to him, how he gets lost in setting limits, how he is unable to ask his employer for assistance. I see that he is, in his mind, trying harder than he ever has at anything. I see that he is lost and does not know how to maintain the awareness that is essential to meeting the drug court requirements. He is overwhelmed at meeting all of his responsibilities.

As Sam and I speak, a solution becomes evident.[43] I need to stand to talk to him—to make the points that I want to make with him. Standing in the courtroom is not something I normally do, but this is where my energy is at the moment and I am moved to stand.[44] I tell Sam that he has gone along now for five months maintaining sobriety, that this is great success, and that he has also reached a plateau, and now it is time for him to learn to do more. We expect him to do more, and we believe he can. But the question, I tell him is, how can we support him?

I describe for Sam that it is like teaching a child to walk. I ask him if he remembers when his daughters were learning to walk, and then I remember that he had served three years in jail just before entering drug court. I ask him if he missed seeing his daughters learn to walk. He bows his head; he missed that. So I demonstrate with my hands and body movement, and describe for him the experience: First, we leave a

---

[43] From a Gestalt therapy perspective, a figure is formed, or stands out, and all else is ground, or context, for the figure.

[44] My increased awareness has mobilized my energy so that I am ready to take some action. I am unsure about where Sam is in his awareness. However, the Gestalt Cycle of Experience is a useful model for understanding "the process by which people—individually and collectively—become aware of what is going on at any moment, and how to mobilize energy to take some action that allows them to deal constructively with possibilities suggested by the new awareness. It assumes that when a disequilibrium in the state of being or functioning of person(s) comes into awareness, the natural human tendency is to want to do something to achieve a new state of equilibrium. The model also assumes that there is an inherent desire in people to function at the most effective, satisfying level possible, and that learning to utilize this process is a key to achievement of optimum functioning" (Nevis, 2001, p. 2). Thus, in the dialogue, both Sam and I are increasing our awareness so that we may optimize our functioning.

short space between us and the child, for the child to walk to us, and as the child gets better at walking, then we step back further and further, encouraging her to walk further to us.

I tell Sam that this is what we expect of him. I decide to impose seven days of house arrest to emphasize the seriousness of the matter and to limit the number of activities on which he will have to focus. I also instruct Sam that he is to keep a notebook for thirty days and he is required to write each day all of the drug court responsibilities as he accomplishes each thing. I explain that this means, for example, that he is responsible to call in every day, and he will write in his notebook the date and time that he called in. I describe each of the responsibilities that he has and tell him that these are all to be recorded in his notebook. I am not adding any new responsibilities, but rather reminding him of all of his responsibilities and telling him that he must record each as soon as he has done it. I ask him if he knows why I am imposing this requirement. Sam responds, "So that it becomes a habit." He understands this much.

Contact with John

And now it is time to address John. John is dressed in the orange-colored county jail garb, having been arrested and jailed since he tested positive for cocaine. His attorney and he come forward to sit at the table with the prosecutor. At the pre-court session, the team struggled over John's needs, the need for a sanction to protect the integrity of the process, and the need for consistency in the sanctions imposed. Everyone concurred that a strong sanction was needed, but the views ranged from house arrest to six months in jail. The treatment provider expressed concern for John's mental health and the need for a psychological evaluation to help us better understand what is going on for him. Those who advocated for a lengthy jail sanction did so because, after all, he had been convicted for trafficking and had come to drug court when the state moved to revoke his probation after his first positive test for cocaine. Since coming to drug court, he admitted to using alcohol in the first month, and then tested positive for cocaine three more times, each use occurring a couple of months apart. By the time of the sanction hearing, everyone understands that John is facing a cap of ninety days in jail if he admits his use this latest time, and that the prosecutor will argue for ninety days, and John and his attorney will advocate for something less. John does not deny that he used cocaine.

I do not know what I will do. I am more informed in this case than I am about most criminal defendants in the regular court process. This is one of the benefits of drug court: I have a fuller picture of this defendant, which I gain not only from the pre-court session, but also from the conversation that will occur between the defendant and me during the sanction hearing.

I will talk to John, first to see how honest he will be about his use, and then to see how much insight he has about his use. And so the hearing begins. I ask first, does he admit to using cocaine? He responds that he does. I ask him to describe how he came to use cocaine that day. John describes his world closing in on him, problems with work, problems with his relationship and his girlfriend's younger sister who lives with them, money problems, and depression. He describes sitting on the couch for hours, not eating or sleeping. Friday night he goes to an AA meeting, looking for something that he does not usually seek or expect from AA—some answers to his problems. No answers come, even though he speaks with his sponsor. He returns to the couch, the not-eating and not-sleeping. Finally, by Sunday, he decides to go someplace to get some cocaine, hoping to feel better, to feel normal again. He thinks about bringing some cocaine home, but states that he had the good sense not to do this. When I ask him about how he felt on Monday, he describes the guilt he felt, and the certainty that he would go to jail for his use. When I ask him how the cocaine affected his depression, he responds that the depression was still there. He describes telling the drug court case manager during the drug test that he had used cocaine.

I ask John whether this use differs from the first two times. The prior use had involved peer pressure and his caving into that. This time he sought out the drug because he was feeling so bad. I ask him about his self-medication. He supposes that is what he is doing, although he seems surprised to admit this to himself.

I ask John questions about his depression. He has never been diagnosed or prescribed medication. His depression did not show up when we screened him for admission into drug court. He is not the first client to enter drug court without our having sufficient information about a mental health diagnosis. John talks to me about a family member's mental health issues, how that individual has taken many medications and, in his view, is still not right. He describes his fear of being like this person, and how he has resisted facing his depression. We talk about when he first experienced depression, and how the depression he felt just before his last use has not changed. The drug court case manager raises concerns about the depth of John's depression, and whether he has had any suicidal thoughts. He asks John some questions to assess the risk for suicide. John and I then discuss whether he was, at the time of the use or now, having any suicidal thoughts. John responds that he is not suicidal. We continue our conversation as I try to understand where John is. John speaks slowly, openly, and honestly.

The prosecutor then makes his recommendation of ninety days. He argues that John has been in the program for seven months and that by now he should have the tools to not use drugs. He should be further along than he is, and that this is his third positive test since entering drug court. He reminds the court of the crimes that brought John into drug court. John's attorney asks for no more than thirty days. He knows John's family, and he talks about the struggle of facing mental health issues, and how drug abuse complicates the struggle. The attorney is clearly moved as he advocates for John.

The treatment provider points out how well John has done in the DSAT program. She says she can hold a space in John's current group for thirty days and help him with making up missed sessions, but incarceration beyond thirty days will mean that John would have to start over with a different group. She advocates for the need to address John's mental health issues. She suggests that house arrest would allow him to get the services that he needs.

I convey my decision to John. I explain that on the simple facts of his case, without regard to the mental health issues, that ninety days would be an appropriate sanction, particularly if I believed that in seven months he should know better. However, I explain that I have a different view. After speaking with him, I conclude that as he has sobered up, his depression has been uncovered. Until we deal with his depression, we cannot know if he can succeed in drug court. So, I sentence him to thirty days, and with credit for the time he has been detained thus far, he will stay in jail another twenty days or so. I also order him on house arrest for ninety days. I order a psychological evaluation and for him to comply with any recommended follow-up treatment. There is a brief conversation about how long a psychological evaluation might take. Someone suggests that it may not occur for quite a while. I order the parties to explore advancing the evaluation because of the apparent seriousness of the depression. In the meantime, I order him to begin counseling right away. I drop him back to an earlier phase of drug court. I also order him during his house arrest to research and write a five-page paper on depression and the relationship to drug abuse.

John takes this all in. He seems relieved. I encourage him to see that today he was taking responsibility for his depression and beginning to face it.[45]

When I look up after speaking with John, I see that Alan is still in the courtroom. It is now 1:30 p.m. This has been an unusually long drug court day. Alan has been in the courtroom since 10:00 a.m. Alan is one of the clients who had a successful week, and who has had many successful weeks. He decided to stay after I told the other clients that they could leave at noon. He has remained attentive throughout the proceedings. At this moment, I wonder what he is thinking, and how Sam and John's stories may have affected him. Normally, the sanctions occur during the regular drug court session so that all of the clients witness each other's progress throughout, and learn about the benefits of program compliance and the consequences for non-compliance. When I see Alan still there, I wished that the other drug court clients had been there to witness Sam's and John's experiences because we learn a great deal from each other. I know that the others will hear soon enough about the outcomes because the rumor mill works well in drug court. The clients keep careful tabs on each other. I only hope that the stories are conveyed to the other clients without any distortion.

I leave to go to another courthouse where I have kept the parties to a post-divorce trial waiting. I struggle to settle down and get engaged in their story, but it pales in comparison to the stories of Sam and John that are now so much a part of me. I think about how the awareness of serving as a witness to the client's progress through drug court affected how I presided in court this morning. I wonder whether I can bring this expanded awareness to the divorce that I am about to hear.

Steve and Sandy: The Beginning of the Stance of Witness for the Client

Several months earlier, I had presided over a sanction hearing for Steve, another drug court client. He had tested positive for cocaine, but he insisted that the test was not accurate and that he had not used. We sent the test for more sophisticated testing and learned that the test sample was not urine but an adulterated sample that Steve was passing off as his urine. Steve continued to deny and claimed that the drug court manager had it in for him. However, at the sanction hearing, Steve decided that he would not put the state to the burden of proving that he manipulated the

---

[45] As soon as the drug court session is over, I telephone the jail and report my concerns about John's mental health and the discussion about suicide. I am assured that a nurse will examine him and that he will be watched carefully.

test; he would admit that the state could prove this, and the court could go ahead and sanction him.

This was not the first time that Steve had come before me for a sanction hearing. The other times were not as serious but evidenced, from my perspective, a power struggle. By the time of this sanction hearing, however, I saw the futility in arguing with him about his behavior. I approached the sanction hearing as one in which I would acknowledge simply where Steve was, and impose a sanction based on what the evidence demonstrated—that he had submitted a false test—and appropriate to where he was in his recovery. I understood that for whatever reason, he could not admit to this violation. I did not need him to admit to the manipulation of the test. It was enough for me that he was willing to accept responsibility at some level, and that he wanted to stay in drug court. My stance broke up the power struggle that had existed between Steve and me. Eventually, long after the sanction hearing, Steve came to accept full responsibility for his behavior with respect to that test, and he was in the first group to graduate from drug court. By accepting where Steve was at that time, I was able to proceed to apply a sanction that incorporated his experience and not one based solely on my judgment of him. While the time that he spent in jail may not have differed significantly, this experience with Steve represented for me a subtle shift in my work as a drug court judge.

It took another client's experience to make this shift clearer to me. I recommended Sandy to drug court when she came before me on a "driving under the influence" charge during a regular criminal docket. She faced a mandatory jail term because this was not her first driving under the influence violation. Sandy came into drug court and appeared to be one of our stars. Her drug tests were negative. She continued working full-time and was successful in her job. She went through a divorce and seemed to handle the divorce well in spite of all of the uncertainties about the financial outcome. She was the mother of teenage children.

As Sandy's year in drug court was coming to completion, we heard rumors about her use of alcohol. She denied. None of the tests was able to confirm the rumors. She was very distraught over our doubting her sobriety. After one drug court session, the treatment provider asked me to sit down with Sandy and listen to her. During this conversation, Sandy continued to deny. I observed how much her hands trembled and, in my need to make meaning out of this experience, I attributed this to the extreme anxiety she must be experiencing with our doubts about her use. Stuck on solutions, and not paying enough attention to the doubts about her sobriety that I continued to have, I encouraged her to ignore the rumors and stick to the program.

Then, a surprise visit to her home one night by probation officers turned up overwhelming evidence that she was using alcohol and may have driven her car that night after having consumed alcohol. I worried about how I had failed simply to pay attention to the phenomena and instead rushed to make meaning out of her story and to find solutions. While worrying about how I had interacted with Sandy, I became aware that I could better serve in drug court if I saw my role as witness to the experiences of Sandy and the other clients. How much more supportive my role would be if I could observe her experience and not rush to explain or interpret it, but simply to observe the phenomena and bring them into her awareness. Just maybe, she would have walked away from our interaction with a greater awareness of where she was, and maybe her denial would have not lasted as long as it did.

Successes and Failures

At the end of the day, Steve and Sandy graduated from drug court.[46] Alan was terminated shortly after the sanction hearing that he had observed not because of continued drug use or crime, neither of which had existed at the time, but because we concluded that he simply was not able to meet all of the conditions of drug court sufficiently for graduation. Because of new criminal activity, and our discovery of their ongoing substance abuse,[47] Sam and John did not graduate. Sam was moved from drug court to probation where the conditions were fewer and easier for him to follow. John violated again and agreed to do a lengthy inpatient program. Shortly, after his return to the drug court program, he again used cocaine. Termination from drug court became the only alternative. I presided over that hearing as well. In the end, John seemed relieved no longer to have to keep up the pretense of succeeding in drug court. He went to jail for a period of time and is now out.

From time to time, former drug court clients stop by to reconnect. I am always curious to see how they are making their way. Very occasionally, we hear from clients who were terminated from drug court, but who are excited about new programs in jail in which they are participating. These former clients still hold hope for their recovery and rehabilitative

---

[46] Both have since been arrested for new crimes, one for an offense related to alcohol use.

[47] After this termination, and serving his sentence, Alan came back into drug court for violating probation again. Alan is the only client to have restarted the drug court program after having been terminated.

process. Periodically, we run into clients who have graduated from drug court, but who have relapsed or run into new legal problems.[48] These experiences challenge how I measure success of the clients, and my own. However, if I hold to my experience as witness, the need to measure success recedes. I know that the clients—even those who have "failed"— have gained greater awareness of their self-destructive behaviors, and they have experienced some positive, reinforcing success. They have these experiences to both motivate them and to fall back on when their old patterns and behaviors begin to resurface.

Final Thoughts About the Atmosphere in the Courtroom

The drug court session discussed in this article occurred when we still adhered to the traditional structure of the courtroom, with the judge sitting behind the bench and elevated above the defendant. As we became more comfortable with the new roles that were possible in drug court, we began moving the courtroom furniture and sitting in a circle for the weekly in-court sessions with the clients. Clients who were arrested for violating the contract during the prior week joined us in the circle, even though they might be wearing orange prison-issued clothing and chains. This change in structure really changed the field conditions and enabled us to interact in "other than in usual ways" (Parlett, 1997, p. 25). We now engage in a more fluid and open discussion that ranges from client check-ins to supportive storytelling to teaching moments. We return to the traditional courtroom structure when certain events occur, such as induction into drug court, imposition of a possible jail sanction, and sentencing. As we "risk doing something differently" (Parlett, 1997, p. 25), we support our clients in taking healthy risks. Although Judge Learned Hand ascribes to the judge's responsibility for the atmosphere in the courtroom, it is each of the drug court participants—the judge, the other team members, the clients, their attorneys, and family members— who share responsibility for the atmosphere in the courtroom and for supporting the client as he or she changes his or her life circumstances. The judge, because of the power inherent in the position, can provide leadership in taking the risks that will support healthy change, but the shared responsibility of the entire community is necessary for real change to occur.

Joyce Wheeler, JD, has been on the Maine Superior Court since June 2005. While a judge in the District Court from 1994 to 2005, she presided in the Adult Drug Treatment Court for criminal offenders and directed the Domestic Violence Case Coordination Project. Justice Wheeler worked with judges in Brazil and Russia about judicial interventions in domestic violence and substance abuse cases. She completed a Three-Year Post Graduate Training Program in Gestalt Methods with specializations in Organization and System Development and Couples and Families. Contact: *Joyce.A.Wheeler@maine.gov*

References

Beisser, A. (1970). The paradoxical theory of change. In J. Fagan and I. L. Shepherd (Eds.), *Gestalt therapy now* (pp. 77-80). New York: Harper & Row.

Beisser, A. (1997). Teacher, collaborator, friend: Fritz. *Gestalt Review, 1*(1), 9-15.

Goldkamp, J. S. (1994). Miami's treatment drug court for felony defendants: Some implications of assessment findings. *Prison Journal, 74*(2), 110-157.

Hepburn, J. R., Johnston, C. W., & Rogers, S. (1994). Do drugs. Do time: An evaluation of the Maricopa County demand reduction program. National Institute of Justice Research Brief, Washington, D.C.: U.S. Department of Justice.

Johnson, S., Hubbard, D. J., & Latessa, E. (2000). Drug courts and treatment: Lessons to be learned from the "what works" literature. *Corrections Management Quarterly, 4*(4), 70-77.

Marlowe, D. B. (2003). Integrating substance abuse treatment and criminal justice supervision. *Science and Practice Perspectives*, 8-14.

Marlowe, D. B., Festinger, D. S., & Lee, P. A. (2004). The judge is key component of drug court. *National Drug Court Institute Review, 4*(2), 1-34.

Matzko, H. (1997). A Gestalt therapy treatment approach to addictions: "Multiphasic transformation process." *Gestalt Review, 1*(1), 34-56.

Melnick, J. (1997). Welcome to *Gestalt Review*: An editorial. *Gestalt Review, 1*(1), 1-8.

National Association of Drug Court Professionals. (1997). *Defining drug* courts: *The key components.*

Nevis, E. (2001). *Organizational consulting: A Gestalt approach.* Cambridge, MA: Gestalt Press.

Office of Justice Programs Drug Court Clearinghouse and Technical Assistance Project. (2004). *Summary of drug court activity by state and county.*

Parlett, M. (1997). The unified field in practice. *Gestalt Review, 1*(1), 16-33.

Peters, R. H., & Murrin, M. R. (2000). Effectiveness of treatment-based drug courts in reducing criminal recidivism. *Criminal Justice and Behavior, 27*(1), 72-96.

Peters, R. H., Hass, A. L., & Murrin, M. R. (1999). Predictors of retention and arrest in drug courts. *National Drug Court Institute Review, 2*(1), 33-60.

Satel, S. L. (1998). Observational study of courtroom dynamics in selected drug courts. *National Drug Court Institute Review, 1*(1), 43-71.

State of Maine, Adult Drug Treatment Court (2002). *Policy and procedure manual.*

CHAPTER 10

From *Inner to Outer Integration* of Refugees and Immigrants in the Swedish Society: A Gestalt Intervention

Sari Scheinberg, PhD

Editors' Introduction

The story that unfolds in this chapter is more than a straightforward description of an intervention. It is an accounting of one woman's quest to make a place for herself in a new country, while at the same time having an impact on a critical social problem. The author herself tells us that she was not simply an objective observer and implementer, but often an intense advocate. This is a personal story as much as it is a telling of a professional assignment. The case is impressive for its work at different levels of system in order to have any kind of impact on difficult social issues. Clearly, the work done at the individual and group levels—supported by considerable experience as a Gestalt-oriented practitioner—was very effective. The more difficult and complex work at the social system and governmental levels seemed to be carried out with equal care and attention but had many obstacles to overcome. This story tells us, once again, how much work is required at that level of system if changes are to occur. It also confronts us with the sobering realization that it takes great effort, and no little courage, to be a social change intervener.

Introduction: "So, Where is Home?"

With the ever-increasing migration of people around the world, the chance of meeting people who are not living in their country of origin—who have moved away from "home"—has nearly a fifty-fifty chance of occurring. While the question of "Where is home?" is natural and simple, the answer is far more profound and complicated. There are many reasons why people move. Categorically, we move either *by choice,* as an immigrant (for work, for education, for love, for the hope of finding better opportunities), or, we move *by force,* as a refugee (when we need to escape war, poverty, natural disaster, political, religious or ethnic persecution, and when we search for a safer haven in another country).

This mass migration of people does not only happen spontaneously. Our society and governments have created many processes and institutions on world, region, and country levels to manage the political, legal, and social aspects of migration. There are laws defining who is a refugee, and political decisions and agreements on how refugees are distributed across countries. There are even conditions and demands that define what a refugee must do in order to settle into a new country.

The phenomenon of migration has characterized world population shifts since the ice age. Even today, when we follow the news, we are confronted with ongoing traumas of forced migrations and horrible stories of illegal movements. We are informed nearly every day how thousands of people try to escape the political, religious, and tribal dangers in Iraq and Iran; how hundreds of thousands or even millions of people try to find and maintain refuge from the genocide in Darfur, Republic of Congo, and Rwanda; and how thousands of Mexicans continue to search for ways to come the United States for better economic opportunity.

The story I relate in this chapter resides within the phenomenon of migration. I will relate to it personally, given that I migrated (for "love") from the United States to Sweden in 1990. And I will discuss it professionally, as I have been working as a psychologist and leader of various "integration" programs for over fifteen years with immigrants and refugees who have moved to Sweden in search of a new home.

Specifically, my aim is to present the program "From Inner to Outer Integration: The Road to Work." This is a one-year program I designed and implemented four times over eight years in Sweden with a friend and colleague. As this story unfolds, I will use two voices—one *descriptive,* where I present more *objectively* what and how we did our work; and one more *personal and reflective,* where I share specific concerns and feelings that arose during our work.

Finally, given that I have dedicated my life for over fifteen years in Sweden to supporting and working with refugees and immigrants in many different capacities, I am not an objective bystander. There is no day that is not touched or affected by my own traumatic experiences of changing country and culture. I am passionate about how I have fought hard to expose the complexity of what it takes to be, and feel, integrated (or not) into a new society. In the program we devised, I have held many intense roles: program leader, educator, supervisor, researcher, advocate, and debater.

The Immigration Phenomenon and Integration: Political Strategy or Psychological Process?

Background

Of all the European countries, Sweden is one of the most open regarding their invitation to political refugees from around the world. As a result, Iraqis living in Sweden today number more than those living in the United States and Europe combined. A large wave of refugees started to flow into Sweden in the 1970s, following the violence in Chile, and then again in the late 1980s and 1990s, when many political and religious refugees arrived from Somalia, Poland, the former Soviet Union and former Yugoslavia. Once the refugees were given official permission to stay in the Swedish system, the national goal and political apparatus for managing this influx of foreigners was primarily geared to helping find them a place to live, a school for their children, and a job. While some of the responsibility of this process remained at the national level, the primary responsibility was given to the regional and Community boards, which oversaw and ran the local employment and welfare and health offices. Nevertheless, much of the responsibility for "landing in Sweden" was up to the refugees themselves.

In 1991(a few months after I had moved to Sweden), I was invited to join a program called "International Competence," which aimed to support unemployed persons from Eastern European and Russian backgrounds. This six-month, full-time program was designed to support participants to create their own businesses, by identifying and developing markets and business opportunities in their (former) home countries and selling this knowledge or service to Swedish companies in order to support their expansion and development into the global market. While the program, delivered five times, was generally successful, several things were lacking: time to support the participants in developing their Swedish language skills, and resources to support them in linking to local business networks. The program lacked the time, values, and resources to support our participants as "whole persons" with significant personal and life needs, rather than "unemployed" persons needing work.

Personal Reflection: My own feelings of desperation mirrored those of my clients:

- *I was constantly frustrated with my role and relation to the participants, feeling that we had no time to reflect, no time to work thoroughly and systematically, and no time to work with their emotions and greater life questions.*
- *I was constantly frustrated with my partners and the other stakeholders (the employment counselors and politicians), as their attitude and philosophy was to "fix them" and to "fix the problem" (even temporarily), rather than to form the partnerships and relationships needed to work together in creating sustainable processes.*
- *I was also frustrated with how our results were measured. It was unrealistic to assume that we could deliver solid, sustainable results after only six months. Our results were shaped into statistics that served only the political agenda, with little consideration of the unemployed person's true situation.*

I tried to convince my two partners and the local authorities that we needed to include more time and space for personal as well as business development. Neither of them saw the need for a change. Their response was: "It just was not the way it was being done." It became clear to me that the culture and systems in Sweden treated *integration* as a political strategy only. All emphasis for integration was political rhetoric and national politics; in reality, the effort was pretence aimed at hiding the numbers of unemployed refugees and immigrants in various "temporary solutions." The more I inquired into the existing possibilities, the more I understood that we were worlds apart: the *politics of integration* versus my view of *integration as a psychological process.*

Although I was committed to continue working with the unemployed refugees in Sweden, I realized I needed to find a new way to approach my work as well as new partners. I searched all of the existing programs for a more innovative and humanistic model, but to my dismay, all were designed in a similar format: short-term action versus a "person development" orientation.

Search For a New Approach

During the years I worked in the above programs (1991-1995) with hundreds of unemployed refugee and immigrant clients, I systematically documented and studied their and my experience. One important finding was that of a "*disintegration process*" the unemployed refugees went through as they moved through a vicious cycle—from unemployment, to practice work,[49] to a personal breakdown, to a breakdown of structures and home process, to continued unemployment, etc. This is illustrated below in Figure 1.

Immigrant Crisis

Figure 1: The Disintegration Process (Scheinberg and Högberg, 2004)

As we observed their disintegration, we saw specific symptoms—behaviors and attitudes that became more prominent as they remained unemployed. My clients and I jointly observed various dysfunctions in their behavior and relationship building, and together we found a series of probable problems that were the root cause to these symptoms (Scheinberg and Högberg, 2004). These observations are summarized in Table 1 below.

Another key observation was how fast the unemployed refugees became dependent, and hopeless, and started acting more as children than adults. We developed a perspective of their behaviors from a "polarity" point of view (Clarkson, 1989) in order to see their choice more clearly and where they might get stuck. We also tried to use the polarities as end marks, so we could look at where people were located and how they felt as they moved along the continuum at different points in time. The polarities identified as being important and present during

---

[49] "Practice work" is a formal means of unpaid employment. It means that the unemployed refugee would be offered a position in an organization for a set amount of time as a "practicant," intending to support them to "learn how it is to work in Sweden" and to get a foot into the workforce. This form of work, while a good idea, unfortunately did not lead to the employment of the refugees as expected. And, in fact, in many cases the practice workers were badly treated and not given the opportunity to develop the skills intended.

Symptoms we observed:	What can lie behind:
— restlessness, inability to listen or perform — hard to hold agreements laziness - even easy tasks are hard, cannot prioritize — don't dare to say truth, give answer they think you want to hear — don't keep track of time - don't show up — feel afraid, insecure, depressed, aggressive, false pride, helpless — poor self identity, loss of life meaning, lose touch with reality — passiveness, don't take initiative — fantasies, unrealistic expectations	— lost ability to focus and concentrate, worried — lost responsibility for relationships, trust — lost ability to meet people — lost ability to plan and manage time — lost memory of why they are and what they can do and have done and what they need to do — lost motivation and will to drive life, depression — lost meaning and place of work in life — lost moral and ethical feelings — loss of social competence — loss or lack of market knowledge — family members not feeling well

**Table 1: Dysfunctional behaviors and related loss of abilities
(Scheinberg and Högberg, 2004)**

the disintegration and unemployment process can be found in Table 2 below.

A New Framework Is Created and the Program Is Designed

I was relentless in my pursuit of a new "integration" model even from the context of being a displaced New Yorker living in Sweden.[50] I searched for politicians and bureaucrats in the employment offices who would be willing to help me develop and then commit to experimenting with a new concept that would break with the norms of the current political model. The concept I presented included the following elements:

- A one-year education and development program for academics who have a refugee or immigrant background; have been unemployed for at least six months; are *tired* and *frustrated* with their vicious cycle; and are motivated to change their work-life situation. (Note the indication of "tired and frustrated"; it was critical to find candidates that were "willing and ready" to change their current life situation.)

[50] The "Jante Law" in Sweden encompasses cultural norms that consider perseverance, ambition and "big ideas" as being "too eager" and not attractive. It is more acceptable to claim you are "not being good enough" and wait for your turn, than to ask too many questions or to want to achieve excellence. This is the common behavioral norm.

— adult	child
— power, empowered	dependence
— control, responsibility	helpless
— confident	hopeless
— self-respect	lack of self-respect
— clarity	confusion
— take initiative	waiting, lazy, inertia
— language	limited understanding, communication
— trust	no trust
— remember	blocked, forget
— data	fantasy
— honest	pretending
— relating	using, manipulating
— feel at home	feeling homeless
— visible	invisible
— curiosity	fear, indifference
— relationship	loneliness
— top dog	underdog
— we	they

Table 2: Polarity Perspective of the Disintegration Experience (Scheinberg and Högberg, 2004)

- A psychological approach to support personal and professional development using a variety of pedagogical methods aimed to improve and sustain well-being.
- A program offering ongoing support for the participants—personal and professional—during all the phases of the work search process.

Together with my partner and my stakeholder group I created *From Inner to Outer Integration—The Road to Work*. If this new approach was ambitious, it also recognized that in order to succeed in getting and keeping an appropriate job, there were a number of critical *milestones* that had to be defined and crossed by each participant. The milestones included the following:

- *Develop a contract:* From day one participants were supported to assess and define their needs and goals both *personally* (emotional, physical, and spiritual health, family, social network, energy use, etc.), and *professionally* (job idea, work experiences, skills, network, etc.), in order to clarify direction and goals. Based upon an assessment, priorities were defined, a plan developed, and a contract written between participant and supervisor and continuously reviewed and updated throughout the year.

- *Develop relationships:* Based upon needs defined above, mentor and participant reviewed the type and quality of relationships needed with teachers, mentors, therapists, and other participants, who would support the participants' development and work search process.
- *Enhance personal well-being:* Through a variety of methods and models, the participants were supported to explore needs, feelings, attitudes, fears and worries, body, successes, and other life experiences and choices in order to create a stronger identity and provide confidence emotionally, physically, and energetically, so that they could make conscious choices and have stronger commitments and motivation in life.
- *Swedish language:* Training was offered to upgrade both verbal and writing skills in order to achieve a workable command of the Swedish language.
- *Define a work platform:* Participants were supported in various ways to identify their work experiences, skills, interests, passions, and limitations in order to define the abilities, professional skills, and social competence they wanted to build on in Sweden.
- *Choice of job idea/niche:* Participants were asked to review their competencies and interests in order to define and prioritize two or three work directions to pursue.
- *Market understanding:* Participants were guided to investigate market trends and job opportunities, and to explore (through a minimum of fifteen information interviews) how their own competence matched the demands of potential employers.
- *Create network:* As they explored the market, participants created a network of professionals in their fields to support their ongoing work search process.
- *Continuous and systematic reflection and analysis:* Various methods of reflection, analysis and learning were introduced and used continuously throughout the program in order to support a systematic way of working that was conscious and responsible.
- *Define professional direction:* Based upon what they learned from the market and from feedback received, participants were helped to make a conscious decision to pursue work opportunities either as an employed person or to start their own company.
- *Develop strategies:* Once the direction was selected to get or create the wanted job, participants developed their *portfolio and action plan*, which they would then follow until they got the desired job.

As the participants followed this full time program over the year and completed each of the above milestones, the hope was that the experience and insight accumulated would support them to become more responsible, self-confident, and self-driven. This experience would enable them to have more of the required flexibility so as to adapt their own interests and competencies to market demands, leading to increased employability. We envisioned that these milestones would be interdependent. For example, enhancing personal well-being would be crucial in allowing professional competence to function effectively in finding and negotiating work opportunities.

Because of the impending trap of longing for the past and getting lost and frustrated in unrealistic fantasies about the future, another important goal was to increase the participants' ability to remain *present* in all they did. A successful job search process requires having knowledge, being organized, and being committed and reflective "in every moment." However, it is easy to lose balance and become distracted if one is not feeling grounded. Thus, we built in a continuous review of the participants' stability in all they did. To reinforce this notion, we encouraged them to take what they learned during each step and apply it at home as well as in their work search process.

Given our conviction that the *inner integration* of the participant's needs, life experiences, abilities, and competences would result in stronger self-esteem and identity, we believed that they would be lead into a quicker and more complete integration *in the work market and in society*. As a result, we aimed to shift the vicious cycle pictured in Figure 1 above to a more satisfying developmental transition from *inner to outer integration*, as indicated in Figure 2 below.

The Search for Ownership

It was important for the program to develop a group of stakeholders that could "own" this idea together with us. After a year of hard work, I was finally able to gather the following representatives from the various stakeholder groups responsible for the unemployed refugee problem:

- An authority from the European Union Office
- A leader from the Swedish National Board of Integration
- A regional Ombudsman for Discrimination
- A regional leader responsible for employment policy and services
- Three community leaders with access to unemployed people
- Various employment counselors to help identify participants

Valuable Citizen of Society

↖

Integration

↖

→ Immigration Crisis   Work

↓   ↖

Disintegration   Better market knowledge

↓   ↖

Unemployment Crisis   More internal integration & self confidence

↓   ↗

From Inner to Outer Integration

**Figure 2: A Healthy Integration Process
(Scheinberg and Högberg, 2004)**

Personal Reflection: This was a complicated but exciting process. It demanded a lot of time and effort over a year without payment. I looked at it as an investment for our community and my potential work. I realized that if I did not make this effort, then who would? I felt responsible for caring for the refugees, and I also wanted to create a piece of work that would follow my own philosophies and values. I was on a crusade.

Program Goals and Priorities

"From Inner to Outer Integration" was accepted for funding by the European Social Fund—Framework 3 (ESF)—in 1997. Because of the complexity of this program, we defined various types of goals:

Individually-Oriented Goals:

- The training program will provide a *holistic psychological approach* for the participants' growth.
- The training program will focus on the *participants' current needs and potential*, and each will develop his or her contract and action plan.
- The emphasis will also be on increasing the *participants' motivation*, self-awareness, and self-esteem and on improving their ability to express themselves.
- The pedagogy will aim to strengthen the participants' "personal competence" and awareness of their *own presence, and their willingness to be responsible and consciousness* of what stops their process in the context of a group and a group's dynamics.
- Productive workers first have to know themselves and be able to *read the job situation and markets around them.* This is how we will

support participants to adapt their skills and competencies in a flexible way.

- Participants will have *better knowledge*, and a *more realistic picture*, of what the market demands, and clear strategies to obtain the job desired.
- Participants will be supported in *making a choice* between seeking employment with an existing organization, or developing their own professional practice or business.
- The overall goal of the training program will be to aid individual participants to use more efficient strategies as they attempt to integrate themselves better into Swedish society, *thus allowing the individual to contribute to society instead of being dependent on it.*

Group Level Goals:

The participants were invited to participate in training in a group setting three days a week. The intention was to support them to:

- Learn how to share their stories in a group in order to develop empathy, and listening and feedback strategies leading to the creation of friendships, trusting relationships, and a social community;
- Learn how to work in groups, on both personal as well as professional issues; and
- Practice on each other what they have learned theoretically: the group as laboratory.

System Level Goals:

Finding and getting the right job is not only up to the individual job seekers. Much of getting into the job market depends on the market conditions and society values. Evidence has shown that in Sweden over the past decade, persons with foreign backgrounds face various forms of structural and systematic discrimination and therefore have a hard time getting into the work market. Thus, three additional goals were defined:

- To follow each participant in order to document their experiences (both past and present), in order to define the structural barriers they have met and are currently meeting as they attempt to find their place in the market.
- To create interventions and develop methods in order to overcome, break down, or meet the various obstacles.
  - To document our methods, approach, and solutions created in

cooperation with participants, authorities, local communities, and companies, etc.

Quantitative Goals

For each of the career-orientation groups we set some specific, measurable targets:

Employment Group (80% of participants):

- By the end of the Program, 90% of the group will have become aware of their needs and key competencies, explored and identified their market niche, tested themselves and gotten feedback on their skills and opportunities in the market, and developed a comprehensive network and strategy for a continued work search.
- 75% of the group will find a job within a year after the course, and the rest will have begun a relevant training within a year.

Entrepreneur Group (20% of participants):

- By the end of the Program, 90% of the entrepreneur group will have finished their business plan, identified the market, and tested their products or services on the market. They will have mapped the processes within their organization and their competitors, and organized a marketing strategy and plan for their continued business activities.
- According to our prognosis, 50% will register a business within a year after the course.

The program was divided into three main phases, with each lasting approximately four months. A comprehensive framework was designed to visually illustrate and demonstrate concretely how we planned to manage the learning process and how we imagined *the inner to outer process of integration* would look. This framework is presented below as *Figure 3 (Scheinberg and Högeberg, 1998).*

Organizing Structures

The Faculty Team

We created a delivery team that would be dedicated to leading, caring, and a long-time active commitment. As the work would be very intense and demanding it was critical to develop a team approach that honored and followed the basic philosophy that we would then deliver to the participants themselves. An implementation team was created as follows:

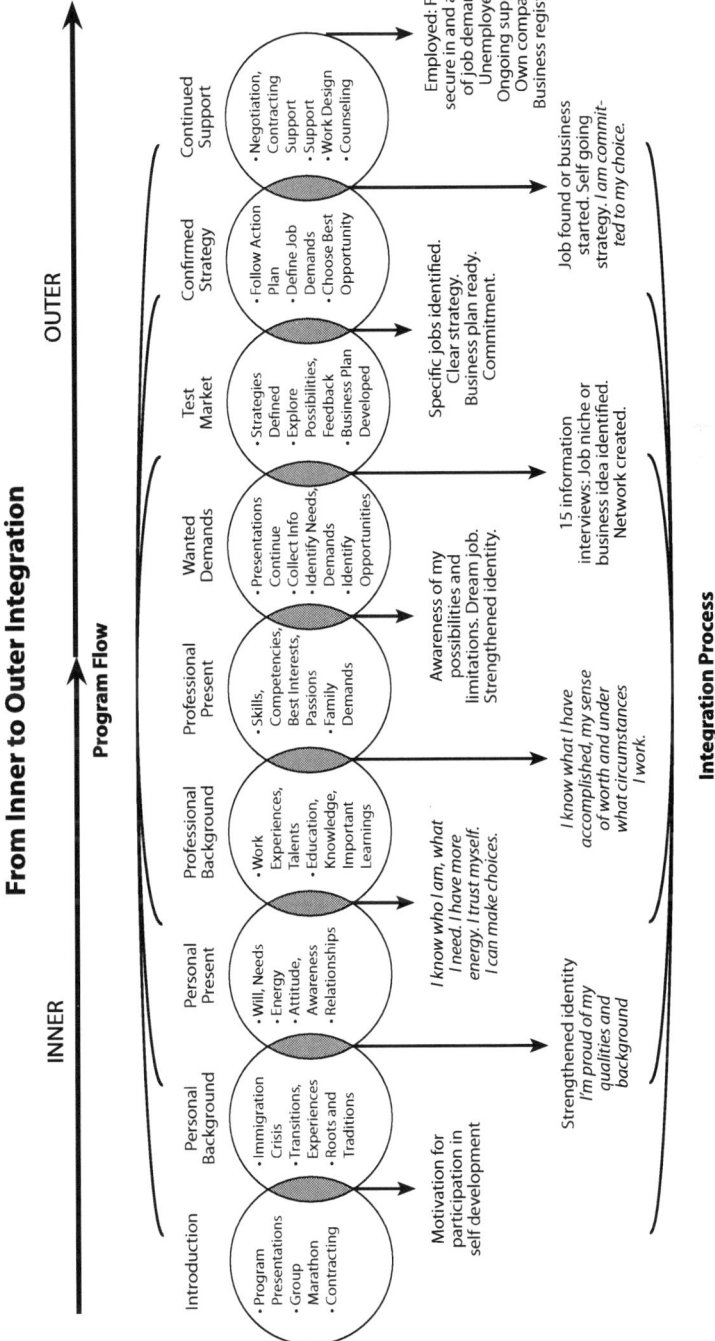

From Inner to Outer Integration

INNER   OUTER

Program Flow

Introduction	Personal Background	Personal Present	Professional Background	Professional Present	Wanted Demands	Test Market	Confirmed Strategy	Continued Support
• Program Presentations • Group Marathon • Contracting	• Immigration Crisis • Transitions, Experiences • Roots and Traditions	• Will, Needs • Energy • Attitude, Awareness • Relationships	• Work Experiences, Talents • Education, Knowledge, Important Learnings	• Skills, Competencies, Best Interests, Passions • Family Demands	• Presentations Continue • Collect Info • Identify Needs, Demands • Identify Opportunities	• Strategies Defined • Explore Possibilities, Feedback • Business Plan Developed	• Follow Action Plan • Define Job Demands • Choose Best Opportunity	• Negotiation, Contracting Support • Support • Work Design • Counseling

Motivation for participation in self development

Strengthened identity I'm proud of my qualities and background

I know who I am, what I need. I have more energy. I trust myself. I can make choices.

I know what I have accomplished, my sense of worth and under what circumstances I work.

Awareness of my possibilities and limitations. Dream job. Strengthened identity.

15 information interviews: Job niche or business idea identified. Network created.

Specific jobs identified. Clear strategy. Business plan ready. Commitment.

Job found or business started. Self going strategy. I am committed to my choice.

Employed: Feel secure in and aware of job demands. Unemployed: Ongoing support. Own company: Business registered.

Integration Process

Figure 3: The Inner to Outer Process of Integration (Scheinberg and Högeberg, 1998)

- Program Coordinator—1
- Lead teachers—2
- Career development expert—1
- Swedish language teachers—2
- Mentors/Supervisors—5
- Therapists—4

Advisory Group

Given the complexities of delivering our ambitious results, and the importance of co-ownership, we asked our original stakeholder group to continue on as an Advisory Council. They all agreed to meet with us on a bi-monthly basis and to commit to supporting our program each year it was running. We planned to use the Council as a sounding board to provide advice and access to their networks.

Even though the various constituents agreed in principle to be part of our Council and wanted to support our program, they were more used to being "controllers" than advisors. We applied some of our teaching to work with the Council. For example, we always started Council meetings with a check in to support their "presence" and readiness to work. There was initial resistance to becoming more intimate, but over time most of the Council members were able to transform their more "objective, bureaucratic" relationship style into a more contactful style. A few did remain skeptical of our approach even to the end.

Participants

The following *criteria* guided our search for twenty-five unemployed adults (over twenty-five years old) living in the area of Angered in Göteborg.

- Academic level (diploma not necessary)
- Foreign background—representing different nationalities
- Basic ability in the Swedish language
- Frustration and motivation to change their situation
- Balance of men and women

The Selection Process

Participation in our program was to be determined by the participants themselves rather than the employment offices. Thus, we developed a two-step process to find participants.

Step 1—*Information Meetings at the Employment Offices*

We returned to our network of employment counselors to review the criteria for selecting participants and to plan how to locate our target group. The counselors searched their data-bases for the names of appropriate people. We delivered a series of information meetings in the various employment offices in the region. Each employment officer sent an invitation to their clients to come and listen to our program. It was mandatory for the clients to attend these meetings. During these series of open and interactive meetings, the clients were able to choose whether the program suited their needs and strategies for finding a job, or creating a business.

Step 2—*Individual In-Depth Interviews*

Each client who chose to explore our program was invited to our office for an in-depth interview. There were two goals for this meeting. First, it was important for the potential participants to gather more information on our program, our teachers, our teaching methods, the demands, etc., so that they could feel that they were making a conscious and clear choice about a one-year commitment. And second, it was critical for us to understand each person's background and psychological frame of mind. Given that many of the refugees had survived war, torture, and very tough traumas, we needed to make sure that they were psychologically fit to be part of a group, be open to personal growth, and be "ready and willing" to drive their life and work process.

There were two clear dilemmas facing most of the participants in choosing whether they would join our program. First, many participants did not want to think of themselves as "sick" and needing psychological support. Only a very small percentage had any psychological training or awareness, so we needed to spend a lot of time helping them to understand the meaning of working psychologically. Second, since the program required the participants to commit to up to a year of working with us, it evoked concern about how much work and commitment might be required. We had to explain that, once a job was found, they were no longer obliged to be connected to us, but that they had up to a year to get dedicated support, if desired.

Key Psychological Concepts

One of the unique features in this training program was the pedagogical approach, where the fundamental principles of both Gestalt and Psychosynthesis psychology would be combined. It was exciting to create a conceptual framework that combined these two psychologies, as they both aim to support individuals to discover, explore, and experience their own way of being in the world and their potential.

Psychosynthesis (Assagioli, 1996) is a psychological approach that aims to give a deeper meaning to the events and crises in life. The methods help the individual to work through the difficulties and to see the opportunity that crisis offers for inner growth. Psychosynthesis supports the development and inclusion of fantasy and intuition as parts of ourselves holding wisdom and deep knowledge.

The Gestalt approach offers many concepts and methods felt to be relevant for working with this target group. Examples include the importance and development of awareness; the value of making conscious choices and taking responsibility; contracting; the management of presence, the quality and development of contact and relationships; and the perspective of wholeness, integrating and respecting the head (thoughts), body (sensations), and feelings (emotions) that all demand attention and care. The cycle of experience was applied to learning how to work more systematically and consciously; learning was enhanced by using "experimenting" as an approach; dialogical encounter was encouraged in all sessions; and the use of phenomenological awareness of self and others was introduced and practiced both in the program and in the job search process. How we applied a number of the Gestalt models and concepts will be presented below.

Personal Reflection: The process of developing the models and approaches was an ongoing experience throughout the program period and throughout its lifetime. My partner (Livia Frischer) and I found that we would spend at least the equivalent number of days preparing for our sessions as the number of days we would be teaching. The creativity and passion that went into the development of the program, its conceptual base and the design, were returned to us sevenfold as we were constantly challenged, nourished, stimulated and inspired throughout the years we delivered it. It felt like a gift.

The Pedagogical Design: Methods and Structures

The design was focused on the participants' development and on the development of a supportive group. "Experiential learning" or "action learning," which encourages mutual support and experimenting, and support for the individual to express his or herself in different ways, formed the base of the methods applied. The training program contained seven structures.

Classroom learning: Lectures, exercises (individual and in small groups), guided meditations, body movement, body awareness, drawings, etc.

Personal reflection: Participants evaluated themselves and reflected on their situation, both privately (in writing, drawing, thinking) and in dialogue.

Support groups: Participants prepared and reviewed homework together, sharing their knowledge and conducting projects. This provided emotional support and helped to create a feeling of belonging.

Individual supervision/mentorship: Participants created contracts with their mentors and were offered individual support for the year to follow. Special attention was given to the individual's needs and goals and to the results achieved. Concrete feedback was given and joint reflection was ongoing.

Individual and family therapy: Participants were offered regular private sessions for working through more personal issues. These included counseling for their family system as well.

Group supervision: Participants engaged in small groups to integrate their new knowledge, to role-play, and to experiment with new techniques and methods.

Fieldwork: Participants were encouraged: to conduct studies of the market and of their competitors; to interview customers, suppliers and network; to search for information on the Internet; to look at trends; to analyze the social, political and economic factors that affect the work opportunities, etc.

Action and Contact: Implementing the Program

The program was divided into three phases (as illustrated in *Figure 3* above), where each phase was approximately four months long. A description of their contents follows below.

Phase 1: Personal Development

The focus in this phase was on the individuals' inner integration process, with the goal of restoring their personal competence. We dealt with the effect of the immigration and unemployment crisis on the participants' loss of identity and self-esteem, and on their stress, fear, confusion, and despair. Through emotional support, the participants were helped to connect to their identity and their roots, and to find meaning in their lives in Sweden. The process led to stronger and more secure self-esteem, and to an improved ability on their part to express themselves and their needs. Finding meaning in the present increased participants' energy level, motivation, and commitment to find work.

We applied a number of models and methods of Phase I, which are listed below in Table 3:

1. Contracting (Knowles, 1975; Block, 1981)
2. Cycle of experience (Nevis, 1987/2005; Scheinberg and Alänge, 1996; Clarkson, 1989)
3. Being and becoming present (zones) (Nevis, 1987/2005; Hostrup, 2002)
4. Quality and building of relationships (Moss-Kanter, 1985; Scheinberg, Frischer and Alänge, 2000)
5. Energetic well-being (Kepner, 1987)
6. Awareness building (Nevis, 1987/2005; Kepner, 1987; Merleau Ponty, 1962; Stevens, 1989)
7. Needs identification (Maslow, 1968; Assiagioli, 1996)
8. Contact and contact styles (Buber, 1958; Perls, Hefferline, and Goodman, 1951; Berman-Zeligman, 2001; Clarkson and Mackewn, 1993)
9. Roots and traditions (Scheinberg and Frischer, 1997)
10. Life transition model (Bridges, 1980, 1991)
11. Field theory (Lewin, 1948)

Table 3: Key Models and Concepts Used during Phase I (First Four Months)

A discussion of how we applied the first three concepts follows.

Contracting:

Since both the participants and our team were committed to working together for up to a year, it was critical to be as clear as possible on what we were agreeing to do. Even if our goals were clear, visible, and presented (over and over again), we did not want to assume that our clients were able to "understand them fully and take them in" with awareness and clarity. Of course, our goals were not the participants' own goals. And, given that this was a pioneering effort to work more holistically with this target group, we made special efforts to be very explicit and create various processes to define what was included in the realm of our work together and what was not included. One of our main efforts was to create a contracting process (Block, 1981; Nevis, 1987/2005), first with the participants as a group and then between each delegate and a mentor. The contracting process was intended to support the philosophy of the self-directed or motivated learner (Knowles, 1975) coupled with an active and engaged mentor working together to help the participants mutually achieve their goals (Scheinberg and Frischer, 1997).

The contract had both a *personal* and *professional* dimension. In the *personal dimension*, we included assessment of their well-being and goals for getting more in touch with their feelings, their body, their family situation, their economic situation and their social relationships. In the *professional dimension*, we included different sub-dimensions of what was needed to build their professional lives, including assessment and goals for the ideal job, market understanding, work and competence (in Sweden and in their homeland), education, networks, Swedish language competence, and the creation of a final portfolio of all formal documentation.

Participants were supported to set both short-term and longer-term goals. They were required to review and reflect on what they had finally formulated (with their mentors), to confirm it, and then to commit to an action plan and set priorities. Over the course of the program, they would meet regularly with their mentors to assess their progress, adjust goals when needed, and set new goals.

Personal Reflection: The process to support the participants to name and be honest about their current status was very challenging and exposing. It was very important that the mentor group work very closely together. It was also necessary for the mentors to bring in therapists to support those participants who were suffering from traumas and unfinished issues that lingered—both from their home country as well as from living in Sweden. Mentors and therapists expressed their own feelings of helplessness and hopelessness, mirroring those of their participants. As a result, it was important for teachers, mentors, and therapists to collaborate and get their own supervision. We needed to attend to the ongoing stress that we ourselves experienced while delivering the program.

Gestalt Cycle of Experience:

One of the key issues plaguing persons with foreign backgrounds who are unemployed for long periods of time (from six months up to fifteen years) is their tendency to become forgetful, unsystematic, and defensive. Thus, it was important to create a common language for the group— to develop awareness of self and a conscious and systematic approach to work and life. To achieve this end, participants were introduced to the Cycle of Experience (see Figure 4 below) as the main operating model of the program. They were taught a revised cycle by Scheinberg and Högeberg (2004) built upon the cycles presented earlier by Nevis (1987/2005), Zinker (1978), and Perls, Hefferline, and Goodman (1951). The main distinguishing feature of this revised cycle was that it included *Integration* as its own stage in an experience and learning process. I recognized that to reflect on experiences and to discover insight out of learning is profoundly complicated. To integrate the impressions, memories, and learning into new behaviors, attitudes, and routines is even more complex and challenging. Thus, it seemed important to divide the reflection stage into two distinct stages to ensure a deeper consciousness and distinction of these two aspects of learning.

The participants were taught and applied variations of the Cycle of Experience at all phases of the program. It was used to support them to learn how to be conscious and systematic in all of their experiences: by being honest about where they started from and how ready, present, and willing they were to focus (*sensation*); by becoming more aware of themselves, their needs, their goals, and their priorities (*awareness*); and then by planning how they would accomplish their goals by recognizing their priorities and preparing and planning for what they needed – resources, competencies, power, energy, etc.–in order to accomplish them (*mobilize energy*). Once ready, they followed their plans working in a conscious and responsible way (*action*) with ongoing contact with themselves and their surroundings (*contact*). And when they had completed their aims or "piece of work," they acknowledged and reflected on their results, assessed the mistakes and successes made, gave and got feedback, and identified the key learnings achieved (*reflection and analysis*). After this analysis ("looking back") they determined how they would integrate these new learnings and insights into their way of working (looking forward), how they wanted to improve their way of working in the future, and how they would share their new routines and relationships (*integration/standardization*). Finally, after they took time to celebrate or mourn the experience, they assessed what remained unfinished or finished, determined what they needed to do next after they withdrew their energy, and got ready to close and withdraw their energy and focus from it (*closure*).

Personal Reflection: In this program, I used the cycle in many ways: from defining the flow of the program over the year, to designing the training sessions, to managing my meetings with my Advisory Council, to

Cycle of Experience

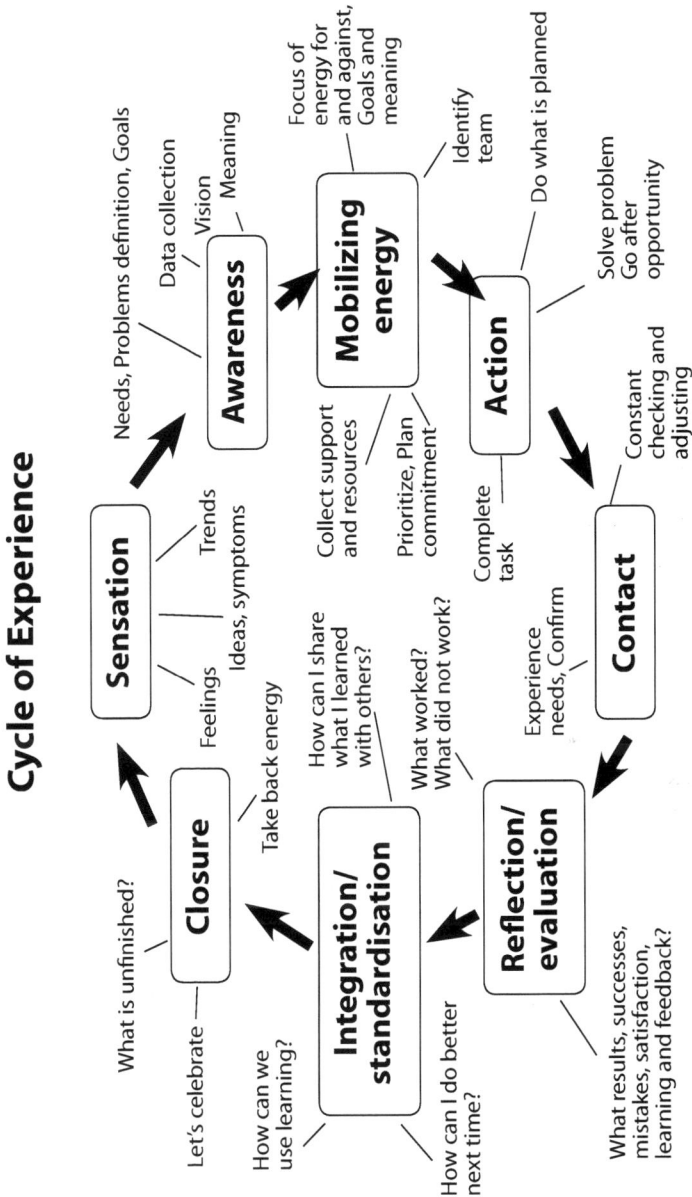

Figure 4: The Cycle of Experience (Scheinberg and Alänge, 1996)

assessing and grappling with not only all of the complexities but also my own learning and insights. One important insight I gained during these years was to observe how people in today's society do not naturally take time to reflect and do not value reflection. I also observed that without reflection and the further integration of the insights into our bodies, minds, and hearts, we risk not maintaining memories, as we do not catch or imprint our impressions into ourselves. For the refugees trying to develop a new life in Sweden, it was critical to support them to assimilate their life experiences truly.

Being and Becoming Present:

We found that it did not take even two months before people would start to "lose their memory" of who they were, what their values were, and what they had accomplished prior to moving to Sweden. Without witnesses, "mirrors," or local reminders, their memories and sense of "self" melted away, and the anxieties of finding the way toward life in a new country took over. In addition, 30% or more of each class of participants had survived torture and trauma experiences, which also stood as a block in their ability to be present and in contact with their needs. These lapses of memories and lost self-confidence affected the unemployed person's ability to recognize their needs, so much so, that experience and competencies often became a "shadow" of their "present" situation.

Another unfortunate effect of being unemployed and a foreigner in Sweden was the gnawing experience of feeling and being invisible. This sense of invisibleness was constantly reinforced: the longer one was unemployed and thus "outside" of most systems, the more one was treated as an object of "programs and measures" to be dealt with. A long term unemployed foreigner was often seen as a nuisance and overlooked entirely. And, to make matters worse, the culture in Sweden had not "valued" foreigners. In fact, all foreigners carried the label of "immigrant" or "refugee" status for their entire lives.

The complication here is that the dominant Swedish values have their foundation in socialistic priorities. Hence, it is "politically incorrect" or not actually possible for the society to acknowledge that there is discrimination ("We only work with integration"), and there are laws that make it illegal to measure the numbers of women, minorities, etc., in a workforce. As a result, this clash of values and sub-cultures in Sweden makes it difficult to admit that there are underlying fears and forces that create a structural discrimination in both the society and the workforce, which makes it even harder to "put your finger on" the issue. As a result, most of our participants have learned to wait (thereby becoming invisible), rather than taking assertive responsibility.

Thus, one key aspect we worked with at all stages of the program was the question of *presence*. We felt it was basic to our learning environment, and to becoming more successful in finding a more visible place in society, to have participants "enforce" their sense of being present. To support this notion, we also introduced the participants to the phenomenological concept of zones (Merleau-Ponty, 1962; Hostrup, 2002). We taught them how to meditate—first checking in with their current experience and then sharing it in the group. We taught them to pay attention to their bodies, their feelings, and their energy, including their breathing. We also developed a program that focused on exercise and well-being. The process of becoming present, and of sharing how folks were in the here and now, helped develop a more honest, responsible, caring, and trusting environment for all of us to work in.

Lastly, we included ongoing, intensive teaching of Swedish, designed to speed up participants' ability to express themselves in that language and thereby become more present in both communication and contribution.

Phase 2: Professional Development

In this phase of the program, the focus was on revaluating the participants' work direction. There was a lot of resistance and fear in both confronting the reality of today's work market and doing the search required to find their place in it. To support the participants' entry into the market, we continued some work in personal development, supporting them to be aware of the way they breathe, use their voices, and hold their bodies. This work was designed to help them manage their presence in meetings in which they participated. In addition, we worked with building cultural awareness (Hofsteder, 1980; Schein, 1985; Phillips-Martinsson, 1981) of their own culture and of the cultural demands and values in Sweden. We looked at the clashes, the difficulties, and the opportunities.

Once the participants had become more grounded personally, the goal of the training was to help them revaluate their professional competence and motivation to work. The participants compiled all their education and previous work experiences systematically and with renewed focus. They sought and obtained validation papers and certificates; afterward, they were supported to come into contact with their dream of a meaningful profession (Bridges, 1980).

Our previous experience showed that many unemployed persons with foreign backgrounds often make unrealistic decisions about where to focus their resources and energy in choosing a direction for work or education. For example, it was common for unemployed persons to send out hundreds of letters to job advertisements—as if shooting in the dark. This resulted in massive rejections, leading to a loss of energy and motivation. To counter this desperation, an important part of the program was dedicated to defining a work-life platform, which is a conscious and structured process around realistic work-life choices. Therefore, choices would be based on a thorough self-evaluation and a solid understanding of the situation in the work market, which would serve as a "stable ground."

Participants were given help to develop a first attempt at defining their *job idea*, based on a link between their competence and their dream. They had to define three work directions simultaneously. Then they had to explore and evaluate where their ideas fit into the market. During this process, they were encouraged to meet with at least fifteen people connected to their *job idea* and working in that field. The goal was for them to get a realistic picture of the job itself, to learn the demands for education and previous work experience, to get feedback on their own capabilities, and to collect new names for additional interviews. The process helped the participants to define and formulate their job idea and direction in a more concrete and systematic way. During Phase 2 we added the following models to our framework:

1. Personal and work platform (Bridges, 1980, 1991; Scheinberg and Frischer, 1997; Stevens, 1993)
2. Job idea and niche (Ericsson, 1999)
3. Cultural awareness (Hofsteder, 1980; Schein, 1985; Phillips-Martinsson, 1981)
4. Network and relationship building (Scheinberg, Frischer and Alänge, 2000)
5. Presence (Nevis, 1987/2005)

Phase 3: Implementing a Career Strategy

By the end of Phase 2, participants were supported to make a decision concerning their continued work direction. This choice was based on a thorough self-evaluation and a deep understanding of the market for jobs and products. Once the group reached a final choice, they were divided into three directions:

- Entrepreneurial Group
- Employment Group
- Additional Education Group

All of the participants created strategies to find or create the right job. Then they established individual plans of action in order to continue reaching their goals. In addition to the regular training, they were offered support in the form of individual and group supervision.

Participants were given help on how to improve their oral and written presentation skills and on how to include their multicultural insights into their job search. They documented their new knowledge of market strategies and of personal strategies learnt during the course. Participants were also offered help to develop their ability to negotiate terms and conditions in different contracts; for example, trial employment, trainee positions, etc.

In addition, participants were offered extra psychological support to help them deal with the feelings that cropped up when they continued to face tough, competitive reality. We had observed that frustration in implementing plans stirred up old feelings of fear and hopelessness, which could be ameliorated with support from faculty.

Entrepreneurial Group

The entrepreneur group was taught the skills required for starting a business, developing ideas and products, conducting market surveys, and creating a business plan with market strategies. Experienced mentors supported group members as they entered the market.

Employment Group

Since it was difficult to find permanent employment during the period of the program, the employment-oriented group had to learn to market themselves and work in a manner similar to the entrepreneur group. The participants in this group learned how to reformulate their skills, both personal and professional, so that they would become assets demanded by employers on the market. They also developed an understanding of the importance of flexibility and a willingness to work either on short-term projects or on a full-time basis. In this segment, the participants learned to explore and analyze the market's demands and to sell themselves as unique and competitive individuals in the market. To help in this work, we introduced concepts of business-plan creation (Ericksson, 2001) and the professional portfolio (Scheinberg, 2004).

Additional Education Group

Based upon the information and feedback the participants had collected during Phase 2, it became clear to a number of the delegates that their particular competence either was lacking or needed upgrading. As a result, a few participants had to search for and apply to education programs that would meet their needs and ambitions. Once they found the best programs, the participants were supported to write applications and prepare for going back to school.

Following the first year's program, the Swedish government required us to adjust our target group to primarily persons who were academics, according to the government's demands. We were assigned the task of preparing a report on the structural obstacles hindering this group from getting into the job market, and of developing methods to eliminate or work around these obstacles. Thus, we broadened our work in Phase 3 to include observations on how participants were met and treated during their search process; and an examination of obstacles or supports they encountered in dealing with the various authorities, community organizations, and industries. We also conducted in-depth interviews with managers in the industry, employment office, and social service organizations with which the participants had contact.

In this segment of the work, we found a very inhospitable environment. Participants had difficulty finding the right person with whom to talk. They encountered unreasonable demands, such as technical foreign language examinations that many Swedes could not pass. Employment interviewers were suspicious of the answers that participants gave to questions, and participants were given little time in their interviews to "show" themselves. Participants had difficulty finding out why they did not get a particular job. The results of the action research was presented to both the participants and the Advisory Group, and finally to the National Integration Board of Sweden (Scheinberg and Högberg, 2004).

Phase 4: Post-Program Transition Association

Once the training year was over, all participants were invited to join an association created with the sole purpose of supporting our "graduates." Our goals in starting the "Transition Association" were to support participants at all stages of the job search and the new job adaptation process, and to address certain acute issues that appeared after our program ended.

First, participants who found *real* jobs often found themselves sitting alone in their offices "not knowing what to do, and too afraid to ask for more information." Rather than asking their bosses to explain an assignment once again and risk looking stupid or losing their job, many participants chose to sit in their offices "frozen" with confusion. It was important for this group to get ongoing mentoring support to help them learn how to clearly define their tasks and goals, to figure out how to work and fit in, and to keep asking questions and not pretend.

Second, participants who found *practice jobs* often found themselves doing work that they were not hired to do. Unfortunately, as they could not manage renegotiating their position in a good way (they were scared of confronting their bosses), they were stuck in a double bind. On the one hand, they were given the message that they should be "grateful" for having been given the opportunity of working. On the other hand, they were being treated unfairly in not being given the opportunity to discuss the fact that they were not doing the work they were hired to do. We often had to step in by going to the employment site to evaluate their situation and help them negotiate the proper terms of the assignment.

Third, participants *not yet placed in a job* were still trying to drive their work or education search process. Thus, it was important for them to have access to a mentor and a support network "as a place to go and belong" during their search process. These graduates were invited to various training and counseling sessions and social gatherings.

Results and Reflections: Outcomes and Our Learning

Conducting European Union (EU) sponsored programs is demanding, with almost more emphasis placed on obtaining financing and analyzing a program than on conducting and driving a program. We analyzed the results of our program in many ways and on many levels. We conducted a comprehensive assessment of each delegate at both the start and the end of the program. We assessed the relationships with all of the stakeholders. We had to reapply to the ESF every time we wanted to conduct our program, which required us to do a thorough evaluation to ensure that all insights and improvements would be "integrated" into the new program. And one of the most exciting assessments we did was to conduct the action research on our participants presented above.

Program Results

The program was conducted four times. Here is an example of the results achieved in our Second Program.

The program for the second group was carried out between May 1999 and May 2000. By the end of the program, eight (38%) of the participants had started working. Two (10%) were working on starting their own companies and three (15%) had trainee jobs (working for experience but not paid) in line with their job idea. One person started a vocational training in August. As Table 5 indicates, fourteen participants (66%) had found their place in the work market at the end of the course, and 90% one year later:

At the end of the course	One year later
8 employed	13 employed
1 in education	3 in education
2 starting companies	2 running companies
3 trainees	1 trainee
7 unemployed	2 unemployed

Table 5. Employment at the End of Program & One Year Later

Based on a survey we conducted at the start and at the end of the program, 85% of the participants felt that they had increased their personal, social, and professional competence and improved their language and computer skills. All of the participants felt they had clearer strategies for continued work search.

Interestingly, the results of the other three programs nearly mirrored those of the second program detailed above. At the close of all four programs, 90% of the participants said that they felt much healthier and happier (as they had developed a more conscious and systematic way of approaching their life), and about 70% had found work, were on their way to starting their own businesses, or had found an education program that suited their needs. A year after the finish of the last program, approximately 85% of the participants were committed to their new directions (work, new business start up, or education).

Our Learning

To summarize the learning that derived from eight years of intense and personally stressful, yet exhilarating, work is not easy. I am amazed at my own determination and energy throughout this period to overcome the various dilemmas and struggles we had to face in order to drive the program. I have included many of my reflections throughout this chapter; below are some other conclusions that stood out for me.

1. When we compared the results from our four programs with those

from previous work in Sweden, it was clear that we made great improvement. This was largely due to the focus on the individual and on inner integration in Phase 1. Though they still had to deal with a difficult environment, our participants were better prepared to do so, and most achieved employment sooner than had been previously possible. A strong Gestalt background helped me both to deal with participants and to handle my own traumatic issues as an immigrant in Sweden.

2. Further success in this kind of initiative requires significant intervention to change the employment system. Sweden is still in the early stages of working with the issues and benefits of diversity in the workplace. In addition to a need to lower prejudice in a relatively open society, there is a need for unemployed persons to get continuous personal and professional support at every stage of the job search process. It is critical to work in lowering discrimination without shaming or blaming anyone. Our experience indicates that most of the employment personnel were unaware of the impact of their behavior and routines. By the end of our years of cooperation, the employment counselors changed their approach to meeting with unemployed clients.

Personal Reflection: To stay with this project over several years, in the face of many obstacles, required a commitment that took over a huge part of my life. The need to accomplish things turned me into more of an advocate than I was at the beginning. I also learned that when an advocate pushes against a system, it is inevitable that there will be a push back. My determination and my stubborn streak helped me to stay positive, and to find ways to overcome resistance, mainly through establishing local relationships that supported our work. We were even able to achieve some change in the Swedish employment system, redefining the relationship and contract the employment officers had with their clients. And, of course, we succeeded in helping a significant number of participants. The key to the success of the program was our active commitment from a long-term perspective. We had clear, mutually agreed upon goals that were led and driven by a generosity of love, respect, co-creation, resources, and energy on the part of all the key stakeholders.

Postscript

"From Inner to Outer Integration" was not allowed to continue after the fourth program. The veil of invisibility and discrimination that effectively kept our clients outside the system affected us as well. Even with all of the successes and all of the visible reports we wrote, the Board of Integration neglected to use any of our work for policy or law. This authority was in fact closed down, and no other authority replaced it. And the ESF decided to prioritize other unemployment issues in Sweden, rather than the one pertaining to refugees and immigrants. But despite our deep disappointment when we learned that we would not be able to continue, our colleagues and clients were still able to celebrate the experience—the relationships we had created, and the deep wisdom we had developed over the eight years of the program.

> *If you are ever asked where home is. . .*
> *Is it where the heart is. . . ?*
> *Is it where you make it. . . ?*

Final Personal Reflection: I can honestly say that from my own experience, and from working with hundreds of refugees and immigrants over fifteen years, home is where the heart is. It is where you have found and developed relationships with people who care about your day-to-day life, and who are committed to supporting your success with love and honesty.

Sari Scheinberg, PhD, has been working as a research-based consultant and program leader for the last thirty years. She has worked with questions of entrepreneurship, innovation, large system change, and leadership in Africa, Russia, Central and South America, and Sweden. Scheinberg studied Gestalt Organization and System Development (OSD) at the Gestalt Institute of Cleveland, and Human Organization Development at the Fielding Institute. In 1990, she emigrated to Sweden, where she has been living ever since. She is a faculty member of the Gestalt Academy of Scandinavia, and of Chalmers University of Technology (Göteborg). Currently, she is leading a long-term project to transform the role of universities in Nicaraguan society.

Contact: *sari@recomate.se*

References

Assiagioli, R. (1996). *The act of will: A guide to self-actualisation and self-realisation.* New York: Daniel Platts.

Berman-Zeligman, J. (2001). Unpublished Gestalt Training Material.

Block, P. (1981). *Flawless consulting* (2nd ed.). San Francisco: Jossey-Bass.

Bridges, W. (1980). *Transitions: Strategies for coping with the difficult, painful and confusing times in your life.* Reading, MA: Addison-Wesley.

Bridges, W. (1991). *Managing transitions: Making the most out of change.* Reading, MA: Addison Wesley.

Buber, G. (1958). *I and thou.* New York: Scribner's.

Clarkson P. (1989). *Gestalt counselling in action.* London: Sage.

Clarkson, P., & Mackewn (1993). *Fritz Perls.* London: Sage.

Ericsson, G. (1997). Course materials. Sweden: New Start.

Hostrup, H. (2002). *Gestaltherapi—en introduction I grundbegreppen.* Stockholm: Bokförlaget Mareld.

Hofsteder, G. (1980). *Culture's consequences: International differences in work-related values.* Beverly Hills, CA: Sage.

Kepner, J. (1987). *Body process: Working with the body in psychotherapy.* Cambridge: MA: GestaltPress.

Knowles, M. (1975). *Self-directed learning.* Englewood Cliffs, NJ: Prentice Hall.

Lewin, K. (1948). *Resolving social conflicts.* New York: Harper & Rowe.

Lewin, K. (1951). *Field theory in social science: Selected theoretical papers.* New York: Harper & Rowe.

Maslow, A.H. (1968). *Toward a psychology of being.* New York: John Wiley

Merleau-Ponty, M. (1962). *Phenomenonology of perception.* London: Routledge.

Moss-Kanter, R. (1985). *Commitment and community: Communes and utopias in sociological perspective.* Cambridge, MA: Harvard University Press.

Nevis, E. (1987, 2005). *Organizational consulting: A Gestalt approach.* Cambridge MA: GestaltPress.

Perls, F., Hefferline, R.F., & Goodman, P. (1951). *Gestalt therapy: Excitement and growth in the human personality.* New York: Dell.

Phillips-Martinsson, J. (1981). *Swedes as others see them: Facts, myths or a communication complex?* Stockholm: Studentlitteratur.

Schein, E. (1985). *Organizational culture and leadership.* San Francisco: Jossey-Bass.

Scheinberg, S., & Alänge, S. (1996). Continuous learning through learning Cycles: A comparative review of schools of thought and application for revolutionary change, culture transformation and development. Department of Industrial Management and Economics, Chalmers University of Technology Göteborg. Unpublished document.

Scheinberg, S., Frischer, J., & Alänge, S. (2000). The learning alliance: Relational aspects to the development of competence. Unpublished document.

Scheinberg, S., & Frischer, L. (1997). Discovering your passion. Course Material: From inner to outer integration. Unpublished document.

Scheinberg, S., & Högberg, A. (1998). From inner to outer integration program: Application proposal to ESF framework 3. Unpublished document.

Scheinberg, S., & Högberg, A. (2004). Structural hinders for unemployed academics who have refugee and immigrant backgrounds in Sweden. Unpublished document.

Stevens, J.O. (1989). *Awareness: Exploring, experimenting, experiencing.* London: Eden Grove.

Stevens, P. (1993). *A passion for work: A lifelong affair.* Sydney: The Center for Worklife Counselling.

Zinker, J. (1978). *Creative process in Gestalt therapy.* New York: Vintage.

CHAPTER 11

Using Gestalt Methods in Training Managers of Development Projects and Programs in Developing Countries

Jochen Lohmeier, PhD, and Chantelle Wyley, MIS

Editors' Introduction

This chapter is about the journey of Jochen Lohmeier and Chantelle Wyley to find the most impactful ways to train managers of developmental projects and programs in third world countries. Lohmeier and Wyley started with a largely problem-focused, cognitive orientation, but soon realized that it could be improved upon. They searched for complementary, impactful methods and came to understand that they needed to learn better what influences human behavior and facilitates societal change. Of equal import, they realized that they needed to develop themselves so that they could fully develop others. They became students of the Gestalt approach, receiving substantial coaching and training. As their comfort and skill increased, they included Gestalt principles and techniques in their training and consulting. Today, they are committed to intervention processes that are primarily Gestalt in orientation and very different from the mainly technologically oriented approach with which they began.

Exceptional about this chapter is that the authors not only detail their change as individuals but also describe how it impacted their intervention design. Then through their own reflections and the inclusion of extensive participant feedback, Lohmeier and Wyley observe how their new approaches and strategies have positively influenced the managers themselves.

Introduction

The managers of socio-economic development projects and programs are tasked with intervening in the lives of poor marginalized people in the economic and societal networks of villages and regions, in sometimes unstable political terrains, and in the threatened ecological systems of the developing world. They are challenged by diminishing resources, increasing populations, widening wealth gaps, tenuous safety and security; but are encouraged by human potential and tenacity.

This chapter records the experience of training managers of development projects and programs, using Gestalt as an orientation for adult learning and behavior change. These development managers came from across the developing world: they worked in rural development initiatives in East Africa, in water management and urban renewal in the Middle East, in guerrilla fighter rehabilitation programs in Eritrea and Somalia, in aquaculture and forestry in East Asia; they came from governments and from non-government organizations. All had an impact on the lives of poor and marginalized people.

The Training Team

For a twenty-year period from the early 1980s to 2004, the German government hosted and sponsored the management training of managers (so-called "counterparts") of German-funded development projects/ programs in Africa, South East Asia, the Middle East, and Eastern Europe. The initial objective of the courses on Project Management/ Development Management was to orient and school these managers in the (useful and rigorous) German government funding agencies' approach to objectives-oriented planning, implementation, and evaluation of projects and programs (see Wyley and Lohmeier, 2003). Early on, the team of trainers widened the scope of the course to include communication and teamwork skills, and a systematic approach to analysis and professional design of development projects and programs, in order to intensify the impact on poverty reduction and sustainability.

A typical course hosted approximately twenty-five participants from approximately fifteen countries of the developing world (often from East Asia, through Central and South Asia, Eastern Europe, Africa, to the Caribbean or even Latin America). The course lasted six to seven weeks and took place in early summer in Germany. The attraction to this training increased and, by the mid-1990s, similar courses were held in the Philippines, South Africa, Indonesia (in Bahasa), Egypt (in

Arabic), West Africa (in French), Ecuador (in Spanish), and Brazil (in Portuguese).

The authors convened/participated in the training teams for these courses as part of private training consortiums[51] contracted by the funding agency. The training team was made up of freelance development consultants; most came from an economic, planning, or community development background. The trainers' team reflected the global diversity of participants: we were from the Philippines, Germany, East Africa, West Africa, and South Africa—women and men, in our thirties, forties, and fifties. As background, the international development aid environment operates as follows:

- Funds originate from the public coffers of developed / "first world" countries and are channeled through national or international government or non-government agencies (an oliopolistic funnel compared to the corporate world) in a package of "projects" or "programs," including structural measures for entire countries.
- Projects/programs are scoped, designed, and planned up front by aid agencies, in order to justify the allocation of public funds (in comparison to the corporate world, and to political and bureaucratic settings).
- Implementation of projects/programs takes place with more or less involvement of the recipients, who again are government or non-government organizations of "third world countries." Projects/programs may or may not be implemented with temporary or permanent presence of a representative from the "first world" or international agency (here intercultural relations come into play).
- The project/program organizations are to have a positive developmental impact on the vast number of ultimately intended beneficiaries (a *societal level* intention with a long-term perspective), who are eligible for an intervention as they are perceived as under-resourced, without capacities, and not sufficiently able to help themselves (this engenders urgency and pressure for results).

Projects and programs come with resources (people, money, equipment, training, advising, networking) that are used to develop local capacity in different ways. Consultants like the authors are hired by aid agencies for short-term tasks like planning or evaluations of projects/programs, or to support implementation and organizations

---

[51] These were COMiT (Berlin, Germany) and, from 2000, Baobab Consulting and Training (Cape Town, South Africa).

in the medium term, or to "build capacities" with sustainable impacts, often through training. Consultants are engaged to fix what is broken for conflict resolution, or for concrete outputs like a plan or a piece of research. Consultants are rarely engaged to support what is already there in people and organizations.

Many development managers are professional planners, trained to be rational, logical, sequential, and cyclic. The approach encompasses the following:

- problem-orientation
- researching situations
- comparing alternative strategies
- appraising and evaluating
- formulating intended solutions
- specifying respective objectives by indicators
- assessing risks of strategies
- involving stakeholders and beneficiaries
- arguing for preferred solutions
- drawing geographical maps and organizational charts
- writing voluminous reports and studies
- operationalizing projects
- aligning and coordinating role-players
- mediating conflicts
- explaining and training
- organizational consulting, monitoring and evaluating
- new problems, researching another situation.

Our Approach to Development

As development practitioners, what made "us" tick was our dedicated search for the emancipation of impoverished societies, for an improvement in poor people's livelihoods, for ways to support people to develop better abilities to cope with their challenges, for ways to facilitate capacity development through participatory processes, and for significant and sustainable impact of our interventions. Even though our intentions were similar, our motivations came from different sources: our own personal experiences of growing up in Africa/Asia and/or in poverty, politicized student years and liberation struggles, religious beliefs, and more.

Our team of trainers already represented the younger generation of development practitioners.[52] Our specialization was that we were people-driven and intervened on multiple levels of system: individual, groups, organizations, regions, and sometimes on the national level. Working in these different levels of government and community systems posed highly complex challenges. Interventions could encompass and be orchestrated on five levels:

- change of globally determined frameworks (like World Bank headed debt relief conditions or poverty reduction strategies for highly indebted countries);[53]
- national level societal and institutional change (like the introduction of a quality check on foreseeable impact of public investments into national planning and monitoring procedures);
- change at the level of sub-national agencies and in organizations (like decentralization of government, or advising local communities);
- change in small systems (like consulting with non-governmental organizations, small enterprises, self-help groups, team coaching);
- personal, individual growth and change (training, coaching, and mentoring of individuals).

We came from an emancipatory position and were well versed in theories of dependency and anti-imperialism, which include corresponding methodologies and tools. We often worked, via facilitating participatory processes, with workshops as key elements. And we trained development practitioners to complement their sector and subject-matter specializations (as agriculturalists, medical persons, managers, engineers, educators, craftsmen, bankers, etc.) with development professionalism and the ability to manage people processes.

Until the mid-1990s, we conducted consultancies, facilitation, and training in the mainstream "management-by-objectives"[54] paradigm: deriving objectives from an analysis of problems; trying to pursue defined objectives with specific and locally adjusted measures.

It is worthwhile to say explicitly that the problem/objectives-orientation was not inappropriate. In strategic aspects our interventions were effective. For example:

---

[52] This generation succeeded those who had adopted a helper-approach to development (1960s), or the economic redistribution-approach (1970s). We built on this with an emancipation-approach (1980s), and were mindful of the global-structuring approach (1990s).

[53] We were not ourselves specialized in the present development mainstream of influencing global (and national level) frame-conditions, although some of our clients were.

[54] An approach to management which orientates all activities and resources to end/predefined objectives.

- At the end of a five-day structured planning process, involving major role-players working on pin boards and flipcharts on an Indian Ocean beach in East Africa, the Ministerial officials, the European donors, the community activists, and the members of women groups reached a joint understanding of what was to be done by whom, when, where, and with what specifications. Plus these people from different backgrounds developed informal personal relationships.
- A well-structured, step-by-step process of designing, testing, and disseminating an inclusive communal planning approach in a country plagued by extreme social divisions laid the foundation for open political controversies and discussions on local public investment priorities. This mobilized civil society to such a degree that transparency has kept corruption in check, irresponsible actions (including non-action) by public servants have caused mass protests, and old divides have started to mend.
- After a three week-long training course in a systematic regional planning process, participants emerged with substantially increased abilities to think strategically. The training used a case simulation that was complex and specific enough to reflect the multiple ambivalences in decision-making, leaving the participants better able to deal with complex, ambiguous situations.
- A week-long facilitation skills course, with video-feedback, was an eye-opener for most participants with respect to personal and professional styles of social interaction, and raised awareness of their own behavior in work and life.

Discovering the Gestalt Approach

By the mid-1990s, however, we were challenged to look beyond the problem and objectives-orientation, as we experienced some inefficiencies and ineffectiveness in our work. For example:

- In planning workshops, we often found out later that we had not dealt with real and major issues. Instead, topics of secondary importance were extensively discussed and elaborated (e.g., in a three-year strategic planning exercise with a non-government organization, the imminent policy change of its main client which excluded the organization from being further contracted was only mentioned; four months after the workshop, the organization went into bankruptcy).

- On other occasions, decisions made during workshops turned out not to be reliable and did not translate into commitments (e.g., promises to allocate resources to a joint undertaking were not kept by one party).
- We were at a loss as to how to influence the participants' workplace application of learning from our courses; participants often were frustrated at the disinterest of colleagues/superiors in what they had learnt, or by the resistances encountered in the face of suggestions for improvement.
- We ourselves were often taken aback at what was happening between ourselves and clients in positive and negative ways.

We wanted to learn not only to understand and empathize with others, but also to stand in observation of ourselves and others in order to become aware of what goes on between/among us and others. We felt the need to explore and influence behavior change in others, knowing that new behavior is always required of others (course participants, community members, women, youth, farmers; in general, beneficiaries of development interventions) when development "happens" (e.g., farmers tend crops differently when new equipment is introduced).[55] We needed to understand human behavior and change better.

So, in the early 1990s, we looked for a qualification in "supervision" that nowadays would be called "coaching." We considered it an opportunity that each summer we worked together as a team of three to five trainers in the Development Management course, and that we could complement our facilitation of the training by being trained ourselves on the same occasion.

In Berlin, a Gestalt center offered Gestalt education for teachers, and we found an English-speaking Gestalt therapist who engaged with us in a special supervision/coaching training of some 150 hours over two years under the auspices of the Technical University of Berlin. The program was geared toward us as consultants and trainers in developing countries. What immediately excited and engaged us about the Gestalt approach was the directness and intensity of dealing with emerging issues in the moment.[56] The combination of self-experience and experimenting in

---

[55] The purpose of a development project/program in our planning methodology always described the changes in behavior of the envisaged beneficiaries to be brought about by the utilization of whatever the development project or program offered.

[56] One of the authors recalls: "I remember that I asked her to give me an in-a-nutshell demonstration of what Gestalt is. She responded by saying: "Are you aware that you shook your head as if to say 'no' when you asked me to demonstrate to you what Gestalt is?"

practice, based on comparatively (to our approach) few core concepts, was fascinating. The principle of identifying and addressing the real issue directly, of going to core needs, was probably the most attractive one.

Next, six out of the ten people in this supervision/coaching training subsequently participated in the Gestalt Institute of Cleveland (GIC) *International Organization and Systems Development (IOSD) Program*[57] (from IOSD 2 in 1995-96 onwards), our Berlin trainer included. The IOSD took our professional and team learning to depths of intensity not experienced before. We went through fundamental changes in ourselves; and we watched and learned how the faculty evoked and provoked these changes. The IOSD changed all of us personally, with issues of identity and motivation being uppermost.

A year after completing IOSD, the late Benny Nganqashe from Transkei in South Africa said: *"I went there as a black female* (= with the hurt and anger of growing up as black non-person in apartheid South Africa), *and I have now become a Xhosa lady"* (= Xhosa is the society and culture in the Transkei, where she and also Nelson Mandela originated) (personal communication).

The most important social competencies we learned in IOSD were to read others and make space for what is, to work with silence, to listen actively for what reverberates within us when working with others, and to work with these data as living materials; in short, the use of self.

Integrating the Gestalt Approach

A week after session 1 of IOSD 2 (May 1995), two of our team began the annual six-week Development Management training in Berlin. Immediately, the training approach shifted and we used what we had learned in the coaching training and the IOSD:

- Instead of asking people to introduce themselves individually (name, job, professional background), we used group constellations/sculpturing to highlight the rich diversity and potential for mutual learning in the group/whole system.
- Instead of ice-breakers, we used body and awareness experiences.
- Instead of leaving more revealing self-presentations to happen by

---

[57] The International OSD Program consists of five week-long sessions over eighteen months, each held in a different venue around the world, offering participants (typically groups of 36 people from about 14 different countries) theory, concepts and methodology, and an experiential grounding in Gestalt OSD. The Program was launched in 1993-94, based on the Cleveland-based OSD Program. It is currently offered jointly with the Gestalt International Study Center (GISC).

chance between individuals, we facilitated sharing data and making contact via collage supported self-presentations.

- Instead of only brainstorming, we also used guided imagery experiences.
- Instead of competition games for team building, we used a step-by-step and process-reflective experience in "temple construction."
- Instead of our randomly organizing task teams, we ventured into choice-evoking group dynamic procedures of team formation.
- Instead of evaluations, we used feedback processes among our participants as well as among ourselves.
- Instead of the trainers advising participants, we used case consultations and coaching groups that train participants to consult with/for one another.
- Instead of a completely planned course schedule, we used unstructured open spaces, we worked with silence, and the schedules became windowpanes to be filled as we went along in the process.

All of the above reflected our initial fascination with a world that we had not accessed before our encounter with the Gestalt approach: we could suddenly reach much deeper waters with others, and we could become more real with and true to them and ourselves. Instead of biting our fingers when we did not cover preplanned schedules, we felt okay with going with participants' abilities to absorb.

The methods acquired through the Gestalt approach increased the depth and impact of our training, all the while that we continued to provide the crucial contents of development management:

- How to *design development interventions professionally*
- How to *plan projects and manage implementation*
- How to *facilitate participatory processes.*

And the change in style was a change in approach as well as in impact.

Predictably, we struggled and encountered resistances in ourselves and with others; here are some instances:

- Our own learning with Gestalt methods had touched us deeply and profoundly; while still open and in process, we were solidifying it into theory, tools, and methods to work with others. Our enthusiasm about Gestalt approaches to learning (open/process-focused, substantial, philosophical, human nature-related) as complementary to our technical training embodied and projected our own need for more. Our focus on tools and methods ("*How* we make our participants have an experience like we had") was coupled with our shallow, beginners' understanding of the context and variations of such methods.

- We struggled to convince our client (the commissioning government agency for the Development Management trainings) to dare do something so weird as to engage in emotional and subconscious aspects of management and leadership behavior, and we confronted a senior manager's mocking of our bodywork exercises.
- In the excitement of the new approach and the demands of the work, we sometimes "forgot" about self-development, self-care, and what happened with us—necessary constituents of Gestalt practice.
- We did not always focus on the real actual process of the group and individuals, as we did not have enough process awareness or skill ourselves. We struggled with facilitating Gestalt methods, putting them into a sequence that made sense for us as incremental learning experience, that also fitted the established technical training of development managers (our brief from the client).
- We did not know what to do with our fear that we might provoke emotions and reactions among participants that we could not contain (in one case, this happened with a borderline participant).
- We occasionally managed to hire a coach for our own supervision during the training course, but generally encountered loneliness as beginners with not enough (affordable) support through really experienced Gestalt seniors.

In the years that followed, we worked more intensively with combining the technical development management learning with evoking in participants an awareness of self, intentionality in intervening, and sense of place and power of self as managers/leaders of development interventions and change. The facility of a residential training over weeks gave us the opportunity to support intensive contact between individuals, powerful subgroup engagements, and effective learning from one another in a complex multicultural environment.[58]

---

[58] These courses, as mentioned above, typically hosted twenty-five participants from fifteen to twenty different countries (in South-East Asia, South Asia, Middle Asia, East Europe, Arab countries, East-/West-/Southern Africa, sometimes the Caribbean and rarely Latin America). As an anecdote: the different cultures posed quite a challenge to the venue cook, who had to prepare each meal for vegetarians and meat-eaters, and for

How Information Technology Reinforced our Gestalt-Biased Shift Toward Management/Leadership as Social Skills Based on AWARENESS

In 2002-03, we introduced a three to four weeks online preparatory phase and reduced the residential training component of the Development Management courses. This made sense in terms of participants' time away from the workplace and the expense of residential training. In this online phase, we introduced participants to the theoretical knowledge and tools aspects, so that we could use the face-to-face training for exercises and experiences. In order to do this, we invested in setting up a 160 mb "learning landscape" on a CD and website (www.baobab-ct.org), which we use as the basis of the online training syllabus. (It covers project planning, monitoring systems, organizational structures, evaluating, communication, facilitation, work groups, emotions, conflict resolution, systems approach, economic and ecological sustainability, participation, target group and gender orientation, self-help, capacity building, and using Gestalt as an orientation for intervening in organizations and systems.)

Importantly, the online phase is also used to introduce the group to one another and to start the contact and group-building process. We struggled with the practicalities of facilitating meaningful contact online: we had ourselves trained in online facilitation,[59] and together with our training in the Gestalt approach, successfully blended technical online training with intentional group interactions in virtual space (e-mail and forum). One aspect of this approach was to pay attention to the senses when communicating online: since we are not all stimulated visually and with words, we introduced the use of pictures and vivid descriptions to share personal data and circumstances. This was rich and exciting as participants communicated from their homes and offices in rural China, southern India, peri-urban Kenya, Zimbabwe, and Cape Town. When these people eventually came together in Germany, they were excited to meet face-to-face, and could "hit-the-ground running" with the residential phase of the training. During the four weeks of residential training, we were engaged in deepening the understanding of topics. We invited participants to facilitate groups, we worked on individual

---

the different preferences/ taboos of Hindus (holy cows) and Muslims (no pork), Asians (sticky rice) and Africans (polenta), as well as the usual demands for high-protein or lowfat, no-wheat or dairy diets.

[59] With Nancy White, Full Circle Associates (www.fullcircle.com).

awareness, we sometimes chose to work with an elaborate simulation case, we organized consulting site visits to local development-oriented projects and programs, we provided space for every person to elaborate systematically on his/her own situation and receive detailed feedback, we used a variety of group constellations and group forming procedures for intercultural contacts. We tried to balance professional development work with self-development. We set up spaces for processes to happen and for participants to work across all levels of systems. Importantly, after closure, already established long distance, internet-based connection allowed for ongoing self-organized networking in the groups across the globe.

The Impact

Here are some comments on the impact of the Development Management course of 2003, elicited seven months after its closure. They reflect the balance of subject matter as well as developmental and personal progress, which we have found to be typical since we added Gestalt elements.

- **Joseline** (Ugandan, working for German Volunteer Service, project manager, Kampala): "I remember the course as an eye-opener, a very rich learning experience especially due to the fact that we were from 19 African and Asian countries. . . . It had intercultural exposure which is necessary for the kind of work I am doing and intend to continue doing. This has built my competence to deal with people of different ethnic backgrounds. . . . Specifically impactful were the field/study groups, group discussions/group work; we were learning by doing. . . . I still feel that there is need for follow-up or continued referral to the Boabab CD: It's like a bible to me."
- **Luisa** (Philippina, National Development Agency, sector specialist for agricultural development, Manila): "I remember this course as a very good learning experience at a personal and professional level. Specially impactful was the personal interaction received from the trainers/facilitators and the participants; this interaction further strengthened my social competence as well as my leadership skills . . . . It has brought about a higher degree of consciousness regarding development work, as well as intercultural and interpersonal relations. I feel that I have yet to make an impact here in my organization. Despite formal re-echoing sessions, it is quite difficult to expect an immediate change in work settings, knowing the

"little" clout I have in the organization. However, I am proud to say that bits, pieces, and chunks of formal and informal experiences and learning from the course are offered and shared. I would like to make a difference, so I wish to continue learning."

- **Mohamed** (Iranian, Rural Development Research for advising government policies and investment decisions, Ministry of Agriculture, Teheran): "I need to admit that my stay in Germany and contact with people from different places of the world with a variety of ideas and thoughts was one of the most outstanding periods of my life. Your remarkable personalities played an important role for this feeling. To tell the truth, facilitation in general, and communication skills in particular, are my most favorite topics from the learning material . . . . I believe now that just spending money for implementing a project, exclusive of setting up a trained monitoring and evaluation system, will not be successful. I'd like to say that in spite of the reward, I had some limitation to enjoying completely during the course . . . and that was my shyness and lack in English speaking capability."

- **Xiaouchun** (Chinese, Technology Department in the Centre of Energy and Environmental Protection, Ministry of Agriculture, Beijing): "I could remember so much, you know, it's my first foreign country what I had been to. It's a study and communication course. Specially impactful is the power of good communication in the interculture cooperation program. Some methodologies, as the too inflexible beforehand plan of operation, were frustrating."

- **Halake** (Kenya, French funded international NGO working for improving frame conditions of children's lives): "I remember the course in some instances as an enabler at personal and organizational levels in terms of adding value to skills development and intervention approaches. At times confusing, particularly awareness raising. Otherwise, the course was enjoyable and interesting. Impactful were the intensive engagement, the systems approach, the experiential learning. Raising awareness was for me frustrating and confusing . . . . I consult the Baobab-CD."

Using the Gestalt Approach in Consulting in Complex Societal Systems

Alongside our training work, we consult to development programs and projects via (mainly) international aid agencies. The uptake of Gestalt

OSD has been more challenging in our consulting work. Development work, since its emergence in the 1960s, deals with unlocking resources, with support for emancipation and self-development capabilities, and with reducing poverty as a mass phenomenon. Development work, especially in the last couple of years, has been publicly criticized for not delivering proclaimed improvements, and for being wasteful or even damaging, probably with the exception of relief operations (which, in our understanding, do not constitute development work but are rather disaster mitigation measures). Development organizations and their representatives are subject to public and political pressures. The vast majority of development managers are actually administrators, as they are government employees and/or donor dependant. What matters from their perspective are: (in this sequence of importance) visible and fast outcomes, which are significant and (lastly) should be sustainable. The pressure to deliver becomes a determining focus and a comfort zone, a place to deflect into, getting active and busy. Development managers are more scared than energized by innovative approaches, and by the adjusting of concepts to the conditions of the here and now. Consultants are expected to know better and to provide advice. Hence as Gestalt consultants, we work with outright resistances to our process-oriented paradigm aimed at unlocking the client group's own resources.

For us, the breakthrough came in 2006 when we learned and applied the Cape Cod Model for Intervening in Small Systems[60] to societal-level work in Africa. For us, the relevant features of the Model were: distinguishing and working with process rather than the content of the client's interactions in the moment; literally seeing and considering the system as a whole with unique dynamics connecting all; affirming the client's strengths/developed aspects as a way of acknowledging and affirming and releasing energy for further work; and the immediacy and power of working in the moment, especially experimenting with new ways of doing things.

---

[60] The Cape Cod Model is an approach to small systems interventions, with roots in family therapy, developed and taught by Sonia March Nevis and her team at the Gestalt International Study Center (GISC), Cape Cod, Massachusetts. The approach is used by team coaches, organizational consultants, psychotherapists and other mental health and social service professionals, executives, educators, and other professionals concerned with small systems. Clients systems are asked to engage with one other, observed by the consultant team (usually of two people); the consultants then give feedback on the client's process by open discussion amongst themselves and directly to the client. (See Nevis, Melnick, and Nevis, 2008)

The Story

First, the context. We were facilitating a profound capacity building program for employees of a South African government development Trust, which supports national and provincial government departments in their implementation of development programs. Many of their programs deal with poverty reduction. There are interventions in infrastructure (schools, health care facilities); local complex support to communities (production centers, business amenities, social measures); and sector-related activities (e.g., in environmental affairs with labor-intensive technologies). The Trust is also involved in policy dialogues on high levels.

Our training with the Trust ran over five months for a total of about sixteen days. It focused on building participants' capacities to deal professionally with typical dilemmas of socioeconomic development interventions. Most program managers in the Trust came from a social worker background. Their familiarity with the challenges of openly addressing the "real" issue with a client, of engaging with required technical expertise, of dealing with sociocultural diversity, and of having a stance in politically conflictive institutional situations stemmed from scattered experience only. This experience remained largely unreflected, and frustrations were high.

Our intention in the training was to arrange for possibilities of impressive alternative experiences. We had packaged the professional development aspects into an instrument, which we call Poverty Reduction Impact Appraisal (PRIA). It allows the rapid in-depth diagnosis of any program or project, provided one comes with the respective background.

We applied PRIA in site visits to five of the Trust's programs. The event was organized as cross-examination (no officers appraised the program for which they were responsible). This is where we brought in the Cape Cod Model—as the way of applying PRIA with clients. We took three days to prepare participants with an introduction to Gestalt theory, awareness experiences, the ability to distinguish data and interpretation, and to stay in awareness; we demonstrated and practiced case consultations on the individual/family level with the focus on supporting the client system; we held a long discussion about optimism and simulated a session with the Cape Cod Model approach in the classroom; and we devoted time to team building. Three-quarters of the participants were in the "doubting Thomas"-state when they went out for the first (of two) visit(s) to their "clients," programs of the Trust. They were also anxious about their technical PRIA capabilities.

When they came back on the first evening (of a two day interaction), three out of five groups were completely surprised at the positive client reactions to the Cape Cod Model approach. Initially, some clients reacted with, "Why are you here if you don't bring money or solve our problems?" Others asked, "What is this?" when faced with the instruction to talk among themselves rather than to the consultants; and to sit in two half circles, which allowed the consultants and the clients to interact with one another as well as among themselves. And one group was so in doubt about the approach that they gave in to the client, forgot to talk among themselves, and slipped up on the process that first day.

Those who used the procedure reported that they found themselves free from their usual role of enquiring about issues. They were free from "being like a teacher" and "having to control all the time" because "the clients are also in control; you sit and listen, and you can think." The engagement between consultants and clients was on an equal footing. One group said: "This is like a traditional African meeting of elders, like when the president and the ministers go to communities and sit with them to listen." Importantly, the Cape Cod Model is culturally "in-synch" with African traditions.

What amazed us most were the full report backs given by the site visit teams after the second and final visit. By then, all were either enthusiastic or firmly positive about the Cape Cod model. Even the doubtful groups had been infected by the positive experiences of those who used the process. The depth of insight into the cases, the detail grasped on what was going on with the clients, the focus on what was important, the learning on alternative options for government departments plus the Trust as implementation agency—all of those things were a qualitative quantum jump compared to our previous trainings. In addition, the feedback from the clients not only referred to insights in strategic aspects of running their programs, but also acknowledged the immediate shifts experienced during the process.

An example

In one community, a land issue had led to intense inner-community conflicts. Previous interventions, over a decade, had focused on the uplifting of the community members by providing infrastructure for irrigation and other agricultural activities, advising farmers, and providing credits and subsidies. All of those are standard measures in a situation of poor agricultural income. Many of the interventions were not appreciated: the nursery was vandalized the evening before the Minister of

Agriculture came to visit, tractors were stolen by one faction and dumped in the bush, and a watchman for the machines was killed by the faction that had no access to the equipment. The Trust, as well as other agencies, referred to this community with sighs of "Oh God, this place/these people!!!" In their second meeting, our PRIA-site-visit team fed back to the community how they themselves had started fighting with each other during and after the first visit, and how drained and angry they were. They made it clear that their fighting was mirroring the situation of the community. At the end of the process, the consultant team and we trainers were told that this was the first time an outsider intervener had acknowledged the real issue dividing the community, and had understood that material "help" actually fueled the conflict rather than resolved it.

Closing Thoughts: on Power, and the Use of "I" in Collective "We" Cultures

With a view toward looking forward to future challenges, we conclude this (minor) success story by touching on some challenges encountered as we develop our practice.

The Special Question of Power in Working with Gestalt Methods in Societal Development

As mentioned above, the mainstream of development institutions since the 1990s have tended toward interventions on the global and national levels of systems, and focused on setting frame conditions[61] right. Some elements that have contributed to this trend are:

- learning from disappointingly little positive impact on livelihoods of the mass of people, in spite of a multitude of efforts and millions of dollars spent with good intentions;
- the funneling of public funds through highly centralized, oligopolistic international and national institutions which fuels the attraction of possibly influencing a multitude of situations through global or national steering mechanisms.

---

[61] Frame conditions constitute the environment in which development projects and programs operate. They affect (adversely or otherwise) the achievement of development objectives, for example: ecological frame conditions (e.g., limited natural resources), economic frame conditions (e.g., limited sales markets, foreign exchange bottlenecks, high level of foreign debt), political-institutional frame conditions (e.g., limited flexibility of state administration) and sociocultural frame conditions (e.g., care of social and client relationships has high importance).

Concrete projects and programs these days are usually in support of economic structural adjustment and sector investment programs, of democratization/good governance and furthering civil society, and of international contracts/resolutions/protocols/regulations. Setting aside discussions on the *legitimacy* of intervening in foreign sovereign countries and on the *competency* to do so, what matters in our case is the debate on where an intervener can best leverage appropriate power. This debate plays out between *structuralist* theories and postmodernist *actor* theories (see Rauch, 2004; and Capra, 2002, pp. 61-82). It asks:

- Is it that the structures, institutions, and systems (which come out of actions of individuals and organizations) establish the rules according to which games and strategies of interest groups and their interplay devolve? And hence is it that the structures and systems are the decisive levers for influencing development/change (e.g., enforcing standards around human rights or good governance)? Or

- Is it that the initiatives and innovative, or even revolutionary, actions of individuals and groups/organizations gain energy and then "structuralize" or change systems and institutions (e.g., digitalization, internet, informal networking, self-help, and interest groups)?

The dilemma for us as Gestalt-oriented development practitioners is to bring together the trend of development institutions towards a *structuralist* approach; and to bring our people-potentials movement paradigm to intervene along the *actor* approach. It has taken substantial effort to sell our process and systems approach to desk officers in state and parastatal development agencies. The agencies deal with rules and regulations first and people development as an afterthought. We have by and large not been completely successful. Thus the "development world" may be a different setting compared to the "corporate world," where competition, initiative, and innovation are inbuilt and provide an actor-oriented bias.

Working with the "I" in Collective/ "We" Cultures

If culture is the common subconscious—values, beliefs, institutions, perceptions, symbols, etc.—that one group has in common and that distinguishes it from other groups, then it should only be possible to perceive one's own culture if members of one group make contact (in the Gestalt sense) with members from culturally different groups. Raising intercultural awareness requires "the other." Boundaries of cultures are arbitrary and dependent on context: there are traditional and ethnic and social movement, and urban and family and national and religious and women and in-group, cultures.

Most of the clients with whom we work come from more collectivist cultures (Hofstede, 1994).[62] We experience difficulties talking about, and even conceptualizing, the 'I' and 'me' in the face of a strong and prevailing "we" and "us" (e.g., "We in India. . ."). Giving personal feedback, taking individual responsibility for sexual behavior in the HIV/Aids-pandemic, and having individually calculated and functional business relationships are difficult. *Clientelistic*[63] relationships within the relevant collective are predominant. One finds that life is about adhering to the "dos and don'ts" of traditions: someone says, "If I have AIDS, I will not die alone"; "we" in business or work treat friends particularly and preferentially; "we" support the children of relatives; "we" give presents to patrons and favors to dependants; "we" prioritize social investment before economic investment. Can you imagine how the famous Gestalt prayer sounds to a person from a collectivist background?

> "I do my thing, and you do your thing. I am not in this world to live up to your expectations, and you are not in this world to live up to mine. You are you, and I am I. And if by chance we find each other, it's beautiful. If not, it can't be helped."(Shepard, 1975, p. 3)

We are constantly mindful of and monitor the potential disjunction. Interestingly, it has been our experience in protected multicultural training situations—like in the above example of the Development Management Course—that personality differences outweigh cultural alliances. An Arab person would rather group with an Indian, a South African, and an Indonesian than with other Arabs; this is how the particular individuals "click" and make contact with one another. It

---

[62] "On the collectivist side we find societies where people, from the time they are born, are integrated into strong, cohesive groups: often their extended families (with grandparents, uncles, aunts) or clans continue to protect them in exchange for unquestioning loyalty . . . . On the individualist side we find societies in which the ties between individuals are loose: everyone is expected to look after himself or herself and the immediate family" (based on Hofstede, 1975, and excerpted from the Baobab-CD's Facilitation learning module/ Group/Intercultural Management).

[63] Clientelism refers to a form of social organization characterized by "patron-client" relationships. Relatively powerful and rich "patrons" promise to provide relatively powerless and poor "clients" with jobs, protection, infrastructure, and other benefits in exchange for votes and other forms of loyalty, including labor. These relationships are typically exploitative, often resulting in the perpetual indebtedness of the client. Abbreviated from: http:// *www.unsp.edu/cnr/gem/ambassador/whatisclientelism.htm*

seems to us that individualism is fostered in such culturally neutralized settings.

Conclusion

Looking back over thirteen years of working with Gestalt methods in our development management consulting and training work, we have shifted focus. We no longer offer mainly technically oriented development project management (training or consulting) influenced by Gestalt methods in supporting individual or systemic change. These days we are contracting mainly around systems change, in which personal growth and team development are primary, and the technical aspects may contribute.

Much of this work has been done in the public sector (government administration) in South Africa. Here, with a history of oppression and racial segregation, Gestalt methods of affirming, acknowledging, and validating the reality of each human being have found resonance and brought healing. New learning and awareness of Gestalt perception theory, and experiencing multiple realities, have brought individually responsible insights into diversity and difference.

We now offer "Gestalt" programs as part of our leadership and team development interventions, and they are usually fully subscribed. We celebrate this and, at the same time, continue to go back and forth with clients on the tension between the technical/content and our process offerings. Sometimes, we wear the technical "hat" and take it off to make a process comment; more often, we wear the process "hat" and lift it slightly to make a comment about the technical content; and as we experience the latter as more impactful, the hat fits more snugly.[64] Ultimately how we hold the two in this tension, showing up authentically and sharing our own dilemmas, is what brings connection and learning between our clients and us.

---

[64] South Africans relate to the "two hats" metaphor. In the early days of liberation, dual membership in the African National Congress and the Congress of South African Trade Unions sparked the "two hats debate"; audiences demanded that speakers identify which hat they were wearing when they made statements about South Africa's future economic policies.

Jochen Lohmeier, PhD, is a Gestalt practitioner, learning facilitator, and Emotional Intelligence leadership trainer. He is a senior consultant in socioeconomic development, specializing in design, planning, management, and assessment of complex projects and programs. He has worked in over thirty countries around the globe for more than thirty years (as planner, manager, trainer, advisor) and speaks several languages. He is passionate about Africa and has lived in Tanzania, the Central African Republic and South Africa. He has run consulting firms in Germany and South Africa (currently as co-chair of Lohmeier-Wyley Associates/Baobab Consulting and Training in Cape Town).
Contact: *lohmeier@iafrica.com*

Chantelle Wyley, MIS is a South African facilitator and trainer. She has a background in antiapartheid work and community capacity building, which led to international experience in training in the management of socioeconomic development; and she also employs computer-based and online learning. Her current focus is leadership development using Gestalt and emotional intelligence, and reintroducing Gestalt training in South Africa. She is co-chair of Lohmeier-WyleyAssociates/Baobab Consulting and Training, based in Cape Town; and is a practitioner of Iyengar yoga.
Contact: *cwyley@baobab-ct.org*

References

Baobab CD: A learning facility for development management and networking (2002). Cape Town: Baobab Consulting and Training/ Lohmeier Wyley Associates. [compact disk]

Capra, F. (2002). *The hidden connections.* New York: Flamingo/Harper.

Hofstede, G. (1994). *Cultures and organizations: Software of the mind: Intercultural cooperation and its importance for survival.* New York: McGraw-Hill; London: HarperCollins.

Nevis, E., Melnick, J., & Nevis, S. (2008). Organization change through powerful micro-level interventions. *ODN Practitioner, 40*(3), 4-8.

Rauch, T. (2004). Bessere Rahmenbedingungen allein beseitigen Armut nicht—eine theoriegeleitete 4-Ebenen Strategie für entwicklungspolitische Interventionen. *Geographica Helvetica, II,* 79-91.

Shepard, M. (1975). *Fritz.* Sagaponack, New York: Second Chance Press.

Wyley, C., & Lohmeier, J. (2003). Development project management. In B. Hazeltine & C. Bull (Eds.), *Field guide to appropriate technology* (pp. 18-29). San Diego, CA: Academic Press.

CHAPTER 12

Using The Gestalt Approach In Developing Social Change Practitioners in The North of Ireland

Seán Gaffney, PhD

Editors' Introduction

This chapter is a brief summary of over fifteen years of dedicated, continuous training, supervision, and consulting in the political "hot box" that is the North of Ireland. Starting out as a trainer of Gestalt therapists, Gaffney quickly realized that the people he was training and developing were just as passionate about promoting social change as they were about individual development, and that the latter was always in the context of the socio-cultural and political situation in which they and their clients lived their lives. Also being extremely passionate about the welfare of all of Ireland, Gaffney then viewed part of his mission as one of supporting people to be more effective in carrying out their social change initiatives, in addition to being good Gestalt practitioners.

There are at least two critical issues raised by this chapter. One has to do with the importance of deep understanding of the cultural forces in any part of the world in which one may be working—whether that be a foreign land or one's own country. This is important not only for providing context and a field perspective, but also for creating healthy environments that may allow growth to take place. And it tells us, once again, that people cannot make "clean" observations of a present situation if they carry a lot of unfinished business from the past.

The second issue—actually more of a dilemma—is how interveners stay open and do not become confluent when they have a strong interest in the trainees' outcome. It would appear that Gaffney has managed this dilemma by being a demanding teacher. Yet, a plausible hypothesis is that strong identification with people who have been living under traumatic circumstances is just what is needed to support their learning. Gaffney's work suggests the challenge of being both tough and supportive at the same time.

Introduction[65]

The development and application of any theory or practice is influenced greatly by the cultural milieu in which it takes place. Indeed, it can be said that a theoretical model is grounded in the time and setting from which it emerges. Gestalt therapy was created and grew in a moment when forces for democracy, individual expression, and an anti-bourgeois movement were prominent. It took root in the Unites States in the 1950s as a radical, powerful approach to self-actualization and self-expression, in the context of a fairly unified country full of itself as a victor in World War II and as an economic and military giant. And as Western Europe began to develop in similar directions, Gestalt therapy was exported back to the area of its origins with a carry forward of the drive for individualism.

As the Gestalt approach has been introduced into cultures that do not match the original setting of its development, it has become clear that its application requires new thinking and modification to fit different societal needs. For example, what are the implications for application in cultures where there has been long internal conflict, where everything is politicized, and where the need for social change may be more critical than individual expression or, indeed, may be a requirement for creating a climate in which people can better flourish? Can the basic model provide ways to deal better with social issues in cultures undergoing conflict, upheaval, and discontinuous change, such as the North of Ireland, Russia and former states of the USSR, and the Middle East? Indeed, how can we modify or expand the Gestalt approach to deal with difficult issues in well-established Western countries, such as the problems of immigration and guest workers in Northern European countries and the United States?

This chapter explores the sociopolitical and sociocultural contexts and the work of Gestalt practitioners in the North of Ireland—in therapy, supervision, group work, community work, voluntary and political

---

[65] With a warm dedication to Edwin Nevis and Philip Lichtenberg.

organizations, and their contributions to the society in which they practice. Whilst the setting is unique, with many cultural and political particulars, it is the author's contention and experience that there is much that can be extrapolated to other areas of such or similar social complexity. In order to conduct this exploration, the author (a southern Irishman resident of Sweden, working regularly in the North) will use his own experience in the Region in various contexts, as well as references to the ongoing work of local Gestalt practitioners. Where relevant, Gestalt-based theoretical models, which wholly or partly originated in the work described in the article, will be used to clarify some issues and to provide a possible framework for Gestalt practitioners elsewhere.

My work in the North and my continued journey there started when I participated in a workshop at a European Association for Gestalt Therapy (EAGT) conference in Cambridge, England in 1995. The workshop was run by the first training organization to have started Gestalt therapy programs in Belfast. In a conversation with the trainers after the workshop, it was apparent that they needed a male trainer, and I wanted to join them. I started as a trainer with Program 3, in 1996. By 1997, I had been approached by a group of program graduates for supervision. Since, then I have been working as a clinical and organizational supervisor, occasionally as a therapist, and as an organization development consultant. The latter work was the source of a paper (Gaffney, 2004) and is briefly mentioned in this chapter. The group supervision work has also been treated in a paper on group supervision in a divided society, with in-text comments from an Australian, a Lebanese, and an Israeli practitioner (Gaffney, 2008).

Being born and bred in Ireland, and now a resident of Sweden since 1975, means that I am emotionally and intellectually close enough to those with whom I work, while living at a distance. I am deeply committed to helping my students, supervisees, and clients have an impact in resolving the political and economic problems in the Region. I make on average six trips a year to Belfast, with up to ten weeks a year spent working there. It is the most stimulating and worthwhile work I do, with exciting people, worthy of respect for their competence, social and political involvement, and willingness to engage fully in their development as persons and professionals—with each of these factors nourishing the other.

Gestalt practitioners have established an influential presence in many areas of society in the North of Ireland. Through the consistent and appreciated application of the core competencies of the Gestaltist—use of self, awareness, contact, figure-ground, and an active acknowledgement of both person and environment as valid forces of the field dynamics of the Region—they have had an impact which is truly a whole that is greater than the sum of its constituent parts. This work is usually with community development; the needs of minorities; rural poverty; people displaced from the North by sectarian and paramilitary activities; and efforts to revive economic activities in areas deprived of investment and stable social development over nearly forty years of armed conflict, and just as many years of previous government neglect.

A Note on the Naming of Things

Before looking at the social context and the work of Gestalt practitioners, it is useful to define some key terms. The term "North of Ireland" is being used here to denote two primary aspects of working in the region: 1. the naming of things—people, places, events, buildings, pets, etc., can always be seen as a political statement there; and 2. recent developments with regard to support from the European Union and other political initiatives have made "cross-border" work more normal and acceptable. With regard to the first aspect, my name—Seán, a Gaelic name—clearly frames me as Irish rather than British, of the Catholic tradition, certainly Nationalist in my politics, and possibly Irish Republican. In addition, using "Northern Ireland" would mean that I agree with the continued partitioned colonization of a part of my home country by a foreign power. I do not agree with it. So, for me, it is the North of Ireland, a geographical description with a political content.

As for the second aspect, the "border" is the now formally rather defunct national border between that part of the United Kingdom of Great Britain and Northern Ireland (UK) known by the British as "Northern Ireland," and the Republic of Ireland to the south and west. "Cross-border" then refers to areas of the Region that straddle the former border, "north and south" politically speaking.

The Social Context of the Work—Political

In the increasingly postcolonial world of the second half of the twentieth century, Northern Ireland long remained an anachronistic anomaly: a British colony, politically and economically supported by the British Government, where the local British colonizers blithely continued with their political, religious, social, and economic dominance and oppression of an indigenous, dispossessed population. The colonizers were English and Scottish Protestants, brought in to supplant the local Irish Catholics. This latter population was the ground from which, in the late 1960s, a civil rights movement emerged. The British Government responded by dramatically increasing the numbers of British Army personnel to act independently of as well as to support the 100% Protestant (British) local police force (Royal Ulster Constabulary—RUC) and the Border Specials (an armed military police force). In the ensuing organic reorganizing of the field, two channels emerged for the energies of the indigenous Irish Catholic population. One was, finally, political representation in the British Government, mainly through the SDLP (Social Democrats and Labor Party), some of whom had been active leaders in the civil rights movement. The other was the definitive position of the IRA (Irish Republican Army) as both a defensive and offensive armed force in respect to the British Army, the Border Specials, the RUC, and the various paramilitary groups that emerged in the Protestant community. The IRA's political wing—Sinn Féin (Gaelic for "We Ourselves")—also became a voice for the Irish population and soon had representatives elected to the British Parliament.

The Border Specials have now been disbanded; the RUC has been dissolved and replaced by the PSNI (Police Service of Northern Ireland); and the British Army has all but disappeared, its camps, border watchtowers, and radio surveillance masts being dismantled and shipped back to England. The IRA has decommissioned its arsenals of weapons, stood down its active volunteers, and called for support for a political solution through its political wing, Sinn Féin (SF). Most recently (January 2007), the Sinn Féin membership voted in favor of the party's participation in the Policing Board of the devolved Assembly of Ministers in Belfast. This is the first time in eighty-six years that the party has recognized such a police force.

The defining concern in local politics is around one issue, and one issue only: the constitutional context. This means either Northern Ireland as part of the UK remaining as a colonial dinosaur in an increasingly postcolonial world, or the North of Ireland as a geographical and economic Region of a reunited Island of Ireland.

The Social Context of the Work—Demographics

The population of the North of Ireland is 1.5 million, of which roughly 55% identify as Protestant and British and 45% as Catholic and Irish. This is changing rapidly: the comparative figures for school-goers are 40% British, 60% Irish. These figures are significant bearing in mind that the political status of the North—as part of the United Kingdom, or reunited with the rest of Ireland—is to be decided by a referendum. They provide optimism for the Irish, and anxiety for the British, populations.

The 55%-45% split was generally reflected in elections to the British Parliament, the Northern Ireland Legislative Assembly, and local councils. Until recently, the Unionist Party (UUP) would always head the polls, followed by the SDLP, with SF third and the more "British Loyalist" parties—the Democratic Unionist Party (DUP) and Popular Unionist Party (PUP)—as minor players.

Following the IRA cease-fire of 1996, and the gradual disappearance of armed conflicts between various sociopolitical forces (though not within the paramilitary groups), the level of socioreligious segregation increased. It is now reckoned that 98% of the population of the North lives in enclaves defined by homogeneity of religious and national/ political identification. In part, this has occurred as a result of people being harassed, burned out, or bombed out of areas to which they did not "belong." In part, it is also a result of there being "safety in numbers"—the more of "us" there are here together, the less chance there is for "them" to sneak in unrecognized and attack us. This is also a throwback to the worst atrocities of the conflict, when innocent people could be lured into hijacked taxis, attacked and killed, simply because of their religion and its political implications. As it is, social and political polarization is a fact of life in the North of Ireland.

The Social Context of the Work—Some Relevant Sociocultural Characteristics

We Irish love to take sides. This is a characteristic which can be seen at its clearest in our national sports—Gaelic football and hurling. Gaelic football is not unlike a mix of rugby and soccer; and hurling is something like fifteen-a-side ice hockey, just as rough, and played in a rink the size of a soccer pitch with a ball that can be handled and struck in the air. Each of Ireland's thirty-two counties and the Four Provinces (Leinster, Munster, Connacht, and Ulster) has a team, as well as each school and parish. To play for a county team, you must have been born in that county, or at least both your parents must have been born there. A game between two county teams is therefore a game between two counties— clearly between them and us! There are no options for whose side to be on as a supporter of either team. Good or bad, winning or losing, they are "our" team, and we are always on their side, of course.

An argument between two individuals can escalate quickly to being between their families, and then their extended families, and then their streets. What began in a rural village can quickly reach a city housing estate, and vice versa.

This aspect of Irish life is enshrined in the well-known story about the man walking along a street in Belfast. He is approached by a hooded figure with a gun, who asks: "Are you a Catholic or a Protestant?" The man replies: "Neither. I'm a Jew." And then the response: "Okay, but are you a Catholic Jew, or a Protestant Jew?" I had always regarded this as an interesting and illustrative joke until Peter Phillipson, co-founder of the Manchester Gestalt Centre, related at a recent conference how exactly this had happened to his Jewish grandmother in Northern Ireland.

Not to take sides is to be suspect, unreliable, passionless, untrustworthy, and not someone who could ever be a friend in a time of need. Closely allied to the taking of sides is the preference for unambiguously taking a stand on any issue of emotional importance. This is reflected in the current polarization of the electorate around the two most diametrically opposed parties, SF and the DUP, and their respective stances on the reunification of Ireland and the union with Britain. The compromising of the UUP has been punished, as has the willingness of the SDLP to work together with the UUP in the Legislative Assembly.

During the worst sectarian-driven violence of the period of the armed conflict, publicly taking a stand was physically dangerous. While this danger has lessened considerably between the communities, it is still a factor between factions within each community. It is now as if the tensions of side-taking were previously held and played out by armed conflict between the paramilitary groups representing the communities, and between the Republican community and the colonial authorities as represented by the Army and the Police. These tensions now seem to be held by the polarizing energies that have emerged in terms of social segregation and political life. Increasingly, taking a stand on sectarian, political, and social issues is more possible, thus giving space for a renewed taking of sides in an increasingly less physically threatening environment.

The Social Context of the Work—Some Implications

As mentioned earlier, the names of people and places are filled with contextual meaning in the North. To repeat and then develop: "Seán" is a give-away at a hotel reception desk or as a listed facilitator: I am clearly Irish, of the Catholic tradition, probably at least politically Nationalist, and maybe even Republican. My name alone can explain why I have not yet been engaged by a clearly Unionist or Loyalist group or organization. My experience is therefore of wholly Irish or of mixed groups. In each case, I am immediately prepared to let my religious and political affiliations be clearly known, and to take a stand on them. This gains me the trust of all concerned. Nobody has to wonder, "where they have me"—of great importance when working in the Region.

Even the apparently most casual conversation is filled with the signs and symbols of affiliation. For the outsider, or the naïve, this is an unmapped minefield of probable misunderstandings, increasingly becoming more complex. Total outsiders, like the Swedish groups mentioned below, are accepted as just not knowing "what's what." For others, like me, with my Irish background and ten years' experience of working regularly in the North, the learning curve just becomes steeper and steeper. More is now expected of me, and my own journey into and through the complexities of contact in this environment informs part of this article.

Incidentally, all the complexities of the move from a colonial to a post-colonial society are brilliantly elucidated by Algerian writer Albert Memmi (1997) in his book, *The Coloniser and the Colonised*. It is important not to neglect this aspect of the situation in the North—it is a colonial society in transition to a postcolonial society, possibly soon to be embedded in another postcolonial society, the Republic of Ireland.

A highly relevant implication of the side-taking and stand-taking aspects of society in the North is the need to recognize just how far this society is from the conditions for change from old prejudices which Philip Lichtenberg, for example, advocates—an ability to see the other as clearly as you believe you see yourself, and an openness to the other seeing you in the same way (Lichtenberg, 1997). Whilst there are small and significant examples of this in the North, the political parties, and perhaps the majority of their voters, are just not there yet and seem to have a very long way to go. In addition, it is in the nature of post-colonial societies to continue all the worst excesses of the past, though now in reverse. Since I have also worked and still work in Estonia and Latvia, I have seen there how the former colonizers, ethnic Russians, were made into second-class citizens (if indeed they ever got past all the barriers to citizenship of the countries in which so many of them had been born).

In both cases—Ireland and Latvia—it is still too soon to forget the colonial injustices of the past, certainly too soon to forgive them. Also in both cases, though still more so in the North of Ireland, the former colonized have not yet achieved full social freedom and economic equality. To understand this situation, and maybe even appreciate its significance, try imagining how you would react if all the ethnic Russians in the former soviet colonies were demanding the return of the Soviet Union and working politically to that end. This simple experiment may give some insight into the context of Northern Ireland as a working environment for Gestalt practitioners.

On Borders and Boundaries

This has become a favorite and fascinating theme for me (Gaffney, 2006), arising originally from my academic work as a lecturer in cross-cultural management, then informed by my Gestalt training, and now reinforced by my work in the Region. As metaphors for ways in which people of different societies and communities may meet, for that which may separate or connect them, and for the dynamics of such complex sociocultural and sociopolitical relationships as occur in the North, the borders and boundaries metaphor has been greatly supportive for both myself and others in personal as well as professional contexts.

"Borders" as a metaphor starts with the notion of national borders, complete with the formalities of crossing them—valid passport, visa where required, permits where required, possible obligations to report to the authorities, as well as the formalities of exiting—by deportation or choice. Worthy of note here is that the inter-member border-crossing openness of the European Union has become entrenched in separate passport controls for "EU Passports" as opposed to "All Other Nationalities"—yet another border. So, "borders" keep others out and allow them in under all sorts of conditions imposed by the "host" country or collective.

Extrapolating the "borders" metaphor refers to the fixed gestalts of identification and the sense of personal and collective identity people may use to find their place in the world. As Amin Maalouf (2003) describes it, identity is something deemed and felt well worth fighting for, especially with "the others." Difference and active differentiation are constituent parts. Any perceived or proposed sameness or even similarity in the other is dangerous, both to the collective and personal identity. Words like "traitor" and "informer" become so explicitly damning within a community that they have become forms of social leprosy—as a terminal illness; and often the termination is at the hands of the betrayed, the informed upon.

Following the Easter Rebellion of 1916, and the subsequent Treaty negotiations, Ireland was partitioned in 1922 into a British (predominantly Protestant) North, and an Irish (predominantly Catholic) South, with a national border and all its trappings formally separating and dividing the two. This soon led to the reinforcement of a more divisive border in the North—between British colonizers and the indigenous population. This latter border was consistently supported by legislation and traditional colonial attitudes and practices, which included institutionalized gerrymandering of constituencies to ensure a Protestant, Unionist majority always. An even more invidious border also emerged, at first slowly and then with momentum. This was the mental border between the Irish of the South and the Irish of the North, now formally separated by a national border between the Republic of Ireland, and the United Kingdom of Great Britain and Northern Ireland. (This has been a painful aspect of my own journey, as I "blew in" from Dublin via Stockholm to Belfast.)

"Boundaries" as a metaphor has a more nuanced set of constructs. My focus here is on the core Gestalt construct of "contact-boundary." As an internationally active Gestalt trainer, I am sensitively aware of the comparative untranslatability of this construct: almost everywhere I teach in a non-English-speaking context, it becomes translated into the linguistic equivalent of "contact-border." This in turn leads to trainees and even trainers thinking and talking about "my" boundary meeting "your" boundary, and about the "boundary of the self." "Contact-boundary" easily becomes a thing, a place, a dissectible something. In my terms here, it has become a border—fixed and changed only by violence or dominance. This is far from what Malcolm Parlett (2005) calls "a revolutionary idea" (p. 55): namely, that the "self is the contact-boundary at work" (Perls, Hefferline, and Goodman, 1951, p. 235). The contact-boundary is not a place; it is an event, an action, a happening, co-created dynamically as an organizing aspect of the organism/environment, self/other fields. It is an experience of being, and of changing into being, other than and similar to before; of influencing and being influenced; of being in process in the presence and company of an environmental other. As an experience, it is always part of our perception. As Gestalt practitioners, our availability to stay open to and with the consummate unpredictability of the impact, on us and on the other, of a co-created and dynamically shared contact-boundary is core to the wonder of our work. As a result, I now use "contact boundary dynamics" to replace the more static and therefore inappropriate "contact-boundary."

My proposal is this: for Gestalt practitioners working in contexts where "borders" may be the path of least resistance, the core and defining feature of our work is precisely our ability and readiness to accept these border conditions, *as well as* our availability to let go of them and engage when "boundaries" (=contact-boundary dynamics) may suddenly become figural. Change occurs in the contact boundary dynamics. And change for both parties. Unpredictable change.

This is both our challenge and our contribution in a context so pervaded by structural and social and mental borders, as is the case in Northern Ireland.

An Example

A Gestalt colleague works with a voluntary agency supporting rural communities of any and all traditions. His name places him firmly in the Irish, Catholic tradition. Part of his work is organizing and distributing funds for the building, and/or upkeep, and/or renovation of community buildings and physical facilities. The agency had been asked to visit an Orange Hall, that is, a building owned and run by the Loyal Orange Order, staunchly Protestant, certainly Unionist, probably Loyalist, and therefore generally anti-Irish and anti-Catholic. My colleague arrived at the hall and was greeted by the Protestant minister in charge, who offered him a cup of tea. The tea and biscuits were brought in and placed on a table. My colleague was invited to move to the table. On doing so, he became immediately aware that he had been seated directly opposite a commemorative stained-glass window in memory of Lodge members "murdered by the IRA." He remained in his seat, drank his tea, and munched on his biscuits. Some thirty minutes later, he was joined by the minister. As my colleague reported this to me, he was clear that every Irish Republican fiber in his body urged him to get up and leave long before the minister's return (a "borders" response). At the same time, his professional stance as a community development worker, reinforced by his Gestalt training, supported him to await possible contact boundary dynamics. This was what happened. As he and I saw it, the "border" issues had been clarified, the stands and sides taken clearly. So, now they could make contact. And change occurred.

Of course, in the North, we Gestalt practitioners mention boundaries in the Gestalt sense, but occasionally we understand that we may sometimes mean borders, fully manned, armed, and active. Passports, visas, permits at the ready. Holding the border issues of my work has become my specialty—and holding my awareness of the possible shifts from borders to boundaries, and remaining as present and open as I can throughout.

This is also a vital issue for local practitioners in communities where everybody seems literally to know everybody. Often, clients have more information on the backgrounds, families, affiliations, connections, and work of their therapist than the therapist may ever get to know of the client or from the client.

From Practice to Theory to Practice

As someone intensely interested in the interplay between theory and practice, and practice and theory, in contemporary applications of what was originally Gestalt therapy theory, I have sketched many a theoretical hypothesis and explanatory, pedagogical model in the Region over the past decade. My interest has been, and continues to be, shared by all of the members of the various constellations of supervision and training groups, both clinical and organizational, with which I have worked there. So, let me here turn to that which is most particularly figural to the ground of my work in the North of Ireland.

The various training and supervision groups have included and still include, members of both community traditions. We have, therefore, often had cause to reflect on the sociopolitical field in which we are embedded, and its impact on the therapeutic, supervisory, group and organizational work of the supervisees, as well as on us together as an embedded part of the field. During one particular group supervision and training session on groups and organizations, I was asked if I could do a field-based model for what was happening around us in the political shifts and changes that had been taking place. Interestingly, I had been informally doing just that, jotting down notes and sketches as I considered how central the impact of the past has been on the present and future of Ireland. This was the aspect I wanted to explore. I did a rough sketch with two continua, time and change, and explored a possible scenario. The sketch is as follows (Figure 1):

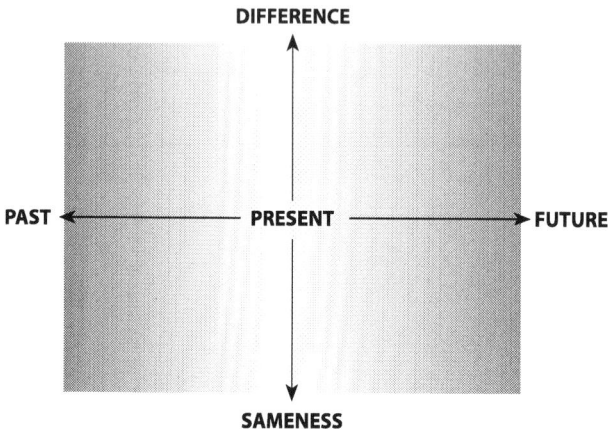

Figure 1

As I saw it, Sinn Féin had looked at its past political vision and policies in the light of current developments, and chosen to: 1. drop some of its former demands, such as "Brits out!"; and 2. reevaluate and change others (a united Ireland by political and democratic means). The Democratic Unionist Party had hung on aggressively to all of its previous policies and demands, until it became clear that the shift in Sinn Féin policies demanded a change. So, they finally agreed to share power in the Northern Assembly with Sinn Féin. The Unionist Party had tried to maintain its past and add some minor new compromises, as had the Social Democrats and Labor Party (SDLP). The two smallest parties, the Womens' Coalition (WC) and the Alliance Party (AP), had each tried something very new in the North—parties across the sociopolitical divide with an optimistic future focus. Both of these latter parties had been voted out of any meaningful position, and WC was soon to disband totally. AP has all but disappeared. My hypothesis was and is that WC and AP had tried something too new, too soon, too ungrounded in past loyalties, in a culture where all "sides" consider loyalty to their pasts as a core value, imbued with emotion.

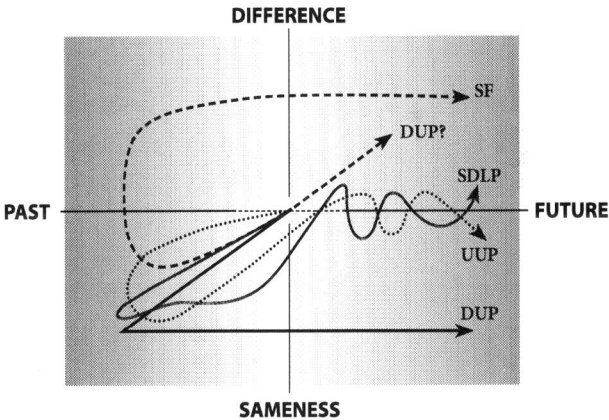

Figure 2

As indicated in Figure 2, Sinn Féin had managed to keep true to its traditional core vision of a united Ireland as a Socialist Republic (holding to a "Past" position). But, as a result of its pragmatic re-evaluation of methods, it had entered into a careful political cooperation with all former opponents in order to achieve it (moving from "Sameness" to "Difference"). By so doing, it maintained its Republican base, yet won over a major share of the Social Democrats and Labor Party's nationalist voters. SDLP had moved too far toward and closer to a Unionist position. UUP had compromised away more of its past values than its voters could accept, so that they now switched to the more hard-line, traditional British "Loyalism" of DUP.

This rough sketch, and the thinking behind it, has since developed into a social and organizational change model (see Figure 3). Moving clockwise, I think of the "Past/Sameness" Quadrant as *"Keep,"* the "Past/Difference" Quadrant as *"Keep and Reevaluate,"* the "Future/Difference quadrant as *"Evaluate and Change,"* and the "Future/Sameness" Quadrant as *"Try/Test."*

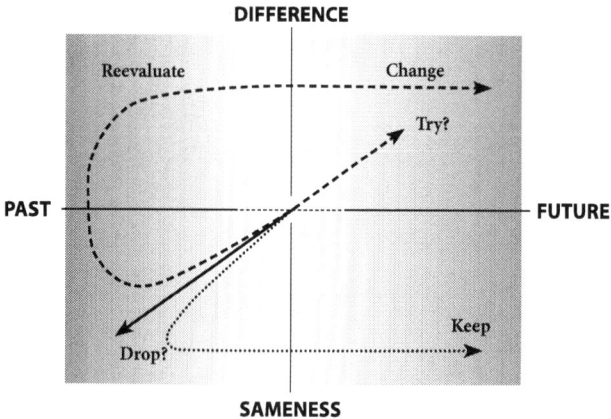

Figure 3

Of great and specific importance, here in the Region, is to respect the past. Many are content to live IN it; all are living WITH it. The emotional loyalty of all involved communities, mentioned earlier, is in allegiance to the historical development of their current identity/identification, so that "what is" is firmly grounded in "what was," and "what will be" needs to be likewise grounded in this "what was = what is." Social and political change involves a change in identity, a collective existential issue. Moving too fast into a "pastless" future will just not work. As a result, when using this model in the North (see below), I always focus on allowing good time for input and discussion of the *Drop, Keep and Reevaluate, and Change* aspects, before moving into any consideration of the future, so that *Try/Test* is firmly grounded.

Gestalt in the North of Ireland—Some Current Practice and its Impact

My work is either a direct result of a recommendation from a colleague in the Region—often with organizations with which the colleague is formally or informally involved—or as a result of an organization preferring a Gestalt practitioner, though one who is not local. I am enough of an outsider, yet also enough of an insider, to fill a useful function. Here is a selection of work I regard as having had a broader impact than its own immediate setting; it indicates the importance of taking sides, and of maintaining a staunch connection to the past.

Triskele Community Development

Triskele is a voluntary organization based in the South, though just over the former border. It was founded by two Gestalt practitioners, both of whom were in my first supervision group, so I have been able to follow it from its birth. It has had three explicit core values since its inception: feminism, republicanism, and a cross-border brief. It now has a professional staff of fifteen community development workers, trainers, and research and policy specialists, representing the traditions of both communities. The Dublin Government is one of its main funders, and Triskele is actively involved in informing Rural and Community Development policies in the Irish Government. Its Director for many years did Gestalt training at the Gestalt Centre London as well as at the Gestalt Institute of Cleveland/Gestalt International Study Center OSD International Program. All of the staff has done further training with Gestalt practitioners from Belfast, as well as participated in the regular Staff and Organizational Residentials, which I and other local Gestalt practitioners have led over the years. Three of the staff have partnered with local practitioners in group skills training within the community sector in the cross-border areas covered by Triskele. And so the ripples spread.

Rural Community Network

RCN is a voluntary organization, founded in order to support isolated Catholic and Protestant communities in the underdeveloped countryside areas of the North. These communities are often surrounded by townlands dominated by people of the opposite religious and political persuasion, or with residents co-existing uneasily in small towns where a bridge was an invisible and impenetrable border between communities. A senior member of staff had completed the GIC/GISC OSD International program and wanted to introduce a Gestalt perspective to RCN and its work. I worked with the whole organization four times a year for five years, as well as with the Management Team. I have supported the agency through a major change as the founder made his decision to move into another area of work and influence, and two others of the three-person Management Team also changed jobs.

There were some complex sociocultural issues that emerged here. One was that community development has long been an aspect of the Catholic/Nationalist/Republican communities. The roots of this are partly the siege mentality of an oppressed minority which has never trusted the authorities, whether represented by police, social welfare, the housing authority, etc., and therefore has always had to be collectively self-sufficient. The Protestant/Unionist/Loyalist communities have the socioreligious tradition of individual responsibility as well as direct connections to "their" power-base of local and regional politics and its formal offices. As such, some RCN staff had a downhill ride with wind at their backs and a warm welcome. Others had to toil uphill with the wind in their faces, including the local reality that the acronym for Rural Community Network—RCN—included the initials of the Roman Catholic Church (RC) and had been founded, and was being run by, a person whose name was redolent of Irish Catholic nationalism.

Another issue was that this first aspect was further reflected in the reality of recruitment: there were far more "Irish" applicants than "British" for any job vacancies. Therefore, the representative proportions of the staff were heavily weighted by one community, in direct contrast to the society of the Region in which RCN is embedded.

A third issue was around the "past-future" perspective. The past was here represented by maintaining a traditional "community development" focus, and the future by offering a more hands-on practical, daily life focus. In this instance, the side-taking was across the divide of the two traditions.

Because of the downhill/uphill difference, as well as the proportional distribution of the two traditions, I tended to support the minority voices. Since I had been clear that my name and whatever associations were made of it were accurate, my support had an extra ingredient in it: my "own side" had to choose between a confrontation with me or support for "their" "whole" side, namely, the RCN staff. We were all walking various tightropes, and none of us fell. The community development or hands-on aspect could be dealt with in a more traditional process manner, supported by the complex ground having been cleared previously.

My closing meeting with RCN was when the new Director had been selected from within the staff, the new Management Team put in place, and the reorganization and change process I had been called in to support completed. One of the dedicated facilitator teams in RCN, I have now heard, has carefully studied my facilitation style and methodology with RCN and incorporated it into their work.

The Northern Ireland Council of Youth Support Forum

This is an umbrella group of the Directors and Senior Staff of both statutory and voluntary organizations involved in youth-work in the field as well as in schools and colleges. One of the agency Directors is Gestalt-trained. Some agencies are focused on specific communities, some on interface areas where the two main communities still occasionally clash, and some openly mixed.

In one intervention, I was engaged to lead a three-day residential where this group wanted to look at the conditions for its continued value and existence, as well as how to mobilize energy to become more proactive should they decide to continue. Having completed the social preliminaries, I described my style of process facilitation—that I would follow them as they explored their needs and expectations with respect to their purpose for this residential. Any interventions I would make would be to raise their and my awareness of my process in their presence, and/or my observations of what I saw or heard as they interacted. As the residential progressed, I would consider the suitability of focused exercises, or even in-the-moment experiments. There was what I can only describe as "subdued" agreement.

From then on, the first day consisted of a mountain of "unfinished business" with all the complexities involved. This could be characterized as "pre-contact" in the Contacting Sequence (Perls, Hefferline, and Goodman, 1951/1994) or "scanning" in the Cycle of Experience model (Nevis, 1987/2005) from GIC. A great deal of time and energy was spent talking about "how it used to be," which sometimes moved imperceptibly into references to specific violent events in the environment.

By the end of the first day, no clear figure had emerged, and the energy seemed to have moved towards dampening energy. Any comment or suggestion which might have created a shift towards interaction was greeted with silence at best, or a "look what happened the last time" comment, both of which added to the energy-dampening energy.

A good social session over dinner and then in the hotel-bar seemed to support some lively reconnecting to one another, which at first continued into and then faded during the second morning. By lunchtime, the mood was somber. My sense was that the group had moved into a self-blaming, self-shaming cycle. So much need, so much concern, so much past energy to work and change—and so many barriers: sectarianism, paramilitarism, political and social polarizing, a depressed economy, a depressed society; a steady increase in youth suicides (currently three times the Great Britain average), self-harming, and domestic and gang violence.

I could feel how I was being called to be "the difference that makes a difference" in Gregory Bateson's felicitous phrase. This is always a choice point in my work: do I go with the flow, do I raise their awareness of our interactive patterns and leave it to them to sort out, or do I await the emergence of another figure?

During lunch, I considered my options, took a walk, and allowed a figure to emerge. The figures were similar—they were of this group committing suicide by disbanding, or cutting themselves in misdirected anger, or splitting into the discrete sociopolitical foci of the past. I made my decision.

After the lunch break, I introduced the Change Model (Figure 3) in full and in its full background in the sociopolitical environment of the North. There were nods and short words of affirmation. I asked if they would like to "give it a go" on themselves. They agreed. I asked them to self-select into subgroups across the organizational borders, and for each group to discuss, in sequence, each quadrant under the headings *Drop—Keep—Reevaluate/Change—Try/Test*, in respect of who/what they had been and done and maybe still did out of habit. Every proposal from each subgroup member was to be listed on a flipchart, so that there was no consensus seeking with a ranked list. Each group would present their flipcharts in the assigned order on their return.

They spent almost three hours doing this task and returned energized and eager to work. Each heading was considered separately, in the sequence outlined above. What followed was memorable as the whole group questioned, debated, and discussed the various lists. When all four headings from each group were posted on the walls, they began the focused process of distinguishing the lively figures that were emerging for them. Some had almost identical "*Drop*" lists; some differed. What others had under "*Drop*," some had under "*Reevaluate/Change*." There was a lively debate around what to "*Keep*," and a lot of laughter around some of the more creative "*Try/Test*" proposals. With a mixture of openhearted and brash exchanges and seriousness, they eventually produced four flip-chart sheets with their consensus opinions under each heading.

The social gathering that night was longer and livelier than the previous one. The third day became a day of contactful action and planning with the energy not only to continue as an umbrella group, but also to plan their next conference—an activity that had faded away, in recent years, from the excitement and enthusiasm around their earlier conferences. By the time we finished the residential, the Forum was up and running again as a force for good in a damaged and deprived population—the young people and future generation of parents of the North of Ireland.

Supporting Local Practitioners

These are the people from all of the main communities who did their Gestalt training in the context of the armed conflict and then the post cease-fire period of the late 1990s, with all of its echoes of warfare carried over into society as a whole. In my own experience as trainer, the interpersonal and subgroup dynamics and controversies natural to any group were magnified, avoided, cut short, diverted, and generally made more complex by the situation and context of the work. The personal became the political, and vice versa. As mentioned earlier, this is a society in which everybody seems to know or at least be somehow connected with everybody, and these entanglements could make unexpected appearances. An example: two women were connected by the fact that the father of one had been a warder in the prison where the partner of the other had served seventeen years of a life sentence, though this was unknown to both with any certainty and had never been mentioned. One of my most moving moments was some years later when the warder's daughter felt able to explore this situation with the lifer's partner. They are now established colleagues doing some of the most well-known and influential work across sociopolitical spheres, including those described below.

Barnardo's "Parenting in a Divided Society" Project and the "Flying Horse" Project

The projects are described in detail by Rosie Burrows and Bríd Keenan in Chapter 4 of *Mending the World*. I mention this reference mainly to indicate that I have served as teacher and supervisor to Burrows and Keenan since they started this work in 2002. Indeed, Burrows and Keenan met in one of my training groups. Since then, my main function has been to support them in managing their differences as they undertook extremely difficult work. The Project Leader (Burrows, the warder's daughter) found herself working with her Gestalt colleague (Keenan, the lifer's partner). Their work was demanding, draining, and filled with anxiety as they carried their own affiliations into their work with each other and, for each of them, with "their own" and with "the others." The result is a brilliant display of Gestalt work at its best: daring, respectful, experiential, experimental, and phenomenological. Published as a Resource Manual (Burrows and Keenan, 2004a) for social workers across the Region, it consists of a main document and five specific workbooks.

Despite its somewhat poetic name, "Flying Horse" is a sprawling estate of mildly substandard housing hastily built by the Belfast City Council in an area well south of the city to house dispossessed families, mainly from the Catholic community. It has long suffered from high unemployment and all its attendant ills—alcoholism, domestic violence, criminality, drug abuse, and high suicide levels. Three local Gestalt therapists (including Burrows and Keenan) have worked there using community development and social research with a view to improving services to this underprivileged community. A report has been published, "Out of Town, Out of Sight" (Burrows and Keenan, 2004b).

Political Parties

Gestalt practitioners have been engaged as process consultants/ facilitators by some of the executives of the various political parties. Because of the sensitivity of this work, we do not feel it appropriate to identify specific people and interventions that were done. Suffice it to say that participants in the Belfast Gestalt training and supervision groups played very active roles in support of those engaged in the peace process over many years.

Wheels within Wheels—the Role of the Supervision Group

All of the local practitioners involved in the work mentioned above have been and/or are still in various constellations of a supervision group that has been running for some ten years. In this way, the learning and experience have become shared knowledge and competence. The Gestalt ripples are thus spread and supported in the Region (Gaffney, 2008).

Summary and Conclusions

The North of Ireland is a complex social context for the theory and practice of Gestalt, which starts from the organism/environment field and proceeds experientially and experimentally, exploring the phenomenology of existence. Use of self, awareness, and contact are further cornerstones. For many years in this particular sociopolitical context, awareness was good ground as a guarantee of survival in a threatening environment, i.e., awareness of "our" sameness and "their" difference. At the same time, such awareness could become rational consciousness and justification, thereby moving towards a fixed gestalt of "borders."

Contact was charged with support or menace or dilemma, so that trust was always a core issue and still is. As such, the environmental other became the focus of the perceived danger or safety of the relationship. The other as person was subsumed into gut reaction "border moments," or met in contact-boundary dynamics. As mentioned earlier, being prepared to take a clear stand on any and all issues, that is, selectively sharing awareness of self and the self/other relationship, is an essential aspect of working in the Region. In supporting clarity, this ability to begin with possible differentiation is a ground for a possibly emerging trust—possibly and *not* probably. This entails always staying with the experience of "what is" and equally always accepting that my "what is" may not necessarily or ever be the other's experience. Convinced and actively committed Irish Republicans are likely to be as loyal to their beliefs as similar people of a Loyalist or even Unionist perspective.

Use of self, awareness, and contact boundary dynamics: these are each and all aspects of a field perspective (see Parlett, 2005), where forces and resonances organize the fields of our experience. A shift in the sociopolitical forces can and will impact unpredictably on both the whole field and its constituent energies. Contact-boundary dynamics in one place, for example, the Orange Hall and/or my supervision work, echo and ripple beyond their physical location and actual participants. Adding the work of the locally-based Gestalt practitioners provides the possibility of a number of "Gestalt" forces—use of self, awareness, contact-boundary dynamics, and field perspectives and their specific impacts in particular pieces of work reverberating around the Region.

And maybe, most of all, respect for the other—wherever the other may be. In the everyday world of Gestalt therapy, this clearly includes straight therapists working with gay, lesbian, bisexual, and transsexual clients; GLBT therapists working with straight clients; churchgoer therapists working with atheists; atheistic therapists working with devout churchgoers, and so on. This is the nature of our chosen discipline, and working with its impact is an everyday part of our work, of our awareness, of our ability to stay open to contact-boundary dynamics, and of our acknowledgement of the field and its impact upon us. It is also a practical acknowledgement of our impact on the whole social field of which we and our clients, and our work together, may seem such a small and unimportant part.

My own experience of working in the North of Ireland, my experience of the Gestalt practitioners there and the amazing and influential work they are doing, has added dimensions and insights to my understanding of Gestalt theory and methodologies. It has also opened my eyes to my own process as a person, as an Irishman and as a Gestalt practitioner. In addition, it has shown me how much impact a mere fifteen or so people, working locally, can have on the society in which they live and work as Gestalt practitioners.

Acknowledgements: My warm thanks to, and appreciation of, the active members of the Gestalt practitioners community of the Region: Michael Ahearne, Rosie Burrows, Fergus Cumiskey, Joëlle Gartner; Bríd Keenan, Paula Keenan, Tom Kiernan, Dominica McGowan, Bernie MacMahon, Maria McManus, Mary Kay Mullan, Joanna McMinn, Norma Patterson, Marie Quiery, Fred Williams; and to Mary Slattery from Cork, South of Ireland.

Seán Gaffney, PhD, is Irish by birth, culture, and conviction, and a resident of Sweden since 1975. He works internationally as a Gestalt therapist and Gestalt OSD consultant and a trainer in both fields. He also is a lecturer in cross-cultural management in various Masters programs.

Contact: *seangaff@gmail.com*

References

Burrows, R., & Keenan, B. (2004a). *Giving children back their future.* Belfast: Bernardo's Northern Ireland.

Burrows, R., & Keenan, B. (2004b), *Out of town, Out of sight.* Unpublished report.

Gaffney, S. (2004). Gestalt at work—A case study. *Gestalt Review, 8*(3), 263-90.

Gaffney, S. (2006). On borders and boundaries—International consulting.

In M. Brazzel & B. Jones (Eds.), *The NTL handbook of organizational development and change* (pp. 355-69). New York: Jossey-Bass (John Wiley).

Gaffney, S. (2008). Gestalt group supervision in a divided society: Theory, practice, perspectives and reflections. *British Gestalt Journal, 17*(1), 27-39.

Lichtenberg, P., van Beuskom, J., & Gibbens, D. (1997). *Encountering bigotry: Befriending projecting persons in everyday life.* Cambridge: GestaltPress.

Memmi, A. (1967). *The colonizer and the colonized.* Boston: Beacon Press.

Maalouf, A. (2003). *In the name of identity.* New York: Penguin Group.

Nevis, E. (1987, 2005). *Organizational consulting: A Gestalt approach.* Cleveland: GestaltPress.

Parlett, M. (2005). Contemporary Gestalt therapy: Field theory. In A. Woldt & S. Toman (Eds.), *Gestalt therapy: History, theory and practice* (pp. 41-64). Thousand Oaks, CA: Sage.

Perls, F., Hefferline, R., & Goodman, P. (1994). *Gestalt therapy: Excitement and growth in the human personality.* New York: Dell. (Originally published 1951)

CHAPTER 13

Making the HIV/AIDS Problem Visible in Cambodia

Frances Johnston, PhD, and Eddy Mwelwa, PhD

Editors' Introduction

The worldwide AIDS epidemic is one of the most pressing social issues of our time. Though it can be narrowly seen as a public health or medical problem, the spread of the disease is in no little way supported by underlying dysfunctional social norms and customs. No wonder that attempts to deal with the problem bring forth intense resistance from the very people who are in danger of suffering the ravages of AIDS.

Frances Johnston and Eddy Mwelwa (together with their colleague Annie McKee) have worked for years in AIDS Reduction Projects in South Africa and Cambodia. This chapter tells us about the intense and emotional aspect of working in this field, and of the ways in which this effort tapped into the social factors that must be dealt with if any progress is to be made. The authors are up-front about saying that they used provocative modes of intervention, sometimes coercing their participants into doing things in order to speed up development of their awareness. While the Gestalt approach uses both provocative and evocative modes (see Nevis, 1987/2005), most of its practitioners have been taught to use provocation very sparingly.

The authors are to be commended for their courage in being willing to deal with confused, irritated, and even angry responses. This story also makes clear the importance of utilizing personal awareness to enhance activities in settings where the major objective of the intervention is to produce action on a frightening social problem. Again, we see the value of creating robust awareness to support action planning.

Introduction[66]

When we walked into the room , the chairs said it all. In front were the lush, cushioned chairs, like thrones. They were for the monks. Next were the chairs with arms for the senators and for us. And behind them were the regular conference chairs for everyone else. The chairs were arranged in rows with a divide in the middle. On one side sat all the men while on the other were the women—the social structure made visible.

In the course of the morning, after the official opening of the program, we rearranged the 100 chairs into six rows in a horseshoe, a challenge to the given cultural norms. We would do this many times over in our work in Cambodia. Each time we knew it was a big risk. Each time we knew we had to take it. But we were as apprehensive of and excited by what we were opening up, as were the participants. We learned to adopt the cultural norm of apologizing in advance of what we were going to say in case what we said would offend somebody. At the same time, we held close to our intentions and experience, trusting that what we were building with them was too important and powerful not to go on building.

From 2002 to today, we have been on a learning journey that has taken us to places, literal and emotional, that we could not have imagined. For five years we conducted comprehensive leadership development processes in Cambodia that would involve men and women from all walks of life and teach us powerful lessons about orchestrating and inspiring social change. This chapter is the story of how we utilized Gestalt theory and applications in our core approach to social change and individual capacity development. We worked with grassroots community leaders, civil service and non-governmental organization (NGO) officials, members of the Senate, people living with HIV and AIDS, and monks. Some of the participants had been part of the Khmer Rouge regime; others had experienced the terror of living under it as children or young adults in concentration camps. Most had seen their colonial prewar society destroyed and were now participating in its rebuilding as a democracy.

In this chapter, we will describe the work we did and the theories and principles that guided us. We will share stories directly from Program participants that speak to the difficulties of cross-cultural change, and

[66] The authors wish to thank Patricia "Trish" Perry for her assistance in organizing and editing this chapter.

the power of the connections made when the walls begin to drop. Our readers will also hear our stories, our fears, and how we were constantly challenged to live and model the mindfulness, hope, and compassion we were trying to develop in others.

The HIV and AIDS Leadership Challenge

Late in 2001, a senior leader from a prominent international development NGO called and said: "The world has spent billions of dollars trying to arrest the spread of HIV and AIDS. As of today we have thirty-three million infected people and many millions more who are affected by the pandemic with no significant reversal of infection rate predicted. HIV and AIDS are radically and negatively impacting entire countries' economies and developmental possibilities. We are convinced that the only path to transformational change is through improved leadership at all levels of the system. Can you help us build leadership capacity with the local leaders in the affected countries?"

We said "yes." How could we do otherwise? All of our work had been about leadership development, using core principles from Gestalt, systems theory, neuroscience, and emotional intelligence. We knew we had the tools to support leaders in creating truly sustainable change.

While the presenting problem was HIV and AIDS, our sponsor believed that education and a medical response to this problem were not sufficient to reduce the infection rate radically. The spread of HIV and AIDS is deeply linked to issues of human behavior, especially sexual behavior. Many of the unsafe practices that contribute to the spread of the virus are the result of long-standing habits and cultural practices (see McKee, Johnston, Mwelwa, and Rotondo, 2009).

Cambodia, the focus of this chapter, presented a few different challenges from some other countries because the HIV and AIDS epidemic was still predominantly hidden. There was little or no public acknowledgment of the disease. Furthermore, the country was facing a long road back from the crippling impact of the genocide under the authoritarian Pol Pot regime, and it was only five years into an emerging democracy. As a result, we would have to begin at ground level, building awareness of the need to even name, let alone address, the problem.

As we began to formulate our process, we had many more questions than answers. How could Gestalt practices and beliefs help us design a program for lasting change? How best to utilize Emotional Intelligence in a country recovering from self-induced trauma? How would participants react to our experiential approach to adult learning? Could we overcome our own lack of first-hand knowledge about this culture and people, while simultaneously engaging participants in a process of self-examination of their own deeply held beliefs and practices? How would we teach, train, explain, and interact when we had no common language and everything we said would have to be translated into Khmer? How would we know when the concepts we wanted to communicate had been understood as intended?

Guiding Principles, Theories of Change, Practices, and Beliefs

There are several theoretical underpinnings to our work drawn from Gestalt, systems theory, neuroscience, and Emotional and Social Intelligence. While the primary orientation of this chapter will be on Gestalt theory, we also wish to acknowledge the importance of several key concepts from Emotional and Social Intelligence, mentioned below.

- The best leaders *move* people (Goleman, Boyatzis, and McKee, 2002). They engage people's hearts and minds, and they help them to direct their energy, individually and collectively, toward a desired end.
- "Resonant Leaders" get results by fostering a climate filled with enthusiasm, hope, mutual support, and commitment. These kinds of leaders are integral to lasting systemic change (Boyatzis and McKee, 2005).
- Effective leaders are emotionally self-aware, adaptable, positive, and able to express emotions in a way that opens others to considering new and creative solutions (McKee, Boyatzis, and Johnston, 2008).

Our goal was to support the people we would work with to become just that kind of resonant leader, bringing self-knowledge, hope, optimism, and energy to the tasks that lay ahead. And as Ghandi said, our leaders need to "become the change you wish to see." This goal was more than fulfilled.

Gestalt Theory

A number of core ideas from the Gestalt theory of change provided both ways of *thinking about* the work and ways of *being in* the work.

Gestalt Theory and Approach Encourages an Optimistic Orientation to Reality. It assumes that people are doing the best they can with what they see and know about their world. The goal of the Gestalt practitioner is to expand possibilities by increasing awareness of what is seen and known rather than by labeling and fixing problems. The fact that we as practitioners wholeheartedly believed this notion created an atmosphere of hope and potential right from the beginning. It also enabled us to be curious and open to what we became aware of. This approach was exactly what we needed in the wholly unfamiliar and urgent situation in which we found ourselves.

Change Takes Place in Overlapping Cycles. The Gestalt Cycle of Experience is a model that charts the flow of energy through an awareness-action sequence. Increased awareness is the starting point for creating the possibility of change. With a rich and full awareness of a situation come multiple possibilities for movement. With further exploration, one of these choices will begin to reflect a "shared awareness" that leads to the mobilization of energy and a focus on action planning. The cycle of change is completed when actions are taken, meaning is made, the change is assimilated, and the process is closed out.

In order for the kind of sustainable, large-scale social change described in this chapter to occur, many overlapping awareness-action sequences at different levels in the system will take place. For example, we went through processes of awareness building many times over. We started with individual interviews of leaders and took what we learned from them to focus groups for confirmation. The data from these groups then was used to continue building awareness in large and small community groups, ultimately ending with the development of multiple action learning projects to address their needs.

Levels of System. Inherent in the Gestalt framework is that there are different levels of system always operating within and across levels. Individuals' actions affect not only them but also the different systems within which they interact: family, friendship network, and/ or community. The process of a social change project involves many systems operating at the same time. In our experience we have found that truly sustainable change happens when leaders inquire, focus, and intervene simultaneously on more than one system level. At the same time, we believe that change at one level will have an impact on other levels.

As we entered into the project in Cambodia, we wanted to pay attention to all levels. This included the individual leaders, both formal and informal, who were making decisions and choices about the HIV and AIDS epidemic. We addressed them as individuals with concerns about their own health and well-being, as leaders who could influence others through policy and practice, and as role models. We started with the former because of our belief in the primacy of the link between emotions and action. When policy makers are emotionally engaged with an issue, they will make and pass policies that make a difference. We also mobilized energy for change by heightening awareness of the negative impact HIV and AIDS was having on the country, since we knew that nationalism ran deep and true across the spectrum of participants.

At the same time, we recognized the need to address concerns for the community and family groups affected by the attention, or inattention, to this problem; as well as for the community and governmental organizations deciding policy and implementing programs. In other words, since we could intervene in any number of places, we wanted to choose carefully in order to have the maximum effect.

Dialogue and Contact—Exploring Multiple Realities. One of the first things reinforced by our initial interviews was how many competing realities existed among participants. This was not surprising, but to address the depth and divisiveness of the differences would take much trust and hard work.

Gestalt theory holds firmly to the power of dialogue to build trust and understanding. It calls for the creation of a space that can hold differences without rushing to resolution. As people speak about their deepest feelings, beliefs, and experiences, individual awareness grows and "contact" between participants occurs more frequently. ("Contact" here is defined as "the point at which boundaries shift, and change occurs.")[67] Our commitment to creating a safe space for this kind of sharing was essential for the program to succeed. In the end, it is where the real learning and healing happened.

Presence and Use of Self. As with the concepts of Emotional and Social Intelligence described earlier, Gestalt theory places strong emphasis on developing leaders' self-awareness and their ability to use themselves effectively to create change. From a Gestalt point of view, this involves the interveners' "supplying what is missing in the system," heightening awareness in others of the choices they are making, and choosing when to work "strategically" (in the service of completing a task) and when to work "intimately" (in service of building relationships) (Nevis, Backman, and Nevis, 2003).

As we began our work, we were aware that we had to pay equal attention to how we were using ourselves as leaders, as well as to how we were developing these capacities in the Cambodian participants. We

---

[67] Definition given in the course of a training program at the Gestalt International Study Center (GISC), South Wellfleet (Cape Cod), Massachusetts.

sought opportunities to learn about ourselves, how we were perceived, and how our untested assumptions, projections, and biases stood in the way of effective leadership. We paid careful attention to how our own process ran in parallel to the experiences of the participants and of the local facilitators and faculty, believing that this inquiry offered important insights.

Program Description and Overview

The different components of the program were clear.[68] We would begin by engaging in diagnostic processes to identify key issues related to HIV and AIDS, leadership practices, and cultural norms relevant to the design of a leadership program. Then we would design a three-week leadership development program interspaced with Action Learning Projects in between the weeks. We intended to deliver it to approximately one hundred people over a nine-month period. Finally, we would develop a process to train a subset of local people to become facilitators and, ultimately, faculty in the leadership program.

Identifying Diverse Participants

We knew that the success of the program depended on finding diverse participants who represented a broad cross-section of the community; thus, the recruitment process was undertaken by the NGO (non-government organization) client system in consultation with us. At the same time, we wanted people who had the capacity to understand, engage with, and utilize the practices we would be teaching. To ensure maximum diversity, program participants were recruited and nominated from many different sectors, including national and local government, non-government and community groups, Buddhist monks, medical doctors, grassroots organizers, and, crucially, men and women living with HIV and AIDS. Participants' ages ranged from twenty to seventy, and they came from both sophisticated urban and remote rural communities. Many of the participants were established, powerful local leaders in their own right.

First Step in the Cycle— Building Awareness and Understanding

As we set out on this journey, the first thing we knew was that we did

---

[68] The descriptions of the program, the selection of participants, and the Dynamic Inquiry process have been adapted from McKee, Johnston, Mwelwa, and Rotondo (2009).

not know enough, about this country, its people, and the objective data related to the current state of the HIV and AIDS epidemic. We needed to raise our own awareness and understanding of what we were dealing with. For the objective reality, we studied, read, interviewed, and were instructed about numbers, rates, intervention, and social and economic costs. We learned about how much the government was responding and what programs were in place.

While this information was important, we knew that these facts were not enough. Even more important were questions about cultural structures and power dynamics, gender relationships, attitudes toward sexuality, and social and emotional realities of life in Cambodia. At the same time, we wanted to identify inherent strengths of the country to draw on as we moved forward. From a Gestalt point of view, our intention was to expand the "ground" from which we operated. We needed to talk to people—lots of people—to listen to what they had to say, and we needed to walk around and feel the place.

Our first steps included dozens of conversations with local leaders, as well as a disciplined investigative process, which we call Dynamic Inquiry (see McMillen and London, 1995). We spent considerable time with local representatives of our sponsor, the NGO that had an international presence and local offices. These meetings were both formal and social. In total, we conducted fifty-five one-on-one confidential interviews in Cambodia.

It is difficult to quantify how important these initial conversations were for us, especially as that was the only time in the whole program when we would be involved in such direct, personal exchanges. As we sat with the Cambodians, we slowly got to know and understand them. Their view of the world became clearer and challenged us to examine what we accepted as given. Not only did we emerge with a better understanding of what we were dealing with, but we also encountered them as people and began to build relationships. For instance, from one woman who identified herself as a Princess, we learned about the current role of royalty in society. Later, we followed our curiosity and read about the political history of the ruling families of Cambodia and their relationships with subsequent regimes. This investigation revealed data about a Cambodian's relationship to and expectations of authority figures. We read about a thousand years of benevolent dependency interspersed with betrayal. We also used these individual meetings to select potential people whom we could develop and train as facilitators and faculty for the program.

After completing the interviews, we reviewed our notes in depth, pulled out key themes, and checked them with a series of focus groups that included people who had not participated in the initial interview process. This process helped us to confirm what we had heard and make adjustments to ensure that the results gave a realistic portrait of the society, which would not be influenced by our assumptions.

What We Heard and Where It Led Us

Through these conversations, we learned about the multiple realities operating in the country and uncovered several core issues involved in the spread of HIV and AIDS. Some of the key issues were: level of awareness/acknowledgment of the problem, gender inequality, and complex power dynamics.

Levels of Awareness of HIV and AIDS Epidemic

As mentioned previously, Cambodia presented a lack of awareness, or acknowledgment, regarding the epidemic. When we began our work, the estimate of infection was "only" 4% and 220,000 people were estimated to be living with the virus. The government had been slow to address the potential severity of the problem publicly, in part because of intense efforts at rebuilding the country.

To address this lack of information, we recognized that we would have to spend a considerable amount of time upfront, in the beginning stages of the Cycle of Experience, getting leaders in touch with the effects of the disease. In the opening session of the program, we began the dialogues with a list of ten questions having to do with the issue of HIV and AIDS in the country. Participants interviewed each other and analyzed the data in small groups. The findings led to a large group discussion in terms of what that meant for Cambodia. Later, we arranged field trips to orphanages, brothels, and hospitals where they could see and talk to the women and children living with HIV/AIDS or affected by it every day.

Gender Inequity: "Bringing What is Missing to the System"

It became apparent quickly that there was a significant lack of gender equity in Cambodia. This was pointed up by how few opportunities there were, and what a critical need existed, for women's leadership in the country. We also knew that beliefs about "maleness" and "femaleness" were deeply implicated in the spread of HIV through the use of commercial sex workers. Men in every social situation utilized prostitutes and enjoyed the attention of "indirect" sex workers such as "beer girls" who promoted alcohol. Men contracted the virus though the practice of unprotected sex and then often carried the virus across regions and social groups.

As we moved into designing the next phase of the program, we knew we wanted to add experiences that would allow and encourage open conversations between men and women about how gender affected the choices and decisions they made. We also knew these conversations would be new, frightening, and fly in the face of established cultural norms. We chose to address the issue in multiple ways, from subtle to provocative.

First, from the start, we focused on women as leaders. We emphasized the importance of women's leadership in society by encouraging the active and visible participation of the women within the program. (Through concentrated efforts, we were able to ensure a 30:70 ratio of women to men within both participants and facilitators). The fact that we, Frances Johnston and Eddy Mwelwa, were a white woman and a black, Zambian man offered a different possibility from the moment we stood up in front of a group. Our modeling of equality and mutual respect between us and for all participants challenged their beliefs and perceptions just through witnessing us work. As a corollary Johnston, as a woman leader leading men, was often the focus of immense attention from the women in the groups; she was told that they never would have imagined such a thing to be possible. For instance, she would approach a man or woman who had gone beyond the time given for presentation and respectfully ask him/her to close it down. Such a practice was new to them, especially coming from a woman.

During the large and small group meetings that would take place over the following years, gender dynamics frequently came up. Some of our first exercises involved men talking with men, women talking with women, and then men and women talking together. In one preliminary session, when participants were asked to mill around the room asking other participants specific questions as part of an icebreaker, everyone "froze" upon hearing the instructions. The older women told us that it would be impossible for a young woman to approach an older man in a position of authority. The rules of social interaction would not allow that to happen. To their surprise, when we followed through on the exercise, one of the young women went right up to one of the male senators without any difficulty, creating an opportunity for a new kind of dialogue, connection, and reframing of the belief.

Power Dynamics and Social Stratification

From our initial interviews, we learned that the power dynamics among and between participants were extremely complex. The degree of social stratification in the country regulated the type and extent of interactions between people at different levels in the stratification, thereby defining who had power. A striking example of the impact of the interplay of power, gender, and social structures is seen in the story one man shared with the group later in the process:

The man in the olive drab clothes of a past Communist era is a leader. You can feel it when in his presence; you can see it in how the other participants sit up and take notice when he speaks. Once deeply aligned with the goals of the Khmer Rouge regime, he had committed unspeakable acts of brutality and cruelty in the past.

Today he is a senior government official in democratic Cambodia. Twenty years after the war, he carried deep shame about his actions during the war years. No manner of rationalizing ("I had no choice") had fully exorcised his guilt. While generally a nice fellow in his everyday life, on the weekends, this leader joined his fellow veterans in heavy drinking, avoiding any discussion of past behavior. As a government official, he had great power and was instrumental in allocating resources and prioritization for many programs.

On the final day of the program, the room hushed as he rose to speak. He recounted losing his parents in the war and the behavior of his youth. He linked that past with his more recent self-destructive behavior and abuse of his wife. He shared that, because of insights he had had during the program, he was changing his behavior. He had curtailed the partying and had even confronted his fellow war veterans about their persistent use of prostitutes. He was more compassionate with himself and his wife.

His Regional Change Group had visited families orphaned by HIV and AIDS and built a house for two families. In his personal life, he knew his behavior put him at risk for infection and that, if infected, he would in turn infect his wife, potentially leaving his children orphans. He did not want that fate for his children, and he now understood the link between his past and his recent unhealthy behavior. Most importantly, he now had a deeper belief in his capacity to change his own behavior.

If that was all, we would have been grateful for his personal transformation, in that one more orphaned family had been avoided.

But institutional change had not yet happened. With the support, challenge, and resources of the Leadership Program, this leader decided to change the way staff in the provincial government worked with the other divisions and with the NGOs in the area. He understood that change needed to happen in his team, and in how his institution interacted with the community.

"We need to add more women in our staff," he declared. He told us how he had brought together some of the people he had met in the program who worked for international aid agencies, as well as those from other key governmental departments, so that they could find a better way to address HIV and AIDS and provide support to poor families. They were invited to call on him directly; a coalition was formed that ended up building wells for water and health centers faster and closer to families orphaned by HIV and AIDS. (McKee, Johnston, Mwelwa, and Rotondo, 2009)

Level of System Focus: The Facilitator and Faculty Group

Having identified the themes, our next step was to enroll not only participants, but also people whom we would train and certify as local program facilitators and faculty to use our materials and methodologies in the future.

As it turned out, working with this facilitator and faculty group proved to be more challenging and critical than we had imagined. We knew from the start that this group had to be a microcosm of the wider society and, as such, would carry all the stereotypes, biases, and long-standing historical differences that were apparent throughout the country. We knew that we needed them to help and support us to build a bridge between the rest of the participants and ourselves. We also knew that we wanted them to carry on the work after we had left. If they could not deal with the pain and mistrust from their past, the divisiveness of gender inequity, and the power differentials they would not be able to engage with and manage the multiple realities in the participant groups they would be facilitating and teaching.

We recognized that we could not leave their learning and development to chance. While we would continue to work with as many different levels of this system as possible, the Facilitator and Faculty Group was one we knew would require maximum attention because they, as a leadership team, would have profound impact on the success of the whole social change initiative. The people chosen had little or no background in teaching or training, but they brought with them a deep commitment to the program goals and their own learning and development. Above all, they shared a deep and endearing love for their country and its citizens.

In the beginning, there was no trust at all. We almost had a mutiny the first week as it became clear how wide the gaps were, how much difficult history was in the room, and how stressful they experienced our unfamiliar approach. We met with them for a day before each program and held three daily sessions during the program itself—in the breakfast, lunch, and pre-dinner hours. Some of the time was spent teaching about leadership, Emotional and Social Intelligence, adult learning, group dynamics, theories and practices of change management, and facts about HIV and AIDS; but most of the time was dedicated to processing the events of the day and what they evoked in them. We supported and encouraged them as they worked through conflict and surfaced often deeply buried stories such as: being forcibly removed from parents and/ or forced to witness or commit violent acts against parents, or being publicly whipped in the concentration camp because a person they thought was a friend had betrayed them to the Khmer Rouge.

The intensity of this effort was challenging and exhausting for us, but we could see how essential it was as they began to take on active roles in the Leadership Program, facilitating and managing the small groups where participants were learning about effective leadership and beginning to develop initiatives to address the problems. They were the "bell weather" (McKee, Johnston, Mwelwa, and Rotondo, 2009, p. 67). When they were open and able to manage their differences, so too was the larger group. When they were having difficulties, we quickly learned that we had to pay attention. They held the emotional realities of all the people, and their developing trust of each other helped make trust possible at all levels of the system.

The bond that was built in the Faculty and Facilitator Group crossed over social, religious, political, and emotional boundaries. It has been transformative. It is a connection that many thought would never have been possible. They have remained as an intact group that continues to meet; it is now running the program at the regional level. The person who led the near mutiny mentioned above became an ardent advocate of the program and an influential faculty member. The following *unedited* excerpt from a letter sent by a Cambodian faculty member captures what the experience meant to one of the participants:

Also, I want to motivate you all that this LDP program is very touched and impressed with us, the facilitators and participants. As one of my female staff, who is also a participant of the LDP round 2 said: that "this program is so good that it can make people who never know and talk to each other in the past becomes very close, sincere and love one another. Everyone keeps contact by calling even though the workshop is finished, and even two monks called me many times, and that never happened to me in the past." Here is just one example, and there are many more to proof as indicators of success of our LDP. And as one of the facilitators, I feel very proud about the result! This result, of course, encourages me to do more work on this LDP. (April 04)

Key Elements of the Leadership Program: Making Contact

There were several components to the program, which reflected our commitment to offering opportunities for contact at ever-expanding levels of system: with oneself, with one's fellow participants, and with the community.

Large Groups. We held three five-day sessions with large groups of 80-140 participants. During these sessions, we used various modalities including: experiential learning and activities, mini-lectures, small and large group dialogue, and reflection. The focus was on effective leadership, awareness, and use of self, as well as on personal and collective explorations of issues related to HIV and AIDS.

These conversations were extraordinarily powerful, especially as they began to move into increasingly difficult areas of stigma, poverty, gender relations, and sexuality. People's stories were wrenching and eye-opening. The courage it took to tell them was immense. Yet, each time one of these stories was told for the first time, both the individual speaker and the listeners became more whole, reclaiming parts of themselves that had been alienated and silenced. As people were giving verbal evaluations of the program on the last day in the third week, a man in his late fifties stood up. He said:

I have an apology to make to my small group facilitator. When we were told that you would be the facilitator of our group I thought, "What can this young woman teach me?" I did not want to work with you. I realize now that you reminded me of a woman who bullied us when we were small boys in the camp, and I saw that woman in you. So, at first, I did not want to listen to you and to what you had to say. But I have come to learn a lot from you, and I have come to respect and trust you. I am sorry for thinking about you like that at the beginning.

In retrospect, we realized that much of the trauma people had experienced occurred in large groups during the *Pol Pot* years, where each day in the camp there were "education" sessions during which individuals were publicly shamed and punished. Therefore, the growing desire to sit, listen, and speak in this setting was significant. Our challenge was to make it "therapeutic" and emotionally healthy. Having a safe opportunity to act and be in this construct helped heal former pain and create new, positive experiences. Tactically, this need often created significant time management challenges for us, as each person who spoke took far longer with the microphone than anticipated.

Small Groups: During the program, participants met regularly in two small, facilitated groups. The "EI (Emotional Intelligence) Practice Group" of eight to ten people focused on building and practicing the skills of establishing and maintaining authentic relationships that supported growth and development in all parties; while the "Regional Change Group" of ten to fifteen people focused on geographically based change projects and mostly met during the workshop intersession periods.

As discussed earlier, Gestalt practitioners think about the use of both "intimate" and "strategic" interventions (Nevis, Backman, and Nevis, 2003). In intimate interactions, the focus is on building relationships and connections through mutual exchange. It is non-hierarchical and emphasizes understanding rather than solutions. Strategic interactions, on the other hand, focus on moving to action and completing a task, using power and hierarchy appropriately. Each of these interventions is critical to the success of a large-scale social process like the one described here.

Our small groups reflected the movement between intimate and strategic intentions. In the "EI Practice Group" interactions were intimate in nature, emphasizing the personal growth of each individual and deep contact among participants. This group met three to four times within each session to reflect on, integrate, and, as the title implies, practice the emotionally intelligent leadership skills that individuals were learning in the large group sessions. Methods of teaching included exercises, discussions about personal experiences and feelings, and both supportive and challenging feedback.

In contrast, the "Regional Change Group" emphasized strategic behavior and learning how to work in diverse, task-focused groups. Over time, the groups had to identify a project, gather information from the community and, ultimately, make a positive difference on real issues. They were encouraged to choose what they cared about, looking for simple, elegant projects that did not require funding. We wanted them to see the impact of their learning.

One example of an assignment undertaken between sessions one and two involved participants using Dynamic Inquiry to interview community members about the root causes of the spread of HIV and AIDS. These data helped them to develop preliminary ideas for change projects that they brought back to the larger community; the data also taught them a technique to remain open, build awareness, and not move to quick and obvious solutions. This was fundamental to our approach to making truly transformational shifts. We wanted to help Cambodia move beyond the existing "solutions" to HIV and AIDS, finding and creating interventions that addressed root cause issues. (For further descriptions, see McKee, Johnston, Mwelwa, and Rotondo, 2009.)

The interplay between these two types of learning and intervening were essential elements in the program. All the time spent on building relations and understanding throughout the first part of the process, as well as in the ongoing groups, made it possible for the participants' energy to be focused clearly and forcefully on the strategic work, unhampered by unaddressed conflicts.

The list of projects that came out of the "Change Group" was (and still is) long and impressive, even to the sponsoring agency and the participants themselves. They discovered how to define, flesh out, and implement change across all levels of system, impacting large numbers of people. Some examples of the projects that spanned 2002-2004 include:

- Creating a ten episode radio drama based on interviews of infected people called *Nothing is Secret* that helped listeners, especially in rural areas, understand the consequences of HIV and AIDS.
- Collecting data on the poor living with HIV/AIDS, including the incomprehensible vulnerability of street children, and presenting the data to the Ministry of Education with a plea to put extra effort into reducing the numbers of street children.
- Designing workshops for government officials about sexuality and gender-related issues tied to the HIV/AIDS epidemic, learning along the way about how much influence and relationship building it takes to make these kinds of workshops successful.
- Developing an initiative focused on educating the "Beer Promotion Girls" about how to avoid infection with HIV/AIDS, and facilitating their involvement in weekly vocational education.
- Producing a play called *I Want to Live*, which stimulated thinking and dialogue to reduce the stigma against orphans and children made vulnerable due to AIDS.

- Providing training that addressed misinformation, discrimination, and a void of service in the garment industry. In all, 900 labor union leaders and workers benefited from this group's training in order to reduce the stigma associated with AIDS.

Outcome Data

Throughout the program we gathered data on its impact. The following data is taken from *Draft Report—Evaluation of the Leadership Development Program* (May 2005) prepared by Development Works for UNDP/Cambodia. Figures 1 and 2 present responses to two of the questions that we asked of participants.

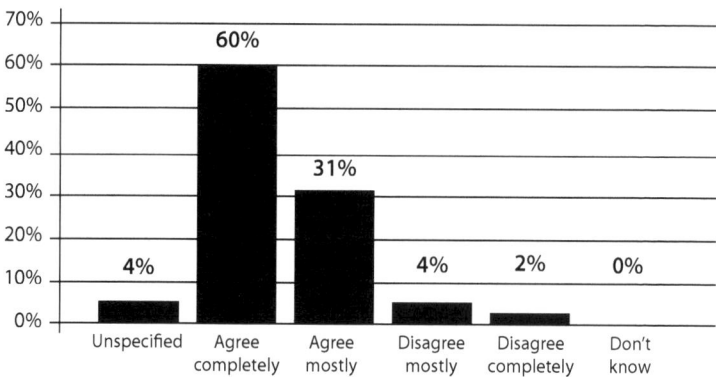

Figure 1: The Leadership Program –
Why our Commitment to Changing the HIV and AIDS Situation Has Changed

Approximately 91% of respondents (60% + 31%) indicated that the program was why their commitment to changing the HIV and AIDS situation had changed (*Draft*, p. 21).

- Participants also indicated that the program had instilled in them a sense of responsibility towards the "poor and vulnerable" in general. Participants reported that they had developed feelings of empathy and a willingness to assist others. In addition, several participants explained that they were now better able to see linkages among the range of systemic social challenges, such as drug abuse, gender inequity, poverty, and HIV (*Draft*, p. 22).
- Participants acknowledged that the program had fostered cooperation among different role-players and stakeholders. Thus, it demonstrated the possibility of generating a cadre of networks

and resource persons who could be mobilized to achieve shared goals. Those networks have been particularly beneficial as a means to foster horizontal and vertical learning and collaborative action (*Draft*, p. 23).

• Participants revealed that the program enabled them to help others around them change their sexual behavior.

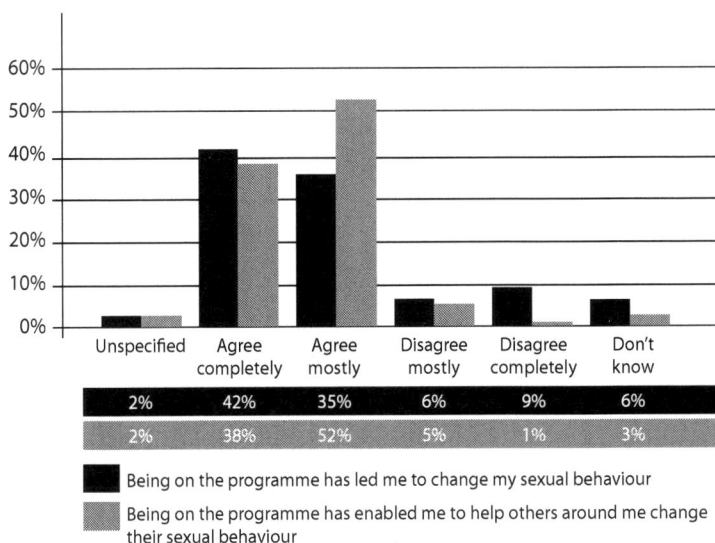

	Unspecified	Agree completely	Agree mostly	Disagree mostly	Disagree completely	Don't know
	2%	42%	35%	6%	9%	6%
	2%	38%	52%	5%	1%	3%

■ Being on the programme has led me to change my sexual behaviour

▨ Being on the programme has enabled me to help others around me change their sexual behaviour

Figure 2: Behavior Change in Me/Actions Taken with Others

About 77% of the participants indicated that being on the program had led them to change their behavior. Further, close to 90% indicated that it also enabled them to help others around them change their sexual behavior (*Draft*, p. 24).

• An overwhelming majority of participants (97%) indicated that they could apply what they were learning in their home environment, the sphere where the applicability of the program's lessons was highest. This could be attributed to the ways in which participants were able to influence relationships among household members; and echoed in the perspective that the home environment was the sphere where most participants (99%) indicated that their action could change the HIV and AIDS situation. Participants noted that they were able to effect transformation first in their personal lives (*Draft*, p. 26).

• Approximately 92% of participants indicated that their actions could change the HIV and AIDS situation in the workplace. Some participants encouraged their colleagues to change their sexual behavior and disseminate HIV information in the workplace. (*Draft*, p. 26)

- On the whole, 354 participants in the "Breakthrough Initiatives" (BTI) groups were able to interact directly with an estimated 2300 persons. The initiatives of the BTI groups have directly benefited 4533. The potential reach of the program through networks accessed is estimated to expand to 62, 000 persons. In addition, three BTIs successfully co-opted and mobilized the mass media. About nine BTI groups have developed video materials used by NGOs, and a further fifteen BTI groups have developed materials that can serve to replicate interventions (*Draft*, p. 45).

Pulling It All Together: What We Learned

As was true for the many people we encountered and worked with, what we learned about ourselves as we undertook this effort in social change in Cambodia was as meaningful on the personal level as it was on the professional level.

You Have to Begin with Yourself. For most practitioners steeped in Gestalt theory, this is not a new idea. Personal awareness is key to effective and powerful leadership practices. In Cambodia, when our every word counted (literally in this case, where translators had to work with exactly what we said), our level of awareness needed to be expanded to include the broadest field possible. We had to take time to think about the intention behind every intervention, knowing that a "provocative" choice could only be useful if we were willing to be fully present to the potential impact of that choice. In the beginning especially, the outraged reactions to our interruptions to the culture, and our insistence on new behaviors, called on us to muster as much clarity and grace as possible to stay centered and available to hear, and respond to, the group. As time went on, we did this with such frequency that it became part of the "show." Participants became very curious about how the group would react to our actions.

In order to sustain the intensity required by the program, we turned to each other for support, debriefing, and challenges as we tried to figure out what to do next and worked on our own issues. When the stress and pressure threatened to overwhelm us, we also drew from the energy in the participants and their commitment to what we were trying to accomplish together. It was a living example of how different levels of system can mirror each other, for good or bad, and we wanted to be sure it that was for good most, if not all, of the time.

Understanding Core Cultural Differences: The "I-We" Continuum. In its attention to working at different levels of system, Gestalt theory talks about how, at times, one level of a system will "optimize itself" over another for the sake of the whole. This is often a source of conflict between attending to the needs of one versus the needs of many, as well as for figuring out who takes responsibility for actions. This dichotomy also raises questions of who I am/who We are; what I/We want; and how will I/We get it. In a well-functioning system, there is balance in the movement from one position to another. At times, however, a system develops in a way that predominantly optimizes one position over the other, to the detriment of both.

At a cultural level, where this conflict shows up is in how much society lets the individual's needs, rights, and voice (the "I") set expectations for how the collective ("We") will meet those needs, versus a society where the communal or collective level is where norms and expectations are set for the individual. The United States is a culture focused on the individual, sometimes to the detriment of the collective; we have operated primarily from this framework. Indeed, our focus on Emotional Intelligence competencies such as self-awareness, self-management, and empathy are examples of focusing on individual behavior. This focus is critical when working on HIV/AIDS, where individual behavior is at the root of prevention and health.

In Cambodia, on the other hand, the "I" primarily serves the "We," sometimes to the detriment of the individual voice. Given this difference, we as facilitators needed to increase our own understanding of the collective and communal orientation, at the same time that we encouraged the Cambodians to consider the value of paying more attention to the individual. In discussing issues related to HIV and AIDS, community responsibility *and* individual responsibility and accountability are equally important.

The Power of Language: Working with Translators. The power of language to bridge cultural, social and emotional gaps cannot be underestimated. Likewise, the power of misunderstandings to increase mistrust is equally important to recognize. As described earlier, all of our interactions with the Cambodian groups took place using simultaneous translation from English into Khmer. We discovered not only that did this process of translation make program delivery take longer, but also that translations of the concepts we wanted to include were sometimes difficult for the Cambodians to understand.

We spent a lot of time working to eliminate any confusing jargon or terminology and looking for clearer ways to explain or demonstrate our theories. Faculty demonstrations including role-plays and fishbowl discussions worked well for some of the concepts difficult to translate and/or understand. We also found that experiential and process learning worked better than didactic instruction.

Our translator team played a critical role in the group's learning and mood. They not only needed to have a deep understanding of the concepts and research, but they also needed to model the kind of presence and use of self that we wanted to teach. They took turns translating our lectures, instructions, comments, and participant interactions. While this was cumbersome and interrupted conversation in many ways, in another way it slowed things down and forced us, as facilitators, to learn to stand in silence and reconnect with ourselves and our intentions while the translators spoke. We fell in love with the participants during these pauses.

Implications and Applications of Gestalt to Social Change

We have attempted above to convey an idea of how we applied Gestalt theories and approaches to large-scale social change in very complex and trying circumstances.

As we reflected on the work, we came to note that combining a clear point of view and structure with "meeting the clients where they were" was integral to the success of our social change initiative. We held our preconceived ideas lightly, or let them go completely, in order to accomplish the change we were hired to help create. Appreciation for the "what is" supported us in responding to situations as we experienced them viscerally.

In using the Cycle of Experience, it was apparent to us that awareness alone was not enough to create the required transformational change. Yes, it mobilized people's energy to want to do something, but the structures we provided offered a *direction* for channeling the mobilized energy through Action Learning Projects conducted in supportive and facilitated small groups. Holding the Action Learning Project groups responsible and accountable for themselves, and to each other, provided further support necessary for sustaining the mobilized energy for action.

Exploring multiple realities through dialogue proved a powerful approach in creating the trust that was needed among the participants in order for them to work together to bring about the desired change.

In particular, the idea of not rushing to solution was most helpful in supporting participants to consider other perspectives and develop empathy. Taking the discussions into other system level configurations enriched the dialogue, so that people were freely able to make informed choices about the need for collaborating with each other in order to move forward in a different way.

In choosing for our interventions the learning community as a microcosm of the larger Cambodian social system, we showed that it was possible to make a realistic and measurable impact on a large social scale. Furthermore, we demonstrated that the Gestalt approaches and principles can be successfully applied in any social system regardless of cultural differences, and that they are extremely useful when one is faced with enormous complexity.

Frances Johnston, PhD, serves on the faculty of the Gestalt International Study Center and the Gestalt Institute of Cleveland, and she teaches at the Wharton School's Aresty Institute of Executive Education. She received her doctorate from Temple University in Adult and Organizational Development. She is passionate about both the use of the Gestalt approach in leadership development and the integral role leadership plays in social change. She has designed and delivered development programs that address complex social issues in North America, Europe, Africa, the Caribbean, and Cambodia. She is co-founder of Teleos Leadership Institute.

Contact *www.teleosleaders.com*

Eddy Mwelwa, PhD., is a consultant with Teleos Leadership Institute and works with companies on leadership and organizational culture change. His consulting integrates Gestalt theory, Emotional Intelligence and neuroscience, group dynamics, and systems theory for transformational change. The interventions he designs and implements positively impact change in complex social issues in Africa, Cambodia, Europe, United States, and the Caribbean. He received his doctorate in Occupational Psychology from the University of Cranfield (Bedford, UK), and he is a graduate of the Organization and System Development program of the Gestalt Institute of Cleveland.

Contact *www.teleosleaders.com*

References

Boyatzis, R., & McKee, A. (2005) *Resonant leadership.* Cambridge: Harvard Business School Press.

Goleman, D., Boyatzis, R., & McKee, A. (2002) *Primal leadership: Realizing the power of emotional intelligence.* Cambridge: Harvard Business School Press.

McKee, A., Boyatzis, R., and Johnston, F., (2008). *Becoming a resonant leader.* Cambridge: Harvard Business School Press.

McKee, A., Johnston, F., Mwelwa, E., & Rotondo, S. (2009). Resonant leadership for results: An emotional and social intelligence program for change in South Africa and Cambodia. In M. Hughes, H. Thompson, & J. Terrel (Eds.), *Handbook for developing emotional and social intelligence* (pp. 49-72). New York: Pfeiffer (Wiley).

McMillen, C. and London (McKee), A. (1995). Discovering social issues: Organizational development in a multicultural community. *The Journal of Applied Behavioral Sciences, 28*(3), 445-460.

Nevis, E. (1987, 2005). *Organizational consulting: A Gestalt approach.* Cambridge, MA: GestaltPress.

Nevis, S., Backman, S., & Nevis, E. (2003). Connecting strategic and intimate interactions: The need for balance. *Gestalt Review, 7*(2), 134-46.

United Nations Development Program/Cambodia (2005). Unpublished Draft Report: Evaluation of Leadership Program.

CHAPTER 14

My Home Is My Castle:
The Use of the Gestalt Approach in Changing the Culture of a Nursing Home Organization in The Netherlands

Frans Meulmeester

Editors' Introduction

It is obvious that, because of medical breakthroughs, people are living longer, but the quality of their lived lives is often compromised. Within this age group is a subgroup of the elderly that struggles with Alzheimer's syndrome, dementia, and an assortment of other psychological problems fueled by aging. It is also obvious that these individuals need treatment that goes beyond the physical and the medical, treatment that addresses their psychological and emotional needs. They need to be met with understanding, compassion, empathy and support.

In this chapter, Meulmeester describes his work in helping the staff change the culture of an Alzheimer unit of a nursing home into a more person-oriented one. Utilizing a Gestalt philosophy, he works "hands on" providing training and support at all levels of system, including patients, staff, and administration.

By increasing the staff's awareness concerning the needs of the patients, while at the same time supporting the management and workers in becoming aware of and meeting their own needs, he is able to create change.

You may wish to notice how Meulmeester uses the Gestalt concepts of working in the "here and now" and employing experimental techniques to help the staff understand the lives of the patients. More specifically, he utilizes a role-playing technique that quickly places the staff in the resident's shoes, generating much learning.

Introduction

Since 1977, I have worked as a trainer/consultant in healthcare, especially the care of elderly populations. I have worked in different positions and functions, such as internal consultant in a nursing home organization, and trainer/consultant in an educational institute for nurses' aides. For the last fifteen years, I have been an independent trainer/consultant and coach in several countries in Europe. From the beginning, I have been interested in the inner worlds and outer situations of people with dementia.[69] I wondered what was going on inside these people, and I was interested in how I could meet them in their world, especially whether it would be possible to deal with them in a more person-oriented way instead of the medical, institutional manner which has been the common orientation.

During that period, I encountered the Gestalt approach, first in 1975 in the field of psychotherapy and counseling, but later as a possible way of dealing with larger groups and systems in education and healthcare. After finishing my Gestalt training, I started to integrate the Gestalt method in my work as a trainer, consultant, and coach. I discovered that the first basic idea of Gestalt therapy—the ability and willingness to stay in the "here and now" and accept a situation the way it is, helped my contact with people with dementia. Being "present," Gestalt therapy's second basic notion, led to many wonderful and deep contacts with people who were diagnosed as demented, which literally means "having no mind" or, in other words, people whose behavior "does not make any sense." From my long experience, I can say that the behaviors of people with dementia do make sense. The only problem is that we do not always understand them. From this background and experience, I started to stimulate and support many teams and organizations to implement a more person-oriented approach and culture in their department or organization.

In this chapter, I will present the case of a nursing home that had asked me to support them in changing the culture of a department for people with dementia into a more person-oriented one. I was involved in their process for about two years, during which time I used a combination

---

[69] In this chapter, I will use the word dementia because it is familiar to the reader. I want to make it clear, however, that I hope that the word dementia will not be used in the near future because it has created incorrect and disrespectful stereotypes. Too often, it is thought that people with dementia do not know what they are doing (no mental abilities), and that what they do does not make any sense. This way of thinking causes a lot of misunderstanding and suffering for people involved: the persons with dementia, their relatives, and the caretakers. See also Feil (1992), and Kitwood (1997).

of team coaching, consulting, workgroups, and education. This case study will offer the following aspects of the work: *intake and contract, getting started, the process, evaluation, the role of the Gestalt approach, and conclusions.* My intervention approach is influenced by the work of Peter Block (2000), Rick Maurer (2004), Edwin Nevis (1987/2005), and Peter Senge (2005).

Intake and Contract

My work began in August 2003, when I had my first meeting with the director of a nursing home and the head of patient care. Our goal was to discuss the management's intention to change the culture of a department into a more person-oriented one. This change was initiated because the department had recently been restructured into a small-scale facility for people with dementia. The management believed that the staff had to acquire new skills in order to care effectively for this new patient population.

At the time of restructuring, the staff of this department was given the choice of either to stay and undergo training or to transfer to other departments within the organization. Some staff members volunteered to stay while others, including the manager of the department, agreed to be transferred. These people were replaced by new staff members. Because of the small scale of the facility, the management decided to not assign a new manager, but to have the facility function directly under the manager of patient care.[70] The time for training was short in that the new facility was set to open in November 2003. I was contracted to support the change process.

After receiving my assignment and clarifying the mandate, I met with the director of the nursing home and the head of patient care to get more insight into the department's functions and person-oriented approaches at various levels of the organization, including management. My questions included:

- What is the quality of the staff, and what is the staff/patient ratio, given the level of pathology of the residents?
- How does the organization define "person-oriented?"
- What does it mean in everyday practice?
- How person-oriented are the staff now, and how person-oriented

---

[70] Later they changed this structure and appointed to the position of coordinator of this department one of the nurse's aides who had become an informal leader. All of the workers involved supported her appointment.

is the management with respect to the elderly population and the staff?

- How was this new department developed?
- Who was involved?
- How person-oriented is the building and, in particular, this new department?

Before describing their responses, it is necessary to provide a brief description of what I mean by a person-oriented approach for the care of people with dementia. *I mean that we are willing to see this population in terms of how they perceive their own world, and how their behaviors relate to their perceptions within the context of their present situation (including our relationship with them). It also means that we are willing to adjust our behavior to the needs, feelings, potentials, and abilities of these people. Finally, it assumes our having an eye for how those with dementia carry whole lives of (positive and negative) experiences with them.*

As I listened to the responses and story of management in our meeting, it became clear that they had a view similar to mine on the meaning of "person-oriented"; management had already done a lot of work thinking through this concept in designing the department and in speaking about the profile to the staff (e.g., in defining patient/staff ratios and the quality of the staff). But somehow I was missing something; by paying attention to my feelings, I noticed that management in cooperation with external advisors had developed the initiative's ideas, including the building itself. None of the present or future staff was involved in this process, and nor were future residents.

I see it as a basic principle that staff in healthcare will only be person-oriented toward their patients or clients when their managers are person-oriented toward them. This means that when we want to develop an organization, department, or facility based on a person-oriented culture, we have to involve the staff in each phase of the initiative: development, planning, and implementation. By connecting to the perceptions, ideas, and needs of the staff in the process of change, our approach to the staff becomes a clear model for how we expect them to relate to the patients or clients later on. It is a perfect illustration of the principle "practice what you preach." And, as a logical next step, we have to include the people who are going to live there. In the case of people with dementia, I knew that we would be confronted with certain limitations, but that did not mean that we could not involve these people at all.

Thus, after complimenting the management for all the work they had done, and for the careful way they had designed the concept, I took the liberty of sharing my awareness and view of missing the input of staff and the residents in the plans; and of asking them if "leaving out the staff and residents in that stage of the process" was a deliberate choice. The first reaction of both management members was that they were surprised by my awareness and view. They realized how easily they had overlooked this principle, and how easily they had gone into a task-oriented approach. We spoke about it, and I suggested that they involve the staff and, as far as possible the new residents, in the rest of the process. They fully agreed, and after our meeting, they asked some future staff members to form a task group with some future residents to look into questions of décor. The staff already knew some future residents because they were already living in other departments and were going to be transferred to the new facility as soon as it was ready.

Significantly, this moment of awareness in our initial meeting stood as a model for the rest of the change process because, in discussing every potential next step, we simply needed to look at each other for the question—"How person-oriented is this strategy or approach?"—to be back on the table. It became a leading, underlying concept for the processes of change throughout the rest of the organization, not only for this department but also later on when I was no longer involved.

In this stage of the work, we agreed upon my contribution to the process. It would consist of the following elements:

- Coaching the management in presenting the project to the staff and later to the residents and their relatives;
- Coaching the management and staff in defining the goals of the project;
- Designing and executing a training program to teach staff about possible person-oriented approaches in the care of people with dementia and the consequences for a twenty-four-hour care environment;
- Coaching the staff in implementing the concepts and theory of the training into their everyday practice, by providing on-the-job training and support for establishing workgroups to figure out specific aspects of a person-oriented approach and culture;
- Supervising the team in dealing with a person-oriented approach in a twenty-four-hour care environment;
- Supervising the team in enhancing cooperation;
- Supporting the team and management in organizing informational

meetings for relatives and volunteers; and
- Informing management about the status of the project.

We also agreed on the time I would spend on this project, which would be intensive in the beginning, especially with the training program, the on-the-job training, and the establishment and start-up of the workgroups. In total, this was about twenty days of work over a period of six months and, later on, one day every three to four weeks to coach and supervise the team and management for about a year and a half to two years. If, during the process, it became clear that more of my time and contributions were needed, we would look into it and, if possible, arrange it.

Getting Started

A few weeks after our first meeting, we organized a meeting with the staff intending to work in the department in order to present the project outline, ask for their opinions, obtain a mutual commitment, and define the goals. These goals had to do with questions such as: What does it mean to be person-oriented? What do you need to be able to be person-oriented? And what does this mean for both our system of working and for the environment in which we work (e.g., the building)?

Management organized the meeting. All of the department's future staff was invited, and almost everyone attended. The reason for absence was in all cases not related to the work, but strictly private; therefore, it was clear that the entire staff was motivated to hear about the new ideas. They asked me for support on two levels: one was as a facilitator, and the other as an expert in the field of people with dementia. These two roles became separate during the two different parts of the meeting, but they also converged at times.

After a welcome by the director in which he presented the purpose of the meeting and then the project itself, I gave a small lecture on person-oriented approaches in caring for people with dementia—some basic information on how they deal with the fact of their "illness," how they perceive their world, the methods and meaning of their communication and needs and, especially, how we can support them. I indicated that the process of dementia can be divided into three stages, and that the affected person has different needs in the different stages. These stages are described below.

1. The *beginning stage* is characterized by the statement, "I know that I don't know, and that bothers me," wherein people feel threatened

by what is happening. The *figure* is "losing your mind" against the *ground* of a clear life story and dealing with the fact of becoming "crazy." Very often people try to finish what feels unfinished, and they are looking for support in holding onto reality. We can offer support by helping them face the fact of having dementia, and by being a "trustworthy anchor in the chaos of life." We can support their feelings of sadness, fear, anger, shame, guilt, and doubt.

2. The *middle stage* is characterized by the statement, "I do not know or bother anymore about the fact that I don't know; my past is bothering me," wherein people are wandering between present and past, where the *figure* is the unfinished past against the *ground* of a chaotic life story. People in this stage relive old, unfinished experiences and express hidden or restricted feelings and needs. We can support them by helping them to face these unfinished experiences and express their feelings; for example, by creating a holding environment, giving words to what is hard to say, and especially by being an empathic and non-judgmental listener.

3. The *final stage*[71] is characterized by the statement, "I no longer know what is bothering me." In this stage, people are withdrawn into their inner world and the *figure* is about basic needs and feelings against the *ground* of a blurred life story. They express their needs and feelings through movement and sounds. We can support them by offering contact through touching, eye contact, verbalization, and singing; by offering security and containment; and by being a "trustworthy contact to the outer world."

At that session with the staff, I wanted to increase their understanding of people with dementia through practical examples and mini role-play situations. It was a nice surprise to see that, in the act of role-playing, some staff members showed that they already understood what it meant to be confronted with dementia and how they could support those people. For others, the information was a real eye-opener.

After a short break, we asked the staff to discuss in small groups the concept of working in a person-oriented way and to formulate questions and ideas about the project. Afterward, we made an inventory of what they had discussed, and this generated a wonderful, lively conversation as to what it meant to be person-oriented, and what they saw as essential in order to be able to work in a person-oriented way. They were also very

---

[71] "Final" here does not mean the end of life but in the process of dementia. Many people with dementia end up in this stage and remain there for many years.

clear on the consequences of that approach on the system of work and on environmental conditions, such as the building.

It was obvious that the staff was enthusiastic about the project and willing to form workgroups to look into specific aspects of a person-oriented approach and culture and have more training on that way of operating.[72] After the meeting, we planned a basic training of seven days, consisting of a combination of theory, supervision, and intervention; and the dates for the on-the-job training were confirmed. We formed workgroups and planned a series of coaching sessions for these workgroups and supervision for the team. It was agreed that all staff who were going to be involved in the department would participate in the training, workgroups, and supervision, including doctors, physiotherapists, occupational therapists, social workers, cleaning staff, and kitchen assistants. The workgroups were formed around the following topics and the questions they generated.

- *Implementation of twenty-four-hour care:* What does a person-oriented approach mean for everyday communication (transfer of information, evaluations, and feedback)? What does this mean for the place and role of the different staff (for example, the place and role of a physiotherapist)? What does this mean for cooperation among the staff? How can we anchor the person-oriented approach within the daily system of care?
- *The function and planning of activities:* What is the place and role of activities? Who will coordinate them? What will be the place and role of the occupational therapist?
- *The function of files and reports:* What do we want to report about? What does this mean for our files? Does the present filing system answer to the needs or conditions of a person-oriented approach? Who takes care of the reports, and who can look at them? What is the place and role of relatives here?
- *The function of patient meetings:*[73] What is the place and role of the meetings? Who will participate? Is it possible for a person with

---

[72] Clearly, the situation would have been more difficult if the base of enthusiasm and good will had not been present. Had that been the case, much more preliminary work would have had to be done with staff and management, because the degree of motivation in an organization is often related to management style.

[73] It should be clear by now that the words "patient" and "patient meeting" do not fit a person-oriented culture. Therefore, from here on, I will use the word "resident," only because it expresses the fact that in a person-oriented culture, we focus on the whole person, and on living rather than on being ill or being a problematic person. In other words, a person-oriented approach is by definition holistic in all its aspects.

dementia to participate? What is the place and role of relatives here?

- *The building:* What conditions should be present in the building to support or facilitate a person-oriented approach? What will be the cost of implementing these conditions?
- *The role and development of a cleaning department, kitchen and storage:* What is the place and role of these facilities and staff? Is it possible to integrate them into the department? Is it possible to prepare meals with the residents? Is it possible to go shopping with residents instead of getting the supplies from storage?

The numbers and combinations of the staff in the workgroups differed according to the complexity and extent of the topic. Some workgroups consisted of four or even five staff with different backgrounds (e.g., to address questions regarding activities or reports), and others just consisted of two or three staff (e.g., to answer questions regarding the building). We agreed that the staff would meet with each other in their workgroups, partly during their working hours and partly on their own time, and that we would have a monthly meeting to evaluate the progress and discuss the results. It was amazing how motivated the staff was to get started. They saw the department and the project as *theirs*, and they were committed to making the most of it.

The Process

During the following months, there were four basic activities: first, *formal training*; second, *on-the-job training* by participatory observation and feedback; third, tasks of the *workgroups*; and fourth, *supervision* and organizing informational meetings for relatives and volunteers.

Formal Training

Formal training took place in the form of a two-day seminar followed by five separate sessions occurring approximately every three weeks. My first aim was to increase the awareness of the staff about the perception and the needs of people with dementia. The second aim was to improve their knowledge of some specific topics related to psychogeriatric care, such as different kinds of psychopathology in old age, the process of crises, the possibilities of group work, and the social history of elderly people.

During the two-day seminar, the focus was on residents' perception and needs, the basic attitude required to be person-oriented (that is, the need of the staff to be empathic), and possible person-oriented approaches. Besides presenting information on the process of dementia, I introduced experiments in which the staff could experience themselves utilizing both a non-person- and a person-oriented approach in daily life:

> In one experiment, half of the group (assigned as B) receives the task of writing a few sentences with their left hand, while the others (assigned as A) receives the task of taking over as soon as the other one has started. They can use statements such as, "Let me do it; it goes faster this way" or "Let me do it; it will be better this way." This small experiment worked within a few minutes: the B group responded in different ways—some got irritated, some gave up, and some fought.
>
> In another experiment, I ask half the group to guide the other half in three ways while blindfolded, as follows:
>
> 1. Strictly task-oriented—A brings B to some place quickly without asking or saying anything, and with no respect for B's needs or fears.
> 2. Totally *laissez-faire*—A does nothing, just follows B while he/she tries to find the way blindfolded.
> 3. Person-oriented—A asks B where he/she wants to go, and how A can support him/her.

The feelings and reactions people show during these simple experiments, especially in the role of B, are similar to the feelings and reactions I have witnessed among residents in nursing homes. The staff often recognizes their own behavior during their daily practices, especially in reference to the first situation above. Other times, they respond with a bit of shame: "Oh my god, this is exactly what I am doing in the department! Now I understand the resistance of the residents!"

Role-play situations provide another way of increasing awareness and, at the same time, of improving the person-oriented approach (attitude and skills). Instead of simply providing information on what a person-oriented approach can look like, I take on the role of an elderly person, present a situation, and invite staff to respond to me. A key to this method is that the participants do not speak about what they would do, but instead really do it—coming into contact with me in the role. In other words, instead of having them say, "I think I would say something like. . ." I invite them to say directly to me what they would say to the elderly person. Afterwards, we review how their response to the experience relates to a person-oriented approach.[74]

Over the five days that followed, I used a combination of presenting theoretical background information on topics mentioned above (e.g., types of psychopathology in old age, the process of crises, possibilities of group work with people with dementia, and the social history of elderly people), and working on their own practical experiences (e.g., discussing their case studies, sharing experiences, and talking about my feedback from observations). By taking time for sharing and discussing their own cases and questions, we created an atmosphere of learning from one another in which it was safe to come with experiences and questions and learn from them.

A specific phenomenon we worked on was that many of the staff had a strong solution orientation tendency in dealing with each other's cases. Instead of taking time to explore a situation and stay with the feelings and questions of the worker involved, these "solution-oriented" staff members immediately jumped into looking for solutions to the "problems." Once staff members' awareness of their solution orientation tendency was heightened, they could look for alternative approaches. More and more, they were able to see that staying with people's questions and sharing their feelings helped them increase awareness about the cases and, surprisingly, supported them more than offering solutions. As the training progressed, staff developed a more person-oriented approach toward their colleagues and, at the same time, became more aware of the usefulness of applying it in their work with residents; previously, in their contact with residents, they had had a similar tendency to want to solve a problem immediately.

Thus, drawing from their own experiences, staff could see clearly the value of sharing questions and emotions, in that the answer was not in bringing about solutions but rather in sharing and showing empathy. This is especially true in working with people with dementia who are reliving unfinished experiences from the past where there is not much to "solve." We cannot solve the loss of a child that happened forty years ago; we cannot solve the feelings of guilt about being a bad husband; we cannot solve the loss of a mother when the resident was very young. We can only listen, share the feelings, and empathize.

During the training, the staff started to see more and more that those with dementia are not some strange aliens from Mars, but people like themselves with the same kinds of experiences, feelings, and needs that they themselves have. This awareness motivated the staff to become more interested in the "person behind the illness" and, in that way, more person-oriented in their approach.

---

[74] To increase further the effectiveness of role-play situations, I regularly introduced an actress (i.e., an elderly woman) into the training. The advantage was that I could stay in my role of trainer and not have to shift from role player to trainer and vice-versa.

On-the-Job Training

During the training period, I visited the department weekly at first for on-the-job training: I observed and gave feedback to the staff on their contact with residents.[75] Most of the time, I observed the staff while I was busy with some kind of activity, like assisting someone doing the dishes or cleaning the table; but other times, I participated in an ongoing activity of the staff member, like having a conversation with a group of residents about the morning paper or preparing dinner with the residents.

My primary aim during observations was to give staff immediate feedback on real, practical situations. It is a well-known fact that feedback on someone's behavior has the most impact or influence when it is given during or immediately after the observed behavior. Thus, by being present in the department and sharing my observations and feedback, I provided staff with the opportunity to learn directly from their practices.

As a rule, I emphasized positive feedback; providing information about situations that worked out well, in which the staff member exhibited person-oriented behavior. I also provided information on situations that did not work out well, even though the staff member used a person-oriented approach. Unfortunately it is common that, even if we are very person-oriented, it is not always possible to reach the resident in his or her inner world. Significantly, when we are dealing with younger people with an advanced stage of Alzheimer disease[76] or some other kind of brain damage, it can be hard to communicate with the affected person. This difficulty of communication is challenging to overcome, even when using a person-oriented approach.

After exploring the positive aspects of the staff member's person-oriented contact, we looked as needed into situations in which the worker was not able to use such an approach. We used the feedback to explore how those situations and contacts were different from the others. Most of the time, this method provided the staff with useful, concrete feedback on their behavior in a specific situation, and how the relationships during that moment of contact had developed. Normally, I give this feedback in a one-to-one conversation with the observed staff member, but when the

---

[75] I sometimes used video recording during my observations; but most of the time it was too intimidating for the staff, and they lost their spontaneity. Therefore, I left video recording out later on in the process.

[76] The original diagnosis of Alzheimer's disease was given to a woman who was fifty-nine years old. Sometimes this disease starts before the age of fifty; and most of the time, these pre-senile diseases are very progressive.

staff member preferred, we also shared the experiences and feedback with colleagues in a small group. Furthermore, if the staff member agreed, I sometimes used the training situation as an example of how situations can develop or, in a less positive situation, how they can escalate.

The main advantage of on-the-job training is that the transfer of knowledge is concrete. People are learning in the same situation in which they will apply their new knowledge at a later stage. In addition, the fact that we are reflecting on concrete, practical situations with residents in their workplace increases the effectiveness of the learning. Although the staff sometimes experienced on-the-job training as uncomfortable or even threatening when I used a video camera, they all were satisfied with the results.

Workgroups

As expected, the workgroups operated in quite a different intensity and frequency. Partly this had to do with the degree of complexity of the topic involved, and partly it had to do with factors such as the intensity of the workload in the department and the potential and capacities of staff members involved in a specific workgroup. However, the people in the workgroups did most of the work; I hardly had to intervene or help. We had agreed that, if they wanted to, they could send me their material by e-mail and I would give them feedback or additional information. Some groups used this opportunity.

In addition, I supported them by organizing a meeting of all the workgroups every three to four weeks in which we discussed the outcomes of each workgroup as well as the cooperation within the workgroup. During these meetings, I functioned primarily in the role of a facilitator and partly in the role of expert.

Whenever possible, the outcomes of a workgroup were implemented immediately in the department, but some items or suggestions for change needed more preparation or had to be discussed with the management first because of the funds involved. For example, one of the workgroups came up with some concrete suggestions for changing the bathroom into a *snoezel* place.[77] Because of the work that had to be done and the money involved, they first had to ask the management for permission. In this case, the management fully agreed with the idea and was able to

---

[77] The word *snoezel* comes from the Dutch verb *snoezelen* (say: "snoozelen"), which refers to a specific activity for people with severe dementia (third phase). The activity consists of different kinds of interventions and materials to improve contact by stimulating the senses in a way that pleases the resident, such as special lighting, sound effects, music, aromas, massage, and bathing.

make some money available. However, it took several months before this change was implemented.

Within the context of this chapter, I will simply mention some of the workgroups' results to provide a sense of the content of the project.

Implementing twenty-four-hour care

This workgroup looked into questions of implementing and anchoring the person-oriented approach and came up with ideas to improve communications/transfer of information, such as organizing a daily moment of evaluation and feedback at the end of each shift to enable people to share experiences and feelings with colleagues about the work and the person-oriented approach. Further, they suggested making each caretaker a "primary caretaker" for one resident, so that all the information/communication concerning a particular resident would go to the same caretaker. That person would also be the first contact for the other professionals such as doctors, physiotherapists, and psychologists, as well as for the family.

Adding and tracking activities

This workgroup came up with numerous ideas for activities that could be part of everyday life, such as preparing meals, washing dishes, cleaning rooms, listening to music, and doing the shopping.[78] Further, they developed a clear and simple system of reporting which residents participated in the ongoing activities and which ones did not, so that staff could easily track whether every resident was getting an opportunity to participate as he or she wanted to.

Another outcome was that activities would no longer be organized and run just by the occupational therapist, but by all staff. Activities increasingly were seen as part of everyday life. The occupational therapist would function more in a support role in organizing activities, especially in terms of exploring the needs and potential of residents whose behavior or pathology was more complex, such as those with brain damage or other severe limitations.

Improving files and reports

One workgroup came up with an improvement for the reports. In the past, and still in many other nursing homes, reports on residents were

---

[78] It might seem logical to do these activities together with the residents; but recalling the roots and history of nursing homes in Holland (i.e., hospitals with medical cultures), this required a change in thinking and acting.

mostly medical and problem oriented; a person was reduced to his or her body and the (potential) problems with that body. Many times reports consisted only of remarks on eating and bowel movements and, of course, problematic behavior, or there was just a short "NS" ("Nothing Special"). Seldom was there any observation as to how people enjoyed their day, how people's needs were fulfilled, or how a person was approached and the effect of that approach. By improving the files with more person-oriented and experience-oriented questions and topics, the staff was motivated to think about them in their daily work.

Another important step was that reports would be created together with the resident as much as possible; those reports were open to the contact person from the family in cases in which he or she was the legal guardian of the resident.

Improving meetings about residents[79]

Similar to the ideas for improvements in reports, another workgroup came up with suggestions about resident-related meetings. Instead of having meetings of only professionals who talk about the resident, they recommended having meetings with the residents. Of course, they realized that in working with people with dementia, this idea could be restricted by the limitations of the residents. But for this workgroup, the basic principle of acting in a person-oriented way was primary, and we had to start there. As the meetings progressed, we would see how far we could go. Although there was some hesitation about the attainability of this idea, people, including the management, were willing to explore it and see what would be needed to implement it. One of the needs expressed by the staff was to have some extra training on communication. They realized that it would be difficult for them to speak in an open, respectful, and sincere way with residents about their situation and illness during these meetings, so we added an extra session to the training program.

Building improvements

This workgroup came up with several ideas for improving the department, such as the *snoezel* place. But unfortunately, most of these ideas had to wait a long time before being implemented, owing to a lack of money. This reality was frustrating for the workgroup; afterward, members correctly criticized both management and me, saying that it

[79] As mentioned before, I replaced the word *patient* with *resident*; I state it here again to make it clear that the meetings have to do with the well-being of the residents.

would have been better to wait with establishing this workgroup until the financial possibilities were clearer.

Developing a cleaning department, a kitchen, and storage

In part, we had a similar experience with this workgroup as with the building group. This workgroup did good research on how other nursing homes had developed systems for cleaning, cooking, and storage, and they offered helpful concepts that were being implemented successfully in one of those nursing homes. One new concept was to integrate the cleaning department into the staffing of the department. This idea was easy to implement in this department because all of the staff agreed to it, and it fit the above-mentioned notion about daily activities.

Another concept involved changing the storage area into a shop and developing the kitchen to be more like a restaurant. Although most staff members preferred the idea—partly because of its success in other nursing homes—everyone realized that a lot of work had to be done to implement it in this nursing home. To begin with, it was not possible to implement it only in the department; the concept would have to apply to the whole organization. And besides the changes to the facility itself and the money involved, it would require a totally new way of managing budgets. In the other nursing home, every department had their own budget for staff, food, supplies of nursing materials, and so on, and they had a system for budget control (monthly reports on income and expenses). It was hard for members of this workgroup to see that, while most of the staff (including the management) shared their ideas, it would take a long time before a totally new concept such as this could be implemented.

Supervision

Where needed, I provided supervision to staff members on individual cases related to the implementation of the person-oriented approach in the twenty-four-hour care environment; their cooperation; and their organization of informational meetings for relatives and volunteers.

One specific topic was how to deal with conflicts among residents, or among relatives and residents: Is it better to let them handle these conflicts themselves or do we need to intervene? How should we deal with relatives who cannot handle the illness of the resident? What should we do with one partner who is rude to his or her partner in front of others? Another topic concerned differences within the team on how to handle cooperation: Do we stick to our own job or task, or do we handle these tasks more flexibly and help someone else with his or her work? How do we handle the dilemma of staff's need—including cleaning staff—to be informed about a resident's background and, on the other hand, the need to respect residents' privacy?

During the process, the team invited relatives and later some volunteers for a few informational meetings. They asked me to supervise them in organizing and structuring those meetings. Most of the time, supervision was a part of our monthly meeting. In some instances, we planned extra time for supervision when a specific topic warranted the time and need to have more staff present.

Evaluation

For workgroups, one of the most difficult aspects of organizational change is maintaining the balance between enthusiasm and good will, and holding on to the reality that implementing change needs time. Especially when people are motivated to improve their way of working, it can be frustrating when an improvement cannot be implemented right away because of a lack of money or time or, worse yet, the bureaucracy involved.

We encountered delays that were due in part to a work overload in the department, in part to finances, and in part to more organizational realities such as the existing organizational structure. It is clear that if the organizational structure does not support or facilitate cultural change, then that change will take much more time and energy, and sometimes it becomes impossible. Before being able to change the culture of an organization, all levels of management must be willing to include structural change as part of the change process. But before discussing the negative impact of the delays on the project, let us first look at some positive outcomes.

The most positive outcome of the process was that the department's staff became more and more aware of what it means to be person-oriented in dealing with people with dementia. Their attitudes and behaviors changed during the process, and there was an increasing willingness to look at their part of the staff-resident relationship. Formerly, it was typical to attribute all "negative" behavior or problems to residents.

In a traditional, task-oriented medical culture, we can draw a line between healthy people (of course, that's us!) and the sick (the patients). Especially in the care of people with psychological, psychiatric, or psychogeriatric problems, the line to be drawn is clear and hard to cross. Disturbances or complex behaviors are seen as part of the illness, regardless of our effect on the ill person. However, in a person-oriented approach such as Gestalt, behavior is always seen as part of the relationship or field, which includes both the patient and me. There is an ongoing interaction between the patient and me, and between the system and the patients. Thus, disturbances are by definition disturbances of the field and need to be explored. This way of thinking became more and more familiar to the staff in the department under discussion. Supervision helped them implement the person-oriented approach in their daily work.

A second positive outcome of the project was that the department staff stayed motivated in their work and in their attempts to make something beautiful of their department, despite the difficulties they encountered such as delays and staff turnover. It is a common fact in healthcare that staff turnover is rather continuous: young women get pregnant and stop working after having their baby, caretakers want to improve themselves and change to hospital work, staff cannot stand the workload anymore, and so on. This department was no different in that respect, although its turnover was less than the average in other nursing homes.

A third positive outcome was the pleasant and constructive cooperation of the different types of professionals in the department. In many nursing homes, there is a distance and sometimes even a lack of cooperation between caretakers: for example, between doctors or physiotherapists, or between caretakers and cleaning staff. In this department, cooperation was high. All professionals, including doctors, took part in the monthly coaching sessions in which we discussed the process and progress of the project, and the staff's cooperation. The atmosphere was positive and constructive. This made it possible to speak openly about cases and handle all questions, as well as to air irritations and other difficulties.

The Role of the Gestalt Approach

In this project, I utilized the Gestalt approach in assisting the staff, including management, to increase their awareness of their way of working, and how that related to their wish to become more person-oriented. That included increasing awareness of their perceptions and feelings concerning people with dementia; and increasing awareness of the fact that people with dementia have the same needs and feelings as everyone else. As I stated above, they are not aliens from Mars, but human beings like us!

These two issues seem contradictory, but they are not. Of course, there is a difference the moment that someone is confronted with dementia, and especially when he or she is in an advanced phase and reliving old memories. Present and past are enmeshed. At the same time, the residents' needs and feelings do not differ so much from those of other people who are confused or unsure. Also, basic daily needs, such as how to have your breakfast, how to enjoy your day, and what time you want to go to sleep, are just typical of needs we all have. By increasing awareness of similarities as well as differences, people's understanding grew enormously.

Another important element of the Gestalt approach which I applied was helping the staff to stay in the here and now, and to accept that what is going on in the moment is fruitful, even if it means staying with someone's sadness or fear. In the beginning, most staff had a strong need and tendency to solve the problems with which they were confronted. It was hard for them to see that many problems the residents were dealing with could not be solved. Some of their so-called problems are existential, such as the fact of having dementia and "getting crazy"; only the resident can find an answer or response to this terrible fact of life. Other so-called problems concern experiences from the past, which cannot be solved because they happened many years ago. We can only support the person in expressing and sharing these feelings, with the hope that expressing and sharing will lead to temporary relief.

My experience, which also stems from my work with people with cancer, is that the Gestalt approach has a lot to offer in these existential crises because it is built on a willingness to stay in the moment. This relates to the third important aspect of the Gestalt approach—presence. Presence means that we are willing to stay in the here and now together, with the other person, with all our qualities and limitations. As supervision progressed, the staff became more and more able to stay present with the residents despite the difficulties that arose. They no longer walked away or escaped into other tasks such as office work, making reports, or cleaning beds, but just stayed in the living area open for contact with residents.

For me as a consultant and trainer, the Gestalt approach offered a continuous awareness of my goals, needs, and tendencies—an awareness that prevented me from imposing them on others. Of course, I was also there in the role of expert in the field of people with dementia, and I used my expertise during training and supervision. On the other hand, I also held back my expertise time and again, in order to allow the staff to find out for themselves how they wanted to work on issues, and in what directions they wanted to develop their department.

This choice sometimes led to situations I might have handled in a different way but, in my opinion, that was not important because, since the staff created approaches and directions, it became their project more and more and only served to increase their motivation. At this point, I am reminded of a Dutch author in the field of consultancy, Willem Verhoeven (1993), who said that instead of asking ourselves how we can motivate staff, we would do better to stop de-motivating them.

Conclusion

It was a pleasure to revisit this case study because it made me more aware of how I had worked with the team, how I had enjoyed the cooperation with them, and how the work had changed me.

I have been working with staffs that care for the elderly for many years. But being involved once again in such a process reminded me of the difficulties and beauty inherent in everyday life in a nursing home, and especially the daily work of the staff. The Gestalt approach helped me to encounter their situation with an open, non-judgmental mind, and to be more connected to their feelings and my own. It helped me to build a closer connection with them and their work, and to appreciate more what they do, day after day. I think that I would not be able to do this work every day and be as patient as many of them are.

After my concrete contribution to the project had ended, I visited the department several times just because of my curiosity to know how things were going. Every time I visited, I left feeling that we had done something beautiful together and, fortunately, that they were able to hold onto the basic principles despite difficult conditions.

In sum, I believe in the possibilities and strength of a Gestalt-oriented approach to effect positive results not only in the work with people with dementia, but also in the work of social change in nursing homes.

Frans Meulmeester has worked as a trainer/ consultant in healthcare, and especially in the care of old people, since 1977. During these years he has worked in different positions and functions, for example, as an internal consultant in a nursing home organization or a trainer/consultant in an educational institute. For the last fifteen years, he has performed this work as an independent trainer/consultant and coach throughout several countries in Europe.

Contact: *info@lifeisaninvitation.nl*

References

Block, P. (2000). *Flawless consulting.* San Francisco, Jossey-Bass.

Feil, N. (1992). *Validation.* Cleveland, Ohio: Edward Feil Productions.

Kitwood, T. (1997). *Dementia reconsidered: The person comes first.* London: Open University Press.

Maurer, R. (2004). *Making a compelling case for change.* Washington, DC: IRC Press.

Meulmeester, F. (2000). *Omgaan Met Complex Gedrag [Dealing with complex behavior].* Brunnik, Denmark: Elsevier.

Meulmeester, F. (2006). Changing is standing still. Unpublished manuscript.

Nevis, E. C. (1987, 2005). *Organizational consulting: A Gestalt approach.* Cambridge, MA: GestaltPress.

Senge, E., Scharmer, C. O., Jaworski, J., & Flowers, B. S. (2005). *Presence.* New York: Doubleday.

Verhoeven, W. (1993). *De Manager Als Coach [The manager as coach].* Amsterdam: Bloemendaal.

CHAPTER 15

"We Are the Ones—But Where Are the People?": Social Identity within a Union Branch in Denmark

Susanne Blom, MSc

Editors' Introduction

Throughout history, unions have been a primary vehicle for social change. They have provided a means for the poor, the downtrodden, the oppressed, and the exploited to join to confront workplace issues. They join not just for higher wages, but also for more fundamental issues such as safe and humane working conditions and, of course, child welfare. Unions in Denmark have historically had a unique and less adversarial place in society than in most countries. Unlike many parts of the world, unions in Denmark function cooperatively with employers and the government, and approximately 80% of the workforce participate in unions.

Yet, just as in many other parts of the world, unions in Denmark are experiencing a decrease in membership. The reasons are complex. Maybe, as Blom points out, it is time for them to die a natural death, having fulfilled their usefulness. However, as she also points out, if the unions were to die, what for many is an essential part of our heritage and social fabric would be lost.

In this chapter, Blom describes her experience of consulting with two branches of a large Danish union that are losing membership. Looking at unions through the lens of identity theory, she helps the leadership become more aware of a number of habits and structures that no longer serve it well. She demonstrates a number of characteristics of a top-notch organizational consultant, such as including as many stakeholders as possible in the process, establishing trust and connectedness, and remaining separate enough to keep her perspective. In the descriptions of her actual work at union meetings, one sees a wonderful example of presence, as she uses herself to join, confront, and take risks in order to facilitate change.

Introduction

The unions in Denmark are on trial; not the type of trial that occurs through public media disclosure, when prominent union leaders are seen as violating the societal etiquette. The trial concerns the *raison d'être* of the unions. Not only have the expectations of the members changed, but so have the market conditions of society, presumably driven by the mega trends of globalization, individualization, digitalization, and value orientation (Silver, 2003). For the unions, these changes have resulted in a life or death crisis; the members are leaving.

One might ask why we should care. Maybe the unions have outlived their usefulness. Perhaps they are like dinosaurs, dying out once their environment no longer supports them. Yet, for many people the unions represent a vital part of the social fabric, not as organizations in their own right but as the societal "watchdogs" of equality. Many believe that, if the union movement were to disband, something important would be lost. One might even argue that this has happened already, that the consistent loss in union membership is the phenomenological evidence for the postulated decline in social capital (Putnam, 2000).

Traditionally in Denmark, when young people reached the working age, joining the union was a matter of course. This action and the values that underlie their joining were passed on through generations without being questioned. It was not just about loyalty and tradition. Being a union member involved an often-unaware emotional sense of solidarity. You joined with a natural pride in being part of something bigger than yourself, a vision with which you identified. Today, however, joining a union is no longer automatic and self-evident, resting more on economics than on closely held political and personal values. For many, the unions have come to represent a form of insurance; important for individual economic safety, but for nothing more. Discussing the matter, a man asked me rhetorically: "Would you give a lot of money for something you don't need?"

In fact, there are a number of reasons for not joining. Most important is the perceived infringement on individualism and liberty. In Denmark, the unions and the employers negotiate working conditions every second or third year. They do that collectively on behalf of their members in order to provide the best overall working conditions, and to provide equality by focusing on the groups with the lowest income. The result of these negotiations, even when positive, can become an impediment for people who want to advance faster, earn more money, or gain more flexible working hours.

This chapter presents the journey of two particular trade union branches with which I consulted over a period of four years. The branches found themselves dying and knew they had to change. During our time together, many changes were implemented regarding structure (mergers, reorganizations, inclusion of new 'business areas'), competencies, and behavior. In hindsight, the profoundness of the change is what stands out most. They changed the very essence of "who they were," or to phrase it slightly differently, their *organizational identity*. That change and how it occurred is the main topic of this chapter.

The Paradoxical Change Consultant

Years ago, I struggled to establish my identity as a Gestalt consultant, which, I assumed, had to differ somewhat from being a therapist (even though the work was grounded in the same theory) and from a management consultant (even though the clientele were similar). Clearly, different authors emphasize different aspects; however, an overview of contemporary Gestalt writings on organizational consulting and psychotherapy shows that the methodology is similar. For example, both fields are grounded in an existential, experimental approach and use concepts such as "the continuum of experience," "the here and now," "experiment," "authentic relationship," "multiple realities," "the paradox of change," and "diagnosis as hypothesis formation" (Melnick and Nevis, 2005, pp. 102-15).

Applying these concepts to an organizational situation, however, shifts the focus from the individual towards the collective-individual, i.e., the behavior of groups, the dynamics between the individual and the collective, the co-creation of relationships, etc. I find that an organizational consultant needs to be knowledgeable as well as experienced in organizational culture, language, politics, and power. As Laura Perls (1992) points out, this sort of preparation is a necessity if you want to establish contact with, and provide sufficient support for, your client. You are in the service of the total system, supporting contacting and meaning-making through creative experimentation (Francis, 2001, p. 21).

A practical basic assumption I have is that an organizational head or board never spends money on a consultant unless he/she/they want to accomplish something, which implies readiness for change. According to Hanafin (2004) one of the ten rules of thumb for change agents is: "80% of consultancy work is simply showing up" (pp. 24-28). I fancy this particular rule of thumb, since in many respects it captures how I experience Gestalt theory at work when executed by experts.[80] "Simply showing up" implies that Gestalt consultants carry their theoretical knowledge "lightly," do not superimpose their beliefs on the organization, and are open to what emerges in the situation. By lightly I do not mean spineless. I firmly believe that being a Gestalt practitioner is a life philosophy that impacts one's working style in a profound way. I mean being able to bracket your theory and values consciously, and knowing that your interventions will be grounded in Gestalt theory: based on existentialism, phenomenology (Zahavi, 2003), Lewin's social psychology (Lewin, 1997; Stivers and Wheelan, 1986), Gestalt psychology, and American pragmatism (Mead, 1934; Hassrick, 2003).

Speaking simplistically, one could say that a Gestalt consultant has two basic perspectives concerning change. The first one is being future based, goal-oriented, with an action plan, deadlines, evaluation, etc. The second perspective on change is grounded in an existential and experimental approach, valuing paradoxical change that takes place through the heightening of awareness of what is going on in the moment (Beisser, 2004), and supporting the client system to deal with dilemmas, make deliberate choices, move into action, and assess a new "what is."

Despite the richness of Gestalt theory, I still felt incomplete when it came to conceptualizing the complexity of the union situation during my work with the branches. I found inspiration in "Organizational Identity Theory" (Hatch and Schultz, 2004). It provided me with an easily comprehensible and manageable macro-level conceptual model that describes what happens when organizations have their very existence threatened,[81] and when life within the organization turns draining, filled with self-criticism and blame. One result is that many of the stakeholders/employees turn their attention towards themselves and their individualistic needs instead of the needs of the collective. Of course, some will work hard to keep business going as usual. Instead of negatively labeling this behavior as resistance, these individuals can be seen as informal or emergent leaders, functioning outside of the formal organizational structure.

---

[80] The term "expert," as understood in Dreyfus's 5 step learning model, is defined as the experienced practitioner who has thoroughly integrated experiences from many different situations, and is able to alter his or her approach based on the shifting contexts of organizational life (Flyvbjerg, 1991).

[81] Some object to language such as "organization's experience" or "organizational identity." They argue that these are human phenomena, which only can be ascribed to an organization when anthropomorphizing it. The founders of organizational identity

Organizational Identity and Identity Dynamics

I refrain from coming up with *a* definition of organizations. Rather I am in line with Morgan (1997) when he talks about *images* of organizations, implying that organizations are many things at once depending on one's perspective. Likewise, the concept of identity appealed to me: "One can only explore it by establishing its indispensability in various contexts" (Erikson, 1968, p. 9).

The concept of Organizational Identity (OI) is used in different ways: by researchers and consultants to characterize aspects of an organization, and by the organization itself to reflect its vision and mission. Today, creating and maintaining an "identity" is a common organizational preoccupation due to the increasingly blurred and complex boundaries between organization and environment. In 1987, Albert and Whetten took on the task of making the concept scientifically tractable. They formulated three criteria for defining OI:

1. What provides the essence of the organization, i.e., its central character?
2. What features differentiate the organization from others, i.e., claimed distinctiveness?
3. What features lead to perceived continuity over time? (Albert and Whetten, 2004, pp. 89-118)

Whereas Albert and Whetten were concerned with describing "measurable" features, other writers have focused more on the dynamics, or how OI is co-constructed. Hatch and Schultz (2004) offer a dynamic model (Figure 1), which builds on Mead's understanding of the "social self." Mead (1934) explains through the concept of *reflexivity* how the social and the personal cannot be understood separately. He argues that the self consists of two aspects, a "Me" and an "I." The "Me" incorporates the attitudes of "the other" (the social world); and the "I" is the mechanism that responds to the "Me," but also acts in unpredictable ways, first comprehensible when reflected in the "Me." Together, and over time, these self-aspects constitute a personality. Hatch and Schultz

theory addressed the dilemma by saying: "We do not wish to treat the organization as an individual, which is to claim that the whole is like one of its parts; nor, while we retain the term organizational culture, do we wish to treat an organization as identical to the society in which it is embedded, which is to claim that the parts are the same as the whole" (Albert and Whetten, 2004, pp. 89-118). Jenkins (2004), questioning the validity of bringing an individual level theory to another level and building on the American pragmatists, argues that when it comes to "identity" and "identity dynamics" the processes by which they are shaped and changed are, in most respects, analogous.

adopt the "Me" and "I" interaction in Mead's theory, using "Me" to refer to the organization's image and "I" to reflect the organizational culture. These two components make up organizational identity. Let me explain the model:

1. Identity mirrors the image of others, i.e., stakeholders have opinions about the unions. For example, "Union managers and employees are more concerned about their own jobs and positions than caring about members and the union mission," or "The union takes care of the 'little man.'"

2. These external images of outsiders are taken in by individuals, who reflect upon the feedback by making personal comparisons with the outsiders. The external images are filtered through the union members' collective self-perceptions as reflections (we work hard, we are not efficient; we are social towards one another). Eventually, they become imbedded in the union culture (its beliefs and values).

3. The reflective process both maintains and changes the organizational members' (also, politicians' and employees' in the case of unions) understanding and explanation of "who they are as an organization."

4. The organizational self-perception (perceived identity) is also projected onto its environment. This occurs both intentionally—as in press conferences, glittering brochures, and corporate symbols—and indirectly through its members' attitudes. All of these projected images, with or without awareness, leave impressions on the external others.

According to Hatch and Schultz, the dynamics must be understood in their interactive complexity and not as orderly organized or linear phases. The extra lines in Figure 1 are drawn to emphasize this point.

What Gestalt theory has to add is the emotional and the relational—it deals with *how* its members regard themselves as an organization. What both theories have in common is a focus on the mutually recursive relationship as formulated in the American pragmatists' self-concept.[82] In Gestalt theory, it is expressed through the notion of the figure of contact against the ground of the organism/environment field. In organizational identity theory it is expressed as the mutual influence and adaptation

---

[82] Being influenced by the American pragmatists, Perls, Hefferline, and Goodman's (1951) self-construct is in some respects similar to Mead's. They claim that "the self" is located neither in the internal world of personal experience nor in the outer world of interpersonal events, but in the creative tension of the two. The "self" is the system of

3. Identity expresses cultural
understandings

1. Identity mirrors the
images of others

Culture   "I"   IDENTITY   "Me"   Image

2. Reflecting embeds
identity in culture

4. Expressed identity leaves
impressions on others

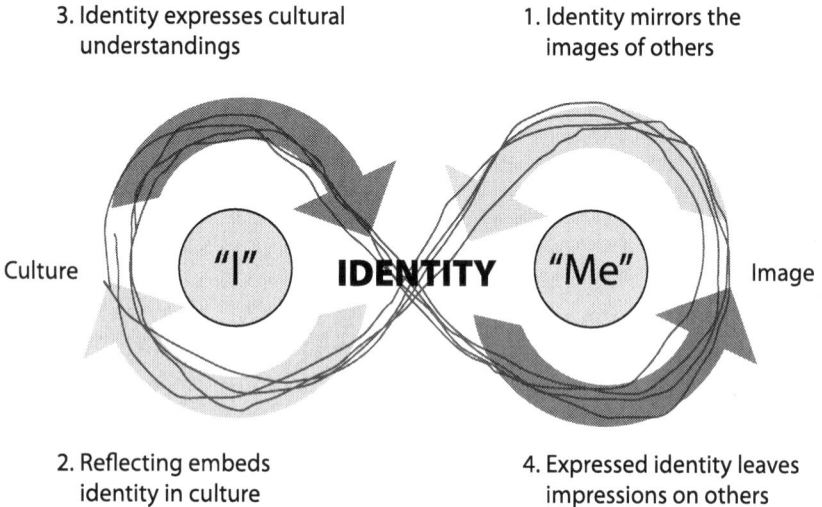

Identity Dynamics: Hatch & Schultz (2004)
Figure 1

between organizational culture and organizational image; as the internal representation or expression of identity, the often unaware perceived ontology of the organization.

Hatch and Schultz (2004) proceed by adding *dysfunctions* to their model. Dysfunction is defined by the degree of discrepancy between the organizations' self-definition (the "I" and culture) and the images of the external other (the "Me" and image). For example, narcissistic organizations are self-absorbed and ignore their environment, while hyper-adapting organizations are mostly concerned with their image and how they impress their environment. Even though it is tempting to "diagnose," I prefer to stay open to "what is." I use the model informed by Gestalt theory's insights of process (what is happening and how) and its emphasis on phenomena in the here and now (what is being done instead of what ought or should be done). The field theoretical strategies

present contacts and the agent of growth. Furthermore, "Self-preserving and growing are polar, for it is only what preserves itself that can grow by assimilation, and it is only what continually assimilates novelty that can preserve itself and not degenerate" (p. 372). Human beings in their pure existence always are both an "I" and a "We." Perls, et al. (1951) state: "So the materials and energy of growth are: the conservative attempt of the organism to remain as it has been, the novel environment, the destruction of previous partial equilibrium, and the assimilation of something new"(p. 373). One of the few times identity is explicitly mentioned is in connection with egotism: "For want of a better term, we call this attitude "egotism", since it is a final concern for one's boundaries and identity rather that for what is contacted"(p. 456).

and the freedom to experiment provide a better way of promoting aware choices and action.

The experiences I had and the problems I ran into while working with the union branches not only had me look for new ways of theorizing, but they also changed my view of traditional Gestalt constructs, such as resistances to contact. I found it meaningful to utilize basic Gestalt concepts of *confluence* and *egotism* as polar contact dynamics[83] that are necessary for identity formation, supported by *deflection* and *introjection, retroflection* and *projection* (Wheeler, 1991, 2006; Gaffney, 2006), as shown in Figure 2 below. Identity formation is existential and basic, always present but not always attended to. The work of identifying and differentiating ourselves is supported by the other contact mechanisms. I move into the "we-ness" through introjection and retroflection and simultaneously differentiate myself through deflection and projection, before or with awareness. Identity work influences the field as the field influences identity formation. Consulting with organizations or groups over time enables one to watch the forming and destruction of subgroups based on this identity work.

In sum, my approach is primarily Gestalt-oriented, with a focus on identity dynamics within organizations. Within the above-mentioned frame, I explore patterns of beliefs (what is or will be), values (what ought to be), and influences and power (who approves or disapproves) that are felt, verbally expressed, and often acted upon in groups/organizations and organizations/society.

Introducing the Fair Trade Union (FT)

"Trade Union" as a construct is understood worldwide. When I say the word union, most people will know what I am talking about. We attribute specific characteristics to the word based on our experiences, as if all unions were alike. Yet unions differ in many respects, based on history, societal and cultural influence, type of union (academic, blacksmith, clerk), etc. Therefore, in order for the client to be understood more fully, I will present a brief history of the union movement in Denmark, followed by a description of this particular union.

The labor movement in Denmark emerged as a collective response to the exploitation of the working force during the industrialization period.

---

[83] I use the notion of contact dynamics (confluence, egotism, deflection, introjection, projection, and retroflection) somewhat differently than do the founders. I do not interpret them purely as defense mechanisms or contact interruptions, but rather as a typology of contacting. We are always contacting something or someone.

Identity Dynamics through Contacting Before and With Awareness

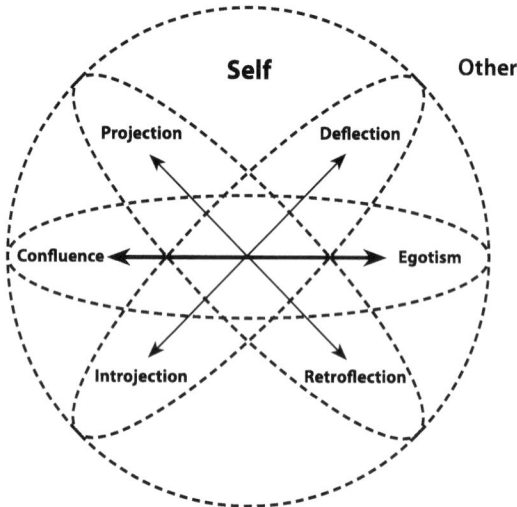

Figure 2

Compared to many other countries, it turned out to be a rather non-violent response. In 1899, the involved parties established the foundation to the later so-called "Danish Model," consisting of binding bipartite and tripartite cooperation agreements between the trade union movement, employers' organizations, and the government. Consequently, almost all collective bargaining is conducted without government intervention, and all significant legislative bodies regulating the labor market are normally tripartite in form. Regional labor market policy is carried out in cooperation between the social partners and the government, and trade unions and employers have a high degree of influence on vocational training in Denmark. This labor market model is still functioning today and influences the working condition for the unions, as well as the living conditions for the Danish inhabitants and companies. More than 70% of the people between the ages of sixteen and seventy years are active members of the workforce, which comprises 2.86 million of the 5.3 million Danes. Approximately 80% of the working population is organized in unions. In Denmark, there are twenty-two unions providing legal assistance for its members and seeking political influence in the Danish Parliament, in the European Union, and internationally. Their members are organized into specific unions, which are specialized in their working areas, i.e., unskilled workers, or skilled workers within differing industries, and so forth.[84]

With approximately 377,000 members, the FT union[85] is the largest trade union federation in Denmark (Figure 3). It consists of forty-one regional branches with the head office situated in Copenhagen. The role of the union is to both coordinate the activities and serve as the information center for all the branches, and also to coordinate and carry out collective bargaining. The FT union can be described as two parallel and interrelated systems; a democratically based, political system, where its members are chosen by voting and the staff of white-collar workers engaged by the political system. The political system debates and decides the strategic/tactical framework, which the staff will carry out. The chair of each branch is selected from the political system, whereas the manager is employed by the branch chair. In each branch, the chair and the employed manager work together in order to implement the overall union strategy,[86] as well as to offer member services according to the expressed ideology. The branch politicians are responsible for providing the local political strategy. It is the employees' task to operationalize the strategy. In order to best serve its members, each branch is divided into four sectors. In this case, the four sectors are: FT/ Retail and Wholesale Trade, FT/Private, FT/Government Institutions, and FT/Municipal Authorities.

The two regional branches that I consulted to were geographically adjacent to each other. They were largely independent when it came to budget, political leadership, local meetings, political process, and governance. They were each responsible for developing their own branch, including marketing and the creation of services.

As I began my work, it became clear that the Fair Trade Union (FT) was in disarray; and that the old ways and beliefs were not working. I realized that the total organization was struggling with its perception of what it meant to be a union. Were they in business to fight the employers for better wages, to increase the union's power and membership, to provide a sense of social connection for its members, or to detect and prevent conflicts between members and their employers? What was to become of the union's role in society? Interestingly, the FT[87] replaced the word

---

[84] It needs to be mentioned that joining the European market also influenced Danish law. The free movement of manpower and the request for flexibility opened up competition amongst the unions, with "new" unions joining the market. These are known in idiomatic Danish as "yellow" unions as opposed to the older "red" unions.

[85] The figures are from 1999. The organizational structure is a description relevant to the time I worked with them.

[86] The union strategy is created every third year in the Congress (the supreme decision-making authority of the union) and by ballot (accepted, adjusted, or rejected).

FT's Organizational Structure Year 1999

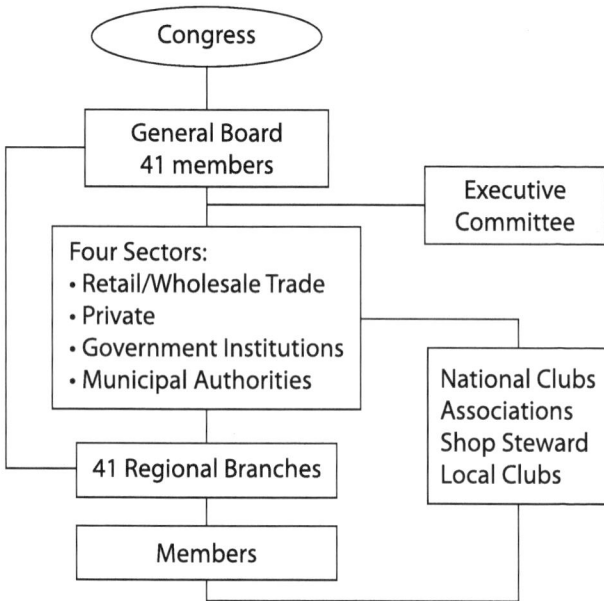

```
                    ┌─────────────────┐
                    │    Congress     │
                    └─────────────────┘
                             │
              ┌──────────────────────────┐
              │   General Board          │        ┌──────────────────┐
              │   41 members             │────────│   Executive      │
              └──────────────────────────┘        │   Committee      │
         │    ┌──────────────────────────┐        └──────────────────┘
         │    │ Four Sectors:            │
         │    │ • Retail/Wholesale Trade │
         │    │ • Private                │
         │    │ • Government Institutions│        ┌──────────────────┐
         │    │ • Municipal Authorities  │        │ National Clubs   │
         │    └──────────────────────────┘        │ Associations     │
         │                                        │ Shop Steward     │
         │    ┌──────────────────────────┐        │ Local Clubs      │
         └────│  41 Regional Branches    │        └──────────────────┘
              └──────────────────────────┘
                    ┌─────────────────┐
                    │    Members      │
                    └─────────────────┘
```

Figure 3

"solidarity" with "loyalty" in a large member survey. Said simply, the FT union and the union branches disagreed as to "who they are," i.e., their organizational identity, how to establish a new "we," and how to agree upon who should possess the power to decide. It soon became obvious to me that the union's very essence was changing, that its basic identity was in question, and that to be effective as a consultant I would have to address this issue at all levels of system, which include the personal, interpersonal, sub group, branch, and union as a whole imbedded in society.

With this brief overview of union history and organizational structure, I will now describe the presenting issues, and how I began my involvement.

Entering and Contracting

In the summer of 1999, I was invited to a college alumni meeting. One of my old classmates, "Sofie," was working as a consultant for branch

---

[87] Because of ethical concerns, I have changed names and events in ways that allow for anonymity. I will call the total union the Fair Trade Union (FT) and the branches I worked with and for, FT-X and FT-Z. I wish to underline that I alone am responsible for the perspectives put forward in the article.

FT-X. We talked about my work as a Gestalt organizational consultant, and she responded with enthusiasm. Some months later she called me and asked if I would help to create a project design for developing her branch in collaboration with a "neighboring" branch, FT-Z. Both branches and, in fact, the entire union were being confronted with a dramatic decrease in membership and, as a result, the budget was being affected. Immediate attention was needed. When FT-X's manager "Jens" benchmarked with other branches within the FT union, he found that in comparison his branch was doing pretty well. He believed, however, that being a competent leader meant acting quickly, before the decrease in membership impacted his branch more seriously. Among the most serious of the projected negative consequences, according to FT values, would be a reduction in staff. Jens and the FT-Z manager, "Karen," were very open concerning how we designed the project. They provided me with their hope for outcomes such as:

- Stop the loss of membership.
- Provide another way of organizing within and between the two branches.
- Increase the competencies of the employees to work in new and creative ways, such as increased outreach.
- Create budget neutral initiatives.

The project was to write an application for monetary support, to be presented to the FT's head office. The application would contain the purpose and goals for the project, an action plan, and a budget. If accepted, I would be assigned as process consultant.

The project team consisted of Sofie from branch FT-X, a consultant from FT-Z, a journalist who wrote articles for the branch newsletter, and me. We met for two days on a small island to discuss previous ideas, formulate the application, and design and submit an action plan. The FT head accepted our application. The project was called "1 + 1 = 3" to emphasize the expectation of synergy through branch cooperation.

Unfolding of the Project

After the project application was accepted we focused on generating local support, for without broad "buy in" from the important stakeholders, especially the politicians, the project would not have enough traction to move forward. In order to win local political acceptance we, the project group, organized a series of informational meetings. We decided to have the first meetings consist of the staffs from FT-X and FT-Z. We chose this course of action because we knew that both staffs had tight personal and often informal connections with the politicians. We also knew that in order for the politicians to accept our[88] recommendations, they would rely on the staffs' thoughts and opinions.

Staff meetings took place at each of the branch premises. The responses of the employees were nearly the same in the two branches. We were met first with silence, followed by a few questions, a few comments, some wisecracks, and then more silence. The first time, after observing this process for a short period, I suggested a coffee break in order to see what kind of dynamics emerged. Luckily, what I hoped for began to take place—a lively conversation. After the break, the shop steward spoke quickly, and directly, to the manager. He expressed his concerns regarding working hours, work overload, payment of wages, and how employees would be involved in the project. He also expressed a fear of a decrease in the quality of member services. Later, my project colleagues explained to me that this was typical of how the union employees addressed and managed change.

We then conducted a series of meetings with the political sectors from each branch. At these meetings, the project team first presented the project design and then followed this up with discussions, first in groups of four and ending with the group as a whole. The politicians' reactions to the project were divided. Some were enthusiastic: "This is great, fun, creative." Some were suspicious: "Who approved this? It's not us; this is nothing but a merger in disguise." And others were despondent: "It will not work anyway; it takes time away from our work with members."

Their responses were extremely important in helping us to plan our next interventions. We communicated to the politicians and the employees the obvious facts—that the union was losing membership—and supported this observation with budgetary and statistical data. Our conclusion was sobering: "The membership loss has to be stopped, and the budget has to be minimized or downsizing will be a fact. Consequently, things have to be done differently." Next, we articulated project values, such as openness, participation and honesty, and discussed how we would incorporate these values into the branches' day-to-day operations. In order to have a chance of succeeding, we were sure of one thing: our process for creating and implementing change would have to include large participant involvement.

---

[88] I was the external consultant, but those who worked with me in the project group felt the politicians' attitude towards them shift over time, as some moved away and others became more interested.

Use of Metaphor: "The Competent Negotiator"

Getting to know the branches, I became aware of enduring patterns of behavior. Being an outsider culturewise, my attention was drawn to other features than those of my colleagues, which gave rise to rich team discussions. One of the values of the branches that seemed to capture much of the essence and competency of its members was that of "the competent negotiator." In general, everybody in the FT system was highly competent at negotiations, approaching most issues in a strategic manner (Nevis, Backman, and Nevis, 2003; Stacey, 2007). They viewed outsiders with a "wait and see" attitude, often projecting that "the others" were holding back information, while having a "hidden card up their sleeve." This willingness to contain information, to use coercion as a method to achieve goals, and to take advantage of power differentials, also had negative consequences. There was mistrust—reflected in a lack of joining around a mutual goal—which could permeate the union as a whole. This mistrust was not just limited to individuals. The branches treated each other in the same manner.

The negotiator metaphor also implied that winning for your clients meant beating the employer. This was seen as a natural outcome of the basic value of "supporting the weak," which has historically been the *raison d'être* of the unions. Learning the role of "competent negotiator" was a fundamental part of the acculturation process of union leaders. For example, high potential individuals were often first selected to be shop stewards, gradually moving to different and more powerful positions within the union while obtaining some kind of legal education along the way. The "competent negotiator" metaphor made sense to most people in the system as the very essence of what they identified with: both the positives and negatives.

We also used the "competent negotiator" as a metaphor for understanding the formal organization and their informal interactions. At an organizational level, it played out in FT's ways of handling democratic values and principals, while at the same time implementing a business strategy. The organizational staff and political relationships were complex. It was difficult to tell which of the two entities was the most powerful. Sometimes they joined; and sometimes they aligned themselves into subgroups, vying for power while pushing their key issues. I soon realized that personal relationships played an important role in decision-making. An informal communication network kept the system updated, superseding the formal decision-making structure and often resulting in blurred boundaries.

At a group level, the branch employee structure consisted of three primary groups. The first one, the *consultants*, had the most influence on strategic branch decisions, received the best pay, and acted as secretaries for the politicians. They worked independently, often outside the branch, dealing with complex member cases and networked with consultants from others branches. The second group was the *case officers*. They saw members in their offices, and if the case turned out to be politically complex, they had the option of informing the consultants. The third group was the *administrative staff*, whose job was to support the other two groups and the members by doing whatever necessary to have the office work efficiently and smoothly. For example, they received members at the front desk, and provided information concerning policies and procedures. They also spent much time giving advice to members by phone. In addition, each branch had a manager. They acted as daily leaders, as well as secretaries for the political heads of each branch, supporting the politicians in a wide variety of ways.

Our next interventions were designed to use the "competent negotiator" metaphor to evoke awareness around these patterns of beliefs, values, and influences. We wanted them to explore how their values resulted in a specific form of interaction, both within and between the staff members in the two branches. We hoped that making these patterns explicit, as well as helping the individuals understand how and to what degree they identified with them, would provide the impetus for change. The identity model supported us in creating a common language during the exploration of how they co-constructed their organizational culture, image, and identity.

Working Episode with the Political System

The local political conference was an annual event and involved the total political system. As indicated earlier, the political system of the union is an elected group that is responsible for the strategic direction of the union, and for selection of the chair of the union branch. At the conference, I was able to observe the group dynamics before presenting the project developments. I recall being fascinated by the visible difference between the sectors and a more subtle sense of competition amongst them. I remember asking myself what keeps them together, when it obviously was not the money. In the middle of my presentation, I asked if there were any questions. Two women began a verbal battle that, while on the surface might have appeared to be about a small aspect of the project, was in fact the latest skirmish in an ongoing struggle between them. They were two gutsy women with long-standing political disagreements. The rest of the twenty-eight people watched, displaying a variety of facial expressions from joy to irritation. A few interrupted in support of each of them.

As it was not my role to work with the process of the group in this setting, I felt caught as to how to proceed. I interpreted the interaction as reflecting a high degree of commitment of the group in general, but also noted that the group was unable to join and create a common shared figure of interest. I also pondered the possibility that the presentation of the project effects had evoked a power struggle between the two branches, with each of the two women aligned with a different branch serving as surrogates. I finally decided to intervene. Relying on the basic Gestalt concept of "use of self as an instrument of influence," I moved into what I term a "provocative mode." I stood up and insisted that the two women stop and listen to me. I asked them to not respond until I had finished, and I then proceeded to selectively share my thoughts and observations. I explained that in light of what I had observed, I needed to talk with my employers—the political heads and the managers Jens and Karen—and renegotiate my task and role. I told them that I wished to have the conversation in front of the entire group. After some hesitation, Jens and Karen agreed.

The three of us sat down in the middle of the room and discussed what had been evoked in each of us and how we could use it in the best possible way. While we talked, the remainder of the participants sat quiet, listening intently. After completing our conversation, I turned to the group and repeated in a more structured way what we had decided. I divided the participants into small groups, making sure that they were with people they knew, and had them discuss their understanding of the project and the impact they thought it would have on them. I also asked them to return with one personal reason for investing their time and energy within the union movement. I then had them list each of their reasons on a flipchart. Finally, I had each group select someone to present the content of their discussion.

There was an amazing energy in the groups. Coming back in plenum, a few of the group representatives expressed concern that FT-X might take over both branches and eventually close down branch FT-Z. Some also expressed frustration about not having direct access to the staff anymore. As mentioned above, each sector had previously employed a consultant from the branch to assist them in creating meeting agendas and taking minutes, amongst other things. However, in order to conserve resources and change the boundaries within the system, the leadership team had eliminated these positions, and the politicians now had to do this work themselves. Others expressed enthusiasm about the project and the possibility of a new way of working and dealing with these difficult issues. All expressed a belief that change was necessary if the union was to survive and members were to be reengaged. I found this meeting to be a critical turning point, especially when some commented on the openness we had shown, and the impact it had had on them. They trusted that we had honestly told them everything that we knew, and that they could actually influence the process. In hindsight, I appreciate the willingness of Jens and Karen to go along with my intervention. This agreement broke the organizational cultural habit of secretiveness and "back door" negotiating.

Working Episode with the Staff

Throughout the entire project, our team worked with the staff. Again, I will focus on how the cultural values and behavior informed the metaphor. For example, socializing and sharing meals was not only an important value of branch culture, but also a way to connect informally. Paying close attention to negotiated working time was another value that was new to me. In most companies I had worked with, flexibility is necessary in order to get ahead. Thus, employees are willing to put in extra time if the organization needs it. This was not the case with the FT employees. They were very clear about the boundaries and expectations. I came to appreciate the positives of what I would once have termed rigidity. One downside of flexibility is the implicit expectation that employees will stay and do whatever is necessary to address unexpected issues and tasks that need attention, often without payment. This norm can also create a culture of uncertainty and anxiety. I remember working with an organization in which nobody ever left before 6:00 p.m. because they were afraid that it would give the wrong signal if they wanted to advance.

The establishment of interest groups was one of the project group's first major interventions. All staff had to be in at least one group, and group membership was based on interest, not competency. The interest groups were designed to meet the project outcomes. Beyond the aim of creating new ways to attract and engage members, the interest groups provided their participants with new skills, developed new working relationships, and changed the view of how "things ought to be" by exploration of "how things were."

For example, one particular interest group wanted to learn how to establish focus groups as a mean of achieving quality improvement, i.e., to learn what their members found helpful and the changes that they wished for. The group consisted of the staff from FT-X and FT-Z, two staff consultants, four members from the administration and two case officers. We decided to meet for five hours, every fourteen days, and to end the project by having two focus groups meetings, and to present the results at a total branch meeting four months later.

At the first meeting, I perceived there to be low energy amongst the group members. There were many good reasons that might lay behind their reluctance to engage fully in the task. For example, some were not familiar with that way of working. Others appeared to regard the design with the "wait and see" approach, so typical of their way of engagement. Also, I was well aware that there were a number of old, unresolved conflicts among some of them. Of course, the reasons behind their reluctance to engage fully were not communicated right away but emerged gradually, and were dealt with as we moved ahead.

At our third meeting, one of the participants started the session with a complaint about how "we always provide food and clean afterwards." This complaint was ignored at first, and then supported by another person who looked directly at me and added: "This is just like at the office. You just leave your cups and stuff floating around, as if we are not busy." I asked her if I was one of those untidy persons she was referring to. My question caused her to laugh and she responded, "No, you do not seem too lofty to help tidy up." She turned to a third woman saying: "And you don't say anything when we are together, but have plenty of things to say when we are alone." I noticed the woman's face turning slightly red, and the other members moving uncomfortably in their chairs and rolling their eyes. I responded by telling the first woman that I appreciated her frankness inn stating her "wants," and that it seemed to me that others in the group might have similar thoughts and feelings. I asked them if it was an issue that they all had dealt with before. One of the consultants nodded affirmatively, whereas the case officer and the other staff consultants argued that "they" had to accept doing their work instead of blaming "us." Furthermore, this issue was taking up "too much time" and they were all fed up with it. There seemed to be a conflict between members concerning the importance of discussing and resolving relational issues vs. a task focus.

I asked the group members if they wanted things to remain the way they had been, or if they wanted a change. They responded with a grunt and nod. Then I asked them to consider silently what each of them had gained from how things had been. After some protests and "don't understand," remarks they became silent. When I asked them to speak, they all came up with their gains. Some had similar gains, and some reported different ones (appreciation, control, tidiness, efficiency). I asked them to explore what the organization gained, both the positives and negatives. They discussed how their self-perception and status affected the work atmosphere, their different perspectives on how things ought to be, and how lack of feedback reinforced their believed status. The meetings that grew out of this discussion, the content and, more importantly, the relational shifts impacted the focus group discussions in positive ways.

The above is just one of many examples of important and long-lasting changes that occurred in the task groups, which impacted branches in multiple ways.

Witnessing a New "What Is"

By the end of 2003, it was time to terminate my involvement. I set up a meeting with the leadership team, in which we did the final evaluation of the project. By that time, the branches had changed their ways from an "us against them" to a "we are in service to promote good working conditions for our members." This change in attitude was important in order to prevent companies from moving abroad and thereby losing jobs, consequently affecting Danish society as well as the unions.

The politicians and the staff employees had established new ways of interacting and working together. For example, if any of the sectors wanted something done or had new ideas, they would talk with the management team instead of one of the staff consultants. This way of contacting each other provided the total organization with a better overview and ability to prioritize and delegate tasks, not to mention making the previously mentioned power dynamics more overt.

The branches had organized themselves into four teams working across the two branches. One of the teams operated partly as consultants, mediating conflicts between managers and employees, contacting new companies, and doing FT marketing on the spot. They worked closely together with a "youth" team, creating workshops for members within the two organizations in order to provide a better working environment, conducting workshops to manage stress, doing outreach work in schools, etc. One team took care of daily administration, membership services, answering phone calls, etc., while the other team provided member services when complicated issues that demanded a more legal point of view arose.

My experience is that building teams (real teams, not just work groups), which can focus internally while at the same time being aware of the organization as a whole, is a difficult task. Teams easily tend to get self-absorbed and forget about other parts of the organization. I noticed that the teams had established a new internal approach to influencing each other. For example, the old hierarchical relationship in which the staff consultants "owned" the information and had more power had diminished. It was replaced by a more collaborative way of interacting. It became of utmost importance to share information in order to contact new members or provide good service to the old ones. If one team heard rumors or complaints concerning issues related to the other teams, this information was passed on, as were creative ideas and potential opportunities that emerged from their field work.

Also, the way recruitment was conducted had changed. For example, the staff started to approach managers in new organizations and forge relationships. They went to sports events in an attempt to meet young people, giving out water bottles with FT logos and contact information on them. Most of the staff was pleased and excited by the new ways of working. However, as was to be expected, some of the staff missed the old ways and found the new team structure difficult, especially when there were conflicts amongst the teams.

As with any change, there were sad and painful experiences. Some of the old staff left. They did not approve of the new approach. A few became physically and psychologically ill during the process and were supported by private psychologists as they attempted to grapple with the profound changes occurring within the organization, as well as within them. For them, the union had always been about getting better working conditions for the working class. It involved the establishing of firm boundaries between employer and employee; and engaging in an adversarial, as opposed to meditative and collaborative, process. The newly appointed staff members were able to adapt to the changes more easily, for most had not "grown up" in the old system with the old values.

The political groups FT-X and FT-Z merged and worked well together after a painful struggle to decide which positions would remain, which would be merged, and which would be eliminated. I had the pleasure of witnessing a political conference arranged by participants from each team in which they discussed excitedly their new ways of working together, such as their recruitment of new members. It was touching to witness their newfound enthusiasm.

The leadership team had become more accepting of its internal differences, personal as well as political. In the middle of the project, Karen said to me: "I can't figure out what you did, but it sure works." At the evaluation, I reminded her about this remark and she laughed, saying that she did pick up on some of the stuff I did. We then had a more serious conversation about the difficult role of authentic leadership in a political system.

During the four-year period that I worked with the branches, there was a decrease of 2% of its membership. This decrease was lower than previously, and better than the union as a whole. Of course, any decrease in membership, no matter how small, has impact on the identity, morale, and functioning of the organization.

Reflections and Learning

Four years of contact with the FT union has provided me with much rich material for reflection and learning. I will confine myself to three points and summarize my learning under these headings:

- Deciding who the client is
- Use of models and metaphors
- Use of self

Deciding who the client is

I was reminded that, when contracting with an organization, awareness of what is co-occurring at all levels of system is important. Contracting is a high-impact intervention. It is necessary to focus on one level in order to develop a clear and phenomenologically supported figure of interest, so that one can intervene without losing track of what is going on at other levels. In this case, these "levels" included society, the government, the unions, this particular union, its branches, the two branches that I worked with, the employees, politicians, and members, to mention a few. Viewing an organization from this perspective allows for sorting out and clarifying what might otherwise be seen as chaotic.

When working with a political system in particular, it is of utmost importance to be aware of the reactions of other parts of the system, so as to heighten awareness of ways of contacting. Looking back, the contracting process began when I was invited in by Sofie, my old classmate. I met the managers, Jens and Karen, and then the political managers from the two branches and the subgroups, prior to the submission of the project application that was accepted by the FT head office. Today, in hindsight, I would have involved the head office in a more extensive way. I believe that inviting them to some of the conferences was not enough.

There is not a simple or consistent answer as to who the client is. Some might say that the client is the entity that provides the money for the work. In this case, the money came from the Head Office, yet I considered my *primary* client to be the two branches, for those were the ones with which I had contracted. In complex systems the client is constantly changing and, as a result, recontracting when the need for doing so emerges. During our work together, I had to renegotiate several times. In fact, each time I was involved with a different "unit of work" I contracted with those involved, not losing sight of specific and overall goals, as well as the dynamics that existed at different levels of system.

Use of models and metaphors

My work with the union branches inspired my search for a model to augment the Gestalt method that would better capture and communicate what was going on in this large system. These models (see Figures 1 and 2) provided a common ground on which we could explore beliefs and values in a non-judgmental way. It supplied us with a meaningful and relevant language, and functioned almost as a map that we could turn to when things got rough. It provided people with a language to understand and describe why they felt uneasy, and why we had to look at their culture and image as well. The Gestalt model, which incorporates an optimistic view and the notion of co-creation, allowed us to be less interested in blaming and finger pointing and to emphasize the response-ability among the stakeholders. For example, in a discussion about solidarity and what that meant for them as a branch in the context of year 2000, they brought out two primary forces that they found were at odds with each other, one for solidarity (collectivism) and one for individualism. The "we" embedded in the concept of solidarity was emphasized in talks and discussions, while the "I" was more hidden and implied in attitudes.

Moving to the cultural dimensions of the identity model and heightening awareness of "what is" through use of metaphors ("the competent negotiator") consequently led most people to feel included without having to repress important values. They noticed that negotiating skills were valued in a narrow way, primarily as "winning your case." "Supporting the oppressed" as opposed to "generating results through dialogue" were other important forces. Lobbying was highly valued and viewed as necessary for survival. However, the FT branches had ambivalent feelings about lobbying. They also valued intimate relations that helped to develop trust with each other (recall how I got involved). Strategic lobbying, which politics is very much about, was kept under the surface.

Throughout my work, I utilized models and metaphors to serve as pedagogic devices that allowed participants to move beyond their own assumptions and perspectives into exploring the current situation, the "what is." For many, this approach allowed them to make sense of what was going on for them and the others in the present moment (heighten awareness), and eventually to find a new platform (I want). Yet for others, the use of models and metaphors was not useful. They were more comfortable with facts and yearned for cause and effect explanations.

As I have mentioned previously, when faced with major changes, and thrown into an unfamiliar, often stressful environment, many withdraw. However, being able to articulate and express their response to these changes reduced anxiety for many, allowing them to withdraw less, and eventually to confront the present reality and move to action. Those who grasped the Gestalt model of building awareness that leads to effective action were the most pleased with our intervention.

I also learned that organizations cannot remain stagnant, especially in a quick changing environment. Exploration is fine, but the unions do not have the luxury of unlimited awareness building and exploration. Decisions have to be made, and they need to move to action, or they will cease to exist. Personally, I always find it a delicate matter as to when to move from exploration to action, to determine when there is enough energy around a common figure of interest to support change. This issue of "when" was magnified in my work with the Danish Unions branches that had for many years held on to values and behaviors that viewed change in a negative light.

Use of Self

I entered the organization valuing clear, straightforward communication, and speaking my truth. I learned to notice and respect the more subtle, indirect movements and exchanges, and to keep my enthusiasm on a short leash. I kept a promise to myself, namely working with "what is," and supporting the system through the heightening of awareness so that they could make deliberate choices. It was not easy. First of all, I am a doer. Second, part of my task was to focus on the future and to be action and goal-oriented.

I was able to look at "what is" in an optimistic way. By optimistic, I do not mean sugarcoating problems but focusing on what the individuals were doing, how they were making sense of it, and what they were gaining from doing it. Often the politicians and employees were not aware of what they were doing well (what worked), since they seldom gave and received feedback. Therefore, embracing the positive qualities of our core metaphor, "the competent negotiator," became an example of focusing on a competency instead of a flaw.

Conclusion

Unions are, and have been for many years, an important part of Danish society. Emerging as a force from oppressed and exploited people, it took an organized form of "us against them" and developed into the Danish model in which unions negotiate with employers' associations. The union movement has provided a way for the poor and weak to stand up for themselves and make a better life. Throughout most of their existence, the unions were an integral part of society in which the values and attitudes were given.

Therefore, unions were able to grow and expand without anyone questioning their existence. The union's values supported their members because the members accepted and believed in them. The "we" was established by a clear boundary between "us, the employees" and "them, the employers." At some point, the changes in society made the unions "visible" in a different way, opening them up to public scrutiny. Joining the EU certainly changed the conditions for the Danish model. The institutional characteristics of unions began to be questioned, not only by society, but also by its members. As a response to public scrutiny the unions turned inward for a while, perhaps investing their energy in maintaining their perceived identity, rather than opening up to a society that was questioning their image and culture.

As such, the crisis facing unions have implications far beyond the small piece of work described above. Surveys tell us that society and the union members, as a whole, still find unions important and necessary as social institutions (http://www.cif.dk). However, a closer look at what people are saying in the surveys indicates that they find unions important, but that, as individuals, they are reluctant to embrace a collective system (i.e., they do not want to pay union dues, to negotiate work conditions collectively, etc.).

Nobody knows what will become of the unions. Will they become totally goal oriented and bottom line focused, more like an insurance company? Or will they insist upon the human values of solidarity and equal rights for humankind, still serving as watchdogs, but on a global level?

Our theory tells us that a change in one part of a system will influence all other levels. My work with the branches changed me. I now have a less ideological and more differentiated perspective, which in fact might mirror social attitudes facing the unions today. Are such values as solidarity no longer supported by our much more individualistically oriented society, or are the ingredients of solidarity just different? Perhaps we, "the people," need to articulate what kind of society and working life we want and do something about it. Perhaps we need to unite around societal responsibility and question global organizational structure and power.

Susanne Blom, MSc, is an organizational consultant who maintains a private practice specializing in leadership training and group development. She has published in the areas of group development and group efficiency and is currently writing a doctoral dissertation on "Organizational Identity: A Gestalt Perspective."
Contact: *Kreos.blom@post.tele.dk*

References

Albert, S., & Whetten, D. (2004). Organizational identity. In M. J. Hatch and M. Schultz (Eds.), *Organizational identity: A reader* (pp. 89-118). Oxford: Oxford University Press.

Beisser, A. (2004). The paradoxical theory of change. *International Gestalt Journal, 27*, 103-107.

Erikson, E. H. (1968). *Identity, youth and crisis.* New York: W.W. Norton.

Flyvbjerg, B. (1991). *Rationalitet og Magt, det konkretes videnskab* (1. Udgave, 4 oplag, 1993 edn). Kobenhavn: Akademisk Forlag.

Francis, T. (2001). The Gestalt brand. *British Gestalt Journal, 10*, 20-28.

Gaffney, S. (2006). Gestalt with groups: A developmental perspective. *Gestalt Journal of Australia and New Zealand, 2*, 6-28.

Hanafin, J. (2004). Rules of thumb for awareness agents. *OD Practitioner, 36*, 24-28.

Hassrick, B. (2003). American pragmatism. *International Gestalt Journal,* *25,* 71-84.

Hatch, M. J., & Schultz, M. (Eds.). (2004). *Organizational identity: A reader.* New York: Oxford University Press.

Hatch, M. J. and Schultz, M. (2004). The dynamics of organizational identity. In Hatch, M. J. and Schultz, M. (Eds.), *Organizational identity: A reader.* New York: Oxford University Press.

Jenkins, R. (2004). *Social identity* (2nd ed.). Abingdon, UK: Routledge.

Lewin, K. (2004). *Resolving social conflicts, Field theory in social science* (3rd ed.) Washington, DC: American Psychological Association. (Originally published 1948/1951)

Mead, G. H. (1934). *Mind, self and society.* Chicago: University of Chicago Press.

Melnick, J., & Nevis, S. M. (2005). Gestalt therapy methodology. In A. Woldt and S. Toman (Eds.), *Gestalt therapy, history, theory and practice* (pp. 102-115). Newbury Park, CA: Sage.

Morgan, G. (1997). *Images of organization: The executive edition.* San Francisco: Sage.

Nevis, S., Backman, S., & Nevis, E. (2003). Connecting strategic and intimate interactions: The need for balance. *Gestalt Review, 7*(2), 134-146.

Nevis, E. C. (1987, 2005). *Organizational consulting: A Gestalt approach.* Cambridge: GestaltPress.

Perls, F., Hefferline, R. F., & Goodman, P. (1951). *Gestalt therapy: Excitement and growth in the human personality* (7th ed). London: Souvenir Press.

Perls, L. (1992). *Laura Perls: Living at the boundary* (J. Wysong, Ed.). Highland, New York: The Gestalt Journal Press.

Putman, R. D. (2000). *Bowling alone: The collapse and revival of american community.* New York: Simon and Schuster.

Silver, B. J. (2003). *Forces of labor: Workers' movements and globalization since 1870.* Cambridge: Cambridge University Press.

Stacey, R. D. (2007). *Strategic management and organizational dynamics: The challenge of complexity* (5th ed.). London: Routledge.

Stivers, E. H., & Wheelan, S. A. (Eds.). (1986). *The Lewin legacy: Field theory in current practice.* Philadelphia: Springer-Verlag.

Wheeler, G., & Backman, S. (Eds.). (1994). *On intimate ground: A Gestalt approach to working with couples.* San Francisco: Jossey-Bass.

Wheeler, G. (1991). *Gestalt reconsidered: A new approach to contact and resistance* (2nd ed.,). Cambridge: Gestalt Institute of Cleveland Press.

Wheeler, G. (2006). New directions in Gestalt theory and practice: Psychology and psychotherapy in the age of complexity. *International Gestalt Journal, 29*, 9-41.

Zahavi, D. (2003). *Foenomenologi.* Frederiksberg: Samfundslitteratur Roskilde Universitetsforlag.

CHAPTER 16

Implications and Conclusions

Joseph Melnick, PhD and
Edwin C. Nevis, PhD

Introduction

Our purpose in gathering this collection of case studies has been to broaden the awareness of all who would venture into the domain of social change. Our hope is that these cases helped bring Gestalt theory alive, that we have given you concrete examples of how the Gestalt approach can be applied to the area of social change, and that you have become encouraged to work in this arena. In short, our goal has been to provide a rich learning experience.

To stimulate your assimilation and integration of the material in this book, we close by discussing briefly some of the themes that have emerged for us. We assume that you will have your own learning, given your background and experience in the area of social change. However, we would like to share some of the major implications and conclusions that we draw from a study of these cases. We have selected four themes that we found particularly relevant in this work: Contracting and Building Credibility, Support, Passion, and Power Dynamics.

Contracting and Building Credibility

In several of the cases, we noticed that the contracting process took quite a bit of time for significant "up-front" negotiation. This may be largely due to the tension and emotionality that are involved in the issues, or to a need to educate the parties as to our methods. In addition, large group interventions involve multiple stakeholders, each with their unique culture and ways of doing things. Each party needs to be convinced of the value of the intervention. Moreover, if the issues are complex or replete with long standing projections growing out of conflict, it often takes a good deal of persuasion to bring the parties together. Because of these issues it may be that, for many social change projects, *the ongoing clarification of the contract is the major part of the work* and cannot be rushed. We saw the value of this in the Blom and Copsey cases. Thus, *readiness-producing* needs to receive as much attention as major follow-up events. Experienced international mediators are well aware of this issue. They spend significant time in preparing all parties for face-face events.

As we contemplate this issue, we also question whether process skills, although of prime importance, are enough for this work. Jochen Lohmeier reminds us that technical and political competencies of the intervener often have crucial value when working with social change.[89] If we look at the cases, some of the consultants gained influence by being seen as experts in relevant content areas. For example, Muellmeester is an expert on Alzheimer's Disease; Lukensmeyer is an acknowledged expert in working with government institutions; Wheeler is highly recognized as a judge; Lohmeier and Wyley and Saner and Yiu are well-regarded as economic development specialists; and Copsey is a highly experienced London-area community worker. Lohmeier considers this expertise to be a significant advantage.

In cases where the intervener is not both a process and content expert, it may often be useful to bring in others who provide such content validity. For example, Kofi Annan, the former UN chief, acting as the chief mediator in the Kenyan post-election crisis in 2008, brought in a high level technocrat from the German foreign ministry who had helped to forge politically a coalition of the two leading parties in Germany under Chancellor Angela Merkel. The consult provided the needed expertise and increased trust that the project was in good hands.

We conclude, then, that Gestalt-oriented social change interveners may want to consider adding a content-knowledgeable person to their intervention team. In their interventions in Cambodia and South Africa, Johnston and Mwelwa added an experienced HIV-AIDS expert to their team. A variation of this model would be for our interveners to work

---

[89] Personal communication, February 25, 2008.

as teachers and coaches of more technically qualified people. Gaffney's work was largely of this nature, enabling the work of people like Burrows and Keenan—who were seen in their world as the experts in working with parents and children. In Cambodia (Johnston and Mwelwa's case), the first rounds of interventions were largely devoted to creating a group of credible locals to carry on the work.

Support

We noticed that many of our cases involved very stressful situations. Interveners often operate in cultures where they are outsiders, where they do not know the rules and the norms, and where the differences among the people involved are sometimes huge. As a relatively unknown entity to many of the individuals involved, interveners must spend a good deal of time and energy becoming known and managing projections. Ongoing support is also needed for other reasons. Because these projects are often so complex and fast changing, it is important to have available as many eyes and ears as possible, to both observe and balance out the biases inherent in all of us when we do this type of work.

We noticed that some of the interventions were conducted by teams of people and some by individuals. Because of the stress involved, it is often important to be able to debrief with colleagues and to share concerns. It is worth pointing out that Lohmeier and Wyley, Saner and Yiu, Johnston and Mwelwa, Sheinberg and her colleagues, and Burrows and Keenan all had more than one pair of eyes and ears. They had ongoing availability of support in figuring out what was happening, or in managing stress. While we do not have enough evidence to say that the projects conducted by teams worked out better than those conducted by individuals, it seems worthwhile to raise this point for future interveners to consider. Even if the outcome differences are limited, it may be that individuals can carry out their work under less stress when they have support readily available.

Passion

Working in the arena of social change touches the interveners' core beliefs about social health and social justice. This is because there are often deeply personal reasons why people choose to work in this area. Even those who start out simply with the feeling that they are embarking on an interesting and challenging assignment soon find that their deeply held values have been aroused and that their heart has been "touched."

This trajectory is certainly true for the authors showcased in this book. Carolyn Lukensmeyer has had a passion for social justice since she was a young girl growing up in Iowa, and she has worked in the political world for thirty years. Seán Gaffney was not just teaching Gestalt skills in the North of Ireland, even though that was his initial assignment. The North of Ireland conflict has been a part of his world from the beginning and touches his "Irishness" in much more than a purely professional way. Sari Sheinberg is not "just training" immigrants to find jobs. She is an immigrant in Sweden herself, and her work grew out of her own journey. Joyce Wheeler is not just a "nine to five" judge. She has spent many years looking to find ways to have more impact on the defendants appearing before her. This journey led to her immersion in Gestalt training programs and resulted in her creative approach in the courtroom. We argue that this work is part of her identity, not only as a judge but also as a person. Rosie Burrows (Protestant) and Bríd Keenan (Catholic) were living products of the conflict in which they chose to become involved long before they reached adulthood. Susanne Blom is deeply identified with the labor movement in Denmark.

We also call attention to a more quiet aspect of passion. There is a caring component to passion, which is reflected in a less emotional, yet equally compelling involvement. This is seen in the way that Neville and Perry invested themselves in their work even though the issues did not affect them personally. They are as dedicated to social justice as the interveners in the North of Ireland.

Thus, we believe that all the interveners in our cases were not dispassionate, objective scientist-observers, but rather engaged and personally aroused action learners. Perhaps the same can be said for psychotherapists or organizational consultants who work at smaller system levels. But we believe that there may be something more pervasive going on when we attempt to "take on" the world at large. At least we offer that as a hypothesis to pursue further.

Because this work seems to touch our core in such a deep way, it makes it difficult to remain neutral, to stay balanced and to take a stance of "creative indifference." It may be extremely difficult, if impossible, not to have a personal interest in the outcome and to focus just on the process. In traditional psychodynamic thinking, the issue we label passion would be viewed as a problem of countertransference (Melnick, 2003). It would also be considered a difficult issue in Gestalt therapy, where we would normally encourage people to be aware of their "issues" and to "bracket" them out of the work.

We propose another perspective. We propose that passion and advocacy can be utilized as a valuable resource, rather than something to be shunted off to the side. Perhaps passion is necessary for doing this type of work, and maybe without it the chances for staying the course will be greatly diminished. Given the long time frame for developing many of the projects discussed, and the significant obstacles to be overcome in achieving a viable contract for the work, it is reasonable to conclude that a great deal of energy and determination is a requisite for social change interveners. Perhaps we should consider passion as a "given" for this type of work.

Yet, we cannot wish away the countertransference issues. We believe that having peer-level colleagues or a board of advisors may be necessary for successful work in this area. Our solution is that a variation of the "control" or supervisory arrangement in the world of psychotherapy may be a useful adjunct to social change projects. This arrangement would provide a presumably independent authority that could act as a check and balance to possible intervener blind spots, or to the loss of objectivity that comes from "being on the boundary." We offer this as a helpful support to interveners, not as a criticism of any of the authors of this book's cases. We believe that it is just too hard to work well out of all the energy and caring that is bound up in passion, without having the objectivity that may keep an intervener from getting stuck, from missing a possible landmine, or from just wearing oneself down unnecessarily.

Power Dynamics

We close with a few comments about power dynamics in these cases. In the Gestalt approach, we see power as an experience occurring *between or among* people and not as something lodged in an individual person or group. In this sense, we concur with Gregory Bateson (1972) and Michel Foucault (Flaskas and Humphreys, 1993) that power is embedded in a process of mutual influence and in micro-level exchanges among people. We do not assume that there are powerful groups and powerless groups: all groups have power. Perls's conception of "Top Dog/Under Dog" shows us that neither of these groups is more powerful than the other.

We recognize that this approach may be at odds with sociological or political perspectives that focus on real or perceived differences in control over resources. Certainly, full-fledged Marxists would take issue with us and, if we were acting as revolutionaries or advocates for the overthrow of a system, we might agree with them. But it seems to us that a more fruitful perspective is to see our interventions as the opening up of relational spaces, with the intent of harnessing the energy of different points of view for a common purpose. We are seeking to promote a joining of energy to achieve collective action around an issue of concern to all involved.

This way of looking at power as a relational concept is similar to what Barry Oshry (1999) has called *"system power."* This concept refers to the system created by people in all forms and sizes of interaction; it asks us to focus our attention on the processes, values, and norms that hold us together. The notion is similar to a key aspect of the Cape Cod Intervention Model (E. Nevis, Melnick, and S. Nevis, 2007), which is designed to focus on the system created by dyads and small groups as they carry out their existence. Most of the time, the people that constitute the system are not aware of their system dynamics, particularly what they do well.

Thus, for us, social change interventions are seen as designed experiences that allow participants to share goals and expectations, attitudes and feelings, and concerns and fears. The objective is to use dialogue to develop a rich shared awareness that leads to useful actions concerning the issues being confronted. Even though we might ask participants simply to listen to each other, and not to change the other, all human exchange carries with it an element of influence; we hope that the participants will have an impact on each other. Much of our work as interveners, then, is to develop readiness and to arrange "containers" to support the exchange that will take place.

With the above in mind, we looked at the cases in this book from the perspective of the following questions:

- Where outcomes seemed limited, or less than desired by interveners or participants, what was missing in the exchange?
- What did that missing part reveal about the process of mutual influence?

We can look at some of the cases with these questions in mind. For example, Scheinberg's domain was initially defined as immigrants needing to find work, and her extensive intervention was initially designed with those people in mind. However, as the work unfolded, we saw that outcome success was highly influenced by employment and government agencies who were only tangentially involved. This observation is not meant as a criticism of Scheinberg's excellent accomplishments; it mainly defines the limits of what is possible to achieve when important parts of the system are absent from potential mutually influential interactions.

Similarly, in Saner and Yiu's UN-based intervention, the results were significantly limited by the decisions of an executive at a higher level. In hindsight, one might say that the real target of intervention was a *triangular system* made up of the three leaders and the organizational units they represented. But interveners start where they are invited in, and Saner and Yiu could only truly see the power relationships in the system after they were well into the work. If the relevant parties are not available for an exchange, there is no way to see and deal with the influencing relationships.

On a smaller scale, we can see how Perry's work was limited by the fact that some elements of the school community system did not make themselves available, even though she knew that their participation was important.

In summary, we do not look at who has power and who does not, but rather at how we can harness the full power of the *system*. This means that an intervener needs to try to define the full system—all the groups and parts that relate to the particular group that is the major target of the intervention—and to try to get them all "into the room" at the same time. All of the cases in this book show some appreciation of this need; indeed, many of our authors devoted significant time and energy to getting all the appropriate parties engaged. In Lukensmeyer's case, the central aspect of the work was to define who belonged to the issue and to get them to talk with each other. Likewise, in Cambodia, Johnston and Mwelwa worked hard to define the system and to have different parts of it represented. Our cases tell us how hard this is to do, and why large system interventions are becoming more critical and widespread.

References

Bateson, G. (1972). *Steps to an ecology of the mind.* New York: Ballantine Books.

Flaskas C., & Humphreys, C. (1993). Theorizing about power: Intersecting the ideas of Foucault with the "problem" of power in family therapy. *Family Process, 32,* 35-47.

Melnick, J. (2003). Countertransference and the Gestalt approach. *British Gestalt Journal, 12*(1), 40-48.

Nevis, E., Melnick, J., & Nevis, S. M. (2007). Organizational change through powerful micro-level interventions. *OD Practitioner, 40*(3), 4-8.

Oshry, B. (1999). *Leading systems: Lessons from the power lab.* San Francisco: Berrett Kohler.

INDEX

A

B

R

S